I0819863

The Andalusi Literary & INTELLECTUAL TRADITION

INDIANA SERIES IN SEPHARDI AND MIZRAHI STUDIES

Harvey E. Goldberg and Matthias Lehmann, editors

The Andalusi Literary & Intellectual Tradition

THE ROLE OF ARABIC IN JUDAH IBN TIBBON'S ETHICAL WILL

S. J. PEARCE

Indiana University Press
Bloomington and Indianapolis

This book is a publication of

INDIANA UNIVERSITY PRESS
Office of Scholarly Publishing
Herman B Wells Library 350
1320 East 10th Street
Bloomington, Indiana 47405 USA

iupress.indiana.edu

The paper used in this publication meets the minimum requirements of the American National Standard for Information Sciences—Permanence of Paper for Printed Library Materials, ANSI Z39.48–1992.

Manufactured in the United States of America

Library of Congress Cataloging-in-Publication Data

Names: Pearce, Sarah Jean, author.
Title: The Andalusi literary and intellectual tradition : the role of Arabic in Judah ibn Tibbon's ethical will / S.J. Pearce.
Description: First edition. | Bloomington and Indianapolis : Indiana University Press, [2017] | Series: Indiana series in Sephardi and Mizrahi studies | Includes bibliographical references and index.
Identifiers: LCCN 2016046942 (print) | LCCN 2016049050 (ebook) | ISBN 9780253025968 (cloth : alk. paper) | ISBN 9780253026019 (e-book)
Subjects: LCSH: Hebrew literature, Medieval—Spain—Andalusia—Arabic influences. | Tibon, Yehudah ibn, approximately 1120-approximately 1190. Igeret ha-musar. | Wills, Ethical.
Classification: LCC PJ5016 .P38 2017 (print) | LCC PJ5016 (ebook) | DDC 892.4/09002—dc23
LC record available at https://lccn.loc.gov/2016046942

1 2 3 4 5 22 21 20 19 18 17

CONTENTS

Acknowledgments · *vii*

A Note on Translations and Transliterations · *xi*

Introduction: "The Preface of Every Book Is Its First Part": An Overview of Materials and Methodologies · *1*

1 "Pen, I Recount Your Favor!": Reading, Writing, and Translating in Memory of al-Andalus · *20*

2 "Examine Your Hebrew Books Monthly and Arabic Books Bimonthly": Autobiography and Bibliography in the Islamic West · *46*

3 "On Every Sabbath, Read . . . the Bible in Arabic": Reading the Hebrew Bible as Arabic Literature · *78*

4 "The Words of the Ancient Poets": Poetics between Jewish and Islamic Scripture · *101*

5 "The Arab Sage Said": Transmitting Arabic Philosophy in Translation · *149*

6 "From Vessel to Vessel": The Reception and Reimagining of the Tibbonid Project · *171*

Conclusion: "This Book Has Been Completed": Looking Back and Ahead at al-Andalus in Translation · *198*

Appendix: Judah ibn Tibbon's Ethical Will: A New Translation · *203*

Bibliography · *229*

Index · *257*

ACKNOWLEDGMENTS

ALTHOUGH IT IS ultimately a very different project, the germ of this book can be found somewhere in my doctoral dissertation, and so I should like to begin by thanking the members of my graduate and doctoral committees in and around the Department of Near Eastern Studies at Cornell University: Simone Pinet, David Powers, and Cynthia Robinson. Kim Haines-Eitzen was not formally a member of the committee but was present at all the key junctures; it was she who encouraged me to apply for the job I currently hold and has encouraged me in nearly everything since. And for having been student and not-student of Lauren Monroe and Shawkat Toorawa, respectively, I learned a tremendous amount about how to read text.

My deepest gratitude, though, is to my Doktorvater, Ross Brann, my intellectual debts to whom will be obvious to the reader. Particularly in the last year of work on this book, it became more and more clear to me the ways in which his thinking has come to shape my own. More than that, though, he shows by example that there is another way within an academy that is so often given to careerism and to demonstrations of ego and cleverness at the expense of a more patient brand of scholarship: that the very best intellectual work and an absolute, decent humanity are not mutually exclusive in one person. I wrote in the acknowledgments section of my dissertation that I suspected that I would find myself forever striving to live up to his example. That is still true.

Much of this book was conceptualized during the academic year 2012–13, which I spent at the Katz Center for Advanced Judaic Studies at the University of Pennsylvania, then under the direction of the legendary David Ruderman. I am grateful to him and to the center's staff—Sam Cardillo, Natalie Dohrmann, Etty Lassman, Carrie Love, and Yechiel Schur—who made life very easy for the coterie of absent-minded professors in their charge; to the library staff—Joe Gulka, Arthur Kiron, and Bruce Nielsen; and to the inimitable Sol Cohen. I would particularly like to acknowledge the generosity of Ione Apfelbaum Strauss, who endowed the Louis Apfelbaum and Hortense Braustein Apfelbaum Fellowship that funded my year at the Center; and the cohort of fellows who created such an enriching intellectual environment there. New York University, as my intellectual and professional home, has been an unusual and wondrous place to write this book. I am beyond grateful to my colleagues in the Department of Spanish and Portuguese Languages and Literatures who were willing to take a chance on hiring an extremely green and untested young scholar and who, like Judah ibn Tibbon, are firmly convinced of the fact that Arabic, too, is a Spanish language. To begin to list names risks inadvertently omitting important ones, so instead I shall thank them here as a group; they know who they are. I would, however, like to acknowledge specifically Jo Labanyi, Robert Lubar, and Jordana Mendelson, who, in their administrative capacities, have been fiercely protective of my time and supportive through the process of writing the book. The writing, as I am told so often happens, came together rather at the end, and I am extremely grateful to NYU's Faculty of Arts and Sciences for the Paulette Goddard Junior Faculty Fellowship that allowed me the time, free of classroom responsibilities, to pull the project together. I am also grateful to the Center for the Humanities at NYU for a generous publication subvention that covered the costs of obtaining image reproductions and of indexing the volume.

I have been fortunate to be able to present sections of this book in a great variety of forums over the past few years; the feedback I received has been instrumental in revising and refining my arguments. I was able to present chapter 2 variously in the spring and fall of 2015: at the Histories of the Book in the Islamicate World symposium organized in Madrid by Sabine Schmidtke, at the Columbia Seminar on Religion and Writing convened by Dagmar Reidel, and more informally in a graduate seminar at Yeshiva University at the invitation of Ronnie Perelis, an exercise that was tremendously helpful in refining the argument. I presented a very early version of chapter 6 at Brian Catlos's and Sharon Kinoshita's Mediterranean Seminar held at the University of California, Berkeley, in the fall of 2012; and at the symposium The Cultural World of the Medieval Translator, convened in the spring of 2013 at the University of Chicago by James T. Robinson, whose subsequent critique of a draft of the manuscript was instrumental in pushing me to give the book the shape that it now takes. Extracts and versions of other chapters have benefitted tremendously from feedback received after presentations at various meetings of the American Oriental Society and the Society of Biblical Literature. Meira Polliack, who has been a supreme mentor and friend to me, facilitated both formal and informal opportunities to talk about my research and so generously and thoughtfully critiqued an early draft of the manuscript, all of which has pushed me to further develop the arguments, particularly those in chapter 3; most recently, she, Camilla Adang, and Benjamin Hary hosted me in Tel Aviv, where I presented that material to the Biblia Arabica Working Group. I am also extremely grateful to colleagues at NYU and at Penn—Gabriela Basterra, Paul Cobb, Sibylle Fischer, and David Larsen—for their comments on various sections of the manuscript and the book proposal and for their advice on navigating the often-treacherous waters of academic publishing. Phil Lieberman was, in a meta-historical twist, my publishing dragoman.

The editorial staff at Indiana University Press has been spectacular throughout. I am grateful to Rebecca Tolen, Dee Mortensen, Paige Rasmussen, and Rachel Rosolina for their guidance and support and to Matthias Lehman, the series editor whose enthusiastic support for the project was key to bringing it to fruition with the press. As copy editor, Eric Schramm made me take a much-needed second look at all the details. I am especially grateful to Jonathan Decter and David Wacks, both of whom unmasked themselves as having been the once-anonymous reviewers of the manuscript for the press. Their comments drew attention to places where I could tighten, refine, and further develop my argument; this is a better book than it would have been without their assessments.

I consider myself very lucky to have colleagues who are also friends, with whom I can talk shop (and not-shop) free of the hazards that can freight many of the interpersonal relationships that we have in this profession, who have patiently listened to and helped me puzzle through both the intellectual and professional difficulties that this project posed: Esperanza Alfonso, Rebecca Goetz, Tara Mendola, Eilis Monahan, and Holman Tse. Quite a lot of this book was written across a table from Abby Balbale at a Manhattan outpost of Le Pain Quotidien; in a field that can be so fractious it is difficult to overstate the value of having confederates who see its fundamental contours drawn in similar ways, and she is one of those. Kathryn Slanski and Eckart Frahm, who have always looked out for me, took me (and my cat—no small feat!) in at two critical junctures over the course of writing this book. Ashley Puig-Herz is a sister forged in the same crucible. And Hamza Zafer and Adam Bursi, my fellows in the Ithaca wilderness, have long been my co-conspirators in all things and willing and sympathetic sounding boards in the personal, intellectual, and professional realms.

And lucky me, as Celia Cruz never quite sang, if not to have been born in Havana, then at least to have been brought up in the academy by someone who was. María Rosa Menocal was a throwback to the days when the university stood *in loco parentis* and took her twin roles as teacher and surrogate mother equally seriously. Finding my own way in the wake of her death far too young has perhaps been the greatest challenge.

Finally, I am most grateful to my family, and especially my parents, Laurie and Stephen Pearce, for their unwavering support through all of this; there is no acknowledgment that could suffice to express my gratitude and love to them.

February 29, 2016
New York City

A NOTE ON TRANSLATIONS AND TRANSLITERATIONS

Except where indicated otherwise, translations are my own. For transliteration of Arabic terms and phrases, I have used the *International Journal of Middle East Studies* system. For Hebrew terms and phrases I have used the transliteration schema of the *Jewish Quarterly Review* with one exception: *ẓ* in place of *ts* for the letter *ẓadee*. In a few instances, when terms (and, in particular, personal names) that have common Anglicized forms appear as a matter of course within the body of the text, I have chosen to use those forms, e.g., Judah and not Yehudah, Samuel and not Shemuel, Maimonides and not Ben Maimon, Halevi and not ha-Levi, Andalusi and not Andalusī. Additionally, I have omitted diacritics from words that preserve a Hebrew or Arabic root within an English morphology even while retaining them in the original terms; thus, *ga'on* but *geonic* and *geonate, shi'ī* but *Shiite, Rekhav* but *Rechabite.* When citing scholarship that contains transliterations following a different system, I have retained orthography as it appears in the original source.

A NOTE ON TRANSLATIONS AND TRANSLITERATIONS

The Andalusi Literary & INTELLECTUAL TRADITION

INTRODUCTION

"The Preface of Every Book Is Its First Part": An Overview of Materials and Methodologies

THE YEAR 568/1172 was monumental in the political life of the Almohad caliph, Abū Ya'qūb Yūsuf ibn 'Abd al-Mu'min. He succeeded his father in 557/1163 to become the second leader of a still young and fervently monotheistic Berber messianic movement, and by 561/1167 he assumed the regnal name Yūsuf I and the caliphal title *amīr al-mu'minīn* (prince of the believers).[1] He then pressed on with his father's program of territorial expansion, bringing along with it a culture that privileged rationalist thought, accommodated prayer and theological reasoning in the vernacular, and ushered into North Africa and the Iberian Peninsula striking new developments in aesthetic and literary production.[2] 'Abd al-Mu'min, Yūsuf's father and the first caliph of the Almohad dynasty, had taken and held Tangier, Ceuta, Seville, Córdoba, and Granada and consolidated his rule by installing loyal family members as governors of those cities; Yūsuf was able to subjugate or win over the remaining provincial military and political leaders who had held out against his father. By that extraordinary year of 1172, following successful campaigns at Andújar, outside of Córdoba, and at Huete, eighty-five miles due east of Toledo and well into the heart of Castile, Yūsuf ordered construction begun on the triumphalist Great Mosque of Seville and considered his conquest of al-Andalus complete.[3]

Where 1172 was a capstone in the political and military prongs of the broad cultural program that Yūsuf inherited from his father, it was just the beginning of a very different kind of familial cultural project that would be carried out by one of the men who fled the advancing Almohad armies and the religious and social restrictions imposed consequently on Andalusi *dhimmī*, the members of the other Abrahamic faiths, Judaism and Christianity, generally recognized as protected under Islamic rule.[4] Having fled the Almohad invasion for the sanctuary offered by his coreligionists in the Jewish community of the Provençal city of Lunel, this well-educated, Arabophone, native son of Granada began to write a letter in Hebrew to his only son in that same year that Yūsuf I's regime reached its territorial apogee.[5] The letter would grow long and its author would return to it over and over, editing and emending it until his death in 1190. Its diachronic composition is self-evident in the strata of the text: here he speaks to a recalcitrant twelve-year-old falling behind in his studies, here to an arrogant young man making intemperate business decisions, and here to someone he regards more as a peer (though never an equal), about to marry and assume the mantle of the family profession. The profession was translation and the family the storied Ibn Tibbon clan whose issue would continue to form a dynastic workshop that would perdure for over a century, dominating and driving the proliferation of philosophical, religious, and scientific texts throughout Europe's Jewish educated elite.[6]

The letter, or ethical will, comprises a wide-ranging collection of personal and professional advice interspersed with a veritable catalogue of medieval insults volleyed at its addressee, condemning him as too lazy, dull, and indolent for anyone's good—least of all his own. Those insults seem to be easily dismissible because they are so incongruous with the dizzying success that the son, Samuel ibn Tibbon, would ultimately achieve as the authorized and canonical translator of perhaps the single most important work of Jewish thought, Moses Maimonides' *Guide of the Perplexed*, an incongruity that has frequently presented itself as an obstacle in interpreting the text. Nevertheless, those insults, along with the rest of the ethical will, in fact encode the most deeply cherished cultural ideals of the father, its author, Judah ibn Tibbon. He berates his thoroughly Occitan son for his messy handwriting and for his unwillingness to study Hebrew, the language of religion and Jewish literary culture in Lunel, and Arabic, the absolute intellectual and literary standard and the language of culture in the Andalusi homeland that Samuel never knew because Judah had left it long before he had been born—without ever leaving it behind. It is the study of the Arabic language and intellectual tradition to which Judah returns over and over again, throughout the ethical will and his other original compositions, conceiving of it as the fountainhead of cultural prestige, in exile as in al-Andalus, and as the bedrock foundation of reading and acquiring knowledge. Judah's is a letter that asserts the primacy and prestige of Arabic and grounds it firmly within the literary and intellectual traditions of al-Andalus. It is a frame within which his other original writings—including translator's prologues, lexicographic work, and epistolary writing—may be viewed; consequently, it represents the backbone for the present study to ask about Judah's attitudes toward the Arabic language and how he used Arabic and Andalusi literature to convey those ideas to his audience in Provence and in wider Europe.[7]

The explicit exhortations to Arabic are striking. In one instance, Judah writes:

> You have not cultivated your Arabic writing as expected: You began to study it seven years ago, when I forced you to [learn] it even though you did not want to. You know that the greatest men of our nation did not achieve their greatness or their lofty heights but through their Arabic writing. You know that the *nagid* explained that the acclaim accorded to him—and to his son after him—was because of it: "Pen, I recount your favor! . . ." and so on. You see that the *nasi*, Sheshet, achieved wealth and honor through his Arabic writing in this land as in a kingdom of Ishmael.[8]

In other words, Judah writes to Samuel of his belief, rooted in his own observation of the trajectories of his contemporaries, that the path to greatness and to recognition for excellence comes through Arabic alone and that this was as much the case in the Romance-speaking north as in the Arabic-speaking south.[9] He invokes the name of a contemporary, Sheshet Benvenisti (ca. 1130–1200), the *nasi* (leader) of the Jewish community of Barcelona, in order to impress upon Samuel that the ability to write eloquently in Arabic was as important and prestigious a skill in the north as it would have been in al-Andalus, in the Maghreb, and in the wider Arabophone Islamic world. He later reiterates this belief in other terms, telling Samuel that aptitude for Arabic would earn him great renown among both "Israel and the other nations."[10] Judah's work—his original compositions as much as his translations—was always underpinned by the idea that there could be no achievement but through Arabic literature and deep engagement with that textual tradition; his aspirations for his son were built up from that same bedrock. But even beyond the explicit praise of Arabic in his writing, Judah's entire endeavor—from his distinctively, persistently word-for-word translations to the prefaces and letters he wrote to justify his method—is a defense of Andalusi culture and its intellectual and literary traditions. For example, in his translator's preface to Baḥya ibn Paqūda's *Duties of the Heart*, he writes about the paucity of the Hebrew language, especially in terms of its vocabulary: "Every matter is better [expressed in Arabic] than it would have been in Hebrew. Because the only Hebrew that has come down to us is what is found in the books of the Bible and that is not sufficient for a speaker."[11] Far more pervasive, though, is his active engagement with the Arabic literary tradition, incorporating it at various levels of his work in such a way that he could ensure the continuity of his preferred language; and it is the prestige of Arabic and the ways in which its readers and writers could express that prestige outside of an Arabized world that is the primary concern of this study.

The letter is most frequently identified as a part of the Hebrew epistolary genre known as *ẓeva'ah*, or ethical will, a type of writing with biblical roots that took hold in Jewish communities across Europe beginning toward the middle of the eleventh century of the Common Era.[12] It has long been observed that the ethical will reads very much like a curriculum and a plan for Samuel's professional education and personal development;[13] but it ultimately tells us much more about Judah's intellectual and cultural biography despite, perhaps, giving the opposite impression at first blush.[14] James T. Robinson argues that although Judah ibn Tibbon places his text within this genre by calling it "*musar av*" (a father's guidance), and despite the existence of other medieval examples of ethical wills, this one is distinctive for its "particular style of writing . . . length, breadth, and coherence," that give it a greater resemblance to medieval Arabic *waṣīya* (bequest) literature than to biblical antecedents and other medieval Hebrew counterparts.[15] This speaks to the ways in which Judah was so thoroughly Arabized in his intellectual outlook and the literary foundations on which he would build his own textual program; both as an author and as a translator, Judah functions, in Gad Freudenthal's words, as a "cultural intermediary,"[16] rendering the Arabized culture of al-Andalus in a form that was legible for a non-Arabophone audience.

Of the many examples of *waṣīya* literature, it is a brief and anonymous one that stands out as an excellent counterpoint to Judah's ethical will for the ways in which it demonstrates the climate of Arabic reading in which Jewish ethical writing was composed, namely, one in which Judaeo-Arabic intellectual figures were engaged, transmitting Islamic and classical Arabic texts and ideas to their own communities and more widely in the Jewish world, as well as developing natively Judaeo-Arabic literature and literary forms. This text, one conserved in the cache of documents found in the Cairo Genizah[17] and now known by the Cambridge University Library shelfmark T-S 13 J 22.19, tells its modern readers and students just as much about the notion of the ethical bequest in the Islamicate Middle Ages as it does about the reading habits of the father who might have copied it out for his son and the access such a Jewish father might have had to Arabic books written by Muslim authors.

The text of the ethical will as it appears in the Genizah fragment is aphoristic in character but touches on similar themes that occur within Judah's ethical will. The anonymous Genizah text, written in Classical Arabic in Hebrew characters, reads:

> (1) My son, I adjure you to piety toward God; to faith; to bearing witness; (2) to speaking truth in favor and fury; to moderation between wealth (3) and poverty; to fairness toward friends and enemies; and to hard work through (4) zeal and laziness, contentment in God in fortitude and solace. (5) My son, the one who recognizes the shortcomings in himself is distracted from the faults (6) of others, but the one who is pleased with the wonders of God will never be saddened by what (7) oppresses him. Whoever unsheathes the sword of injustice will die by it; and whoever digs a well for his (8) trusting brother will find himself at the bottom; and whoever humiliates his brother (9) will find his whole house likewise exposed. Whoever forgets his own sins exaggerates the (10) sins of others. Whoever overestimates his own opinion goes astray, and he who [enriches himself through his wits][18] is making a mistake. (11) He who gossips about people is weak. He who associates with (12) scoundrels is contemptible and to be scorned, (13) but the one who confers with scholars is honorable. He who jokes will be treated as a lightweight for it. (14) A man who makes a choice will be known by it. The one who is verbose (15) errs greatly. The one who errs greatly has very little shame. (16) The one with very little shame also has very little piety. [As for] the one with very little piety, (17) his heart is dead; and the one with the dead heart will enter into the Hell-fire. (18) My son! A courtly education (*adab*) is the best inheritance and the finest of creation is the best (19) companion. My son! Vitality has ten parts: (20) Nine of them lie in being taciturn except in matters of meditating on God (21) the exalted, while one of them lies in ceasing to confer with fools. My son! (22) It is burden that adorns poverty and gratitude that adorns wealth. O, (23) my son! There is nothing more noble than fearing God, no refuge (24) a better keeper than piety, no intercessor more successful than repentance, (25) no clothing more beautiful than good health. Greed is the key, (26) is the key, is the key[19] to hatred and the conveyance to roguishness. (27) Reflection before work guarantees against regret. Misery (28) increases hostility and is the enemy of humanity. Repentance (29) is possible for him who is loyal to God and who knows Him and serves him in his love, in his zeal, in his despair, in his words, in his laughter, in his speech, and in his deeds.[20]

This is an ethical will that is principally concerned with instilling in its recipient a sense of his place within a community and care for his reputation. Despite the overlap in themes and concerns between this text and the Ibn Tibbon ethical will, it is not the content that offers insight into readership practices among Arabophone Jews in the medieval Mediterranean, but rather the source of the text: the *waṣīya*, the ethical bequest, attributed to ʿAlī ibn Abī Ṭālib, the fourth rightly guided caliph and, along with his two sons, the figurehead founders of shiʿī Islam.

The ethical will found on T-S 13 J 22.19 was initially compared in form by S. D. Goitein to the late-eleventh-century epistle written by the theologian and philosopher Abū Ḥāmid Muḥammad ibn Muḥammad al-Ghazālī (d. 1111) to his disciple, a text that the modern editor and translator characterizes as "a kind of epitome"[21] on the summa *Revival of the Religious Sciences*. This epistle, known by the vocative phrase that begins nearly every paragraph, *ayyuhā al-walad* (O, son!), a call that echoes Judah's frequent repeated exhortations to Samuel beginning with a hortative "*beni*" (my son), is an ethical bequest in which Ghazālī directs his interlocutor to avoid rationalist philosophy generally and alludes specifically to the tenets of neo-Platonist thought as those to be most avoided.[22] However, by the time he published the text, Goitein was able to identify a better source. Ultimately, in *A Mediterranean Society* and in a related publication, following consultation with the Arabist Meir Kister,[23] he concludes that it was drawn, impressionistically and incompletely, from the *waṣīya* attributed to ʿAlī ibn Abī Tālib as recorded in the twelfth-century *shiʿī-nuṣayrī* compilation of discourses attributed to the prophet Muḥammad and members of his family, compiled by Ḥasan ibn Shuʿba al-Ḥarrānī;[24] the text on the Genizah fragment appears to draw elliptically and selectively from that version of the sermon. However, I should like to emend Goitein's identification somewhat; it is a minor point but helps to get at the notion of Judaeo-Arabic ethical writing occurring in a bookish and readerly context. It has been amply demonstrated that a number of versions of the *waṣīya* attributed to ʿAlī were in circulation from its earliest existence in written, rather than exclusively oral, form.[25] The text reflected in the Genizah fragment is, in fact, nearly identical to a different classical Arabic version of the text that would also have been in circulation in the twelfth century,[26] namely the one attributed to the third/ninth-century Muslim historian and genealogist Zubayr ibn Bakkār.[27] The version of the *waṣīya* of ʿAlī reflected on the Genizah fragment in Hebrew characters matches the version recorded by Ibn Bakkār exactly except in the case of a few errors and the substitution of a single phrase for another in order to make the text theologically palatable to a Jewish audience. Where Ibn Bakkār's version of the ethical will includes the assertion "*lā āshraf min al-islām*"[28] (there is nothing more noble than Islam), the Genizah fragment reads: "*wa-lā maʿqil aḥraz min al-waraʿ*" (there is no refuge a better keeper than piety).[29] The version recorded by Ibn Shuʿba is nearly twice as long, containing additional admonitions about hard work and thorough study, fidelity to God and man, the honest assessment of character, and resistance to dwelling on negative thoughts and events in life; and so to argue that the Genizah copyist independently edited the Ibn Shu'ba version and coincidentally arrived at omissions that nearly exactly resemble Ibn Bakkār's version would suggest (and require accounting for) the broader exercise of editorial judgment and demand an almost supernatural belief in editorial coincidence; comparing it with a nearly identical source text is a nearer and more sensible match. Instead of concluding, then, that the scribe adapted the text, we must conclude that he had access to another, more closely related version that was in circulation in addition to the one that Goitein identified with Kister's assistance. This is notable because it suggests the possibility that not only did many versions of 'Alī's *waṣīya* circulate within Muslim communities, but many versions circulated among Jewish readers as well. Arabized Jewish readers and writers were engaged not only with ethical questions in a written form but also with a wide range of Islamic sources for ethical bequests as well as other types of writing.

This adaptation of the ethical will attributed to 'Alī ibn Abī Ṭālib is hardly the only instance in which Arabized Jewish writers drew on Shi'ī sources in developing the component texts of their intellectual programs.[30] The significance of this instance of borrowing is that it situates the anonymous Arabized Jewish copyist-adaptor with a written copy of the book, demonstrating access to written Shi'ī sources not dependent on teaching or oral transmission. This *waṣīya* in particular is much more aphoristic and list-like in character than Judah ibn Tibbon's, lacking a certain development of and elaboration on the various ideas and admonitions that the author has for his son (although we shall revisit the role of aphorism in Judaeo-Arabic ethical writing toward the end of chapter 2). Ultimately, though, both spring from an ethical culture grounded in books and in written, rather than oral, transmission of text. Errors reflective of a copyist working from a text that contains only the consonantal structure of the Arabic text can be found on the Genizah fragment and these demonstrate that not only were versions of 'Alī's ethical will in circulation, but that Jewish copyists were working with them. For example, where the word *al-'ibād* (humanity) appears in Ibn Bakkār's version, in the Genizah fragment the word *al-ghinā'* (wealth) appears in its place;[31] absent the diacritical marks that distinguish some letters from others, the *rasm* (consonantal skeleton) of each word is virtually identical.[32] This is a mistake that can only be accounted for by assuming that the Genizah copyist was looking at an unpointed text and supplied his own, different diacritical points. Changes in the version of the text written in Hebrew characters that are explicable as mistranscriptions of the consonantal structure of the text written in Arabic characters suggest that it was made from a written copy of the Arabic text to which the translator-copyist had access, thereby illuminating a world in which fathers who were readers wrote and borrowed ethical bequests to their sons rather than simply relying on popular sayings to give shape to their ethical writing, making an excellent counterpoint and comparison for Judah's ethical will. Both texts were produced in Arabized Jewish settings in which readers and writers had access to Islamic books and the will to use them.

Although Judah's ethical will is occasionally discussed in scholarly literature, it still represents a tremendous wealth of unmined data and information. The cross-cultural, genre-bending characteristics that we have just begun to see here render it strange; and furthermore, it has, by and large, simply not yet been fully rescued[33] from the nineteenth-century morass of positivistic historiography that "was then largely devoted to the identification of what could be accepted as historically 'true' in chronicle accounts of the past and the radical expurgation—most often in the form of scornful neglect—of everything that could not."[34] Judah insults his son's intelligence and work ethic forcefully and extensively for failings and traits that the historians of the Wissenschaft des Judentums movement,[35] who drew modern attention to this text and laid the groundwork for its study, knew to be ultimately unreal and untrue; the text did not comport with the truth and so largely fell through the interpretive cracks.[36] The terms and the framing set down by the Wissenschaft have persisted even as historiography has moved forward, taking a linguistic turn that can resolve many of those false tensions. Through a careful reading of the ethical will that is at once close and contextualized, carried out in conjunction with readings of Judah's other writing, this study argues that his adherence to Arabic syntax in his translations is just one prong of a textual program that emphasizes the continuing cultural prestige of the Arabic language for the Arabized Andalusi Jews who had been driven out of the Islamic world and into Latin Christendom. If, "at the dawn of Islam, written Arabic functioned . . . to create a community out of signs, not sounds,"[37] then by the time Islam's Jews were exiled into Christian France the signs had changed shape but their meaning persisted. Over the course of this book, we shall see how Judah uses his ethical will to transmit both Jewish and Islamic thought, assert the primacy of Arabic, and preserve Andalusi culture. Look at the text of Judah's ethical will one way and it is simple medieval Hebrew ethical prose writing from Europe; tilt it into the light and it glints with the gilt of al-Andalus that runs, in veins, to its core. Ultimately, that it is a fundamentally Andalusi and Arabizing text is not in doubt despite its origins in Provence and its wider audience's Arabic illiteracy.

The necessarily almost dialogic character of the open letter from father to son becomes reflective of what Mikhail Bakhtin referred to as "social heteroglossia."[38] The letter speaks in multiple registers and to many audiences as it simultaneously employs the "unitary language [that] constitutes the theoretical expression of the historical processes of linguistic unification and centralization, an expression of the centripetal forces of language."[39] In other words, the ethical will is not only heteroglossic at the linguistic level—in its use of Hebrew in the service of Arabic—but also at the social and receptive level. If the Tibbonid project is unitary, with an interplay of authorial voice and admonished intended audience quite literally pulling together a form of cultural expression and, indeed, a language—scholars properly refer to the texts that come out of this workshop as being written in "Tibbonid Hebrew"—then it is simultaneously that and an other's monolingualism,[40] with the single cultural idiom of Andalusi Jews expressed in a Hebrew that speaks as Arabic. The central paradox of the Tibbonid project is its ability to accommodate both a unitary monolanguage and a social heteroglossia, both of which are articulated in the textual and cultural Arabizing elements of the work and delineated most explicitly in Judah's ethical will. All these admonitions offer up details of a reader's life and all are reflective of Judah's particular values as a translator and a reader. The exasperation that has historically made this letter such a challenge for modern readers to dissect is in fact vexation directed at a son who was indeed a dutiful protégé but who also sought to answer the big literary, intellectual, and cultural questions for himself, drawing on distinct Andalusi models and writing as someone born into exile and so, perhaps, simultaneously much less and infinitely more of an exile than his father. Ultimately, the frustrated disdain that comes through in the text is a byproduct of the loss of al-Andalus that Judah is watching, knowingly, in real time.

This book represents a literarily guided study of one particular aspect of Judah's work as a translator that helped shape that work not just as a textual program but rather a full cultural one; that aspect is his attitude toward the Arabic language itself. This study examines the myriad ways in which his translations and his original writing about those translations advocate for recognition of the cultural prestige of the Arabic language and the Andalusi culture from which it emerged.[41] Closely identified with a word-for-word approach to translators that had, by the twelfth century, largely fallen out of fashion among Arabic translators, Judah is known for translations that are often described as "slavish"[42] in their adherence to the originals in vocabulary, syntax, and style, in effect making the resulting Tibbonid translations Arabic texts written with Hebrew words. This is an intellectual and aesthetic choice that has often proven puzzling in light of the popularity of sense-for-sense translation among other translators. Yet Judah, too, was translating cultures and ideas as much as texts and words. Even in exile and even while translating into Hebrew, the rhetoric Judah employed in his translator's prologues and in what has survived of his correspondence reveals a much more systematic program of preferring and privileging Arabo-Andalusi language and literature, of which word-for-word translation was just another part. For an audience resident in Christian Europe, that which was Arabic came to symbolize al-Andalus as a metonym. In *The Arabic Role in Medieval Literary History*, María Rosa Menocal writes:

> Under the rubrics Arabic and Andalusian, just as under the rubric of any other highly productive culture, we find a great diversity of ideologies, literary genres, and philosophical postures. In the tri-partite culture of al-Andalus, the Christians' and the Jews' contributions and adaptations of cultural and intellectual material were often expressed in the prestige language, Arabic, and many of the traditions of pre-Islamic as well as pre-Christian Iberian antiquity were important parts of the intellectual and artistic tradition. We must furthermore assume this to be even more true in the case of medieval Europe than in cases in history where these cultures have been more homogenous. These examples, a small number of the many available, should serve to point out the essential fallacy in assuming that what is Arabic in medieval Europe is necessarily Islamic or that what was originally something else (Greek or Persian, say) was not received as Andalusian, as part of the great outpouring of material of al-Andalus was so much a feature of the period. It is thus untenable to reject instances of possible Arabic-Andalusian influence on Christian Europe on the basis that the texts in question were not really—that is, originally—Arabic or Andalusian.[43]

By the time, Menocal asserts, that these texts arrived in Europe, the fact of their Arabic language and character was enough to make them Andalusi in the eyes of the audience. Judah ibn Tibbon's project was a part of that transformation.

The shapes of the literature govern the progression of the present study.[44] The first chapter comprises an overview of the concepts of prestige language and cultural transmission operative within the Judaeo-Arabic environment that Judah inhabited and also establishes the Andalusiness of the project and Judah's understanding of that geographic-cultural frame of reference as an especially meritorious one for literary production. Chapter 2 looks at the library as a way of containing these types of cultural knowledge and the library catalogue as a specific form of writing that further preserves and disseminates them; it sets up the material text as the key unit of transmitting text and culture within Judah's immediate orbit. The third chapter examines the role of the Hebrew Bible, both in Hebrew and in Arabic, as a counterpoint to the Qur'ān in establishing the sacred foundations of the secular aspects of Judah's cultural project. The fourth chapter focuses on Arabizing Hebrew poetry and poetics as a way to set poetry apart from all other types of Arabic literary production and to leverage the unique character of poetry in the service of addressing multiple audiences regarding a multiplicity of thematic concerns. Chapter 5 focuses on the quotation of classical Arabic prose of various modes and genres as another means to that textual and cultural end by examining works that are not themselves Andalusi in origin but formed an important part of the intellectual curriculum that prevailed there in the last days of the taifa kingdoms and Almoravid rule. Finally, the sixth chapter is a reception history that focuses on the literary contiguity (and lack thereof) of Judah's ideas about the Arabic language and the possibilities for an afterlife for those ideas in an intellectual environment increasingly removed from Islamicate culture and the Arabic language.

Methodologically, this is a work that does not observe the traditional distinctions between the academic study of literature, philology, philosophy, and history; this principle, grounded in an unwillingness to impose modern epistemological categories on medieval texts that transgress them, is crucial and fundamental to understanding medieval literature within its own cultural and temporal contexts. Even as we speak of the philosophical and theological texts that Judah translated into Hebrew, the textual and linguistic implications of the life of the language within these lives ultimately makes this a literary-critical concern and is thus heavily reliant on the practices, discourses, and even standards of evidence of that discipline. At the same time, despite this book's imperfect fit in the field of history at large, I still consider it to be a work of cultural and literary history. At the end of the day, however, I also think that it is less important for a researcher to respect the boundary between history and literature when it limits the discursive and investigative possibilities available for a certain corpus or context and more important to mix methodologies, to read these texts as literature, and to take the text as far as it will go—though no further—rather than to throw up our hands at what we might never know; in fact, this approach is not a lesser alternative for dealing with a weaker textual record than is ideal but rather adds value through the additional perspective. In this respect, I have relied heavily on the foundations of the New Historicism, its drive to contextualize literature, its directionality toward the linguistic turn, and its disruption with detail of the grand narratives that obtain and govern.[45] This work depends on the idea of history and text as a continuum; yet it does so in the service of a grander narrative, sustained rather than disrupted, by literary anecdote. Readers may find a greater reliance on literary-critical methodologies—close reading, cartographic attention to the observation and transgression of the boundaries of genre by medieval writers, careful philology and concern with the histories of the languages in play, and other types of rhetorical analyses among them—than expected in a typical work of history because it conceives of cultural history, perhaps definitionally, as more a subdiscipline of philology and literature than of History writ large.[46] This kind of work fulfills several important historiographical functions—answering questions of causality and change and interrelationship—but it is ultimately Gabrielle Spiegel's "genuinely integrated literary history"[47] that through its pure and realized interdisciplinarity stakes out "a theoretical position capable of satisfying the demands of both literary criticism and history as separate yet independent disciplinary domains with a common concern for the social dimensions of textual production in past times" and unequivocally adopts the "critical posture that does justice equally to textual, historicist, and historical principles of analysis and explanation."[48] In a certain respect, as unfashionable as these thinkers have become in recent decades, this is history as Auerbach or Vico might have written it.

This work is deeply indebted to the modern theory and the scholarship that has come before it, including the framework of the Tel Aviv poststructuralists, principal among them Itamar Even-Zohar,[49] and the scholars who subsequently applied their work to the Iberian readers and writers who sought to navigate the textual options available to them within the literary polysystem they inhabited.[50] Ultimately, though, it is a study that is guided by its subject, texts that are themselves works of literary theory. The number of Arabists reconsidering the relationship between Arabic and western literary theory, and reasserting the primacy of Arabic thinking within the study of Arabic literature, a position so self-evident that it seems almost tautological, has only grown in recent years;[51] yet it is still a very necessary tautology. And so, faced with the curiously inevitable question "Oh, and do you use *theory* to do that?" when I tell my interlocutors that I work on the history of translation from a literary perspective, my answer has changed over the course of writing this book. What began as outright rejection became grudging admission, which ultimately yielded an acceptance that is possible to balance text and theory, history and literature, medieval and modern, in an organic way. What has not changed, though, is my own view of these texts as a coherent poetics of translation and my conviction that they themselves therefore provide the best guidance through the material. And so it is to these texts that stand as both object of study and as cipher that I have chosen to give a wide berth in which they can speak for themselves.

NOTES

Chapter title from Samuel ibn Tibbon, *Commentary on Ecclesiastes*, trans. James T. Robinson (Tübingen: Mohr Siebeck, 2007), 28.

1. On the four-year discrepancy between Yūsuf taking power in 1163 and formally receiving the caliphal title "prince of the believers" in 1167, see Hugh Kennedy, *Muslim Spain and Portugal* (New York: Routledge, 1996), 216–17. Generally I use only Common Era dates throughout the book, rather than the combination of *hijrī*/Common Era dates that I have used here initially both to contextualize what follows within the field of Islamic history and historiography and because this introductory paragraph fits more squarely and cleanly within that silo than does the rest of the book, which more messily straddles the fields of Islamic, Judaic, and Iberian studies.

2. On the Almohads, see Maribel Fierro, *The Almohad Revolution: Politics and Religion in the Islamic World* (New York: Routledge, 2012); Madeleine Fletcher, "Al-Andalus and North Africa in the Almohad Ideology," in *The Legacy of Muslim Spain*, ed. Salma Khadra Jayyusi (Leiden: Brill, 1992), 235–58; Ambrosio Huici Miranda, *Historia politica del imperio almohade* (Granada: Editiorial Universidad de Granada, 2001 reprint); María Jesús Viguera Molins, *Los reinos de taifa y las invasiones magrebíes* (Barcelona: Mapfre, 1992).

3. Kennedy, *Muslim Spain and Portugal*, 216–31. On the Great Mosque see Fatima Roldán Castro, "De Nuevo sobre la mezquita aljama almohade de Sevilla: La versión del cronista cortesano Ibn Sāhib al-Salah," in *Magna Hispalensis: Recuperación de la Aljama almoade*, ed. A. Jiménez Martín (Sevilla: Hernán Ruiz, 2002), 13–22, and Leopoldo Torres Balbás, "La primitiva mezquita mayor de Sevilla," *Al-Andalus* 14 (1946): 425–39.

4. The nature of these cultural limitations is just beginning to be reassessed after decades that cast the Almohads as the absolute villains of Andalusi history. An initial step was taken by David Corcos, "The Nature of the Almohad Rulers' Treatment of the Jews," *Zion* 32 (1967): 137–60. Subsequent studies include Maribel Fierro, "La religión," in *Historia de España*, ed. María Jesús Viguera Molins (Madrid: Calpe, 1997), 437–546; and Amira Bennison and María Ángeles Gallego, "Jewish Trading in Fes on the Eve of the Almohad Conquest," *Miscelánea de estudios árabes y hebreos* 56 (2007): 33–51. With renewed attention to the founder of the movement, Ibn Tumart, scholarship has more recently turned to the religious foundations and implications of the movement, as in chapters 5–7 in Mercedes García-Arenal, *Messianism and Puritanical Reform: Mahdis of the Muslim West* (Leiden: Brill, 2006), and political changes such as those outlined in Pascal Buresi's history of the Maghreb from the eleventh to the fifteenth centuries, and delineated in more detail in his editions of governance documents in *Governing the Empire: Provincial Administration in the Almohad Caliphate* (Leiden: Brill, 2013). The status of Jews under Almohad rule has also long been a subject of interest, in no small measure

because of the seemingly paradoxical response of the Maimonides family to the political changes in their hometown of Córdoba, namely fleeing Almohad rule there and heading directly into the heart of the empire: Fez.

5. I have reckoned the initial date of composition after accepting the scholarship that posits 1160 as the year of Samuel's birth (1150 and 1165 have also been suggested) and concluding that Judah appears to have composed the earliest stratum of the text addressed to a twelve-year-old Samuel.

6. Evidence from the ethical will tells us that Judah and Samuel earned their living principally as merchants and that Judah also worked as a physician. I am using the word "profession" here to describe their translation activity because the vicissitudes of the English language mean that the alternatives—avocation or hobby, to name a few of the possibilities—minimize the seriousness of the endeavor and investment of time and effort that they put into it, as well as the impact of the work. Ultimately, the choice of term is in line with Isidore Twersky, who described translation as the Ibn Tibbon family "profession" in the same sense in his "Aspects of the Social and Cultural History of Provençal Jewry," *Journal of World History* 11 (1968): 200.

7. While I principally use this text in the service of cultural history—and, more specifically, of literary and intellectual history—it is a wide-ranging document that encompasses many topics and should also be of considerable interest to social historians with interests in economic, medical, and even domestic history.

8. Judah ibn Tibbon, "Musar Av," Bodleian Mich. MS 50.3 (Neubauer 2219), folio 16a. The published edition appears in *Hebrew Ethical Wills*, ed. Israel Abrahams (Philadelphia: Jewish Publication Society, 1926), 59. Two other editions of this text were published, both in 1852: H. Edelmann, *Derech Tovim* (London); and Moritz Steinschneider, *Ermahungsschreiben des Jehuda ibn Tibbon und Sprüche der Weisen* (Berlin). Abrahams considered Steinschneider's edition to be uncharacteristically flawed; the Edelmann edition followed Steinschneider rather than the manuscript. Sections of the letter also appear in the revised and expanded 2002 version of Simha Assaf's *Sources for the History of Education in Israel,* ed. Shmuel Glick (New York: Jewish Theological Seminary of America, 2006), 129–32. Two new complete editions have also appeared more recently, edited by Pinhas Koraḥ and by Simon Iakerson and E. Yuzbashyan. Excerpts from and partial copies of the text can also be found in three additional manuscripts: Frankfurt Hebr. Oct. 266.1, Florence Biblioteca Laurenziana 45.7, and in Biblioteca Palatina Parma 2484.5 (De Rossi 1046). The Bodleian manuscript is the earliest and most complete surviving copy of the text, bearing a colophon with an encoded date revealing it to have been copied sometime between the fall of 1340 and the spring of 1341; this colophon and the dating scheme of the manuscript are discussed in greater detail in chapter 4. Because of that manuscript's antiquity and completeness, work for the present study is based on the text as it appears in the Bodleian manuscript with recourse to the Abrahams and Koraḥ editions and other, later and less complete, manuscripts as necessary. Citations from the text refer to the Bodleian manuscript. Although Abrahams's version includes an English translation, it sounds quite antiquated a century on, and so all quotations from this text appear in my own English translations (with the full text translated in the appendix), as are all others except as noted.

9. Ross Brann has already called attention to this statement as an assertion of Judah ibn Tibbon and Samuel ibn Naghrīla's cultural integration into an Arabophone, Islamicate society in his *Power in the Portrayal* (Princeton, NJ: Princeton University

Press, 2002), 39, as has María Ángeles Gallego in her "The Languages of Medieval Iberia and Their Religious Dimension," *Medieval Encounters* 9, no. 1 (2003): 117.

10. Judah ibn Tibbon, "Musar Av," 17a.

11. Judah ibn Tibbon, preface to *Ḥovot ha-Levavot*, 8.

12. The dying instructions of the biblical figure Jacob to his sons (Gen. 49) and Moses' farewell exhortation to the Israelites in the desert (Deut. 32:1–43) are often seen as models for the types of discourse and content found in medieval and later ethical wills. Judah's ethical will is published along with other medieval ones in Israel Abrahams's *Hebrew Ethical Wills*.

13. Carlos del Valle Rodríguez identifies the ethical will as a school-type text (497–99); his characterization, based on the ethical will, of Judah as an unrepentant bibliophile is discussed further in chapter 3. In the section "Stereotype and Individuality in the Handwriting of Medieval Scribes" of his *The Making of the Hebrew Book* (Jerusalem: Magnes Press, 1993), Malachi Beit-Arie situates Judah's critique of Samuel's handwriting within the calligraphic training that scribes received. Beit-Arié concludes from Judah's remark about the similarities between the hand of Patur's son and that of his teacher that young scribes were taught to write by directly mimicking the handwriting and calligraphic style of their teachers, and that success was measured by how closely they were able to emulate the original sample. Judah even comments that "script is made up of shapes, like any others, and any man can copy it from a model with sufficient scrutiny and drive" (16a and again, similarly, on 17b). The fourteenth-century Ḥanbalī jurist and theological commentator Shams al-Dīn Muḥammad ibn Qayyim al-Jawziya attested a similar practice among Muslim scribes. This is described in Franz Rosenthal, "Significant Uses of Arabic Writing," *Ars Orientalis* 4 (1961): 15–23. Judith Olszowy-Schlanger also mentions the curricular function of the text in a study of school texts found in the Cairo Genizah in her "Leaning to Read and Write in Medieval Egypt: Children's Exercise Books from the Cairo Genizah," *Journal of Semitic Studies* 48, no. 1 (2004): 47–69. Like Beit-Arie, Lawrence Fine, in his "The Arts of Calligraphy and Composition and the Love of Books," *Judaism in Practice: From the Middle Ages through the Early Modern Period* (Princeton, NJ: Princeton University Press, 2001), ties the value of the document to its comment on scribal practice, noting that it "so richly reflects the aesthetic values of Islamic culture during this period. These include the importance of cultivating the art of calligraphy and fine composition style in both Hebrew and Arabic" (321).

14. To my eye, the fact of this text being not only an intellectual autobiography as much as a curriculum but also a very fundamentally Andalusi text are self-evident and inherent characteristics of the text. Nevertheless, it must be noted that James T. Robinson has already made those observations in earlier work, namely in his "The Ibn Tibbon Family: A Dynasty of Translators in Medieval Provence," in *Studies in Memory of Isadore Twersky*, ed. Jay Harris (Cambridge, MA: Harvard University Press, 2005), 202–4, wherein he writes: "This interesting and amusing document has been published several times, translated, cited and discussed, and exploited as evidence that the young Samuel did not excel in his early studies. But I would suggest that, in fact, this ethical will tells us more about Judah than his son . . . a document expressing Judah's cultural ideology. . . . In the course of his Testament, Judah touches upon every aspect of the broadly conceived Jewish culture of Islamic Spain. He emphasizes the importance of the Bible, Talmud, Arabic language, Hebrew grammar, literary style, astronomy, medicine, and

other 'foreign sciences,' articulating Spanish ideals with greater clarity than was done in Spain itself. In light of the Arabic literary background, I would suggest that Judah is not only addressing his son and mapping out the latter's educational curriculum but is also addressing the community of scholars of southern France. His Testament accordingly can be read as a Sephardic manifesto of sorts, a call to adopt the broad cultural ideals of the Jews of al-Andalus and a plan to reeducate the children of southern France. In light of this interpretation of the Testament, Judah emerges not only as a man of language and literature, law, and science, but also as a reformer, and translation can be seen as the essential tool in transmitting his uniquely Spanish vision of Judaism to the communities of southern France."

15. Robinson, "The Ibn Tibbon Family," 203.

16. Gad Freudenthal, "Abraham ibn Ezra and Judah ibn Tibbon as Cultural Intermediaries," in *Exchange and Transmission across Cultural Boundaries: Philosophy, Mysticism, and Science in the Mediterranean World*, ed. Haggai Ben-Shammai et al. (Jerusalem: Israel Academy of Arts and Sciences, 2013), 68.

17. On the Cairo Genizah cache and its role in Andalusi historiography, see notes 9 and 57 in chapter 2.

18. Lacuna restored based on the Arabic original.

19. This emphatic repetition, which appears to be part emphasis and part scribal stutter or homeoteleuton, does not occur in the text as attributed to 'Alī ibn Abī Ṭālib.

20. TS 13 J 22.19.

21. Tobias Mayer, Introduction to Al-Ghazālī, *Letter to a Disciple* (London: Islamic Text Society, 2005), vii.

22. Goitein's comments comparing the ethical will to al-Ghazālī's epistle are found in his notecard files, specifically Card 100775. Al-Ghazālī's text is published as his *Letter to a Disciple*. The place of al-Ghazālī in the Andalusi and wider Judaeo-Arabic intellectual canon is the subject of chapter 5.

23. On whom, see http://www.kister.huji.ac.il.

24. S. D. Goitein, *A Mediterranean Society*, vol. 5 (reprint, Berkeley: University of California Press, 2000), 399 and 619.

25. Dimitri Gutas, "Classical Arabic Wisdom Literature: Nature and Scope," *Journal of the American Oriental Society* 101, no. 1 (1981): 49–86; and Riad Kassis, *The Book of Proverbs and Arabic Proverbial Works* (Leiden: Brill, 1999).

26. Muḥammad ibn Abī Bakr al-Tilimsānī al-Birrī, *Pearls of the Lineage of the Imam 'Alī and His Family*, ed. Muḥammad al-Tūnaji (Beirut, 1994), 87–89; Ibn Shu'ba, *Gifts of the Intellect from the Family of the Messenger.* The differences between the two versions of the ethical will are accounted by the wholesale expansion of the earlier text by the later one and should be self-evident to any reader looking at both versions.

27. Stefan Leder, "Zubayr ibn Bakkār," *Encyclopedia of Islam*, 2nd ed., http://ezproxy.library.nyu.edu:2313/entries/encyclopaedia-of-islam-2/al-zubayr-b-bakkar-SIM_8190, accessed January 23, 2016.

28. Al-Birrī, *Pearls*, 88. This sentence occurs in the part of the text that is reflected in lines 23–24 of the Genizah version. In chapters 4 and 5 there is further discussion of how Arabized Jewish writers handled the translation and transmission of texts that contained explicit references to Islam.

29. T-S 13 J 22.19, line 24. On the procedures by which Jewish authors engaged in substitution as a kind of theological editing process, see Jonathan Decter, "The Render-

ing of Quranic Quotations in Hebrew Translations of Islamic Texts," *Jewish Quarterly Review* 96 (2006): 336–58.

30. Perhaps most famous is Shlomo Pines's "Shiite Terms and Conceptions in Judah Halevi's Kuzari," *Jerusalem Studies in Arabic and Islam* 2 (1980): 165–251. More recently, see Ehud Krinis, *God's Chosen People: Judah Halevi's Kuzari and Shiʿi Imami Doctrine* (Turnhout: Brepols, 2014).

31. T-S 13 J 22.19, line 28; and al-Birrī, *Pearls*, 88.

32. Following the definite article *al-*, which is attached to both words, the two are spelled with the following combinations of letters: *ayin-bāʾ-alif-dāl (ʿibād)* and *ghayn-nūn-alif-hamza (ghināʾ)*. *ʿAyin* and *ghayn* are formed identically and distinguished only by a single point over the latter; *bāʾ* and *nūn* are of an identical shape, distinguished by a point below the former and above the latter; the *alif* in each word is the same; and depending on the hand of the scribe, it is not at all implausible that a *dāl* could be mistaken for a *hamza* resting on the line.

33. This is not to suggest that this is in any way an unknown text, just an underutilized one. Some examples of studies that have centered on or referred to the text include the following: Avriel Bar-Levav writes about the phenomenology of Judah's criticism of Samuel within the generic frame of the "egodocument" in his article "When I Was Alive: Jewish Ethical Wills as Egodocuments," in *Egodocuments and History: Autobiographical Writing in Its Social Context Since the Middle Ages*, ed. Rudolf Dekker (Rotterdam: Verloren Publishers, 2002), 49ff. Menachem Ben-Sasson identifies the text as one that articulates a kind of Andalusi cultural supremacy when it "alluded to the claim that Sefarad in their time—and even before—was the divinely-chosen, temporary center . . . for Jewish refugees from Islamic Spain to the Christian North there were obvious reasons for developing such a claim, especially when they began to encounter Jewish intellectuals of different cultural backgrounds." See his "Varieties of Inter-Communal Relations in the Geonic Period," in *The Jews of Medieval Islam: Community, Society, and Identity*, ed. Daniel Frank (Leiden: Brill, 1995), 29. Hayim Schirman mentions the ethical will, particularly the instruction to Samuel that he read Samuel ibn Naghrīla's *After Proverbs*, among the medieval Hebrew texts that can, in part, be considered works of poetics in "The Function of the Hebrew Poet in Medieval Spain," *Jewish Social Studies* 6, no. 3 (1954): 238.

34. Gabrielle Spiegel, *The Past as Text* (Baltimore: Johns Hopkins University Press, 1997), xii.

35. Wissenschaft des Judentums was a nineteenth-century humanistic movement dedicated to applying scientific principles and precision to the study of Judaism. Some among the most significant members of this movement were Leopold Zunz, Heinrich Graetz, Solomon Schechter, and Moritz Steinschneider.

36. A somewhat comical appraisal of the state of the question about the ethical will comes in the English introduction to a recent study, edition, and Russian translation of the text: "As far as I know, there are two English translations and one translation into Spanish. However, the testament has never been translated into Russian and consequently has never been the subject of serious study" (Simon Iakerson and E. Yuzbashyan, *Testament of the Sage Judah ibn Tibbon to His Son Samuel Written in the Days of His Youth* [Saint Petersburg: Center for Oriental Studies, 2011], 197). While one might—and perhaps, indeed, should—dispute the causal relationship in which modern Russian translation necessarily predicates the serious study of medieval Andalusi Arabizing

Hebrew *belles lettres*, its author's description of the state of affairs is, nonetheless, not wholly inaccurate.

37. Benedict Anderson, *Imagined Communities* (New York: Verso Books, 1983), 13.

38. Mikhail Bakhtin, "Epic and Novel," in *The Dialogic Imagination*, trans. Michael Holquist (Austin: University of Texas Press, 1981), 270.

39. Ibid., 269.

40. This alludes, of course, to Jacques Derrida's 1992 essay *The Monolingualism of the Other: or, The Prosthesis of Origin*, trans. Patrick Menash (Stanford, CA: Stanford University Press, 1998). Although it principally deals with the modern period and is both somewhat autobiographical and typically Derridian, its treatment of the linguistic and cultural situation of Arabophone Jews in France makes it a useful text to read with the Tibbonid translators in mind.

41. In "Introductions of the Thirteenth-Century Arabic-to-Hebrew Translators of Philosophic and Scientific Texts," in *Vehicles of Transmission, Translation and Transformation in Medieval Textual Culture*, ed. Robert Wisnovsky et al. (Turnhout: Brepols, 2011), 223–34, Steven Harvey alludes to two unpublished papers read at European Association of Jewish Studies colloquia in 2001 and 2002 in which he argued for the centrality of the translator's preface in interpreting philosophical works in translation, pre- and post-Maimonides.

42. The origin of this term to describe the Ibn Tibbon translations appears to originate with Albert Loewy's 1872 translation of the letter from Maimonides to Samuel: "Whoever wishes to translate and aims at rendering each word literally and at the same time adheres slavishly to the order of words and sentences in the original will meet with much difficulty and his rendering will be untrustworthy"; the term becomes a common descriptor of Tibbonid translations going forward.

43. María Rosa Menocal, *The Arabic Role in Medieval Literary History* (Philadelphia: University of Pennsylvania Press, 1987), 37.

44. This is not an uncommon way of tracing the development certain cultural and intellectual phenomena. The *Cambridge History of Arabic Literature* volume focusing on the literature of al-Andalus is another volume that organizes itself according to a principle of the "shapes" of the literature and culture ("Introduction," *The Cambridge History of Arabic Literature: The Literature of al-Andalus* [Cambridge: Cambridge University Press, 2000], 18).

45. Here, in addition to the broader principles of the New Historicism/New Medievalism, I am also following Miriam Frenkel's approach to resisting the classification of texts (in her case specifically those from the Cairo Genizah) as either documentary or literary, as delineated in her "Genizah Documents and Literary Products," in *From a Sacred Source: Genizah Studies in Honour of Professor Stefan C. Reif*, ed. Ben Outhwaite (Leiden: Brill, 2010), 139–56.

46. It has been in the course of framing this current project, particularly in preparing what is now chapter 5 for inclusion as a stand-alone article in a special 2013 issue of the journal *Medieval Encounters* populated otherwise by articles written by historians more traditionally construed, that I began to formulate my ideas about the relationship of cultural, intellectual, and literary history to philology and history as major disciplines. Particularly helpful in articulating this idea as a part of the theory of history that governs the present study was the subsequent appearance of Ryan Szpiech's "The Convivencia Wars: Decoding History's Polemic with Philology" in *A Sea of Languages: Rethinking the*

Arabic Role in Medieval Literary History, ed. Suzanne Conklin Akbari and Karla Malette (Toronto: University of Toronto Press, 2013), 135–61.

47. Spiegel, *The Past as Text*, 21.

48. Ibid., 23–24.

49. Even-Zohar's foundational statement of polysystem theory is found in his "Polysystem Theory," *Poetics Today* 1, no. 1 (1979): 287–310.

50. The earliest systematic application of polysystem theory to the Iberian context came in the work of Rina Drory, *The Emergence of Jewish Arabic Literary Contacts at the Beginning of the Tenth Century* (Tel Aviv: Ha-Kibbutz ha-Meuḥad, 1988), published in English as *Models and Contacts* (Leiden: Brill, 2000). Subsequently, the same approach is applied across a wide range of topics in Andalusi literary history. See, inter alia, Ross Brann's *Power in the Portrayal* (cited above) as well as his earlier book *The Compunctious Poet: Cultural Ambiguity and Hebrew Poetry in Muslim Spain* (Baltimore: The Johns Hopkins University Press, 1991); Esperanza Alfonso, *Islamic Culture through Jewish Eyes* (Routledge: New York, 2008); and Jonathan Decter, *Iberian Jewish Literature: Between al-Andalus and Christian Europe* (Bloomington: Indiana University Press, 2007).

51. Perhaps the best example of an achievement of this balance can be found across the work of Abdelfattah Killito; in a more standard vein of writing about this issue within the profession itself, see Alexander Key, "Arabic: Acceptance and Anxiety," *American Comparative Literature Association State of the Discipline Report*, 2014–15, http://stateofthediscipline.acla.org/entry/arabic-acceptance-and-anxiety, accessed September 15, 2015; and Mohammad Salama, "Arabic and the Monopoly of Theory," *Arcade: Literature, the Humanities and the World*, http://arcade.stanford.edu/blogs/arabic-and-monopoly-theory, accessed September 15, 2015.

1 "PEN, I RECOUNT YOUR FAVOR!"

Reading, Writing, and Translating in Memory of al-Andalus

THE NATURAL AND cultural wonders of al-Andalus are among the most powerful forces and prevalent tropes in the Arabic and Arabizing Hebrew literature of Spain's native sons and their descendants. In poetry and prose, Andalusis lavish high praise on their land and on the superiority of their landsmen in all respects—especially their cultural and literary skill. The place is, of course, lauded in works of *futūḥ* (conquest narratives), *masālik wa-l-mamālik* (geographic surveys), and *ṭabaqāt* (sociological categorization). Poetry praises the lushness of the land and the wisdom and general superiority of the people; and when those authors and their intellectual descendants are forced to leave, we see loss, exile, and nostalgia as common refrains in Arabic and Arabizing Hebrew poetry. Ibn Shuhayd writes perhaps the most famous lament over the city of Córdoba after the collapse of the Umayyad caliphate.[1] Ibn Ḥazm praises the lush land and the expressions of its cultural values in a work of courtly love and, subsequently, to counteract what he saw as the barbarity of the Almoravid and Almohad invasions, writes a treatise in the *faḍā'il al-Andalus* (merits of al-Andalus) mode highlighting the achievements of the Andalusi literary class.[2] And perhaps most salient for the discussion that follows, Abraham ibn 'Ezra' (ca. 1093–ca. 1170) wrote a mournful lament over the collective exilic fate of the Jews of al-Andalus and over the loss of the land:

> Calamity came upon Spain from the skies,
> And my eyes pour forth their streams of tears.
> I moan like an owl for the town of Lucena,
> where Exile dwelled, guiltless and strong,
> for a thousand and seventy years unchanged—

until the day that she was expelled,
leaving her like a widow, forlorn,
deprived of Scriptures and books of the Law . . .
I shave my head and bitterly keen
for Seville's martyrs and sons who were taken,
as daughters were forced into strangeness of faith.
Córdoba's ruined, like the desolate sea . . .[3]

With respect to the general shift from praise to lament, Ross Brann comments: "The trope's persuasive power rests not only on the ritualized remembrance of experienced and imagined loss, but also and more particularly on the community's recollection of exactly what was lost."[4] The lament over the land and the culture that sprang from it grows out of the praise that preceded it.

Judah ibn Tibbon was unabashedly a "cultural nationalist,"[5] elevating a national Israel above all others. For example, in the ethical will, he exhorts Samuel to charity so that he "will be respected by both great and small, and by Israel and the other nations,"[6] establishing a parallelism that equates a national Israel with great men and the other nations with lesser men; yet he was also a thoroughly Arabized thinker and writer, exiled from a place where those two things represented no contradiction. Even so, Judah never wrote any sort of explicit defense of or lament for al-Andalus and its Arabic literary culture; nor did he hold himself as an Andalusi apart from the Jewish communities in the north once he found himself in their midst as did his near contemporary, Moses ibn 'Ezra' (unrelated to the aforementioned Abraham ibn 'Ezra'), who, like many of his contemporaries, consistently tied the superiority of Andalusi Jewry to its lineage as the descendants of the exiles of Jerusalem.[7] It is worth noting that Brann has described this type of nostalgia as motivating in Ibn 'Ezra' a desire "to present himself as a teacher and transmitter of Andalusian Jewish culture";[8] in other words, the model of an Andalusi cultural translator in exile already existed. Nevertheless, in time Judah adopted the pieces of that model that were useful to his textual program without ever explicitly taking on the mantle of the rhetoric of nostalgia. His program of translation serves the needs of his adopted community in medieval Lunel, a city in southern France just a few kilometers away from the modern city that bears the same name, for works of religion and philosophy in a language at least nominally accessible to them. In doing so, Judah telegraphs that same profound longing for and pride in al-Andalus to readers who have been receptive to it while writing a prideful defense of Arabic into his compositions; and he uses translation and his writing about translation to articulate these correlated sentiments.

The cornerstone of Judah's intellectual project was the translation of Arabic texts, word for word, into Hebrew. In doing so, he created philosophical and religious texts that preserved the features and complexities of the original work as well as the linguistic features of the source language, and he wrote about the importance of both of those aspects of textual conservation. By examining the relationships between Hebrew and Arabic and secular and sacred writing, this first chapter delves more deeply into Judah's program of literal translation and examines the ways in which it allowed him to transmit his ideas about Andalusi texts and textual culture. Furthermore, it sets the process of word-for-word translation into a broader context of the transposition and adaptation of Andalusi literary models and cultural ideals for non-Arabophone audiences outside of the Islamicate world. As much as Judah was meticulously literal in his rendering of text, he was also a cultural conduit who channeled his belief in the superiority of the Arabic language and of al-Andalus to transmit and preserve a wide range of texts.

THE TIBBONID WORKSHOP

Judah ibn Tibbon was born in Granada around the year 1120, the scion of a family that, if the Arabic etymology of the family name is to be any guide,[9] may have originally made their living as grain millers.[10] Although he is most closely and regularly associated with the city of Granada (a place that factors into his thinking about the Andalusi character of Arabizing Hebrew poetry, as is discussed in chapter 4), there is also some evidence connecting his family's origins to the city of Seville.[11] The first direct evidence that we have of Judah's presence in Lunel as a resident of that city comes, as do the whereabouts of so many itinerant thinkers and writers, in Benjamin of Tudela's *Itineraries*, in which he writes about the various scholars he meets in towns with substantial Jewish populations in the south of France:

> From there [Montpellier] it is four parsangs (*parsa'ot*) to Lunel, where there is a Jewish community that studies Torah day and night. It includes the great rabbi Meshullam and his sons, all wise, great, and well-to-do: Joseph, Isaac, Jacob, Aaron, as well as the contrarian Asher, who rejects worldly matters and abstains from meat, always occupies himself with books, and is very learned in matters of Talmud. Also: Moses, the brother-in-law of the rabbi Samuel the Elder; and Ulsarnu; and Solomon ha-Cohen; and Judah ben Tibbon the Spaniard, a physician (*Yehudah ha-rofe' ben Tibbon ha-Sefardi*). They support, teach, and provision everyone who comes from a far-off land to study Torah, for as long as they study in the college there. They are wise, generous,

> and holy men who observe the commandments and have great munificence toward their brethren, wherever they are. There are about 300 Jews in this community; may the Rock preserve them. From there it is two parsangs to Posquieres.[12]

However, it has long and consistently been suggested that by the time Benjamin encountered him there in such illustrious company, Judah would have already been living in Lunel for close to a decade, perhaps having left Granada as early as 1148 with the advent of Almohad rule in the Iberian Peninsula. Although the ethical will is a text of tremendous autobiographical character, James T. Robinson calls it "notable" that it never refers to the political and cultural changes that ostensibly drove Ibn Tibbon out of al-Andalus and north across the Pyrenees. In Judah's work we do not even see the kinds of hints to the political upheaval and advent of North African rule in al-Andalus that we find in the work of Abraham ibn 'Ezra', who wrote that he found himself in Rome to escape "the oppressors."[13]

Once in Provence, Judah began to translate works of Arabic philosophy into Hebrew for his coreligionists there, since they were not uniformly literate in Arabic, and for a wider European audience as well. Some of his translations were created for specific patrons in response to specific requests: The first parts of Judah's *Ḥovot ha-levavot*, the Hebrew version of Baḥya ibn Paqūda's *Hidāya ilā farā'id al-qulūb* (*Duties of the Heart*), are dedicated to Judah's teacher Meshullam ben Jacob (also mentioned in the passage of Benjamin of Tudela's *Itineraries* cited above and whose role in Judah's intellectual formation is discussed in chapter 3) and the other parts to Abraham ben David; Solomon ibn Gabirol's *Kitāb iṣlāh al-akhlāq* (Improvement of Moral Qualities) was translated into Hebrew as *Tiqqun Middot ha-Nefesh* for Meshullam's son Asher (whose role as patron and fellow is discussed in further detail in chapter 4). The specific impetus behind some of his other translations is less clear—except perhaps to say that they were chosen "methodically and prudently, for he was writing for popular consumption"[14]—but still form part of a coherent Andalusi philosophical and religious corpus: an additional work by Ibn Gabirol, namely his *Kitāb mukhtar al-jawāhir* (*Choice of Pearls*) translated into Hebrew as *Mivḥar ha-peninim*; Judah Halevi's *Kitāb al-radd wa-l-dalīl fī l-dīn al-dhalīl* (Book of Proofs and Refutations in Defense of the Despised Faith), which came to be known in both Arabic and Hebrew more simply as *The Kuzari* and, although not Andalusi in origin but certainly popular in the region, Sa'adya Ga'on's *Kitāb al-amanāt wa-l-itiqadāt* (Book of Beliefs and Opinions) translated into Hebrew under the title *Sefer emunot ve-de'ot*. Judah also translated a pair of reference works for the study of the Hebrew Bible, known together in Hebrew as the *Maḥbarot ha-diqduq* (The Grammatical Notebooks). These two works, originally compiled by Jonah ibn Janāḥ (b. ca. 985), were entitled *Kitāb al-Lum'a* (Book of Variegated Flower Beds), a style guide and grammatical resource that was translated into Hebrew as *Sefer ha-riqmah* (Book of Woven Patterns), and *Kitāb al-Uṣūl* (Book of Roots), an Arabic-language lexicon of the Hebrew Bible translated into Hebrew as *Sefer ha-Shorashim*. As a translator, he coined many words for scientific and philosophical concepts that existed in Arabic, a consequence of the by-then longstanding Greek-to-Arabic translation movements, but that did not yet exist in Hebrew. Although Judah is not typically characterized in the scholarship as having been a writer in his own right, his considerable output of text paints a coherent and compelling picture that is worthy of further attention. He wrote prologues and epilogues to these works as well as epistles in which he delineated his own principles for translation. In addition to the prologues and epilogues, his original compositions included a letter to Asher ben Meshullam of Lunel describing his process of translating the *Tiqqun Middot ha-Nefesh* and the aforementioned letter to Samuel written in the genre of the ethical will, which generally advises on how to lead a correct personal and professional life, transmitting values from an older generation to a younger one. In the latter, Judah also references an original composition on grammar and style; but as far as is known, that work was never completed and does not survive even in quotations or fragments. Additional treatises are attributed more insecurely to Judah; so, too, is a Hebrew translation of one of al-Farābī's treatises on logic, although that text is unknown other than in a reference to it by Judah's grandson Moses.[15] The letter to Samuel also gives additional information about Judah's activities as a physician, merchant, and important participant in Andalusi and Provençal Jewish life, and offers a picture of Judah's ideals for a satisfying and harmonious family life.[16]

Judah's nickname "the father of the Hebrew translators"[17] was bestowed on him by the person who regularly called him father, the addressee of his ethical will, his son Samuel.[18] As noted in the introduction, Judah turned to writing an ethical will as a way to transmit both his professional and personal values to Samuel and to other readers in the Provençal Jewish community who would encounter the text after his death. Judah's entrée into the genre is most often identified as a repository of over-the-top criticisms of a son deemed too indolent and dull for his own or anyone else's good. For example, Judah expresses his disappointment in Samuel by telling him: "But you, my son, belied my expectations and my hopes. You did not see fit to make use of your vision. You have separated yourself from your books, and have shown no interest in them—not even in their titles or tables of contents";[19] he also complained that "even now you rely on me to wake you from your lazy slumber."[20] Judah laments that "God has not given you a heart with which to know, eyes through which to see, or ears through which to hear"[21] until finally the document deteriorates into rhetoric of pure hysteria, crying out at the shame and humiliation wrought by his son's ineptitude.[22] Judah does ultimately temper his criticisms with the concession that the reputation Samuel has earned in his father's eyes and in the wider world for his poor judgment and lousy work ethic is "mostly a lie" (*rovo sheqer*);[23] however, despite such small concessions and the success and repute Samuel would ultimately enjoy in the profession his father chose for him, evidence internal and external to the ethical will suggests that Judah largely believed genuinely in the harder line.

After Jonathan of Lunel,[24] a rabbi and the leader of the community in which Judah had relocated himself, commissioned its native son, Samuel, to translate Moses Maimonides' *Guide of the Perplexed* (following Maimonides' own declining of the commission on the basis of his advancing age),[25] Samuel wrote to Maimonides to ask him to resolve a series of questions and doubts he had about his Hebrew interpretation of the text. The pair corresponded over the course of at least four letters back and forth; of these, only two survive and only in Hebrew translation rather than in the polyglot of Hebrew and Judaeo-Arabic in which they were originally written. The surviving letter from Maimonides, which dates to the year 1199, a mere five years before his death and the same year in which he wrote the first of the two letters to Jonathan of Lunel, is the first one he wrote in reply to Samuel.[26] Following typical salutations at the start of the letter, Maimonides writes:

> Years ago, I had already heard of the honored prince, the sage, your father Judah and we all were aware of the breadth of his knowledge and the clarity of his language, both in Arabic and in Hebrew. Learned men from Granada, and one from Toledo, came here and told us about his great honor. The wise, dear Meir . . . also gave us examples of your father's wisdom and showed me all of the books that he translated, from the grammar books to the works of wisdom literature. *But I did not know that he had a son.* However, since your letters in both Hebrew and Arabic arrived and I considered them and saw the places that caused you doubt in *The Guide of the Perplexed* and places where you thought there might have been a scribal error, I quoted an ancient poem: The father's excellence has passed to the son. Blessed is the One who compensated your father for his wisdom by giving him a son like this.[27]

In a setting that might fairly be described as prosopographically obsessed, Maimonides' report of not even knowing that Judah had a son speaks to Samuel's extraordinary exclusion from the salons of Andalusi-exile high society. It also represents a slight that would seem to suggest that Judah very much believed what he wrote about Samuel's professional inadequacies and thus did not offer him entrée into the intellectual world that Judah himself inhabited. Where Maimonides praises the elegance of Samuel's handwriting,[28] Judah lambastes its messiness and its non-conformity to the hand of his teachers.[29] Furthermore, Judah describes contracting a certain Provençal teacher, Jacob ben Ovadiah, to teach Samuel to write in Hebrew and recounts the conversation between the two men. After writing about Samuel's lack of progress in learning good Arabic style, he adds: "Nor have you progressed as expected in your Hebrew writing. Do you not remember that I have been paying your wise teacher, Jacob, the son of the most generous Ovadiah, thirty gold dinars per year? When I pressed him into the service of teaching you how to write the letters, he said to me: 'Wouldn't it be enough for him to learn one letter per year?'"[30] It seems that Jacob might have been cracking a joke about the generosity of the salary Judah was paying him and suggesting that he would like to collect it for the upward of two decades it would take to teach the Hebrew alphabet at the rate of one letter per year; yet Judah, predisposed to think ill of Samuel's skill, understands it as a deserved dig at his son's intelligence and abilities. Even as other medieval and (eventually) early modern and modern readers would consider Judah's criticisms to be unfair or inaccurate, that Judah believed them himself becomes more difficult to dispute in light of the external evidence.[31]

The current state of the question places Samuel's birthdate around 1160, although earlier scholarship has fixed it as early as 1150 (based on Henri Gross's monumental survey of Jewish communities in France)[32] and as late as 1165; he was born in Lunel and also resided in Toledo and in Marseilles, where he died in 1232. He was responsible for Hebrew translations of many of Maimonides' works: most famously, the *Dalālāt al-ḥā'irīn* (Guide of the Perplexed), translated into Hebrew as *Moreh ha-nevukhim*, with a glossary of new coinages entitled *Perush ha-millot ha-zarot* (Explanation of Foreign Words) appended to the second edition of the translation; but also the *Commentary on Mishnah, Avot*; the *Treatise on the Doctrine of Resurrection*; as well as the *Epistle to the Yemen* and Samuel's own bilingual epistolary correspondence with Maimonides. He further translated scientific philosophical works in the Greco-Arabic tradition, including the Arabic translations of Aristotle's *Meteorologies* and ʿAlī ibn

Riḍwān's commentary on Galen's *Ars Parva*. His translation of the *Treatises on Conjunction*, written by Averroes and his son, received widespread attention in Europe and served as an aid to the Latin translators of that text, who rendered it as *De Anime Beatitudine*. He also translated short excerpts from other, related texts, including Avicenna's *Kitāb al-Shifā'*. Samuel's original compositions included an Aristotelian meditation on the nature of the elements grounded in the biblical verse from which its title, *Ma'amar Yiqavu ha-Mayim* (Treatise on 'Let the Waters Be Gathered'), is drawn; a short treatise on ritual sacrifice that draws on the *Guide of the Perplexed* and is entitled *Ta'am ha-shulḥan, va-leḥem ha-panim, ve-ha-menorah, va-reyaḥ ha-niḥoaḥ* (The Reason for the Table and the Showbread and the Menorah, and the Pleasant Smell); and a philosophically minded commentary on the biblical book of Ecclesiastes.[33]

While Judah and Samuel are the best-known members of the family, they were only the first of a dynastic line of translators that would carry on their work and extend the influence of their translations and the Arabic texts they prioritized throughout Jewish communities in France and Italy. Samuel's grandson, Jacob ben Makhir ibn Tibbon (1236–1307), also widely known by his Provençal name, Profiat Tibbon, in particular picked up the mantle of the scientific texts. Among his many Hebrew translations from Arabic were works of Averroes and al-Ghazālī's, alongside his Arabic versions of Euclid's *Elements* and *Data*. He also translated from Arabic into Latin, producing versions of Azarchiel's treatises on astrolabes and astronomical charts. Samuel's son Moses (second half of the thirteenth century) was also a translator; his work is the only source of information that has survived that indicates that Judah may have also translated al-Farābī's treatise on logic. Jacob Anatoli (ca. 1194–1256), Samuel's son-in-law, is also a well-known member of this dynasty of translators and was likewise principally interested in translating astronomical texts. Members of the Ibn Tibbon family were crucially important in coining the Hebrew vocabulary that would allow the discussion of science and philosophy among Jewish communities in Europe and perpetuating the transmission of knowledge that had begun in the ninth century in the eastern Mediterranean with the first Arabic translations of Greek texts.

JUDAEO-ARABIC AS A CULTURAL DESIGNATION IN AND OUT OF EXILE

These translators translated from classical Arabic and Judaeo-Arabic into Hebrew (and later and in a more limited fashion into Latin). Yet although their translations and compositions were in Hebrew, we may still describe the translators as Arabized Jews or as culturally Judaeo-Arabic tradents.[34] The term *Judaeo-Arabic* appears most often in linguistic contexts, where it refers first to the Middle Arabic dialect utilized by Jews living in Arabophone contexts. In its written form, this dialect uses Hebrew script rather than Arabic, and in both its spoken and written forms it shows certain Hebraizing and colloquializing features.[35] Two of the most prominent twentieth-century historians of the language disagree with respect to the reasons why Jewish communities in Islamic lands adopted an Arabic dialect as the language of commerce, intellectual activity, and culture; while A. S. Halkin has argued that Arabic was a better-suited language for the types of activities in which Arabized Jews were engaged and was therefore actively selected,[36] Joshua Blau has argued that it is a more simple matter of assimilation over time.[37] Perhaps not incidentally, support for both positions may be found within Judah ibn Tibbon's writing about the Arabic language: Judah's own assessment of the situation supports both positions. In his prologue to *Sefer ha-Riqmah*, he wrote that Jewish writers utilized Arabic because it was the language with which they and their readers were familiar but also because it was better suited for writing about certain topics:

> These books were composed in the Arabic language, since that was the language of the nation in whose midst they dwelled most of the authors from among the ranks of the wise leaders (*ge'onim*) and sages (*ḥakhamim*) were in the kingdom of Ishmael; and since that was an expansive and clear language, lacking nothing (while the sacred tongue did not put but the books of the Bible into our hands and isn't sufficient for all we need to discuss); and since only the exceptional ones from among our nation could understand it because all of their peers knew Arabic; as such they elected to compose their discourses in it.[38]

In essence, he suggests both that assimilation within the "kingdom of Ishmael" as well as the insufficiency of Hebrew for both philosophical and theological discourse push the drive toward Arabic within Mediterranean Jewish communities; both Halkin and Blau's interpretations of the role of Arabic and Judaeo-Arabic are firmly grounded within the medieval sources that allow for both takes on the material.

More recent sociolinguistic and historical-linguistic studies of the Judaeo-Arabic language, particularly those that survey the day-to-day Arabic of Jewish speakers in the Iberian Peninsula and elsewhere in the Mediterranean as reflected in the documentary sources in the Cairo Genizah, have begun to describe the bi- and multilingualism of culturally Judaeo-Arabic writers and speakers as a more organic and perhaps less freighted phenomenon than it might first seem to modern Western scholars.[39] However, Judaeo-Arabic can also be used as a term more broadly than as a simple linguistic designation, and in spite of their not making overwhelming active use of this language, the Tibbonid translators can nonetheless be described as culturally Judaeo-Arabic. Arabized Jews like the Tibbonids, both in central Islamic lands and in the Western Mediterranean, were fully participatory in Arabic modes of thinking, writing, and cultural production.[40]

Judaism in Iberia predates the rise of the Arabic language and the arrival of Islam there, and Jewish culture changed radically with that watershed event. Tombstones dating to the third century of the Common Era offer the earliest evidence of a Jewish presence in the Iberian Peninsula. When a more complete picture comes together in documentary sources by the sixth century, Jews appear as important members of the merchant and bureaucratic classes; but their fortunes changed by the end of the seventh century, when the sixteenth and seventeenth councils of Toledo prohibited them not only from owning but also from dealing in land and other types of property.[41] But just as in the eastern Mediterranean and the *ḥijāz*, where Jewish cultures tended to flourish after the rise of Islam owing to the increased economic freedom and various political safeguards that were the consequence of the protected status afforded by Islam to the other monotheistic faiths,[42] all aspects of Iberian Jewish culture blossomed after the arrival of the Umayyads in the eighth century.[43] Under Islam, Jewish thinkers and writers adopted Arabic as the language of culture and also began to develop literary and theological responses to what were for them the challenging notions of Arabic as the divine language of Islam and of the inimitability of the text of the Qur'ān; and as this culture developed, it ceased to be one of influence or reaction, but rather became the local artistic and intellectual vernacular in which Arabophone Jews existed in Islamdom. In the Muslim East, Arabized Jewish writing generally fell into theological genres (broadly construed by modern standards to include even grammatical and lexical aids for exegetes), while in the West, and in al-Andalus in particular, prose-fiction and poetry in both Arabizing Hebrew and Arabic were among the many generic vehicles for this kind of response, reflection, and creation. In addition to translating texts in the most literal sense, Jewish writers, poets, and philosophers began to adapt the forms of Arabo-Islamic literature to serve the needs of a Jewish population through a kind of *cultural* translation, an adaptation of a mode of thinking and a transformation of the target language "in order to translate the coherence of the original."[44]

The memory of a Judaeo-Arabic culture continued to be important to Andalusi Jews even as they left their immediate Arabophone environments, and this nostalgia for language and modes of thinking comes to bear on the literature of the Arabized Jews in exile from al-Andalus.[45] Although he was writing in Provençal exile rather than in Granada and to a son who would grow up in an environment that was mostly not Arabophone, Judah repeatedly emphasized the value of the Arabic language for Samuel's education. From within the text of the ethical will he criticizes Samuel's laziness in studying Arabic even though, he writes, "you know that the great men of our nation did not reach their lofty achievements but through their Arabic writing." He also offers the example of Sheshet Benvenisti, a fellow physician and a *nasi* (community leader) of Barcelona, whom he praises for his skill in Arabic in spite of residing in the northern environment of relative linguistic paucity where Judah likewise found himself. Again, he writes in the letter: "You can see that the *nasi*, Sheshet, achieved wealth and honor through his Arabic writing in this land as in a kingdom of Ishmael."[46] Judah exhorts Samuel to see the value in excellence in Arabic even in a place governed by Romance speakers and inhabited by a Jewish population that was not the culturally Judaeo-Arabic one that would necessarily or automatically value that kind of excellence.

Judah's Provence[47] was a place with a flourishing scientific culture and a drive, consistent with wider trends in the Almohad and post-Almohad world, toward the philosophization of religion. Ultimately, philosophical reasoning would come to permeate exemplars of nearly every type and genre of writing[48] and to inform and drive the brand of Maimonideanism that governed and counter-governed religious theory and praxis there;[49] as Twersky comments almost poetically, "There are students of philosophy and philosophers and devotees of philosophy, as well as patrons and protagonists who are responsible for preserving and transmitting philosophic and scientific learning of Arabic-speaking Jewry as well as for interpreting it, disseminating it, and extending its frontiers."[50] It was also a time and a place that produced a wide array of writing within a variety of other literary and documentary genres, and those in between.[51] As much as Provence was developing its own Jewish intellectual culture, rooted in the work both of native sons and immigrants from Spain and elsewhere, an even briefer moment circumscribed within this very brief cultural renaissance[52] demands an ongoing connection to the Andalusi Arabic roots of those ideas. Where it was Samuel who would go on to fully philosophize and Arabize the religious practice and religio-legal traditions of the Jews of Provence, helping to promote Maimonides' replacement of the weight of faith with the more Almohadizing weight of authority itself,[53] it was his father's program of cultural and textual Arabization and Andalusization that paved the way for that possibility; this was a culturally Judaeo-Arabic society even as it ceased to be so linguistically.

FAḌĀ'IL AL-LUGHA, FAḌĀ'IL AL-ANDALUS, AND THE LIMITS OF AUTHORITY

What allows for the possibility of all of this is, of course, the special place of Arabic within Islam and the cultural ramifications of that framework. The cultural prestige of the Arabic language, through a range of pre-Islamic and Islamic periods and in a wide geographic swath, is a well-attested phenomenon, with implications in both the theological and cultural spheres; here we focus on the Islamic-period implications of the status of Arabic, with special attention to the ways in which the theological gives way to the cultural, and with further specification to the western Mediterranean. The sociolinguistic notion of a prestige language, to which speakers ascribe particular status within a given society, is complicated in a diglossic case such as Arabic, in which prestige carries not only cultural but theological implications.[54] Despite the need to proceed with caution, however, prestige is an especially apt way to look at Judah's attitude toward the propagation of Arabic as a language that confers cultural capital and serves as a link to a much-vaunted external literary and linguistic culture. The presence within medieval Arabic literary theory of a concept that speaks to the same idea further bolsters its suitability as a lens through which to view Judah's work. The medieval Arabic concept of *faḍā'il* (merits) is one that natively addresses those issues and allows writers to laud the best qualities of texts (especially the Qur'ān), the places they inhabited, and the Arabic language itself. This section offers an overview of the development of Arabic as a prestige language in the Middle Ages and then explores the ways in which that idea became a cornerstone of Judah ibn Tibbon's translation program.

But let us begin at the beginning. As the central linguistic and theological pillar of the Islamic world and perhaps the most significant touchstone for Islamicate culture, the Qur'ān can, in places, be described as being an incredibly self-conscious text. A number of verses draw attention to the fact that the language of the text is Arabic: "We have bestowed it from on high as a discourse in the Arabic tongue that you might encompass it with your reason";[55] "We know that they say 'It is but a man that imparts this to him.' The tongue of him to whom they so maliciously point is wholly unformed, whereas this is Arabic speech, clear and clearly showing the truth";[56] and "If we had revealed it in a foreign tongue, they would surely have said, 'Why is it that its messages have not been spelled out clearly? Why in a foreign tongue when he is an Arab?'"[57] That linguistic self-consciousness and the equation of clarity with the Arabic language together become, first, a major theological principle within Islam that crosses all sorts of sectarian divides and, second, a challenge to be addressed within the textual thinking of the minority faith groups that existed within the Islamic world.[58] The doctrine of *iʿjāz al-Qurʾān*, or the inimitability doctrine, grew up beginning in the second half of the third Islamic century, built on the belief that the revelation of the Qurʾān was an unrepeatable intervention of the divine in human history and that, therefore, the language of that intervention was as much a part and a proof of the miracle as the act of the revelation itself;[59] this would come to inform a wide range of areas of investigation within the Islamicate world, including linguistics and philosophy and, crucially for our purposes, literary work, translation, and notions of Arabic as a translatable language.

Jewish thinkers and writers naturally sought to respond to the perceived gauntlet thrown down by a sacred language claiming to be not just holy but divine. As the idea of *iʿjāz* developed and took hold within the Islamic world, Jewish responses fell broadly into two camps: polemic on the one hand and literary competition on the other.[60] However, in Iberia and in the Andalusi diaspora by the twelfth century, acculturated, Arabized literary production quickly became the local mode of operating rather than a direct response to any particular challenge and ultimately didn't serve apologetic purposes as much as very lightly sublimated proto-national ones. Besides the tensions, both theological and aesthetic, that were manifest in the literary sphere, questions of language in a purely theological context persisted, particularly with respect to the use of Arabic in Jewish devotional activities, ultimately giving way to elevation of Arabic and Arabizing literature. One example of such a response is the introductory poem that opens Abraham ibn 'Ezra''s comparative grammar of Hebrew, the *Safah Berurah* (Clear Language). He praises the merits of the Hebrew language and uses the same epithet, the clear language, that is applied to the language of the Qurʾān. The last four lines of the poem read:

> This is the brilliance of the language of *Torah* and *Miqra*ʾ:
> It exceeds all other languages in truth,
> praised like a precious stone, it will sit as a crown upon Solomon's brow.

Guarded by Abraham, son of Me'ir
it will be remembered from generation to generation
For in his wise heart and enveloped in his mouth,
this shall be called the clear language.[61]

Indeed, the entire governing principle of the work is a direct response to the challenge to Hebrew that the self-declared clarity of the Arabic message of the Qur'ān,[62] even as Ibn 'Ezra''s work marked a thematic shift in Hebrew poetry as these culturally Arabized writers adapted their rhetorical toolkit for a more culturally varied and Christian audience in northern Spain.[63]

Within and aware of this cultural environment, Judah ibn Tibbon's devotion to word-for-word translation may be seen as part and parcel of the fastidious cultural dedication of Arabophone Jews to the Arabic language itself. Both Yom Tov Assis and Ross Brann have made similar observations about Moses ibn 'Ezra''s literary output, with the former writing that Moses ibn 'Ezra' and others "felt the necessity of formulating the essence of their Andalusian tradition as a result of their contact with the Jews of Christian Spain. In many respects, Moses ibn 'Ezra' tried to justify the deep debt of Andalusian Jewish culture to Arabic and show that the result was not at all harmful . . . the history of the Jewish communities in Christian cannot be understood without reference to these dual influences"[64] and the latter noting, regarding Ibn 'Ezra''s own nostalgia-filled peregrinations in Christian Spain, there was "no choice but to privilege lineage and learning over place and political economy. At least their cultural identity was portable, as long as they nurtured its aesthetic, literary, and scientific values in Arabic and Arabic-to-Hebrew translation."[65] So it was, too, for an Arabophone exile in Christian Provence such as Judah ibn Tibbon.[66]

It is precisely that cultural prestige of the Arabic language that is telegraphed through the details of Judah's translation project. There is no textual trait more closely associated with his work than word-for-word translation, a method that, as closely as possible within the limits of the grammar and syntax of the target language (and sometimes pushing up against those limits), renders each word from the source text into a corresponding word in the target language. Judah justifies his choice in terms that highlight the value of Arabic within his enterprise, explaining that the *ge'onim* and other sages in the "kingdoms of Ishmael" wrote in that language because it is "broad, and clear, and not wanting for a single word," whereas Hebrew "places in our hands only what is in the Hebrew Bible (*miqra'*), and that is not enough to say what we need to say."[67] He then goes on to define his strategy for translation as being one that "changes nothing but the language" (*lo yishtaneh ki im ha-lashon levadah*) and not its "meaning" (*'inyan*) or even its "style of expression" (*meliẓah*).[68] While it seems obvious, at first blush, that a translation should change only the language and not the meaning, it becomes clear that Judah is making a distinction here between the language as a system that includes vocabulary only and every other aspect of the text, which includes not only the sense of the content but also the rhetoric and modes of expression. When he delineates the few cases in which an exception might be made at a translator's discretion, he makes completely clear that when he talks about the language (*lashon*) he is referring to its individual constitutive lexemes: "We might use a [grammatically] masculine word (*lashon zakhar*) in place of a [grammatically] feminine word (*lashon nekevah*) or a word in the singular in place of a word in the plural (*lashon rabim*), or change one word for another that is similar to it."[69] Judah recognizes that there are some minor changes that must be made for the sake of a bare minimum of readability in spite of his insistence on translating word-for-word; but even by describing those exceptions he affirms the general principle. In other words, through this distinction Judah sets out his poetics of translation, in which the words are the only things that change between the two languages while everything else that makes the source language a valuable mode of communication must remain the same.

Both word-for-word translation and its alternative, sense-for-sense translation, in which the translator treats phrases or sentences as the base unit to be translated instead of single words, have benefits and drawbacks. Literal translation can preserve the ambiguities of the source language, as the modern English translator of the *Guide*, Shlomo Pines, observed:

> As I see it, there are two legitimate ways of translating the *Moreh*. One of them (which is the way spontaneously adopted by Ibn Tibbon) is to endeavour to provide a translation as ambiguous and as esoteric as is the original text. In other words, the uninitiated reader should have as great a difficulty in penetrating the sense of the translated work as he would have in reading the original text. On the other hand, such a translation, inasfar [*sic*] as it succeeds in being an entirely exact reflection of the original, would give the reader the possibility of appreciating Maimonides's method of exposition and all that is involved therein.[70]

However, by adhering so closely to the syntax and lexical peculiarities of the source language, this method also tends to sacrifice the intelligibility and readability of the text in the target language.

As Pines rightly signals, and in spite of Judah's conviction that translation *ad litteram* took the right to authorship out of the hands of the translator, the method is every bit as much an intervention in interpreting the text as is translation *ad sensu*, in no small measure because of the demands that it places on the reader to engage with the original language.[71] The usual paradox of the culturally Judaeo-Arabic writer is that he uses Arabizing literary forms to glorify and promote the Hebrew language. Judah's approach represents a variation on this paradox, however. Even though he is translating into Hebrew, the Arabizing nature of the translations means that Judah, in effect, uses Hebrew to promote Arabic and to preserve the authority of the author of the original text.

Moses Maimonides also wrote letters about the process of translation; especially relevant here is the aforementioned correspondence with Samuel, in which he praises his addressee even in the face of Judah's scorn and neglect, and offers advice about how he would like to see the *Guide* translated. Maimonides adopts the opposite position to Judah's and grounds it firmly in the innovations that came about at the ninth-century start of the Greek-to-Arabic translation movement.[72] Maimonides advocates a holistic sense-for-sense method of translating that places interpretation firmly in the domain of the translator before a translated text is handed over to a reader. An illustrative excerpt from the letter reads:

> Whoever wishes to translate, and proposes to render each word literally, and at the same time to adhere slavishly to the order of the words and sentences in the original, will meet with much difficulty; his rendering will be faulty and untrustworthy. This is not the right method. The translator should first try to grasp the sense of the subject thoroughly, and state the theme with perfect clearness in the other language. This, however, cannot be done without changing the order of the words, putting many words for one word, or vice versa, and adding or taking away words, so that the subject may be perfectly intelligible in the language into which he translates. This method was followed by Ḥunayn ibn Iṣḥāq, with the works of Galen, and by his son Iṣḥāq with the works of Aristotle. It is for this reason that all their versions are so particularly lucid, and therefore we ought to study them to the exclusion of all others. Your distinguished college ought to adopt this rule in all the translations undertaken.[73]

Maimonides advocates for an eminently readable translation that is explicitly based on the translator's interpretation of the original text and even echoes the self-identification of ninth-century Nestorian Ḥunayn ibn Iṣḥāq,[74] credited with founding the movement to translate Greek texts into Syriac and then into Arabic, who attributed his own preeminence in translation to the fact that he translated sentences as units of meaning rather than translating literally, word-by-word, with individual words as the units of meaning.[75] This stands in stark contrast to Judah's theory.[76]

The cornerstone of Judah's translation program was the conservation of an Andalusi Arabic curriculum for non-Arabophone readers. He envisioned his role as a translator to be the custodian of the text, claiming that word-for-word translation allows the translator to transmit the text without intervening in it or interfering with it, drawing a sharp distinction between the acts of translation and authorship. In addition to giving specific examples of the allowances that he would or would not make, Judah situated his translation method within his conception of the respective roles of authors and translators, writing extensively in support of literal, word-for-word translation from Arabic into Hebrew, distinguishing between the act of translating and the act of composition *de novo*. For example, in his prologue to *Sefer ha-Riqmah*, Judah wrote that "many times, translators approach [a text] and exert their own influence on the books of the sages, slaying their lovely words."[77] He also distinguishes between translation and authorship when he describes the process of his translating Solomon ibn Gabirol's *Kitāb iṣlāḥ al-akhlāq*. He explains that after studying Baḥya ibn Paqūda's *Duties of the Heart* with Meshullam, he decided to translate Ibn Gabirol's elaboration on that text: "I have finished [lit., freed myself from the burden of] translating it, which I had been cautioned against doing . . . by our teacher, your father. Remember that when you and I were studying that chapter under his tutelage? Among the things I told you about in our conversations was finding a short composition by the sage and philosopher Solomon bar Judah ibn Gabirol called *The Improvement of Moral Qualities* in which he mentions all of the things from those nine chapters of that book and also adds to them."[78] In this passage, then, Judah describes Ibn Gabirol as a composer of a new text in which he adds to the extant discussion already begun by Ibn Paqūda on divine unity, commenting that in the new composition, Ibn Gabirol adds to what has already been written on the topic. This characterization is significant in light of the contrast he then goes on to draw between composition and translation. In the above passage, Judah adopts a tone that is neutral, if not largely positive, in describing the addition of more material in a wholly new treatise to a summary of what Ibn Paqūda had already written on the matter as an act of composition. This stands in stark contrast to the tone Judah adopts elsewhere in the body of his work, as in the prologues to the *Maḥbarot ha-diqduq*, when describing translators who add additional material to their translations. Original composition, then, is not part of the translator's brief.[79] It is this very criticism of sense-for-sense translation, from the medieval to the modern, that further illustrates the value placed on cultural and linguistic Arabization as a way of ensuring a kind of accuracy of the text in transmission and guarding against the supposed deficiency in those same texts and processes. Preserving the ideas requires preserving the language. For Judah it was the Arabic language and for his later readers it was the consequences of the Arabic language that were preserved in a translation *ad litteram*.

Just as the term Judaeo-Arabic can describe both a language and a culture, we have begun to see here the idea that will be the main thread of this book: as much as Judah ibn Tibbon is best known for adherence to the Arabic language when translating into Hebrew, he too, like the broad notion of Judaeo-Arabica that he inhabits, can and does leverage cultural meaning to serve his literary and cultural ends. He is a representative microcosm of this tension encapsulated in the notion of a culturally Judaeo-Arabic translator who adapted culture as much as language. As a translator, Judah was a full participant in an Islamicate culture of translation that we might describe more specifically as an Andalusi Judaeo-Arabic one. His own practice rejected, at least overtly, the notion of cultural translation, translation *ad sensu*, and the adaptation of cultural and sense units in such a way that they would resonate and be intelligible to readers. What we might call Judah's sociolinguistic underpinning is grounded in a sophisticated and broad conception of literature and his own peculiar definition of what constitutes the role of the author, text, and book. Ultimately and fundamentally, what he was translating was an Arabic text corpus as an Arabic text corpus, but inherent in that program is a fundamental paradox: the preservation of Arabic so literally as to create a particular and difficult-to-parse Arabized Hebrew is as much an instance of cultural translation as it is of literal translation. The cultural translation inherent in the literal translation is not one that adapts metaphors and toponyms and idiomatic expressions but is rather one that conveys the sociocultural prestige of the source language through literal translation. Judah's is not a conservative textual program as much as it is a conservationist one: of the Arabic language even in Hebrew; of Arabic authors; of references to the idealized and pragmatist pasts of a rapidly changing culture, even as they might not make sense to readers in a target culture; and of the library as the material support and the vehicle through which these things could all be sustained. The impulse to conserve is the manifestation of a foundational approach to Arabic that sees the language itself as a manifestation of a culture—present or lost, real or imagined—of intellectual and literary value and prestige.

NOTES

Chapter title from Samuel ibn Naghrīla, lost "Ode to the Pen," cited in Judah ibn Tibbon, "Musar Av," 16a.

1. Abū Amīr ibn Shuhayd, *Diwān*, ed. James Dickie (Cairo: Dar al-Kātib, 1969), poem 26.

2. 'Alī ibn Aḥmad ibn Ḥazm, *Rasā'il*, vol. 3, ed. Ihsan 'Abbas (Beirut, 1981), 171–88.

3. Abraham ibn 'Ezra', *Yalqut*, ed. Israel Levin (New York: Keren Yisrael, 1985), poem 35. English translation, Peter Cole, *The Dream of the Poem* (Princeton, NJ: Princeton University Press, 2007), 181–82. For an even more comprehensive survey of exceptionalist and lament literature, see Ross Brann, "Andalusi Exceptionalism," in *A Sea of Languages*, ed. Suzanne Conklin Akbari and Karla Mallette (Toronto: University of Toronto Press, 2013), 119–34.

4. Brann, "Andalusi Exceptionalism," in *A Sea of Languages*, 124.

5. Cultural nationalism is a kind of collective identity grounded not only (or especially not) in a group's relationship to a particular territory or state, but is rather one that coheres around a set of texts, values, ideas, etc. I have chosen to render "cultural nationalism" within quotation marks because the term *nationalism* itself is so closely associated in current English usage with the modern ideology of the nation-state. And so, while "cultural nationalism" is an ideal framework for understanding the ways in which the medieval Jewish communities of Spain and France articulated their cultural identity, the extra punctuation helps to distinguish it from the anachronistic implication of a state-based supremacy. For a discussion of Jewish cultural nationalism, and in particular its suitability as a framework for analysis of pre-modern Jewish societies, see David Aberbach, *Jewish Cultural Nationalism: Origins and Influences* (New York: Routledge, 2007).

6. Ibn Tibbon, "Musar Av," 17a.

7. Brann, *The Compunctious Poet* (Baltimore: The Johns Hopkins University Press, 1992), 67–70. See also Nehemiah Allony, "The Reaction of Moses ibn 'Ezra' to 'Arabiyya," *Bulletin of Jewish Studies* 3 (1975): 19–40; and Raymond P. Scheindlin, "Moses ibn Ezra," in *The Cambridge History of Arabic Literature: The Literature of al-Andalus*, ed. María Rosa Menocal et al. (Cambridge: Cambridge University Press, 2000), esp. 260; and Scheindlin, "Rabbi Moshe ibn "Ezra' on the Legitimacy of Poetry," *Medievalia et Humanistica* 7 (1975): 101–15.

8. Brann, *The Compunctious Poet*, 61.

9. See the etymological discussion of the family name *Ibn Tabbān* and its relationship to *Ibn Tibbon* in *The Poems of Levi ibn Tabbān*, ed. Dan Pagis (Jerusalem: Israel Academy of Arts and Sciences, 1967), 29–30.

10. This section largely replicates the overview of scholarship written by James T. Robinson in his article "The Ibn Tibbon Family: A Dynasty of Translators in Medieval Provence," in *Studies in Memory of Isadore Twersky*, ed. Jay Harris (Cambridge, MA: Harvard University Press, 2005). 193–224, in which he surveyed the work and cultural context of the Ibn Tibbon family in the interest of pursuing the possibility of viewing the members of the Tibbonid workshop as a case study and the basis for a formal typology of the medieval translator, in the mode of Jacques LeGoff. I write this section with no quarrels whatsoever with Robinson's work, but rather because such an overview is also

a necessary and integral part of this kind of study of Judah's work vis-à-vis his attitudes toward the Arabic language that the following chapters represent. In other words, this section duplicates work that has already been done but that needs to appear here as well in order to orient the reader.

11. In his *Shekel ha-Kodesh*, Joseph Kimḥi places Judah's origins in Seville, in response to which Robinson postulates: "Perhaps Judah himself came from Granada but his family originated in Seville?" ("The Ibn Tibbon Family," 199).

12. Benjamin of Tudela, *Itinerary*, ed. Marcus Nathan Adler (Oxford: Oxford University Press, 1907), 4. María José Cano Pérez identifies the individuals named in this passage in "Los notables judíos de Cataluña y el sur de Francia según el Sefer Masa'ot de Benjamín de Tudela," *Miscelánea de Estudios Árabes y Hebreos* 53 (2004): 84–86.

13. Robinson, "The Ibn Tibbon Family," 199; Ḥayim Schirman and Ezra Fleischer, *Hebrew Poetry in Christian Spain and Provence* (Jerusalem: Magnes Press, 1997), 13–28.

14. Isadore Twersky, *Studies in Jewish Law and Philosophy* (New York: Ktav Publishing, 1982), 193.

15. Moses ibn Tibbon explains in an original conclusion to his translation of al-Farābī's abbreviation of Aristotle's *Prior Analytics* that he was motivated to undertake that translation because his grandfather had translated the abbreviation of the *Posterior Analytics*. This translation does not yet exist in a published edition; Robinson cites the conclusion from BNF MS Heb. 917 ("The Ibn Tibbon Family," 201).

16. For editions of all the texts cited in this paragraph, see the relevant entries in the bibliography.

17. This appellation was given to him by Samuel in his preface to his Hebrew translation of the *Guide of the Perplexed* (17). The sixteenth-century Italian talmudist and kabbalist Gedalyah ibn Yaḥya modified the phrase to "head of the translators." In his *Die Hebraieschen Uebersetzungen des Mittelalters*, Moritz Steinschneider repeated the epithet as Samuel coined it and also noted some of the variants (see his *The Hebrew Translations of the Middle Ages and the Jews as Transmitters*, ed. and trans. Charles Manekin et al. [New York: Springer, 2014], 77), and it appears consistently in scholarly discussions of Ibn Tibbon since Steinschneider.

18. Evidence from the ethical will tells us that Judah and Samuel earned their living principally as merchants and that Judah also worked as a physician. I am using the word "profession" here to describe their translation activity because the vicissitudes of the English language mean that the alternatives—avocation or hobby, to name a few of the possibilities—minimize the seriousness of the endeavor and investment of time and effort that they put into it, as well as the impact of the work. Ultimately, the choice of term is in line with Isadore Twersky, who described translation as the Ibn Tibbon family "profession" in the same sense (see his "Aspects of the Social and Cultural History of Provençal Jewry," *Journal of World History* 11 [1968]: 200).

19. Ibn Tibbon, "Musar Av," 15b.

20. Ibid., 15b–16a.

21. Ibid., 15b.

22. Ibid., 16a.

23. Ibid.

24. The correspondence may be found in Isaac Shailat, *Epistles of Maimonides*, vol. 2 (Ma'ale Adumim: Birkat Moshe, 1995), 491–559. See also S. M. Stern, "Maimonides'

Correspondence with the Scholars of Provence," *Zion* 16, no. 1 (1951): 18–29, and Carlos Fraenkel, *From Rambam to Samuel ibn Tibbon: The Path from Dalālat al-Ḥā'irīn to Moreh ha-Nevukhīm* (Jerusalem: Magnes Press, 2007), 35–53.

25. The text of the 1199 letter to the rabbis of Lunel, in which Maimonides himself suggested that they request that Samuel translate the work in his stead, is published in Isaiah Shailat's *Iggerot ha-Rambam* (vol. 2, letter 36). Of particular interest is Isaiah Sonne, "A Unknown Copy in the Archive of the Jewish Community in Verona," in which Sonne contends that the Verona copy of the letter, which significantly omits the list of books that Maimonides advises Samuel not to bother reading, is an autograph copy made by the recipient.

26. A new study and synoptic edition of the correspondence between Moses Maimonides and Samuel ibn Tibbon has appeared very recently: Doron Forte, "Back to the Sources: Alternative Versions of Maimonides' Letter to Samuel ibn Tibbon and Their Neglected Significance," *Jewish Studies Quarterly* 23 (2016): 47–90.

27. Moses Maimonides, "Epistle on Translation," in Shailat, *Epistles of Maimonides*, vol. 2, 525–54 (emphasis mine). My English translation here is based on the Hebrew translation (tentatively identified by Steinschneider as Samuel's) of Maimonides' Arabic original since a complete version of the Hebrew text still exists whereas the Arabic text exists only in a badly damaged copy. It is worth noting that the inability to consult the Arabic original of the introductory paragraphs in which Maimonides comments about Judah and Samuel's skill and repute as translators does raise questions about the reliability of that discussion as by Maimonides or whether it was a later addition.

28. Maimonides, "Epistle on Translation."

29. Ibn Tibbon, "Musar Av," 16a.

30. Ibid.

31. Just as a side note, it is interesting to mention that this is not the only place that Maimonides himself directly contradicts Judah's assessment of Samuel: where Judah laments the state of Samuel's handwriting, Maimonides praises his "elegant hand" in recommending him to the rabbis of Lunel as his translator.

32. Henri Gross, *Gallia Judaica* (reprint, Leuven: Peeters, 1997), 282.

33. Because this is principally a book about the intellectual-cultural life of Judah, it does not devote a lot of space to the biography of Samuel, although he is arguably the better known and more studied of the two. Foundational in this area is Aviezer Ravitzky, "The Thought of Zerahiah ben Isaac ben Shealtiel Hen and Maimonidean-Tibbonid Philosophy in the Thirteenth Century" (PhD diss., Hebrew University of Jerusalem, 1978). See also entries in the bibliography for other works by Fraenkel, Harvey, Ravitzky, Robinson, and Sermonetta. In his *From Rambam to Samuel ibn Tibbon,* Carlos Fraenkel has demonstrated thoroughly the extent to which and the means by which Samuel rejected advice from other mentors and intellectual and religious elders in order to adopt his father's technical professional style of translating and to adopt other pieces of his father's advice, thereby ensuring the intellectual unity and integrity of the Tibbonid project and allowing it to function as a workshop as such. Fraenkel's particularly attentive discussion of Samuel as a reader responsive to his father and to Maimonides appears in his third chapter.

34. Ross Brann, "The Arabized Jews," in *Cambridge History of Arabic Literature: The Literature of al-Andalus*, ed. María Rosa Menocal et al. (Cambridge: Cambridge University Press, 2000), 435–54; Raymond Scheindlin, "Merchants and Intellectuals, Rabbis

and Poets: Judeo-Arabic Culture in the Golden Age of Islam," in *Cultures of the Jews*, ed. David Biale (New York: Schocken Books, 2002), 313–88.

35. This is not the place for a full discussion of the Middle Arabic dialect bundle and the history of its study; for such a discussion, see Kees Versteegh, "Middle Arabic," in *The Arabic Language* (reprint, Edinburgh: Edinburgh University Press, 2001), 121–49; and Joshua Blau, "The Emergence of Middle Arabic," in *The Emergence and Linguistic Background of Judaeo-Arabic* (Jerusalem: Yad Ben-Zvi, 1999), 1–58. Recently, in her "The Question of Judaeo-Arabic," *Arab Studies Journal* 23, no. 1 (2015): 14–78, Ella Shohat has contended that Judaeo-Arabic is a wistfully fictional construct of the Wissenschaft des Judentums and later scholars who, for political reasons, sought to wrest Arabized Jews away from the primacy of Arabic in their cultural identity; however, because her argument from the outset seeks to discuss the terminology of the Judaeo-Arabic language but "does not concern itself with the extremely rich, indeed invaluable scholarship in the related fields of Judaeo-Arabic and Jewish languages," it is given to privileging speakers' personal identities and to making cultural and linguistic comparisons with Yiddish that many scholars of Judaeo-Arabic would challenge.

36. A. S. Halkin, "Judaeo-Arabic Literature," in *The Jews: Their History, Culture and Religion*, ed. Louis Finkelstein (Philadelphia: Jewish Publication Society, 1960), 116–48. See also Halkin's "The Medieval Jewish Attitude towards Hebrew," in *Biblical and Other Studies*, ed. Alexander Altmann (Waltham, MA: Brandeis University Press, 1963), 233–48.

37. Blau, *The Emergence and Linguistic Background*, 20.

38. Judah ibn Tibbon, preface to *Sefer ha-Riqmah*, 4.

39. Esther Miriam Wagner, *Linguistic Variety of Judaeo-Arabic in Letters from the Cairo Genizah* (Leiden: Brill, 2010), and "The Weakening of the Bourgeoisie: Social Changes Mirrored in the Language of the Genizah Letters," *From a Sacred Source: Genizah Studies in Honour of Professor Stefan C. Reif*, ed. Ben Outhwaite (Leiden: Brill, 2010), 343–56; Benjamin Hary, *Translating Religion: Linguistic Analysis of Judaeo-Arabic Sacred Texts from Egypt* (Leiden: Brill, 2009), *Multiglossia in Judaeo-Arabic* (Leiden: Brill, 1992); Hary, "Judaeo-Arabic as a Mixed Language," in *Middle Arabic and Mixed Arabic: Diachrony and Synchrony*, ed. Arie Schippers (Leiden: Brill, 2012), 125–44; Hary, "Religiolinguistics: On Jewish-, Christian-, and Muslim-Defined Languages," *International Journal for the Sociology of Language* 220 (2013): 85–108; and Mark Cohen, "On the Interplay of Arabic and Hebrew in the Cairo Geniza Letters," in *Studies in Arabic and Hebrew Letters in Honor of Raymond P. Scheindlin*, ed. Jonathan Decter and Michael Rand (Piscataway, NJ: Gorgias Press, 2007), 17–35.

40. In fact, the notion that language is just one aspect of a broader cultural frame very much underpins the current state of the field of Judaeo-Arabic studies. See, for example, Haggai Ben-Shammai and Benjamn Hary's introduction to their volume of essays, *Esoteric and Exoteric Aspects in Judaeo-Arabic Culture* (Leiden: Brill, 2006).

41. Norman Roth, *Jews, Visigoths, and Muslims in Medieval Spain: Cooperation and Conflict* (Leiden, Brill, 2004), 26–34 and 37–86.

42. Mark Cohen, "What Was the Pact of Umar?," *Jerusalem Studies in Arabic and Islam* 23 (1999): 100–157. Cohen's analysis is revisited in Phillip Ackerman-Lieberman, "The Muḥammadan Stipulations: Dhimmī Versions of the Pact of 'Umar," in *Jews, Christians and Muslims in Medieval and Early Modern Times*, ed. Arnold Franklin et al. (Leiden: Brill, 2014).

43. For brief overview of the Jews of Islam, see Scheindlin, "Merchants and Intellectuals," 313–88. Other studies include Mark Cohen, *Under Crescent and Cross: The Jews in the Middle Ages* (Princeton, NJ: Princeton University Press, 1995); S. D. Goitein, *A Mediterranean Society* (reprint, Berkeley: University of California Press, 2000); and Moshe Gil, *Jews in Islamic Countries* (Leiden: Brill, 2004). For a historiography of the field, see Mark Cohen, "Medieval Jewry in the World of Islam," in *The Oxford Handbook of Jewish Studies*, ed. Martin Goodman et al. (Oxford: Oxford University Press, 2002), 193–217.

44. Talal Asad, "The Concept of Cultural Translation in British Social Anthropology," in *Writing Culture*, ed. James Clifford and George Marcus (Berkeley: University of California Press, 1986), 157. On the phenomenon of cultural translation in al-Andalus, see Michelle Hamilton, "Translating Desire," in *Representing Others in Medieval Iberian Literature* (New York: Macmillan, 2007), 47–88; and Esperanza Alfonso, introduction to *Islamic Culture through Jewish Eyes* (New York: Routledge, 2007).

45. Gad Freudenthal, "Abraham ibn 'Ezra' and Judah ibn Tibbon as Cultural Intermediaries," in *Exchange and Transmission across Cultural Boundaries*, ed. Haggai Ben-Shammai et al. (Jerusalem: Israel Academy of Sciences, 2013), esp. 54–55; Brann, "Andalusi Exceptionalism," 128; and Alfonso, *Islamic Culture through Jewish Eyes*, 74.

46. Ibn Tibbon, "Musar Av," 16a.

47. Provence is admittedly an imperfect, insufficiently specific term to designate the southern French region under discussion. In the field of French history, it is applied in discussions of Jews in the south of France specifically to those who had papal protection and special legal status; however, in Jewish history it is used more broadly, and that is the sense in which I shall continue to use it here.

48. James T. Robinson, "Secondary Forms of Philosophy: On the Teaching and Transmission of Philosophy in Non-Philosophical Literary Genres," in *Vehicles of Transmission, Translation, and Transformation in Medieval Textual Culture*, ed. Carlos Fraenkel et al. (Turnhout: Brepols: 2011), 235–48.

49. Carlos Fraenkel, "Beyond the Faithful Disciple: Samuel ibn Tibbon's Criticism of Maimonides," in *Maimonides after 800 Years*, ed. Jay Harris (Cambridge, MA: Harvard University Press, 2007), and "From Maimonides to Samuel ibn Tibbon: Interpreting Judaism and a Philosophical Religion," in *Traditions of Maimonideanism*, ed. Carlos Fraenkel (Leiden: Brill, 2009): 171–212; and James T. Robinson, "We Drink Only from the Master's Water: Maimonides and Maimonideanism in Southern France, 1200–1306," *Studia Rosenthaliana* 40 (2007): 27–60.

50. Twersky, "Provençal Jewry," 186–87; he further develops this idea on 202–7.

51. Frenkel, "Genizah Documents as Literary Products," in *From a Sacred Source*, ed. Ben Outhwaite (Leiden: Brill, 2010), 139–55.

52. The characterization of this period of cultural flourishing between the eleventh and fourteenth centuries as a brief and well-defined one is, in fact, Twersky's ("Provençal Jewry," 185); everything about the Tibbonid project makes it an exceptional and even briefer moment within this brief, circumscribed period.

53. Fraenkel, "Legislating Truth," in *Studies in the History of Culture and Science Presented to Gad Freudenthal on His 65th Birthday*, ed. Resienne Fontaine et al. (Leiden: Brill, 2010), 209–25.

54. Versteegh, *Arabic Language*, 3; and Reem Bassiourey, *Arabic Sociolinguistics* (Edinburgh: Edinburgh University Press, 2009), 18–19. These two works offer two dif-

fering perspectives on the relationship between the prestige form of a language and the standard form; I would tend to agree with the latter, which argues that prestige and standard are not necessarily correlated.

55. Qur'ān 12:2, trans. N. J. Dawood (reprint, New York: Penguin, 2005).

56. Qur'ān 16:103, trans. N. J. Dawood.

57. Ibid., 41:44.

58. Margaret Larkin, "The Inimitability of the Qur'ān: Two Perspectives," *Religion and Literature* 20, no. 1 (1988): 31–47.

59. Geert van Gelder, *Beyond the Line: Classical Arabic Literary Critics on the Coherence and Unity of the Poem* (Leiden: Brill, 1982), 97–100.

60. Some of the initial Jewish responses to *i'jāz* did, indeed, take the form of polemic; among these is that of Yūsuf al-Baṣīr (d. after 1048), whose works remain largely unedited. An overview of the state of the manuscript evidence may be found in David Sklare's chapter on the theologian in *The Jews of Medieval Islam*, ed. Daniel Frank (Leiden: Brill, 1995), 249–70; and in an article by Sabine Schmidtke, "Yusuf al-Baṣīr's First Refutation," *Arabica* 53 (2006). A portion of al-Baṣīr's polemic against the Qur'ān is published in David Sklare's "Responses to Islamic Polemics by Jewish Mutakallimun in the Tenth Century," in *The Majlis: Interreligious Encounters in Medieval Islam*, ed. Hava Lazarus-Yafeh (Wiesbaden: Harassowitz, 1999), 137–61.

61. Abraham ibn 'Ezra', *Safah Berurah*, p. 1*. The prose translation here is mine; for a versified translation, see p. 97 in the same volume.

62. Qur'ān 14:102–6, trans. N. J. Dawood.

63. Ḥayim Schirman, *Hebrew Poetry in Spain and Provence*, vol. 1, p. 569; and Joseph Sadan, "Identity and Inimitability: The Contexts of Inter-Religious Polemics and Solidarity in Medieval Spain, in Light of Two Passages by Moše ibn 'Ezra' and Ya'qov ben El'azar," *Israel Oriental Studies* 14 (1994): 325–47.

64. Yom Tov Assis, "The Judaeo-Arabic Tradition in Christian Spain," in Frank, *The Jews of Medieval Islam*, 111–24.

65. Brann, "Andalusi Exceptionalism," 31.

66. Assis extends his argument for the medieval Christian kingdoms of what today is Portugal as well, and despite the geographical and topographical differences in the boundaries between the two pairs of places, extending the argument to Provence as well is hardly a stretch.

67. Judah ibn Tibbon, preface to *Sefer ha-Riqmah*, 4. However, it is worth noting that in his preface to *Duties of the Heart*, Judah makes some greater allowances for sense-for-sense translation when the text will be used as a supplement to or commentary on, rather than a replacement for, the original text or a word-for-word translation. This alternative line of reasoning is discussed in greater detail in the reception history in chapter 6. In this respect, he follows Sa'adya Ga'on's approach to text, which Lenn Goodman describes as having been designed "not to make the work accessible to nonreaders of Hebrew. . . . He expects his readers to be familiar with the text and its expressions." "Sa'adya Ga'on's Interpretive Technique," in *Translation of Scripture*, ed. D. M. Goldenberg (Philadelphia: Annenberg Research Institute, 1990), 49.

68. Judah ibn Tibbon, preface to *Sefer ha-Riqmah*, 5–6.

69. Ibid., 6. In his preface to the *Guide of the Perplexed*, Samuel would echo this statement very closely, but in terms that mark him as someone who learned Arabic rather than as someone who grew up with it as a native tongue. In his discussion of the

need to sometimes use a word of a different grammatical gender when translating, he remarks with a tone of alarmed didacticism that is familiar to anyone who has begun the study of Arabic: In his preface to the *Guide*, he writes: "Many times there will be call for one word that is grammatically masculine in the Hebrew language but that is grammatically feminine in Arabic; and the same is true for singulars and plurals. And what's more, in Arabic verbs come before nouns, and so it goes according to their custom; and even though a noun might appear in the plural, they will put the verb in the singular form in many instances. So it happens that in certain places the masters of the language have needed to render a verb in the singular in our language when it refers to every single one of the plural nouns that come after it. Furthermore, there is no distinction in Arabic between uses of the feminine singular and the masculine plural" (118).

70. Joel Kraemer and Josef Stern, "Shlomo Pines on the Translation of Maimonides' Guide of the Perplexed," *Journal of Jewish Thought and Philosophy* 8 (1999): 21. It is worth noting that despite the apparent tone of approval in this passage, Pines generally preferred for his own translation the more holistic method of translation preferred by Moses Maimonides himself, with a critical apparatus to serve as entrée into the places where precision or original mystery (to which Pines did pay tremendous attention) might be lost to a reader in translation.

71. The idea of translation *ad litteram* as an active intervention in the transmission of text is examined in chapter 5.

72. For an overview of Greek-to-Arabic translation, see Dmitri Gutas, *Greek Thought, Arabic Culture* (New York: Routledge, 1998).

73. Moses Maimonides, *Iggerot ha-Rambam*, trans. Adler, 222–23.

74. Maimonides was hardly the only commentator on the Judaeo-Arabic translation movements (both into and out of Arabic) to be aware of his professional heritage; Miriam Goldstein also demonstrates the extent to which Karaite commentators such as Yefet ibn ʿAlī were aware of the Greek background to their work. See her "Arabic Composition 101 and the Early Development of Judaeo-Arabic Bible Exegesis," *Journal of Semitic Studies* 55, no. 2 (2010): 456–57.

75. Ḥunayn ibn Iṣḥāq, *Risāla*, 2–6; throughout the epistle there are additional references to translation technique, as well as critiques of earlier translators whose work contains errors or was, to Ḥunayn's mind, overly literal.

76. Ultimately Samuel would work in his father's mode rather than Maimonides', justifying his decision in terms that closely echo his father's. For more on Samuel as a faithful disciple of his father and critic of Maimonides, see Fraenkel, *From the Dalāla to the Moreh*.

77. Judah ibn Tibbon, translator's preface to *Sefer ha-Riqmah*, 6.

78. Judah ibn Tibbon, "Letter to Asher ben Meshullam of Lunel," in *Otsrot Chajim: Katalog der Michaelschen Bibliothek*, ed. Moritz Steinschneider and Leopold Zunz (Hamburg, 1848), 367. The letter is appended to only one of the more than half-dozen manuscripts of the *Tiqqun Middot ha-Nefesh*: Bodleian Neubauer 1404.3, formerly Munich Michaelschen 327.3. It appears in only two of the printed editions (Hamburg, 1848; Lyck, 1859), each of which seems, at a minimum, to reflect textual problems in the manuscripts. An English translation and additional bibliography can be found in Appendix A of Stephen S. Wise, *The Ethics of Solomon ibn Gabirol* (New York: Columbia University

Press, 1902), 105–7. A new translation appears as an appendix in Freudenthal, "Cultural Intermediaries," 80–81.

79. Here we touch up against a similar issue within the Latin and Latinate world, namely the question of *auctoritas*. I have not yet been able to demonstrate that Judah's ideas about the authority of the author versus that of the translator developed in response to contact with Romance-speaking writers, thinkers, and translators, but I am pursuing this line of inquiry for a future study.

2 "EXAMINE YOUR HEBREW BOOKS MONTHLY AND ARABIC BOOKS BIMONTHLY"

Autobiography and Bibliography in the Islamic West

Arabic and Islamicate literatures manifest a particularly close relationship between biographical and bibliographic writing, with books being a central focus of meditations on their owners' lives. That relationship is strengthened when we note that biographical dictionaries are some of the most prominent sources for information about libraries, particularly Andalusi ones. In fact, the focus on books and curriculum in Judah ibn Tibbon's will is not correlated only to its function as a prescriptive curriculum but also to its autobiographical functions. The classic, authoritative study on the theme of bibliography and the library in the Islamic West, the century-old *Libros y enseñanzas en al-Andalus* by Julian Ribera y Tarrago, recently reedited by María Jesús Viguera Molins,[1] is based heavily on the information in the libraries enumerated in the biographical notes in *Kitāb al-Ṣila fī ta'rīḥ al-Andalus* (A Continuation of Andalusi History) of the *mālikī* jurist and bibliophile Ḥalaf ibn Bashkuwāl (d. 1183); in a sequel to *Kitāb al-Ṣila*, namely *Kitāb Takmila li-Kitāb al-Ṣila* (Completion of the Book of Continuation) by Muḥammad ibn al-Abbār (d. 1199), a poet and diplomat whose literary, official, and historical writings have survived to the modern period; and in the original book to which both of the aforementioned refer when they call themselves a "continuation" and a "completion," namely *Tarīkh 'ulamā al-Andalus* (History of the Learned Men of al-Andalus), written by 'Abd Allāh ibn al-Faraḍī (d. 962), who viewed biographical and historical writing as an integral part of his role as a *qāḍī* in Valencia.[2] The relationship in both modern and medieval writing between biography and bibliography gives Judah's ethical will and its extensive discussions of books yet another anchor within the forms of Andalusi Arabic literature, tying it as much to bibliographic as to ethical writing. Individuals write about their lives just as surely as they write about their libraries; and the catalogues that document those libraries are frequently not simply lists of books but rather records of reading and, more significantly, repositories of ideas about the family and ethical writing. Biographical and autobiographical writings commonly include a bibliographic section, one that affirms the author or subject's own corpus or enumerates the contents of his library; this feature of the genre comes into Arabic writing in the ninth century with Ḥunayn ibn Iṣḥaq's translation of Galen's *My Books* and *The Order of My Books*, which opens with a brief, autobiographical lament over the loss of his own library.[3]

Judah ibn Tibbon likewise makes bibliographic writing an important part of the autobiographical writing that is his ethical will; thus, by situating his bibliographic and library writing within his autobiography and, more specifically, within the sections that discus the role of an intellectual within a community, the ethical will becomes an important source for demonstrating the role of the library for the continuity of Arabic literature and Arabizing intellectual culture within exile communities. Returning to the brief quotation in the general introduction as illustrative of Judah's belief in the cultural value of Arabic, we see it in a bit more of its context, namely Judah writing about the cultural value of his library:

> You see that great sages seek *me* out and try to come here from the far corners of the earth to avail themselves of fellowship in *my* salon. They yearn to see *me and my books*; but you, despite finding yourself here at no cost, do not. God has not given you a heart with which to know, eyes through which to see, or ears through which to hear. May God give you a new heart and spirit, and a desire to secure what is gone and recuperate what is lost. May He set you on the path you should walk and guide you along it. You have not cultivated your Arabic writing as expected: You began to study it seven years ago, when I forced you to [learn] it even though you did not want to. You know that the greatest men of our nation did not achieve their greatness or their lofty heights but through their Arabic writing. You know that the *nagid* [Samuel ibn Naghrīla] explained that the acclaim accorded to him—and to his son after him—was because of it: "Pen, I recount your favor! . . ." and so on. You can see that the *nasi*, Sheshet, achieved wealth and honor through his Arabic writing in this land as in a kingdom of Ishmael.[4]

In this passage, Judah situates his library within the context of his role as a teacher, demonstrating belief that the chief utility of philosophical works, and especially philosophical works in translation, comes when they are taught rather than studied alone. Here the library is manifestly the anchor that could uniquely ground the teaching of a literary and intellectual heritage. He also highlights the financial value of access to his library and tutelage by pointing out the costs that scholars were willing to incur to visit and emphasizing Samuel's good fortune in not having to expend his resources similarly: "Even though you find yourself here at no cost, you are not interested." The notion that numbers of people were seeking out Judah's library as well as his companionship and instruction also speaks to the cultural and intellectual capital of his library and salon. It clearly ties this to his lamented Andalusi past when Judah asks God to give Samuel "a new heart and a new spirit and the urge to recuperate the past and reclaim everything that has been lost" and then draws on the Ishmael-Edom dichotomy that so often represents al-Andalus in contrast to Christian Spain and France when he hearkens back to the "kingdom of Ishmael" as the standard bearer for literary prestige. This section of the text progresses through three main points. First it begins with a discussion of Judah's prestigious salon and his financially and intellectually valuable books; second, it moves on to his aspiration for Samuel to reclaim the past—the national-diasporic past and the national-familial past in al-Andalus that were his heritage—and to pursue a new future; and third, it returns to the theme that is always just below the surface of the text or bubbling up there, namely, that same value of Arabic as a source of literary and cultural prestige. The temporal component and the directional thrust of this passage, from the past and the library down the path to a continuation of linguistic trends, asserts Arabic as the language of libraries past, present, and future.

The relationship between biographical and bibliographical writing is forced to the fore precisely because of the important role of books and libraries in the ethical will, where they are the focal point of Judah's admonitions about acquiring wisdom and preserving cultural and intellectual capital. The presence of books in the ethical will is among the factors that situates Judah's work firmly within the realm of the textual and frames the ethical will so as to require that the text as a whole be read with an eye toward genre, literacy, and literariness; it is a work produced within a book culture by a reader of text. The ethical will is typically situated within a northern European milieu when it comes to considering its value as a library document that can aid our understanding of twelfth-century scribal, reading, and book-collecting practices. Malachi Beit-Arie deftly parses the discussions of handwriting in the ethical will to connect them to what we know from other sources about the education of scribes;[5] Israel Abrahams hears the evocation of the libraries of the Cambridge colleges in Judah's discussion of cataloguing and storage practices;[6] and Carlos del Valle Rodriguez has helpfully indexed all references to library, book, and writing activity throughout the body of the text.[7] All these interventions, however, situate the ethical will comparatively against the libraries and scribal practices of Christian Europe; and regardless of how apt some of these European comparisons and counterpoints might be, it is also important to consider this text and its reflection of library practices within its own cultural context. As such, the analysis within this chapter considers the ethical will against a range of other types of library writing in Hebrew and Arabic in the Judaeo-Islamic western Mediterranean (with a few counterpoints drawn from more easterly contexts). This analysis is aided by (though not limited to) the monumental volume of library documents from the Cairo Genizah published by Nehemiah Allony, Haggai Ben-Shammai, and Miriam Frenkel. Prior to his death in 1983, Allony, who among his scholarly roles was the director of the Jewish National and University Library in Jerusalem, sought to collate the documents from the Cairo Genizah pertaining to library collections in such a way as to propose an archetype of the Jewish library in the Middle Ages.[8] The potential value of such a composite or Platonic form of the library remains to be seen; upon Allony's death, Ben-Shammai and Frenkel elected to publish the documents in a sourcebook rather than pursuing Allony's more synthetic and, perhaps, quixotic analysis.[9]

The Ibn Tibbon ethical will itself serves many distinct purposes and contains within it elements that conform to a variety of genres of writing, from the more documentary to the more literary; it is a text that can speak, as it does in the context of this study, to both cultural-historical and to more poetic concerns. However, this is not a unique feature of this text; Frenkel goes as far as to advocate for a literary treatment of Genizah fragments that seem, on their faces, to be of the most documentary character. She argues for this type of consideration along a spectrum because of the extent to which modern distinctions of form and genre do not make sense in a medieval context in which the literary and the documentary were never as wholly separate as modern readers would like to believe them to be.[10] A very different example of a documentary source that more explicitly walks the line between its practical, everyday function and the literary universe from which it emerged is a fragment that appears, on the basis of the monumental script, to be a label for a bookcase; but instead of listing the volumes contained in the case, it offers a boastful dialogue between the bookcase to be labeled and a Torah scroll, perhaps a metonym for the sacred books it was destined to contain.[11] The text takes a common form from the toolkit of Hebrew prose writing, where we find many examples of dialogues full of boasting and one-upsmanship between pairs or triads of inanimate objects:

> (1) I am a bookcase. Open me and [lacuna] everything you find within me. (2) I am an ark. I have been elevated and honored above all other bookcases because of what sits [on my shelves]. (3) Other cabinets might have silver, gold, and valuable instruments placed in them, but they aren't useful and cannot save from the flames and brimstone. (4) But I, the bookcase, guard the tree of life from the Garden of Eden which is the inheritance of the beloved. (5) What has the wheat to do with what is kept in me? (6) Turn and behold the perfection of its words and tell it: Be my confidant, my sibling, and my intimate.
>
> (7) I am the Torah, full of beauty, with no defects to be found. (8) How great are the gifts and pleasures that can be found within me! (9) Every man seeks three things for himself that he cannot achieve except by pursuing them through me. (10a) Gifts and pleasures are increased with greatness, honor and praise, and freedom from hardships and ills. (10b) They call these things desires and preferences. (11) I also have a fourth thing that is not ever [lacuna], and it flourishes within me. (12) What is it? Never-ending, eternal life, as He said through His beloved man [lacuna]. (13) Many of those who sleep in the dust of the earth will wake; they [will wake to] the eternal life reserved for those who pursue me. (14) This life also creates honor and grandeur and a radiant countenance to those who are educated by me; (15) those learned men will shine like the firmament and will forever guide the masses like the stars.[12]

This text is a materially functional example of a particular type of writing that is quite recognizable within the context of the Arabized Jews of Spain, namely the competitive dialogue between writing implements, books, and the other objects and paraphernalia of a readerly culture. As a label for a bookcase, it gives only limited information—that the case should have contained sacred texts—but also demonstrates the role of literary prose in describing library collections even in very practical ways. Judah's ethical will, then, as a work that has a literary function but also serves, remarkably, as at least a partially descriptive catalogue, sits on the same spectrum as this label; the literary universe in which a bookcase could be labeled with an imagined rhymed-prose dialogue between itself and its contents is the same universe in which a father's letter of guidance to his son can also double as a record of the library he built. In sum, the relationship between documentary texts used in the care and organization of libraries are not such a far cry from the more literary texts that they housed.[13]

Arthur Bahr writes that it is scholarship's tendency toward treating texts as documentary or as literary that itself demands a reassessment of any of those texts in a more literary light, suggesting that "such binaries evoke the vexed concept of literariness."[14] He continues by arguing for an inherent poetics of the historical-documentary aspects of works traditionally seen as the purview of either social history or codicology:

> The aesthetic, and more particularly what we might call literariness, cannot be reduced to mere or transparent expression of external social and political facts . . . the selection and arrangement of texts in manuscripts, like that of words in poetry, can produce those 'metaphorical potentialities,' discontinuities and excesses, multiple and shifting meanings, resistance to paraphrase, and openness to rereading that have deservedly become resurgent objects of critical value. In proposing this analogy between words in poetry and texts in manuscripts, I do not mean to suggest that manuscripts are inherently equivalent to poetry either in goal or effect. Not all medieval manuscripts readily offer those literary rewards that Pearsall eloquently describes.[15] It is also the case, however—our now normalized passion for canon smashing notwithstanding—that not all medieval literature equivalently offers them either. In short, neither words in poetry nor texts in manuscripts inherently produce such literary effects, but both have the potential to do so.[16]

Bahr is writing specifically about compiled texts, and not just documentary ones. Both the ethical will and several of the library documents to which it will be compared in this chapter are, themselves, compilations according to Bahr's working definition; but the principle holds more broadly for thinking about the literary elements of documentary texts. As such, this chapter looks at library writing along a continuum from the documentary to the literary, acknowledging that texts closer to one pole nonetheless conform in certain ways to the characteristics of the other. While it does not seek to create an archetypal medieval Jewish library, it aims to provide an overview of writings about libraries that parallel Judah's writing about his own library in the ethical will and to offer a contextualization for them.[17] Within this framework, it is possible to consider the ethical will as, itself, a library document and to use it to place Judah's activity within a completely bibliophilic context; this examination of one little corner of what might have been Allony's Jewish library of the Middle Ages serves to assert that Judah's transmission of texts examined in the following chapters is informed by his book-dense environment and his access to Jewish, Islamic, and secular-Islamicate texts alike.

GENRE AND THE FORM OF THE MATERIAL LIBRARY

The relationship between orality and literacy, and the cultural hierarchy of the oral and the written transmission of texts, is still very much an open question in the intellectual histories of both Jews and Muslims in the Middle Ages, when a fluid relationship existed between text and codex and between the two types of transmission.[18] Ultimately the split between the oral and the written also creates a split between the material and the abstract text. Franz Rosenthal writes meditatively about the tension within medieval Arabic writing between books as material objects and the knowledge contained therein. Some of his subjects go as far as to encourage the burning of their books upon their deaths; others wish to avoid allowing access to a written version of a text so that its very transmission might not be called into question; and still others request the same in order to avoid leading future generations away from piety in the way that they themselves had been distracted from it by those books, invoking a common trope in Arabic bequest literature, or *waṣīya*.[19] Judah ibn Tibbon's ethical will is as reflective of time spent with books as these Arabo-Muslim examples. Although he never renounces his love of books and instead glorifies them, seeing them as a key part of his material bequest to his son, his is in fact the other side of the very same impulse; to either laud or renounce books with equal vehemence requires a life spent in their presence. This study is not only based on the premise that Judah was a reader and a transmitter of written texts, but draws that presumption from the centrality of the library within the ethical will. Judah frames his life as a bookish one and so his recourse to the vast fount of Hebrew and Arabic literature must be understood to be done on material, rather than aural, terms.[20]

It is clear that Judah situates himself within a textual culture that privileges access to books, a facet of his intellectual profile that is demonstrated throughout the course of this chapter. But to begin with a provocation, perhaps, I would like to propose that Judah ibn Tibbon's ethical will can itself be read as the catalogue of his own library as he reassembled it in Provence. To describe the type of catalogue document he would like Samuel to prepare, Judah uses several terms. He tells Samuel to compile and refer to an *iggeret* (missive) to know which books are in his library. Abrahams interprets this to mean the list affixed to the end of a bookshelf in line with the practice of medieval European institutional libraries: "This method was often adopted in old libraries, see the example in the fine book-cases in St. John's College, Cambridge."[21] Indeed, Judah specifies that this is to be the fate of the memorandum, encouraging Samuel to facilitate searching for books by placing it on the shelf: "If you were to write down the spot of all the books on the shelf in a missive (*iggeret*) that you would then put in that very shelf, you would then be able to find a book promptly by reviewing the memo that covers that shelf instead of rifling through them. Do the same thing for every book case."[22] However, in this passage Judah uses two words to describe the catalogue, also referring to it later as a *mazkeret-sefarim* (memorandum of books).[23] This passage, using two words to describe the library catalogue, opens up the question of Judah's understanding of the genre to which a library catalogue belongs and the relationship he sees between essayistic autobiography and autobibliography.

The term *iggeret* itself is a surprisingly broad one; its use here to denote the library catalogue that Judah would like Samuel to write opens up the possibility that the ethical will itself has a library cataloguing function. Elsewhere in the text, Judah describes the entire ethical will as an *iggeret*,[24] demonstrating that he envisions both this kind of epistolary, along with library catalogues, as falling into the same generic category of text. This assessment on Judah's part is borne out in the wider use of the word as well: in the talmudic context to which Judah recourses to ground his discussion of libraries, bookmaking, and cataloguing, the Aramaic cognate term, *igarta*,[25] refers to a secular document that can be subject to change, sometimes frequent and regular, which is suggestive of a more substantial prose composition than a simple library list, perhaps a discussion of the books in question.[26] In the Hebrew dictionaries available to him, including Sa'adya's *Egron* (although, interestingly, not in Ibn Janāḥ's *Kitāb al-Uṣūl*), an *iggeret* is portrayed as a collection of written comments.[27] Judah's choice of words is significant on formal grounds in that it suggests that the catalogue is a formal mirror of the ethical will, a long-form document written in prose and subject to editing and change over time. If Judah conceived, eccentrically, of library catalogues as epistles, then the ethical will conforms to that vision of a library catalogue and we, too, may think of it as such. The text becomes (if it was not always already and at its origins) a catalogue in exile of the library that Judah left behind in Granada and rebuilt in Provence; the catalogue is, through time and space, the portable conservation and microcosm of the library. Even the stratigraphy of the text—the editorial history that saw it composed, compiled, and revisited over time—is itself suggestive of a catalogue updated as books come in and out in conjunction with or parallel to the events documented within the bio-bibliography. It is ultimately the content of the library that we can reconstruct from the ethical will that is the most significant contribution to understanding Judah's particular predilections and the ways in which he clings to the memory of an intellectual culture of al-Andalus. The collection of books enumerated in the ethical will acts, at a minimum, as a kind of proxy, portable library catalogue, a textual analogue for the movement of knowledge and the remnant of the libraries that might have been north and south of the Pyrenees.

The term *iggeret* is a fairly broad one that can refer to many types of documents, almost always intended for at least some kind and range of public distribution. Medieval Judaeo-Arabic biblical lexicographers invoke a passage from the book of Nehemiah to define it as a general term for written material, either private correspondence or a document—a legal writ, an epistle, an announcement, or message—intended for a wider public:

> They sent for me four times in the manner described, and I answered them in the manner described; but then Sanballat sent for me a fifth time in the manner described, his messenger [came] with an open letter (*iggeret petuḥah*) in his hand in which it was written: "It is rumored amongst the nations that you and the Judeans mean to revolt."[28]

Although Jonah ibn Janāḥ did not seek to define the term in his dictionary, and consequently we do not have a translation of such an entry by Judah ibn Tibbon in *Sefer ha-Shorashim*, Saʿadya Ga'on defines the term as an anthology (*kitāb jāmiʿ*), which highlights the definition of the term as the kind of text that could contain many different things; Abraham ibn 'Ezra' likewise comments on the nature of the word *iggeret* as a collection of words, or a list.[29] Judah uses the word *iggeret* in the ethical will with a range of semantic valences that nonetheless manifest a certain elegant degree of consistency: Judah tells Samuel that he has copied out certain books for him and written certain other original compositions, including an *iggeret*, undoubtedly referring here to the ethical will itself as a kind of open prose text that its author knew would be read out among a wider audience. He also admonishes Samuel to write an *iggeret* listing his books, here using the word to describe a kind of library catalogue. And so we see that the term *iggeret* is used in several different places with slightly different valences under the same broad semantic umbrella, once to refer to a catalogue-type document and the second time to refer more generally to written material that Judah has prepared for Samuel. As has been noted throughout, the ethical will, while directed specifically to Samuel, was always destined for a wider audience; it, too, is most definitely an *iggeret*, both on the face of it and as defined by its author. While this is a significant consideration in framing the reading of the text as a whole and certain other characteristics within it, such as the critique of Samuel and the overall characterization of Arabic literacy and its value in Christendom, it becomes the axis on which the discussion of the library and the library catalogue hinges. When Judah tells Samuel to write an *iggeret* as a reminder of all the books that he owns, he is signaling the ethical will itself as a model of a library document written long-form and intended for public consumption. By placing the ethical will in the same category as a library catalogue, he gives an additional function to the text that he is writing and sets up future expectations for the genre itself. The ethical will might not be the exact catalogue that Judah would place at the end of each bookcase, but his inclusion of the two texts in the same documentary category invites further examination of the features that it shares with other library catalogues more conventionally drawn up. The coincidence between the use of *iggeret* to mean *catalogue* within a text that is, itself, explicitly an *iggeret*, is a thought-provoking invitation to the reader to consider the ethical will, which already contains much evidence about Judah's library, as evidence *for* the library itself.

Yet regardless of whether one sees fit to accept the terminological argument, the comparative documents from the Genizah still lend validity to the contention that the ethical will is a model library catalogue within a personal narrative. Thus we may use it to the fullest to determine the contents of Judah's library and assess its typicality as the library of a Judaeo-Arabic thinker and the outsized place of the Andalusi curriculum within it.

Some of the library lists in the comparative corpus drawn from Allony, Ben-Shammai, and Frenkel's publication of the Genizah documents are organized according to genre or reflect an interest in one particular area over others; for example, Allony 95 is a legal library and Allony 39 is largely a collection of geonic works.[30] The fragment published as Allony 95 (Firkovitch II Evr-Ar 1.127.1a) is a particularly important document when trying to situate Judah's library collection in his historical context, not because of the contents of the library that it enumerates but because it has been closely associated with a near contemporary of Judah who, similarly, left al-Andalus in the wake of the Almohads' arrival there. Allony 95 is associated, if not with Moses Maimonides himself, then at least with other members of his family, making it not only a temporal, geographic, and geopolitical match, but also the book list of someone who was in direct contact with both Judah and Samuel. The list appears on an early page of a manuscript of Sa'adya Ga'on's *Kitāb al-amanāt*. The codex was split and its pages are now found in the Firkovitch and Jewish Theological

Seminary collections; the half that is now in the Firkovitch collection bears an owner's mark identifying it as Maimonides' copy.[31] Both Bacher and Scheiber identify the hand of the book list as that of Maimonides;[32] Ben-Shammai affirms the identification but also approaches it more cautiously, noting that "it is possible that the entire list is connected to the Rambam *or to his circle*."[33] The contents of the list are largely juridical in nature: a specialized library for that part of Maimonides' professional life (or the work done in his wake by those in his religio-legal circle). The list enumerates many works of law (*hilkhot*). Some of these are identifiable, such as the two copies of Isaac al-Fāsī's *Hilkhot ha-rif* and the single copy of Simon Kiyara's *Hilkhot Gedolot*; others are described in a more vague way that does not allow them to be identified as specific works or with specific authors. The list betrays a special interest in the writing of Hai Ga'on and Sa'adya Ga'on, containing three identifiable works by each author and others that might pertain to their oeuvre. It also contains reference resources, such as al-Fāsī's grammatical work *Kitāb jāmi' al-alfāẓ*, that, as we shall see in the next chapter, are also crucial instruments of biblical exegesis. The list also includes one unidentified work of *adab* (belles lettres), suggesting breadth of reading even within a more narrow subsection of a medieval reader's professional, intellectual, and readerly life. In Maimonides we have an example of a reader whose library list contains only a fraction of what we know him to have read.[34]

Conversely, other lists catalogue more general collections that reflect a wide range of interests, including biblical, rabbinic, exegetical, grammatical, and literary texts; this is the type of library collection that Judah shows to be his own through his enumeration of his books in the ethical will. For example, the fragment published as Allony 5 (TS NS 312.84) is particularly evocative because of the large size of the collection in documents and its particular interest in Andalusi works. This is perhaps the most analogous to what Judah's collection might have looked like: the personal collection of a single individual who owned a wide range of books on various topics, with a particular concentration of Andalusi authors, with at least twenty of his sixty-eight volumes[35] containing texts written by Andalusi authors; these include poetry by Dunash ben Labraṭ, Moses ibn 'Ezra', and Samuel ibn Naghrīla; "two volumes of the sayings of the Andalusis" (*kanāsayn fīhā aqāwīl*[36] *li-ahl al-Andalus*); grammatical works by Ibn Gikatilla, Ibn Bil'am, al-Kanzī, and Ḥayyūj (North African by birth, but heavily implicated in the Córdoba grammar wars);[37] and an extensive selection of Jonah ibn Janāḥ's grammatical, lexical, and polemical works. The library is described as having contained many works by Sa'adya and other geonim; four medical works containing texts by both Jewish and Muslim writers;[38] volumes of liturgical poetry, and a range of exegetical works. It also contains works of philosophy and theology by Muslim authors, including a stand-alone fascicle of a single book excerpted from al-Ghazālī's *Iḥyā' 'ulūm al-dīn*;[39] Radī al-Dīn al-Ta'ūsī's *Kitāb maḥāsibah al-insān ilā nafsihi* (Man's Accounting of His Soul); and *Sharḥ kitāb al-'ibāra*, al-Farābī's commentary on Aristotle's *De Interpretatione.* As a whole, this library reflects a representative cross-section of books being read by Arabic-speaking Jews in the twelfth century, strikingly similar to Judah's in range and in its preoccupation with the book culture that emerged from al-Andalus. The material texts were sites for transmitting wisdom not only through the books they listed but also through paratextual elements; and because of this secondary function, we see Judah's ethical will, at least in part, as conforming to that model and solidifying his place in the readerly culture of al-Andalus, even from afar.

The ethical will is what remains of that *iggeret*, a catalogue incorporated into an epistolary form that could naturally accommodate it. With that text as a guide, we may say that Judah's library contained the text of the Hebrew Bible in both Hebrew and in Sa'adya Ga'on's Arabic commentary-translation, with particular attention to the books of Numbers, Deuteronomy, Kings, Isaiah, Jeremiah, Malachi, Psalms, Proverbs, Job, and Jonah, some of which might have been copied out in individual volumes, as reflected in the book lists. Judah's library would also have contained copies of the Babylonian Talmud and commentaries on the Mishnah. It would have included Andalusi works of prose—Solomon ibn Gabirol's *Choice of Pearls* and Samuel ibn Naghrīla's oft-cited *After Proverbs*—and poetry, including some form of the *dawāwīn*, though perhaps not the canonical ones, of Samuel ibn Naghrīla, of Judah Halevi and of Dunash ben Labrat. The library would also have contained Islamic and secular-scientific books, including the *Iḥyā' 'ulūm al-dīn* in the first category and, in the second, the works of Hippocrates in Arabic translation[40] and al-Jāḥiẓ's *Kitāb al-Ḥayawān*.[41] Judah was also a compiler of scientific miscellany and perhaps also of *shamā'il* literature and proverbs, as we learn when he describes that activity: "Pay attention to conserving loose leaves in the bound volumes and those that are in the archival files; and do not lose them because there are great and wonderful things in them that I have compiled and written out for you. Don't lose any of the written documents or essays (*al-te'abed ketav ve-lo iggeret*) that I have collected for you."[42] This represents Judah's most active intervention in his own library collection, moving beyond being its collector and curator and director to becoming an anthologist, creating not only a set of specific books and commissioning new ones where needed, but copying and creating books himself. We see these types of personalized collections reflected across many of the Genizah lists, including volumes of poetry with selected commentaries preferred by the patron or owner,[43] selections of the biblical text and correlated liturgical selections or lexicographic aides,[44] and personalized compilations of works of Jewish law.[45] Finally, there are the invisible works,[46] the ones whose existence we know only through mention in this text. These include a lost poem by Samuel ibn Naghrīla, the so-called "Song of the Pen," of which we have one line preserved in the ethical will, "O, pen, I recount your favor!"; as well as two phantom prose works by Judah ibn Tibbon himself, a commentary on the biblical book of Proverbs and a guide to writing that he called *The Purity of Language*. In terms of its content, Judah's library, as enumerated by his quoted works and the other books he describes owning or using, closely mirrors many of the book lists that survived in the Genizah; this coincidence, combined with Judah's insistence on the value of curating a careful personal library collection, means that we may read the ethical will as a catalogue, if even only a partial one, of Judah's own personal library in exile in Provence.

FATHERS AND SONS IN THE LIBRARY

Even though the ethical will is a great many things and even though its readership has always been wide, Judah ibn Tibbon's ethical will is also always first an aspirational and self-reflective mandate from a father to a son; and so, even as the text is ultimately Judah's and not Samuel's, any aspect of the former's autobiography must be viewed within a framework that includes the latter. It is the intellectual biography of the father; but the shadow that the son casts on the text as its permanent, presumed interlocutor cannot be dismissed in the course of reading and interpreting it. Every aspect of the text, including the role of books and libraries in an Andalusi education, must be viewed from beneath both sheets of this dialogic overlay. As noted in the general introduction, it seems likely that Judah himself truly believed his negative assessment of his son's potential in spite of what he would go on to achieve for himself; this is a curriculum for a wayward son. In her recent book, Avital Ronell develops the theory of "loser sons," men she defines as those "who fail to live up to [their] fathers' repute or aspirations, who lose out and deform the world with this sense of 'counterfeit legacy,' even when they win out, often tilting the scales of justice and warping the playing fields on which fateful moves are determined."[47] On the one hand, it seems anachronistic and out of proportion to place Samuel ibn Tibbon in a theoretical category that includes George W. Bush and Osama bin Laden; on the other hand, Ronell's idea is well suited to a son whose chief legacy was the twinning of a berating and a professional-familial mantle to be taken up and carried forward. Perhaps rather than calling Samuel a "loser son," then, it might be best to think of him as a son for whom something was lost in translation. Be that as it may, in light of Samuel's ultimate achievement, the reader is left wondering what he himself might have said about his own education and his work ethic as a student, and even about his father's role in it. Samuel's own prefaces, though clearly dependent on his father's, do not offer us enough insight to determine the extent to which his career was a response to or a reaction against his father's criticism. Yet as we see fathers and sons across a range of Judaeo-Arabic library writing, we may begin to assess the nature of that relationship as it played out within the institution[48] of the library.

Judah writes to Samuel about the importance of sharing his good fortune to have a library by lending books to other young men studying in his community, an ethic that we see corroborated in some of the Genizah book lists. In one instance Judah connects communal study to the lending of books,[49] with the sly recognition that lending books is an imperfect system that does not always see them returned to their owner:

> Neither take your studies with your teacher for granted nor cease to study with the younger men, even if you do not leave your teacher's study until late at night. You should always share everything that you have learned from me and from your teachers with other worthy students to keep your knowledge fresh at hand; by teaching them, you will learn it by heart and by answering their questions you will remove any doubt. Nor should you refuse to lend books to anyone who does not have any or the ability to buy them, as long as you are sure he will return them to you. You know what our sages wrote: 'Wealth and happiness reside with him and his righteousness remains forever.' So, do not keep the benefit of your possessions [from others] or guard your books closely. Cover your book cases with lovely tapestries and guard them against moisture, bookworms, and damage, because they are your treasure. When you lend a book to anyone, inscribe his name in the catalogue before it leaves your house; and when it is returned, cross it out with a pen. On Passover and Sukkot, recall all of the books that you have lent out.[50]

In this passage, Judah highlights the special responsibility placed on Samuel as his son to share the windfall of books available to him precisely because that father-son relationship within the library reinforces the kind of personal and communal connections that he views as crucial for learning. Throughout the sections of the text that discuss library practice, Judah emphasizes that Samuel's fortune in having a library is a fortuitous consequence of being his son. And in another place Judah highlights the importance of lending in light of the fact that the library he created for Samuel contained multiple copies of the most important works, a phenomenon that is observed in the richest of the personal libraries documented in the Genizah book lists: "You," Judah writes to Samuel, "praise God, can lend and do not have to borrow since you have two or three copies of most of your books."[51] Furthermore, some of the lists situate libraries and the movement of books in and out of them within and among members of specific and well-defined families and communities. Borrowers as well as lenders keep track of the movement of books in and out of their collections. With respect to borrowing and lending, some lists show evidence of exactly the type of practice of crossing out and reentering items in a catalogue that Judah enjoins to Samuel, as noted in the passage cited above that concerns crossing out and reentering borrowed and returned volumes.[52] Lending within families and communities, or as the familial obligation of the sons of elite religious and cultural leaders, is also in evidence in the documentary material: The list found on the fragment TS NS 228.3, published as Allony 42, begins with the descriptive heading "This is what I have in my bookcase" (*allaḏī lī fī l-khizāna*) and is clearly an inventory rather than a property list. The document lists books that this anonymous cataloguer owns, and then also goes on to note that many of the books on his shelf are on loan from other owners; the list is of the contents of his library, as distinct from books that were his own property. The borrowed books on his shelves included "a copy of the Gemara that belongs to my uncle Sālim"; as well as "a copy of the Mishnah that belongs to my uncle Abū 'Alā"; a bound codex containing the text of the Torah (*muṣḥaf*) that was "property of the *cohen*, Ibn al-Tāqī"; and a volume of midrashim that "belongs to *the son of* Rabbi Zakkai."[53] The now-nameless library cataloguer has borrowed books not only from his own relatives, but also from community leaders and, crucially, from *their* sons, too. Although this document does not offer any insight into the circumstances that led Rabbi Zakkai's son to lend books to this anonymous reader, he is, in fact, doing the same thing that Judah wishes Samuel to do; the book list of this anonymous reader, as well as Judah's own discussion of his personal obligation to create a library that serves a community and his expectation that his son follow in his footsteps, both demonstrate the significance and common cultural value of caring for a heritable book collection and making it available to members of the community for their use.

Similarly, other book lists admit the delineation of familial relationships and the assertion and description of relationships between fathers and sons: Allony 85 (TS 10 G 5.7) is a catalogue and bibliography of a collection of works written by Sa'adya Ga'on. The list was compiled by his three sons and begins with an introduction that goes beyond the formulaic to express, even if only briefly, their respect and affection for him.[54] In this example we see a book list as an expression of filial piety, one in which sons seek to make arrangements for copies of their father's work. In line with the other examples, we begin to see book lists as a site of transmitting familial values and aspirations through explicit statements of advice and piety and through more literary avenues like quoting from poetic wisdom literature; with this as a feature that occurs in documentary book lists, we must see the listing of books in Judah's ethical will explicitly couched as a father's moral instruction much more in line with those documentary sources for the libraries. And formulaic though this catalogue written by Sa'adya's sons is, it nonetheless reflects a similar expectation that sons will ultimately care for their fathers' library collections.

But perhaps the best comparison to Judah's ethical will in terms of its integration of autobiography, bibliographic detail, and the pedagogical relationship between a father and son is not a book list at all, but rather an autobiographical statement that melds religious belief, filial piety, and a detailed, book-rich statement of curriculum with its origins in the western Islamicate world;[55] by virtue of the many planes that it presents for equal comparison, the conversion narrative of Samawa'l al-Maghribī might be thought of as a kind photographic negative of Judah ibn Tibbon's ethical will. Almost an exact contemporary of Judah ibn Tibbon, Samawa'l al-Maghribī (d. 1175) was from a North African and Andalusi family and was educated in Baghdad in mathematics and medicine; after his conversion to Islam, he earned a reputation as a noted polemicist against his former faith, although in this he, too, may have been speaking to multiple audiences, a mathematician using an assailable faith tradition to argue against faith more broadly as it impinged on his own particular brand of rationalism.[56]

One chapter of his polemical work *Ifḥām al-yahūd* (The Silencing of the Jews) is an autobiographical narrative in which he narrates his turn toward Islam.[57] In it he frames his conversion in terms of the books he read in his youth, both as a part of his education and, with the teleological certainty of theological hindsight, as part of his path toward Islam. The history of Samawa'l's polemic and conversion narrative is complex, with longer and shorter versions of the text extant; and it has been suggested that he refrained from writing the autobiographical portion of the text until after his father's death so as not to insult him in light of the efforts he made in educating his son, which are themselves evident in the text. Samawa'l's description of his early education, his father's role in it, the books that he read, and his memories of his reactions to them are worth quoting at length in order to facilitate a contraposition of the text against the Ibn Tibbon ethical will. In describing his early education, Samawa'l writes:

> My father had me learn Hebrew writing, and then study the Torah and the commentaries until, by the age of thirteen, I had mastered this knowledge. Then he introduced me to the study of Indian reckoning and the solution of equations under Shaykh Abū l-Ḥasan ibn al-Daskarī, and the study of medicine under the philosopher Abū l-Barakāt Ḥibat-Allāh ibn ʿAlī, and the observation of current surgical operations and the treatment of diseases as practiced by my maternal uncle Abū l-Fatḥ ibn Baṣrī. As to Indian reckoning and astronomical tables, I mastered them in less than a year, by the age of fourteen, and at the same time continued to study medicine and to observe the treatment of diseases. Then I studied administrative accounting and the science of surveying under Sheikh Abū l-Muẓaffar al-Shahrazūrī, as well as algebra and equations also under him and the administrator (*kātib*), Ibn Abī Turāb as well. I then frequented Master Daskarī and Abū l-Ḥassan ibn al-Naqqāsh for the study of geometry, until I had solved the problems from Euclid that they used to solve. At the same time, I was so devoted to medicine that I absorbed whatever I could from the above-mentioned two teachers of science. There remained parts of the Book of Euclid, the book of al-Wāsiṭī on arithmetic and The Book of Ornament on algebra by al-Karkhī. But I could not find anyone who knew anything of these books, or beyond these, on the mathematical sciences, such as the book of Shujāʿ ibn Aslam on algebra, and others. My passion and love for these studies were so strong that I would forget food and drink when pondering on some of them. I secluded myself in a room for a time and analyzed all those books and expounded them; I refuted their authors wherever they committed mistakes, demonstrated the errors of their compilers, and undertook to verify or correct where other authors had failed. I found Euclid's arrangement of the figures in his book faulty for by rearranging them I could dispense with the superfluous; this after the book of Euclid had been considered the acme by the other geometricians, so much so that they had introduced nothing new either by changing Euclid's set of figures or by eliminating any of them. All this I achieved in that year, namely, by the age of eighteen. Since that year my writings in these sciences followed one another continuously down

> to the present. God has revealed to me much that had been withheld from my predecessors among the eminent scholars; all this I put into shape for the benefit of whomever it might reach.[58]
>
> Before I took up these sciences, that is, in my twelfth and thirteenth years, I was fascinated by records of the past and by stories, and was eager to learn what had happened in ancient times, and to know what had occurred in ages past. I therefore perused the various compilations of stories and anecdotes. Then I passed on from that stage to an infatuation with books of entertainment and long tales. And later still to the larger compilations such as the tales on 'Antar, Dhū l-Himma, al-Baṭṭāl, Iskandar Dhū l-Qarnayn, the stories of 'Anqā', Ṭaraf ibn Lūdhān and others. On reading these I recognized that most of the material was derived from the works of the historians. Therefore I sought the real historical accounts and my interest shifted to the histories, of which I read the book of Abū 'Alī ibn Miskawayh entitled Experiences of the Nations, the History of al-Ṭabarī, and other historical works.[59]
>
> I saw the miracle of the Qur'ān, which human eloquence cannot rival, and well did I recognize the truth of its miraculous character. Then, after I had trained my mind on mathematical sciences, especially on geometry, I asked myself about the differences among men in religious faiths and tenets. I received the greatest impulse to inquire into the subject from reading the epistle of Bardhawayh the physician in the book of Kalīla and Dimna.[60]

Within the framework of Samawa'l's description of his conversion to Islam and his delineation of the proofs that convinced him of the truth of that religion, readers are also offered many details of his early intellectual formation, including the subjects, authors, and books that he studied; the conversion narrative includes specific mathematical treatises, historical chronicles, and works of *adab*, in addition to more general instruction in Hebrew and medicine: a curriculum that, in broad strokes if not in the specific works, is quite similar to the curriculum that Judah lays out for Samuel in the ethical will in which he enjoins him to read theology and philosophy, but also mathematics and scientific texts, all the while drawing in the literary texts that formed so much of the core of the belletristic readerly culture he inhabited.[61] We see further indications of the bookish and readerly character of Samawa'l's education. He explains that his interest in history had grown out of literature when "I recognized that most of the material [in the literary works] was derived from the works of the historians. Therefore I sought the real historical accounts and my interest shifted to the histories."[62] His sensitivity to genre and his attention to the relationship between literary accounts and historical chronicles speaks to a recognition of the fluidity of textual forms; and his discussion of his own emendation of the mathematical works in particular make clear that he is an active participant reader in a material-readerly culture and that his intellectual and religious developments are equally the consequence of the material transmission of the written text. This is a literary education adjacent to an extensive personal library, and its student demonstrates its impact in his reflections on it as an adult.

In certain respects, this narrative is the mirror image of Judah's ethical will: Samawa'l, the student, writes about beginning to study Hebrew and to take instruction in the common curricular subjects around the age of twelve or thirteen; he portrays himself as an eager student of the language whereas Samuel, at the same age, is described as a reluctant one. In his conversion narrative, Samawa'l describes undertaking both sacred Jewish (and later and, at first, covertly, Islamic) subjects as well as "foreign" or secular ones, just as we learn that Judah procured tutors in secular subjects for Samuel. In fact, the confidence with which Samawa'l speaks of his mastery of all these areas of inquiry, above and beyond all of his predecessors and fellow students, offers the view from the other side and raises questions about the role of hyperbole in this kind of writing, both in terms of Samawa'l's aggrandizement of his own achievements and quick path to knowledge and of Judah's denunciations of Samuel; notwithstanding the earlier observation that external evidence seems to suggest that Judah's complaints about Samuel reflect sincerely held beliefs, even the ethical will allows some room to concede the role of hyperbole in the expression of those beliefs, as when Judah observes that Samuel's reputation for laziness is "mostly a lie"[63] and his frequent hedging that Samuel should accomplish certain goals "to the best of your ability."[64] Samawa'l's contrasting account leads the reader to wonder what the other Samuel in question, Samuel ibn Tibbon, might have said if we had record of his own version of his education and personal intellectual history rather than relying solely on his father's.

Yet the significance of filial ties in education is also evidence of Samawa'l's preoccupation with his own father's tutelage and, when it comes to describing his conversion, with sensitivity to his father's reaction to the news after having taken such pains to ensure his Jewish and secular education. Furthermore, both texts participate in perpetuating the significance of publicizing the intellectual lineage of young writers and scholars as a part of establishing their authority. Like Judah's ethical will, which draws on conventions of a specific Arabic literary genre, so, too, do Samawa'l's conversion narrative and texts more typically viewed as documentary instead of—and not also—literary, namely on the conventions of Arabic autobiographical and broader prose writing;[65] and in all of the cases discussed in this section we see the authors integrating a detailed discussion of their reading habits, preferences, and influences into this wider framework of genre-based personal narrative and literary form.

THE "SON" OF PROVERBS IN THE ETHICAL WILL AND THE LIBRARY

A great many of Judah ibn Tibbon's cultural admonitions to his son are drawn from the oeuvre of the poet Samuel ibn Naghrīla, an eleventh-century poet, grammarian, and jurist who also served as scribe, vizier, and battle commander to the Zirid emirs of Granada; he is also identified as the *nagid*, or leader, of the Jewish community of Granada, the term by which Judah often refers to him in the ethical will. Judah holds Samuel ibn Naghrīla as a model for his namesake son in everything from moral conduct to neat handwriting; as he directs his son to make a greater and more self-directed effort toward writing well, Judah exhorts: "Choose one of your Arabic books that is written in a hand that appeals to you aesthetically and try to learn from it by imitating it. No one taught the Arabic script to the *nasi*, Samuel [ibn Naghrīla]; rather, he took one of the documents written by an important scribe and tried to write using it as a model."[66] Most notable, though, throughout the ethical will Judah draws extensively from Ibn Naghrīla's collection of aphoristic poetry known as *Ben Mishlei*—literally "The Son of Proverbs," but more sensibly rendered into English as *After Proverbs*.[67] *After Proverbs* is a collection of cycles of poems; each cycle features one letter of the Hebrew alphabet as the first letter of each line of each poem in the given cycle, and the cycles run in alphabetical order. It is one of three collections of poems by Ibn Naghrīla that stake an explicit—if internally more complex—claim to biblical models of writing: *Ben Mishlei*, *Ben Qohelet* (After Ecclesiastes), and *Ben Tehilim* (After Psalms). Responsive to the form of its "father" text and the clarion call to wisdom and rectitude that it issues in its first chapter, the poems included in *Ben Mishlei* are largely, but not exclusively, aphoristic in character, challenging the reader to grapple with their meaning.[68] This group of poems was collected and edited by Ibn Naghrīla's youngest son, Eliasaf; the preface that he added to his father's work tells the reader that Eliasaf began to copy out his father's poems beginning from the age of six, a curricular and conservationist indication against which Judah ibn Tibbon's admonition to Samuel that he copy out the ethical will for himself can be measured, as well as an additional data point by which to gauge the age at which the sons of the literary elites began their formal educations.[69] The poems in the collection lived on vividly in the literary lives and history of medieval Jews, including that of Judah ibn Tibbon. In his introduction to the text edition, Israel Abrahams goes so far as to describe Ibn Naghrīla as Ibn Tibbon's "hero."[70] The program of text citations within the ethical will certainly bears out the high value that Ibn Tibbon placed on Ibn Naghrīla's work: while the text of Judah's ethical will draws on, alludes to, and cites a whole range of Hebrew and Arabic, sacred and secular, ancient and medieval texts, *Ben Mishlei* is far and away the most cited and most referenced text, outpacing by an eight-fold margin the next most popular text in Judah's writing. Over twenty-five citations of and allusions to *Ben Mishlei* may be found there, while the next most cited texts, Solomon ibn Gabirol's *Choice of Pearls* and the biblical book of Jeremiah (the use of which is discussed in greater detail in the following chapter), are each cited only three times.

In this respect, Judah was a fairly typical reader; he was far from the only one for whom Ibn Naghrīla's work has tremendous significance. As the text lived on with later medieval readers,[71] it, too, became an important component of the medieval Andalusi Jewish library and as a literary component of library documentary practice. Documentary sources continue to reveal the broader cultural significance of the Ibn Naghrīla *diwān* and the lengths to which medieval readers would go in order to come into possession of copies of the work; these sources include prose texts such as the stunning letter written in Judaeo-Arabic recently discovered by José Martínez Delgado bound into a codex in the Firkovitch Collection (Ebr-Arb I 4575). This letter, which Martínez Delgado identifies as having been written in al-Andalus and quite likely during the lifetime of Judah ibn Tibbon,[72] stands as an excellent counterpoint to the ethical will because it reflects the literary tastes of an Andalusi book collector and the fervency with which he sought excellent copies of Andalusi literary texts, specifically two by Ibn Naghrīla. The rhymed-prose literary epistle is bound in with a personalized miscellany replete with Andalusi and North African works, including Ḥayyuj's grammatical treatise on verbs formed from geminate roots; a poem by Moses ibn 'Ezra'; an anonymous commentary on ibn Janāḥ's grammatical works that focuses, according to Martínez Delgado's reading, on "liberties taken" in the work; and a copy, written in a distinct hand, of a poem written by Hai Ga'on and sent to a confederate in Qairoan.[73] The letter in question represents an example of a personal epistle written in combination with bibliographic cataloguing and anthologizing; it speaks of an accompanying book list although that list is now separated from the letter and apparently lost.[74] Yet even the central concern of the letter similarly reflects bibliophilic, acquisitive, and cataloguing values and priorities as it focuses principally on the procurement of Andalusi works of poetry.[75] The recipient has apparently sent his agent or personal secretary to procure for him copies of *After Proverbs* and *After Ecclesiastes*,[76] copies that would be of better quality than the ones that he already owned. The letter writer, the agent, explains that he sought but could not obtain autograph copies of both of the requested parts of the Ibn Naghrīla *diwān*:

> I understand my lord's (*mawlī*) instruction with respect to the matter of *After Proverbs* and *After Ecclesiastes*. I will not let his glorious letter out of my hands until I shall have succeeded in seeking both of them out. I set out on my task and have seen many of them, excellent copies in the handwriting of the author of our lord (*adoneinu*), the memory of the righteous is a blessing. I requested both of them for less than a dinar but the owner declined and so I offered him double but he was completely unwilling to agree. So I was unable buy them. I still have my lord's [copies of the] volumes with me, but they are not complete; they contain an authorization (*tawkīl*) but are not copied beautifully and as such the value is corresponding.[77]

This letter offers some sense of both the monetary value of these books and the cultural capital with which they were imbued. Meta-analysis by Maya Shatzmiller of texts discussed in Eliahu Ashtor's *Jews of Moslem Spain* and of other documents found in the Cairo Genizah that contain information on wage payments suggests that an average monthly salary for judges, teachers, and municipal officials in the twelfth century ranged from one to two dinars.[78] Furthermore, although none of the twelfth-century lists published in *The Jewish Library in the Middle Ages* indicate the cost of volumes of poetry, other libraries that do not contain poetic works are both enumerated and priced; and so by way of comparison we see that the price offered and refused for these volumes was extraordinary. In contrast to the two dinars that were insufficient to purchase the books of poetry, a copy of Sa'adya Ga'on's *Kitāb al-amanāt* sold for 4 dirham,[79] volumes containing individual books of the Bible cost between 2 and 5 dirham, biblical commentaries cost between 10 and 12 dirham, a codex containing the full text of the Pentateuch cost 17 dirham,[80] and a damaged Torah scroll was sold for 25 dirham.[81] In comparison with the cost of these books, we see the dramatic value placed on the copies of Andalusi poetry that the writer was seeking for his patron; it further gives context for the comments that we shall see presently that Judah made about the great expense he incurred in creating his library for Samuel's benefit and the benefit that Samuel reaped from not having to pay for books or for access to them.

Time and again, we see that Samuel ibn Naghrīla's *After Proverbs* represents a central touchstone in the lives of Jewish readers and book collectors in the Islamic West.[82] The book list published with the number Allony 25 (ENA 2687.5) forms the basis of another fascinating comparison with the text of Judah's ethical will, preoccupied as it is with that particular work. One of the shortest lists recovered,[83] it enumerates only four items: a partial copy of the *diwān* of Judah Halevi; a complete copy of the *diwān* of Samuel ibn Naghrīla; a miscellany of liturgical poems including a glossary with definitions of difficult words; and a copy of the liturgical-legal work *Seder Rav 'Amram Ga'on*.[84] In many respects, despite the brevity of his list it appears that the bibliographic needs and preferences of this anonymous collector are similar to Judah's, albeit on a much smaller scale: like Judah, the owner of this collection had interests that ranged from the explicitly religious to the secular-literary and included reference works that, while growing out of the exegetical tradition, could assist in the interpretation of both types of texts as well as those that sit on the boundary. Of particular and exceptional interest, though, is the facing side[85] of the fragment, which contains excerpts from *After Proverbs*, a component part of Ibn Naghrīla's poetic *diwān*, a copy of which the book list shows us that the collector owned. The fragment quotes the first two lines of two poems from the cycle of poems whose first lines begin with the letter *vav*. The two short poems, like most of the others in the cycle, take the form of Sphinx-like riddles, common in Andalusi poetry, about certain characteristics of human nature (such as happiness and hatred) and the natural world (such as the chicken and the egg). The full text of the two poems is reproduced here in translation, with the lines quoted in the library catalogue shown in italics:[86]

> *And he asked: Is there anyone who waits for no man?*
> *I replied to him: The one who awaits the God of man.*
> And who can die while keeping his spirit, the void cast out
> in the streets, while he keeps his soul? I answered him: The one who has fallen asleep.[87]
> *And he said: Is there anything that eliminates strife*
> *and adds to the heart's love? I answered him: A gift.*
> And could there be anything that nourishes the body without food
> or drink? I answered him: Happiness.[88]

The brevity of the two couplets excerpted and quoted provides a particular interpretive challenge, not leaving much to grab hold of with respect to the significance of those verses in this context; but Bahr's theory of the compiled text provides a clear way in to analyze the placement of the two couplets alongside the book list. As Bahr signals, the interpretation of an assemblage or juxtaposition of texts is always inherently a subjective and reader-centered endeavor that ultimately renders the final product more inherently literary. He defines a compilation as "the assemblage of multiple discrete works into a larger structure whose formal interplay of textual and material parts make available [certain] literary effects," and then goes on to delineate a methodology for approaching a text that is compiled and at least twice-composed: "By defining *compilation* as a way of apprehending and interpreting objects, rather than as an inherent quality of the objects themselves, I make central to my study the question of what constitutes a legitimate invitation to compilational reading, what makes it profitable interpretation rather than willfully idiosyncratic or anachronistic imposition."[89] Bahr further insists on the subjectivity of the interpretation and the inevitability of skeptical reception: "Compilational interpretation is interesting only as long as and to the extent that we can imagine a reasonable interlocutor disagreeing with us."[90] The conjunction of book list and poetic citation in the fragment ENA 2687.5 is a compilation of the type that contains two texts that perhaps echo each other or, perhaps, are simply on the same page because it is what a scribe had at hand but that nonetheless invites an interpretation that considers the juxtaposition of the two. A specific connection between the two poems that could explain their joint selection from within the *vav* cycle of *After Proverbs* is not immediately apparent beyond their proximity in the cycle. Not only is there a paucity of text, but the two poems within the cycle are not connected through the substratum of biblical verses that run through each as *shibbuẓim* (references and allusions to the biblical text or quotations from it); there is no overlap in biblical verses quoted or alluded to by both poems and even only the second of the two poems alludes to the text of Proverbs. Yet juxtaposed against each other and outside of the context not only of the two full poems but the wider cycle of *vav*-poems, these two couplets counsel piety and patience; juxtaposed against the book list, perhaps they cast the books contained in the library and enumerated on their same page as a gift that could eliminate strife and increase love in the life of a pious reader. Ultimately, though, while it is difficult to discern a purpose for those specific verses in a library catalogue as they are not immediately suggestive of particular bibliophilic values but are instead demonstrative of a readerly culture much more generally, the juxtaposition of the most canonical of the poets and the anonymous collector amplifies the volume of that collector's voice as he articulates his literary tastes. By inviting a list of literary works itself into the realm of the literary, the presence of those two couplets highlights the presence of the Ibn Naghrīla *diwān* within the collection, thereby drawing attention to and emphasizing the fact that this collector owned such a culturally significant work; by writing out verses from within one of the books after the collector made a list of all the books he owned, he asserted the literariness of the document and the materiality of the library.

And finally, their presence in a library catalogue as brief as the quoted poetry itself, the interpolation of a book list with quotations from *After Proverbs*, is deeply evocative of the same juxtapositions of an enumeration of volumes and quotations from this particular text by Ibn Naghrīla that we see throughout the ethical will. In both the instance of this book list and the much more narrative and expansive ethical will, reference to *After Proverbs* serves as a literary framing device within a larger text that deals with the creation of a library and the care for and value of a collection of codices. The book list found in Allony 25 is so very fragmentary that it is difficult to assess the function of the citations from *After Proverbs* juxtaposed against the library list in this specific case beyond serving as quotations from one of the books in the library; the content of the quotations does not immediately connect it to a book list, nor does it seem to function as a kind of proof of the book's presence in the library collection delineated on the list. However, it does serve to tie Judah's ethical will more closely to the form of library catalogue in the Genizah society, where we see other listings of books, deliberately and clearly designated as such, embellished with text from *After Proverbs*. And so, perhaps invited by the literary nature of that which is being documented, the literary quickly bleeds into the documentary, and always spelled out in black and white; and it is in these terms that the book culture backdrop against which Judah's program of translation is defined.

NOTES

Chapter title from Judah ibn Tibbon, "Musar Av," 19a.

1. Julián Ribera y Tarragó, *Libros y enseñanzas en al-Andalus*, ed. María Jesús Viguera Molins (Pamplona: Urgoiti Editores, 2008).

2. On both of whom, see the eponymous entries in the *Encyclopaedia of Islam* by Ambrosio Huici Miranda and Charles Pellat.

3. The Arabic translations of Galen's autobibliographies may be found in Max Meyerhoff, "Autobiographische Bruschstücke Galens auz arabischen Quellen," *Sudhoffs Archiv für Geschichte der Medizin* 22 (1929): 72–86. For analysis of these texts, see Franz Rosenthal, "Die arabische Autobiographie," *Studia Arabica* 1 (1937): 1–40. For a contrasting opinion, see Gustave von Grunebaum, *Medieval Islam: A Study in Cultural Orientation* (Chicago: University of Chicago Press, 1946), 258–61.

4. Judah ibn Tibbon, "Musar Av," 15b. Emphasis mine.

5. Malachi Beit-Arie, "Stereotype and Individuality in the Handwriting of Medieval Scribes," in *The Makings of the Medieval Hebrew Book* (Jerusalem: Magnes Press, 1993), 77.

6. Israel Abrahams, notes to "A Father's Admonition," in *Hebrew Ethical Wills* (Philadelphia: Jewish Publication Society, 1926), 81n.85.

7. Carlos del Valle Rodríguez, "El testamento de Yehudah ibn Tibbon: Notas para una historia de las bibliotecas en la España medieval," *Revista de archivos, bibliotecas, y museos* 82 (1979): 495–524.

8. For a general introduction, see Stefan Reif, *A Jewish Archive from Old Cairo* (London: Curzon, 2000); and the studies included in Joshua Blau and Stefan C. Reif, eds., *Genizah Research after Ninety Years* (Cambridge: Cambridge University Press, 1992). On the terminology, see Haggai Ben-Shammai, "Is 'The Cairo Genizah' a Proper Name or a Generic Noun?," in *From a Sacred Source*, ed. Ben Outhwaite (Leiden: Brill, 2010), 43–52. And finally, for an excellent overview of Genizah history and historiography that is scholarly while still aimed for a more general reader, see Peter Cole and Adina Hoffman, *Sacred Trash: The Lost and Found World of the Cairo Geniza* (New York: Nextbook, 2011).

9. Nehemiah Allony, Haggai Ben-Shammai, and Miriam Frenkel, *The Jewish Library in the Middle Ages: Book Lists from the Cairo Genizah* (Jerusalem: Ben-Zvi Institute, 2006). By and large I read with Allony, Ben-Shammai, and Frenkel. Where it is relevant, I shall note where my readings differ from theirs on the basis of my own consultation with the manuscripts in Cambridge, New York, and digitally via the Freidberg Genizah Project; these differences are largely matters of interpreting which texts listed should be considered to be comprised within a single volume and which are to be counted as separate volumes. Frenkel in particular documents meticulously where her readings differ from the ones that Allony left in the unfinished work. As such, I shall not note the differences between the authors here; the interested reader may look those up herself.

10. Miriam Frenkel, "Genizah Documents as Literary Products," in *From a Sacred Source*, ed. Ben Outhwaite (Leiden: Brill, 2010), 139–55.

11. S. D. Goitein, "Books, Migrant and Stationary: A Geniza Study," in *Occident and Orient: A Tribute to the Memory of A. Scheiber*, ed. Robert Dan (Leiden: Brill, 1988), 174–98.

12. TS Ar. 5.1r.

13. Although I mention this label here in the service of contextualizing Judah ibn Tibbon's library, it is a fascinating exemplar undeserving of the contempt that Goitein heaped upon it, meriting a fuller treatment on its own terms.

14. Arthur Bahr, *Fragments and Assemblages: Forming Compilations of Medieval London* (Chicago: University of Chicago Press, 2013), 2.

15. Here he is referring to Derek Pearsall, "Towards a Poetics of Chaucerian Narrative," in *Drama, Narrative, and Poetry in the Canterbury Tales*, ed. Wendy Harding (Toulouse: Presses Universitaires du Mirail, 2003), 99–112.

16. Bahr, *Fragments and Compilations*, 10.

17. The analysis in this chapter is qualitative in nature. Quantitative analysis is another matter; this project does not conceive of itself in the mode of, nor does it leave room for, the big-data approach that immediately suggests itself when one is confronted with the kind of information published by Allony, Ben-Shammai, and Frenkel, although this is an avenue that I hope to pursue in a future project centered entirely around Andalusi and Castilian library culture. Nevertheless, a byproduct of beginning the work on this chapter and orienting myself in the Allony et al. volume is a database of the information contained in the fragments that record the contents of personal libraries datable to the twelfth century. I have chosen to exclude institutional book lists, such as those that document the contents of the library of a particular synagogue, judicial body, or school, as well as lists that were primarily economic, that is, those that were purchase orders or records of sales; book lists written as part of the dispensation of the property of an individual after his death are included in the comparative corpus; in order to maintain the best possible comparison to the type of library Judah might have had and the practice that he as an individual might have used to catalogue it, my comparative corpus is likewise limited to personal collections. These fragments include Allony 4 (TS Misc 26.147 and TS 10 K 20.9); Allony 5 (TS NS 312.84); Allony 6 (TS NS 53, formerly TS NS J 94.53); Allony 25 (ENA 2687.5); Allony 27 (TS NS 298.9); Allony 29 (TS 8K 1); Allony 30 (TS Misc. 36.150); Allony 31 (TS Misc. 36.149); Allony 37 (TS K 3.16); Allony 38 (TS Ar. 51.79); Allony 39 (ENA 1290.5); Allony 41 (Bodl. MS Heb. d 66 f.129); Allony 42 (TS NS 228.3); Allony 65 (TS K 3.32); Allony 67 (TS NS 108.151); Allony 70 (TS NS 108.151); Allony 84 (JRL Gaster Parch 47); Allony 85 (TS 10 G.57); Allony 89 (TS Misc 28.42); and Allony 95 (Firkovitch II Evr.-Ar. 1:127). Owing to the generally poor state of access to the Firkovitch collection in St. Petersburg, I am wholly reliant on their reading for the book list Allony 95, the only document among those listed here that I did not collate for myself, either in person or from photographs.

18. On the early development of the relationship between oral and written transmission of text within Islamic societies, see Gregor Schoeler, *The Genesis of Literature in Islam: From the Aural to the Read* (Edinburgh: Edinburgh University Press, 2009). On oral law within Judaism, see Daniel Boyarin, *A Traveling Homeland: The Babylonian Talmud as Diaspora* (Philadelphia: University of Pennsylvania Press, 2015).

19. Franz Rosenthal, "Of Making Many Books There Is No End: The Classical Muslim View," in *The Book in the Islamic World*, ed. G. N. Atiyeh (Albany: State University of New York Press, 1995), 33–56. Several of the deathbed requests for the destruction of books offer specific instructions on how to proceed with that ultimate disposition of the library, with many specifying that they be burned. However, Rosenthal also identifies the deathbed request of Shuʿbah ibn al-Ḥajjājj, who asked that his son "wash off and bury his books after his death" (41); Abū Ḥayyan al-Tawḥīdī similarly asked that his own work be obliterated through washing so that later generations could not condemn his mistakes in his absence after death (40). The request that the

books be washed off and buried is striking in the similarities it evokes with Genizah-type practices within the Islamic world as identified by Joseph Sadan in two articles on the subject.

20. For a contrasting perspective on translation as an aural activity rather than a written one, see Dimitri Gutas, *Greek Thought, Arabic Culture*, 23.

21. Israel Abrahams, notes to "A Father's Admonition," in *Hebrew Ethical Wills*, 81n.85.

22. Judah ibn Tibbon, "Musar Av," 19a.

23. "Musar Av," 19a. For *mazkeret-sefarim* I am translating with Abrahams (81, folio 19a) to give the term the twin valences of catalogue and *aide-memoire*.

24. Ibn Tibbon, "Musar Av," 20a.

25. Shlomo Na'eh, "On the Meaning of 'Igarta,'" *Meḥqarei Talmud* 3 (2005). I am grateful to both Judith Olszowy-Schlanger and Matthew Morgenstern for pointing me to this reference.

26. Shmuel Safrai, *The Literature of the Sages*, vol. 2 (Assen: Fortress Press, 2006), 425–26.

27. Sa'adya Ga'on, *Sefer ha-Egron*, ed. Nehemiah Allony (Jerusalem: Academy of the Hebrew Language, 1969).

28. Nehemiah 6:4–6.

29. Abraham ibn 'Ezra', *Dos comentarios al Libro de Ester*, ed. and trans. Mario Gómez Aranda (Madrid: CSIC, 2007), 90–92.

30. Allony, Ben-Shammai, and Frenkel read the first entry in list 39, "books by the ge'onim," as the heading of that library, understanding it to be formed as a collection of geonic books. However, the presence in that library of extra-geonic material, which they note and comment upon its incongruity, makes me wonder whether "books by the geonim" is not simply the first entry in the catalogue, seeing that general terms are not unknown in these lists (as, for example, "some books on language" in list 6). That said, the list does contain a majority of geonic works, and so for our purposes here, we can consider it a specialized library even if it is not named as such in its catalogue.

31. Alexander Scheiber, "Autograph Manuscript of Maimonides from the Leningrad Genizah," *Acta Orientalia Academiae Scientarum Hungaricae* 33 (1979): 188.

32. Ibid., 188–89.

33. Haggai Ben-Shammai, in *The Jewish Library in the Middle Ages*, 28. Emphasis mine.

34. Mordechai Cohen enumerates what he calls Maimonides' "exegetical library," which offers the far broader picture of Maimonides as a reader in *Opening the Gates of Interpretation* (Leiden: Brill, 2011), 21–22. For a different take on Maimonides and the question of poetry, see James T. Monroe, "Maimonides on the Mozarabic Lyric: A Note on the Muwashshahat," *La Corónica* 17, no. 2 (1989): 18–32.

35. Allony, Ben-Shammai, and Frenkel count sixty-five volumes in this library list; three items that they counted together do not show evidence of necessarily having been a part of the same volume consistent with other bound volumes on the list.

36. Allony, Ben-Shammai, and Frenkel (29) translate *aqāwil* into Hebrew as *mizmorim* (songs). In his dictionary of Judaeo-Arabic, Blau suggests that this term should be understood even more broadly than I have rendered it, preferring instead *matters*

(570). For Andalusi Arabic, Corriente indicates that *qāla* can be used as the verb for singing songs; but in the nominal form, he does not admit *qawl* as song and also prefers a broader semantic sense that includes *sayings* and *remarks* (448).

37. These are addressed in chapters 3 and 4.

38. These four medical works include *Al-Kāfī fī ʿilm al-ṭib* by Abū ʿAdnān ibn Naṣr al-Aynzabī, a twelfth-century Faṭimī court physician; a second copy of this work and another, unspecified work of medicine, both written in the hand of Shlomo ben Zakai; and a medical work by al-Rāzi, with no title given (TS NS 312.84).

39. The section in question, identified in the book list as *Kitāb al-Khawf wa-l-rajāʿ* (*The Book of Fear and Hope*), constitutes part 4, book 33 of the *Iḥyāʾ*. Readership of the *Iḥyāʾ* in the Judaeo-Arabic cultural milieu, and in al-Andalus and the Islamic West in particular, is the subject of chapter 5.

40. For references within the ethical will to all of the works mentioned up to this point, see the apparatus in Abrahams's edition of the text.

41. On this text, see the discussion in chapter 5.

42. Judah ibn Tibbon, "Musar Av," 19a.

43. As in Allony 39 (ENA 1290.5).

44. As in Allony 6 (TS NS 53).

45. As in Allony 42 (TS NS 228.3).

46. Readers will, of course, recognize the phrase "the invisible work" as borrowed from Georges May's description of Antoine Galland's contribution to the *1,001 Nights* in French. See Muhsin Mahdi, in the introduction to his critical edition of the *Nights* on the difference between invisible and unknown works: Introduction to the *Thousand and One Nights* (Leiden: Brill, 1995), 36.

47. Avital Ronell, *Loser Sons: Politics and Authority* (Urbana: University of Illinois Press, 2012), 2.

48. Just as I have elected to use the term *profession* to describe Tibbonid translation activity despite their not receiving remuneration for it, I use the term *institution* here not to describe libraries as large or extensive public cultural institutions. Although *The Jewish Library in the Middle Ages* and other sources offer evidence for some of these types of libraries, my interest here, as already noted, is in personal libraries; and so, when I speak of these as institutions, I mean simply to say that they are a fixture of the lives of the literate elite.

49. The significance of teaching and communal study for the dissemination of translated texts will be discussed in the reception history in chapter 6.

50. Ibn Tibbon, "Musar Av," 19a–b.

51. Ibid., 15b.

52. See examples of this in Allony 5 (TS 314.84).

53. TS NS 228.3; published as text 42 in Allony, *The Jewish Library in the Middle Ages*. Also published in Nehemiah Allony, "Four Book Lists from the Twelfth Century," *Qiryat Sefer* 43 (1968), 121–39. Emphasis mine.

54. Also cf. Allony 84 (JRL Gaster Parch. 47).

55. Even more than the notion of a "Genizah society" or a "Mediterranean society," the natively Islamicate geocultural framework of the Maghreb, the western region that includes Spain and North Africa, is part of a coherent, if varied, geographical and cultural unit. The term Maghreb simply denotes the geographic west and represents

North Africa and Spain, unified under Umayyad rule. Even though Judah ibn Tibbon's lifetime saw major distinctions drawn between those who saw themselves as Andalusis and those they envisioned as North African interlopers, the flow of text, commerce, and humanity across the Strait of Gibraltar dictates that both sides be treated as the parts of a coherent, if not unitary, system.

56. Steven Wasserstrom, "Sharing Secrets: Inter-Confessional Philosophy as Dialogical Practice," in *New Directions in Jewish Philosophy*, ed. Aaron Hughes and Elliot Wolfson (Bloomington: Indiana University Press, 2009), 209–12.

57. Although some of Samawa'l's contemporaries and later medieval writers, prominent among them Ibn Kammūna, cast doubt upon the sincerity of his conversion, that will not concern us in this section, which is only concerned with the relationship of Samawa'l's self-fashioning and his discussion of his reading practices. On the question of the sincerity and longevity of the conversion, see Sarah Stroumsa, "On Jewish Intellectuals Who Converted to Islam in the Middle Ages," in *Medieval Islam: Community, Society, Identity*, ed. Daniel Frank (Leiden: Brill, 1995), 191–96.

58. Omitted here is further discussion of Samawa'l's medical education.

59. Omitted here is further description of what he read in the historical chronicles, without specific reference to any additional books or authors.

60. Samawa'l al-Maghribī, "Conversion to Islam," trans. Moshe Perlman, *Proceedings of the American Academy of Jewish Research* 32 (1964) 74–80. The Arabic text may be found in the same volume, 97–101.

61. Intellectuals are perhaps the best case studies about conversion since "because the intellectuals were literarily included, we may expect them to have recorded the circumstances of their decisions to convert, thereby affording us a glimpse of the apostates' inner world" (180); for more on this phenomenon see Stroumsa, "On Jewish Intellectuals."

62. Samawa'l al-Maghribī, "Conversion to Islam," 74.

63. Ibn Tibbon, "Musar Av," 16a.

64. Ibid., 17b, 18b, 19a.

65. Esperanza Alfonso, *Islamic Culture through Jewish Eyes*, 48.

66. Ibn Tibbon, "Musar Av," 19b. Like the above-cited comment about Patur's student's handwriting resembling that of his teacher, this observation, too, is an indication that stereotype handwriting was the ideal.

67. The relationship between *After Proverbs* and its companion texts, *After Ecclesiastes* and *After Psalms*—to each other and to the Ibn Naghrīla *diwān* as a whole—remains a matter of debate, although there is broader consensus for the idea that those three texts are constituent parts of the *diwān* than for other theories.

68. In his preface, Eliasaf comments upon the difficulty of the text; and Peter Cole, in the notes to his collected volume of Ibn Naghrīla's poetry, suggests that it was *Ben Mishlei* that Judah al-Ḥarīzī had in mind when he suggested that reading Ibn Naghrīla's poetry would require commentaries and interpretive aids.

69. In chapter 6, we see that the age at which the children of the literary elite began to write, copy, and translate is one of the linchpins in the debate in secondary literature about whether the Hebrew translation of an Arabic Alexander romance that is attributed to Samuel ibn Tibbon is, in fact, a part of the canon of Tibbonid translations or a spurious attribution; one of the arguments against the possibility of Samuel's participa-

tion in that translation is that the dating of the text means he might have been too young (possibly ten years old when the text was translated) to have successfully worked with a text of that complexity and length. Comparisons with individuals like Eliasaf suggest that this prong of the debate should be reconsidered.

70. Abrahams, *Hebrew Ethical Wills*, 53.

71. Among the desiderata and directions for future research that presented themselves while I was writing is a reception history of *Ben Mishlei*.

72. José Martínez Delgado, "Una carta literaria de la Guenizá de El Cairo en judeo-árabe," *Sefarad* 75, no. 2 (2015): 254, where he writes: "Sus contenidos nos sugieren que podría tratarse de una carta redactada en Alandalús, a finales del siglo XI o a lo largo del XII."

73. The description of the contents of the codex is drawn from the overview in ibid., "Una carta literaria," 255–56.

74. Ibid., 256.

75. The letter suggests that both the collector and the agent have themselves at least dabbled in writing poetry. This is another way in which external sources can demonstrate the typicality of Judah ibn Tibbon's literary activity within the Arabophone world; he, too, dabbled in writing poetry, as discussed in chapter 4.

76. It is worth simply noting that the patron and his agent are looking for these two collections of Ibn Naghrīla's poetry, while *After Psalms*, the volume of the poetic trilogy whose contents and history have been most contested and least clearly identified in modern scholarship, is absent from this medieval discourse.

77. Firkovitch Ebr-Arb I 4575, f. 30v, ll. 8–15, ed. Martínez Delgado, 265.

78. Maya Shatzmiller, "Measuring the Medieval Islamic Economy," http://www.medievalislamiceconomy.uwo.ca/cost_of_living/egypt/index.html, databases for cost of living based on Ashtor's data accessed from this site September 15, 2016.

79. Per Shatzmiller's data sets, during this period 1 dinar typically equaled between 40 and 50 dirham, but could command as few as 20 or as many as 60.

80. Allony 48.

81. Allony 41.

82. The prevalence of references to and citations from *After Proverbs*, and aphoristic "wisdom-type" poetry in the context of library catalogues more broadly, is another aspect of this material that will be developed more fully and on its own (rather than simply as a context for Judah ibn Tibbon's library) in my next book project.

83. Frenkel and Ben-Shammai propose in their notes that this fragment may have been the last page of a longer list, any other surviving pages of which remain to be identified.

84. See chapter 3 for further discussion of the role of this text in the Andalusi intellectual environment.

85. The leaf is laid out with the book list on the right-hand side of the obverse and the quotations on the left-hand side of the same page. The page has been folded down the middle. There is no writing on the reverse.

86. As noted at the outset, these broader issues raised within this chapter represent the jumping-off point of a second book-length project that deals in greater detail with the libraries of al-Andalus and Castile; one of the aspects that I plan to treat there is the use of advice, wisdom literature, and aphoristic poetry, and *After Proverbs* in particular, in conjunction with library writing and documentation.

87. Samuel ibn Naghrīla, *Ben Mishlei*, ed. Dov Yarden (Jerusalem: Libov School of Graphic Arts), 1982, poem 474.

88. Ibid., poem 475. As in the text appendix, I have translated the poetry into prose while still maintaining the line breaks.

89. Bahr, *Fragments and Assemblages*, 10–11.

90. Ibid., 3.

3 "ON EVERY SABBATH, READ . . . THE BIBLE IN ARABIC"

Reading the Hebrew Bible as Arabic Literature

THE QUR'ĀN WAS a text perpetually in the background of the intellectual and religious lives of Arabic-speaking Jews living in the Islamicate world. In parallel with some of the literary responses to the theological challenges posed by the doctrine of the Arabic Qur'ān's divine inimitability that is discussed in chapter 1 and is to be revisited in chapter 4, translating the Hebrew Bible into Arabic was an additional way to grapple with the question of Scripture in an Arabic-speaking environment and, crucially, to make the biblical text more accessible to a readership living day-to-day in Arabic. Judah ibn Tibbon's position as a translator of Arabic texts into Hebrew for a non-Arabophone audience might seem on the surface to exclude him from making any kind of significant contribution to biblical study in Arabic in the Middle Ages. Nevertheless, despite the fact that his community did not have the need or desire for an Arabic translation of the Hebrew Bible as Arabophone Jewish communities did, the development of a distinct Arabic-language exegetical tradition, especially in al-Andalus, meant that there was plenty for Judah to transmit back to a Hebrew-speaking community. Ultimately, through Judah's role as a transmitter of Arabic exegesis and exegetical tools and, especially, as an exilic Arabophone reader of the Hebrew Bible, we also find a more subtle, integrated engagement with the text of the Hebrew Bible, both as a source of text and a source of language, that allows Judah to interrogate the relationship between sacrality and secular prestige, and between Arabic and Hebrew themselves.

Where the Qur'ān helps to shape the linguistic and literary landscape for Arabophone Jews, the Hebrew Bible, translated into Arabic, is both one of the most important outcomes of that tension and one of the greatest driving forces in the further development of the literary tradition and textual production more widely in the Judaeo-Arabic world.[1] The Hebrew Bible as an Arabic text, in the many forms that such a construction takes, has been the subject of intense and renewed scholarly interest and scrutiny in recent years. While this section focuses primarily and specifically on Judah ibn Tibbon as a reader of the Hebrew Bible and his placement of that text within an Andalusi Arabic exegetical and literary tradition, a brief, bibliographically focused survey of Jewish bible translations for Arabophone readers is in order.[2] Christian translations of the Bible into Arabic appear to have begun as early as the end of the seventh century, although the earliest surviving written evidence of the practice is dated to the middle of the ninth century.[3] Robert Hoyland argues that the transition from oral to written Arabic that accompanied the first writing down of Arabic Bible translations is closely connected with the increasing prestige of the language in Arabian society around that time.[4] As for Jewish exemplars of the biblical text in Arabic, in the course of discussing the oral origins of the form Ronny Vollandt cautions: "The infant stage of Judaeo-Arabic Bible translation is invisible today and largely a matter of scholarly conjecture. The intellectual environment in which it emerged is likewise unknown."[5] Nevertheless, the earliest Jewish Bible translations raise similar questions as the Christian ones, including those about the prestige of the language and its place in sacred contexts in the face of its pride of place in and constitutive of the text of the Qur'ān. The first exemplars that we have of text from the Hebrew Bible in Arabic translation are generally acknowledged to be those of Daniel al-Qūmisī, a commentator best known for two innovations in reading, responding to, and translating the Hebrew Bible in the Arabophone world. First, in imitation of the Islamic practice of writing exegesis in the sacred tongue, Arabic, he began to write his commentaries in Hebrew instead of Aramaic; and second, he added Arabic glosses that became such an integral part of the text itself that he essentially forced the issue of Arabic in a Bible-reading context.[6] The first circle of translators whose work more resembled a full, running translation of the Hebrew Bible into Arabic, the self-styled "Mourners of Zion" (*avalei ẓion*), grew up around al-Qūmisī after his relocation from Baghdad to Palestine.[7] These Karaite translators of the Hebrew Bible not only reflected debates over language between Jewish and Muslim exegetes but also begin to show the adoption of natively Arabic modes of thinking and exegeticizing, specifically the particular brand of rationalism known as mu'tazilism; two of the major translators in this vein were Yefet ibn 'Alī and Ya'qūb al-Qirqisānī.[8] Yefet's inter-sectional translations (that is, those running section by section rather than line by line) and his particular attention to the question of who, precisely, can be considered the narrator or composer (*mudawwin*) of the biblical text opened up the realm of biblical exegesis to greater interest in elements beyond the purely linguistic.[9] In his *Kitāb al-anwār wa-l-murāqib*, Qirqisānī lays out a programmatic foundation that stands as a watershed within Karaite exegesis: an explicit statement of exegetical principles.[10] Both his exegetical model and his interest in Moses' role as the *mudawwin* of the Pentateuchal books make him, in effect, a direct successor to Yefet as a commentator and mark a shift toward narrative as one of the frameworks for Judaeo-Arabic exegesis.

The translation that would ultimately have the greatest impact in Andalusi and wider Maghrebi circles and that would force the question of Arabic as a devotional language and the fount of relevant and appropriate literary models would be Saʿadya Gaʾon's translation and commentary, known as his *Tafsīr*. Saʿadya, head of the Talmud academy at Sura and the author of many of the Arabic works of philosophy, theology, and lexicography that were translated into Hebrew by Judah ibn Tibbon and others, is largely regarded as the preeminent biblical exegete of the medieval Rabbanite world.[11] In keeping with the prevailing notion within the Arabophone world that the study of language and grammar was an inextricable part of scriptural exegesis, he conceived of his biblical dictionary as an integral part of that endeavor. Known commonly as *Sefer ha-Egron* (The Thesaurus), the title given to it by its Hebrew translator, Judah ibn Tibbon, the dictionary begins even from the first words of its Arabic title, *Kitāb uṣūl al-shʿir al-ʿibrānī* (The Book of Fundamentals of Hebrew Poetry), to indicate the close relationship between biblical and poetical texts.[12] The relationship between the Hebrew Bible and poetry is discussed in greater detail in chapter 4, but more central to the present discussion is Saʿadya's *Tafsīr*, his Arabic commentary-translation of the Pentateuch and many of the prophetic books, which he viewed as an integral part both of a rationalist project and a defense of Rabbanite Judaism against its Karaite counterpart.[13] Among his major innovations was the incorporation of Arabic literary methods into the orbit of Bible translation and biblical commentary;[14] and, as we shall see below, Saʿadya's *Tafsīr* became a site of methodological argumentation over approaches to literal and literary translation and the permissibility of Arabic within Jewish religious and liturgical contexts.[15] Its spread into the Jewish communities in Spain and North Africa was as swift and overwhelming as it was in the Jewish communities of the rest of the Arabic-speaking world.[16] The notion of the Arabic-language Hebrew Bible as a part of Jewish cultural nationalism can be seen as early and as far east as in Saʿadya's oeuvre. Aaron Hughes suggests a tension within the Saʿadyanic corpus that on the one hand praises and leverages the merits and advantages of the Arabic language, while on the other strives to even the linguistic playing field on which it appears with Hebrew.[17] In the wake of Qirqisānī's and Saʿadya's interventions, translation came into its own in both Karaite and Rabbanite communities as a form of exegesis in its own right,[18] as its own particular kind of literary production.[19]

Judaeo-Arabic exegesis and translation also became an important foundation for the articulation of a linguistically grounded cultural-national identity and for biblical reading and interpretation more generally in al-Andalus.[20] As in the Islamic east, Arabic-language biblical interpretation in the Islamic west begins with grammatical and lexical study. Where Saʿadya principally studied the language in terms that he referred to as "foundational," the grammarians of al-Andalus more closely approximated and anticipated what would become the standard for the grammatical and morphological analysis. Dunash ben Labraṭ, a North African student of Saʿadya who returned to the western Mediterranean after the death of his teacher, both adapted quantitative poetic meter from Arabic for use in Hebrew and sought to better understand Hebrew grammar through comparative study with the well-established works of the Arab grammarians and linguists. This grammatical approach was cemented by Judah al-Fāsī, better known as Ḥayyūj, was also implicated in the grammar controversies in tenth-century Córdoba and drew explicitly on the work of those earlier Arab grammarians. This Arabizing approach brought Dunash in particular into conflict with Menaḥem ibn Saruq, likewise a poet and grammarian. Ibn Saruq placed prime value on the elevation of Hebrew above Arabic and his grammatical program reflected his emphasis on that principle. Their debates over the permissibility of what today we would call comparative Semitics are recorded in their own letters and those written by their students and defenders, notably Yehudi ben Sheshet as a partisan of Dunash and the triumvirate of Isaac ibn Chiquitilla, Isaac ibn Qapron, and Judah ben David defending Ibn Saruq's position. The study of Hebrew grammar and lexicography through the Judaeo-Arabic intellectual tradition and in support of Arabic Bible-reading and exegesis continued in the Islamic west with Jonah ibn Janāḥ, whose works were subsequently translated into Hebrew by Judah ibn Tibbon. All of this work, written in the Arabic language and within the Judaeo-Arabic intellectual milieu, proved to be the foundation of subsequent study of the Hebrew Bible in al-Andalus.[21]

That foundation was amplified by Moses ibn Chiquitilla, who was among the first Arabic-to-Hebrew translators of al-Andalus and who laid the foundations of his rationalist biblical interpretation on his Hebrew translation of Ḥayyūj's work; his translation of these lexical and grammatical works is a sense-for-sense work par excellence, updating and amplifying much of the work based on developments since the author's original composition of the work.[22] His biblical interpretation was still largely linguistic in nature, an interpretive choice that would have a major impact on Andalusi exegesis moving forward.[23] This is particularly exemplified in the works of Abraham ibn 'Ezra', specifically in his approach as a commentator on the biblical text. Although his commentaries were produced subsequent to his exit from al-Andalus and in the second half of his life spent in Christian Europe, they still drew on many of the rhetorical strategies and exegetical priorities of the commentaries written in Arabic-speaking lands. From Ibn 'Ezra' forward, the Andalusi school of biblical interpretation solidly reflected the *peshat* (plain sense, linguistically informed) method developed by Sa'adya Ga'on in deference to the integrity of the linguistic structure and textual and historical context of the text, in contrast with the *derash* (metaphorical, extratextual extrapolation) method preferred in Jewish communities in parts of the Levant and throughout Christian Europe.[24] Joseph Qimḥi is representative of this approach; like Judah ibn Tibbon, he left al-Andalus for Provence and became the first of a dynasty of exegetes, followed most famously by his youngest son, David Qimḥi; and just as Judah ibn Tibbon's translations were staunch defenses of the Andalusi intellectual tradition, Joseph Qimḥi's biblical commentaries were steadfast examples of Andalusi *peshat*-style commentary and explicit rejections of the *derash* method preferred in Provençal communities.[25]

Contact with the Arabo-Islamic model that centers and emphasizes the Arabic language, its study, and its correct interpretation, preservation, and dissemination also bore on Arabic-speaking Jews' approach to their own forms of exegesis and sacred history. As such, lexicography, grammar, and comparative linguistics became central aspects of Jewish biblical exegesis, first among Karaites and subsequently among Rabbanites.[26] And so rather than a feat of translation, Judah's significant contribution to an already-established mode of studying the Hebrew Bible within non-Arabophone communities was the aforementioned translation of two vocabularies—*Kitāb al-Uṣūl* (Book of Roots) and *Kitāb al-Lum'a* (Book of Variegated Flower Beds), which Judah translated into Hebrew as *Sefer ha-Shorashim* (Book of Roots) and *Sefer ha-Riqmah* (Book of Woven Patterns)—that could bring Hebrew lexicographic advances from the Arabic-speaking parts of the world to the rest of it. However, it is in his deeply idiosyncratic reading of the Hebrew Bible itself and the clear situation of that reading within a culturally Arabized context that we begin to see the fast bind between the text of the Hebrew Bible and the Arabic literary culture in which Judah could understand it.

REVEALING AND CONCEALING THE ARABIC LEXICOGRAPHIC TRADITION

Paradoxically, it is by partially concealing the Arabic source material for his lexicographic-exegetical tools that Judah's work as a translator is able to bolster an argument for the prestige of Arabic. Yet despite the apparent paradox of this framework, Judah adopts the practice of many Andalusi-exilic readers of and commentators on the Hebrew Bible of his day; perhaps most prominent among them is Abraham ibn 'Ezra', who not only adapted Judaeo-Arabic exegetical strategies for use in Hebrew prose but also consistently and deliberately concealed the Arabic nature of his sources and influences.[27] It is in the introduction and conclusion to his grammatical works that Judah sets out the central paradox of his task, rendering intelligible texts that deal in concepts for which even the basic vocabulary does not exist in the source language; in this case the problem is one of explaining Arabic rationalism as applied to theology in a deeply insufficient Hebrew that had not yet been made to keep up with the intellectual developments made in al-Andalus and the wider Arabophone world. In fact, in his preface to *Sefer ha-Riqmah*, Judah utilizes a literary trope that occurs from Saʿadya to Saʿadya—that is, from the work of Saʿadya Ga'on in the tenth century through that of Saʿadya ibn Danan in the fifteenth[28]—when he writes that the paucity of Hebrew vocabulary makes the language inferior to Arabic. Although this complaint is clearly a literary trope with a long history before Judah and a long perfect-future following him, it is nonetheless a guiding principle that comports nicely and directly with the rest of his program of lexicographic analysis and translation. Part of his effort was to develop, through translation, the vocabulary that would allow for those very translations to be carried out.

It is in the development of that vocabulary that we see Judah at the height of his ambivalence in mediating between Hebrew and Arabic, their distinct linguistic traditions, and the multiple audiences served differently by them. In his lengthy study of the medieval linguistc tradition, Aharon Maman identifies one of Judah's key strategies in transmitting Ibn Janaḥ's Arabic grammatical exegeses as the "omission of explicit comparisons," seeing this technique in those instances in which "Ibn Tibbon ignores inner Arabic discussions on grammatical or semantic topics, due to these having no direct relevance for the meaning of the Hebrew word."[29] In other words, despite his conviction that the Arabic lexicon was, at least at his starting point, superior to that of Hebrew, he refrains from elaborating all of the technicalities of the Arabic grammar, and especially morphology, that contributed to the superiority of that vocabulary.

However, he not only omits but also substitutes a way that retains a sense of the prestige of the Arabic without miring non-Arabophone readers in details that would prove inaccessible to them. Maman continues: "Ibn Tibbon's 'omission policy' at times even went to the extreme of dispensing entirely with the definens and merely entering the mark '*yaduʿa*' (well-known)," this regardless of whether the omitted term was, indeed, actually well-known or not.[30] Ibn Janāḥ himself sometimes shortened explanations in his original dictionary with an Arabic term that Ibn Tibbon calques with his *yaduʿa*, namely, the Arabic *maʿaruf* (known). However, although Ibn Tibbon is using a lexical calque of the term that appears in his source text dictionary, he uses it much more extensively and in a wider range of places in the text. He may, as Maman suggests, have adopted the turn of phrase from Ibn Janaḥ;[31] however, he does not use it to translate Ibn Janaḥ word-for-word, instead using it as part of an elegant holistic translation that privileges sense and both cultural and linguistic intelligibility for the target audience.

This example of translation by omission, according to an Arabic lexicographical model, illustrates a greater willingness than is usually attributed to Judah to translate culturally and adaptively for sense and simultaneously—and herein begins the paradox—for the sake of the Arabic. This kind of adaptation, this translation by omission, shows that sense translation can privilege the source language just as much as word-for-word does, further contextualizing Judah's work in a culturally and literarily Arabizing mode, rather than in an obsessional, narrow, linguistic one. By replacing internal explanations of Arabic terms and concepts, Judah simultaneously conceals the Arabic foundations of the exegetical reference works he was translating and defers to the authority of the Arabic and Judaeo-Arabic grammarians by accepting their conclusions, even in the absence of the reasoning that led them to those conclusions and explanations, and through the rhetorical conventions that they had developed for the task. The omission of Arabic source material is one that arises frequently within the world of Andalusi Hebrew-to-Arabic translators as a way in which a writer, thinker, or translator can substitute his own judgment for that of his readers who might not possess the background or judgment to handle ideas or texts in the way that the author saw as correct.

For example, in his letter of advice to Samuel ibn Tibbon on how to translate the *Guide*, Maimonides enumerates which Graeco-Arabic texts Samuel should read and translate and which ones are not worth his while. In the former category are those of Joseph Ẓadik, al-Farābī, and Ibn Sīna (Avicenna, whose works Maimonides deems to be more superficial than al-Farābi's but useful nonetheless). The latter category is much longer, containing the works of many more writers and many varied reasons for not reading them: Isaac Israeli and al-Rāzī are dismissed for being "mere" physicians, while Empedocles, Pythagoras, Porphyrius, and the authors of the entire Hermetical corpus are dismissed simply for being ancient philosophers. Maimonides also cautions Samuel to approach the works of Aristotle with care and only with the assistance of the commentaries by Alexander of Aphrodisias, Themistius, and Ibn Rushd (Averroes); he also cautions him against reading works spuriously attributed to Aristotle, like *Kitāb al-Tufāḥ* and the *Risāla al-Ḏahabiyya*. This section of the letter is lengthy and allows Maimonides to vest textual authority in the hands of those thinkers he considered responsible and worthwhile; this is another instance of a medieval thinker establishing a hierarchy of sages, something that is critical and consistently concomitant to discussions of translation. In the Verona manuscript that contains the text of this letter, a copy believed to be translated from Judaeo-Arabic by Samuel ibn Tibbon himself and copied out in his own hand, in place of that lengthy passage is the simple observation that "after this [Maimonides] indicated the books in these sciences that one ought to read and the books that are not worth my time wasted in reading them. I do not need to copy them for you."[32]

Such a comment would indicate that he took Maimonides' advice on board and even extrapolated from it that he should not even make the existence of the ostensibly worthless texts known to the rest of the community in Lunel and, by extension, more widely in Europe. In this instance, he substitutes the transmission of Maimonides' judgment—in this case an omission—for even the potential of anyone else's. Because of the seriousness with which Maimonides' opinion was taken, as reflected here, this letter became critical in determining how philosophy would be studied by the Jewish thinkers who succeeded him and Samuel.[33] In the case of the Ibn Janāḥ translations, though, Ibn Tibbon *père* does not seem to be protecting less-educated readers from esoterica and sloppy thinking; rather, he is deferring to the judgment of the Maghrebi grammatical tradition that so informed the literary world of al-Andalus while simultaneously and seamlessly sliding it, cleanly, into non-Arabophone Europe.

ARABIC AS A SINGLE DEVOTIONAL AND PROFESSIONAL LANGUAGE

The writing of several of the *ge'onim*, or heads, of the major Jewish academy at Sura proves illustrative of intellectual and religious issues that arose as a result of the process that integrated scientific study of language and devotion in a changing linguistic landscape; these writings even anticipate the ways in which they are addressed in the Tibbonid canon. One of the earliest discussions of these issues was taken up by Naṭronai Bar Hilai, a mid-ninth-century *ga'on* whose connection with Iberian Jewry included the correspondence with the Jewish community in Lucena that formed the basis of the prayer book known as *Seder Rav 'Amram Ga'on*.[34] At a time when Jews were just beginning to translate the Hebrew Bible into Arabic, Naṭronai Ga'on penned a responsum that would ultimately be incorporated into a fourteenth-century compilation of *halakhah* known as the *Orakh ḥayim*, in which he holds that devotional reading in Arabic is not valid. In that responsum, he writes: "Those who do not translate, saying 'we do not have to recite the translation of the rabbis, we should rather translate in our language, the one used by the public,' those people do not fulfill their obligation."[35] Although the second half of the responsum does admit the possibility of using Arabic in a liturgical setting as an interpretive aid to explain readings and rites to an Arabophone congregation that might not comprehend them fully in Hebrew and Aramaic, my reading of it nonetheless holds Arabic apart as something liturgically and devotionally invalid; a language's place in a devotional context is as a mere interpretive aid separate from the mandatory act of devotion. In addition to drawing Arabic apart from Hebrew and Aramaic, the sacred languages of Judaism, and eliminating the possibility of its use in prayer contexts, Naṭronai Ga'on implicitly creates a hierarchy of translations and translators, vesting authority in the translations of certain sages (both of these issues reappear in Judah ibn Tibbon's work, where they are handled very differently); the revolutionary aspect of Sa'adya's program, by contrast, is that while he takes up Naṭronai's hierarchical position, he also adapts it, ensuring the sacral, if not sacred, status of Arabic for Jews in the Arabic-speaking world.

It speaks to the foundational role that the Hebrew Bible, the Hebrew Bible in Arabic, and the Hebrew Bible read with an Arabizing lens play in the intellectual and textual life of the Arabized Jews of and exiled from the Islamic west that these are not only sacred text in Judah's literary cartography but also a mile-marker-zero for professional development and a sextant for his cultural horizon. Judah pushes the boundary between sacred reading and profane profession through his leveraging of the Arabic Hebrew Bible itself—not just the reference works used to study it—as a translator's source. Advocating that religious dogma be put to work in the service of what today we might call professional development, Judah writes: "On every Sabbath, read the weekly portion [of the Bible] in Arabic because it will be useful to you in developing your Arabic vocabulary[36] and in translation, should you wish to become a translator."[37] In other words, Judah instructs Samuel to prioritize his professional aspirations even while performing devotional acts like the prescribed weekly reading of a portion of the Pentateuch. The temporal phrase that begins this admonition—"on every Sabbath"—demonstrates the devotional character of the advised reading. Judah does simply advise Samuel to undertake reading specifically designed to improve his vocabulary and draw his attention to the features and nature of translated text so that he might eventually be able to replicate the process on a different, working day of the week, or simply weekly, without specifying a day. In other instances he does precisely that, telling Samuel, for example, to study medical texts simply "one day each week."[38] The contrast represented by the specificity of this instruction highlights it as a meaningful and deliberate turn of phrase. By making Arabic-language Hebrew Bible reading in the interest of translation an activity to be undertaken on the Sabbath,[39] Judah is, in essence, advising Samuel to instrumentalize at least a portion, if not all, of his devotional weekly reading, thereby closely connecting the notion of Bible reading to that of pursuing translation.[40] Although various Jewish communities harbored periodic debates over the possibility of accepting remuneration for devotional acts,[41] Judah's represents a distinct twist. I have consistently described him here as a professional translator, but it is important to note that Judah does not fall into the category of scholars who would accept remuneration for devotional acts because we have no evidence that he accepted any kind of remuneration at all for his work as a translator.[42] Judah is at once instrumentalizing devotion in the service of studying Arabic and elevating the translation of Jewish *kalām* texts to the level of sacred study to be done on the Sabbath.

A BIBLICAL HERITAGE FOR BEDOUINS AND ARAB GRAMMARIANS

At the literary level as well as at the cultural-historical one, the text of the ethical will utilizes the Hebrew Bible as an instrument to make a cultural argument about Arabization and about the merits and drawbacks of cultural and linguistic assimilation more broadly. As noted in the introduction and the first chapter, the ethical will is populated by Jewish, Arabic, and Andalusi sources, some of which are cited and identified directly and others that are quoted without identification or are paraphrased. As noted earlier, of the sources in the former category, Samuel ibn Naghrīla's *After Proverbs* far outstrips all the others; Solomon ibn Gabirol's *Choice of Pearls* and the episode in the biblical book of Jeremiah about the Rechabites come in a distant second. On the face of the text, Judah directs Samuel to Jeremiah 35 because, he says, the story of a confederation of people who live according to the precepts of their ancestor should be an adequate lesson in obedience and example for why Samuel should take to heart all of Judah's own advice. This coincides with Judah's desire for Samuel to take his advice on board, a trope that recurs throughout the text of the ethical will.[43]

In addition to telling Samuel in general terms to read the Hebrew Bible in Arabic every Sabbath, and in addition to quoting a variety of biblical books, Judah makes several specific, salient recommendations to Samuel for which books and passages to read in which we begin to see the deeper depths of the Yehonadav[44] story coming into play within Judah's Andalusi-Arabizing intellectual program through allusions to the trope of the Arab Bedouin. Toward the end of the prose section of the ethical will, Judah writes, "On the Sabbath and the holidays, the members of your household should read the Bible and peruse books of grammar, the book of Proverbs, and After Proverbs as a matter of habit. My son, I also encourage you to peruse, on every Sabbath, the biblical portion concerning the descendants of Yehonadav ben Rekhav so that you will be fastidious in observing my admonitions to you."[45] In addition, then, to having told Samuel to read from the Bible weekly in Arabic alongside secular works from the Andalusi canon, he specifies further that Samuel should pay particular attention to chapter 35 of the book of Jeremiah. Judah portrays this parable as one that should instill a lesson of filial piety in its readers, one that will impress on Samuel the importance of following the "directives" of his elders. The tale does, indeed, manifest that thematic character, with the Rechabites refusing to drink the wine that is offered to them because of the injunctions established by their ancestor, Yehonadav, but also carries other implications for Andalusi readers. In this section of the ethical will, Judah has juxtaposed *After Proverbs* as the Andalusi work par excellence with a biblical pericope that speaks both to questions of filial piety and of cultural conservation and resistance to assimilation; he thereby frames his own interest in the biblical book of Jeremiah as a multifaceted one that links the devotion of his son to devotion to Andalusi literary culture.

To contextualize this further it is necessary to consider the relevant excerpt from the biblical text:

> I set out goblets full of wine and other drinks for the Rechabites, telling them: Drink the wine. But they said: We do not drink wine because our ancestor, Yehonadav ben Rekhav, ordered us thusly: Neither you nor your descendants should ever drink wine. Do not build houses for yourselves or plant or possess crops or vineyards; instead dwell in tents all of your days so that you might live long lives from the fruits of the land that you dwell upon. We have heeded the opinion and every instruction of our ancestor, Yehonadav ben Rekhav, to the effect that we, our sons, and our daughters never drink wine, we do not build houses to live in permanently, we have no vineyards, fields, or crops, and we dwell in tents. We heed and we obey everything that our ancestor, Yehonadav, instructed us.[46]

While the main thrust of the passage may assert the value of filial piety, it is a message bolstered by a depiction of a community that refuses to assimilate into the majority Judahite culture[47] and give up its own local set of customs, a set of customs that happens to bear a striking resemblance to the depictions of Bedouin grammarians who served as the archetype for linguistic purity in medieval grammatical discourse, depictions that resonate with Judah's own discussions of grammatical correctness, linguistic purity, and the preservation and historical memory of his own Arabized culture. The repeated references in the ethical will to the Rechabites do as much to further Judah's project of preserving Andalusi culture through the transmission of Arabic language and literature and their sensibilities as they do to bolster Judah's admonitions to his son to be dutiful.

The description of the customs, acts, and behaviors of the Rechabites tell another story, one that goes beyond filial piety to address questions of cultural and national assimilation in ways that speak very directly to writers concerned with preserving the Arabized, Islamicate aspects of their Andalusi Jewish culture as they reside in a kind of cultural exile in Christian Europe. In chapter 35 of the eponymous prophetic book, Jeremiah is instructed to offer wine to an insular community, the Rechabites, who traced their origins back to Yehonadav ben Rekhav, a figure who appears in the book of Kings. The Rechabites decline the offer of wine, and go on to describe the nomadic lifestyle handed down to them by their ancestors going back to Yehonadav himself, in which they abstain from drinking wine, inhabit tents, and do not make use of fixed farming lands (and especially do not plant vineyards). The description of tent-dwelling nomads who, as a rule, do not imbibe[48] and place high value on familial ties is evocative, at least in broad strokes, of an image of Bedouins who were revered in the Arabic lexicographical and grammatical traditions as the guardians of the true and pure Arabic language.[49] And so, we see Judah pushing Samuel toward a text that, from within the Hebrew Bible, deals both with cultural Arabization and resistance to assimilation.

The figure of the Bedouin is a conflictive one in Andalusi literature and it is worth revisiting places in which that figure occurs before moving on to engage with Judah's development of it within the ethical will. A number of distinct terms that refer broadly to Arabs and Muslims occurs within the Hebrew-language literature of Arabized Jews.[50] The designation "Arab" is not exclusively associated with Bedouins, though; as we see in chapter 5, it is a term that can also be applied to individuals associated with the most urban and urbane of lives. Ultimately, though, when it or any of the other terms that refer to Arabs or Muslims is deployed in order to designate a figure as one with Bedouin associations, it can carry a wide range of connotations for Arabized Jewish writers and readers and can evoke both biblical and secular textual antecedents; and it is against this literary backdrop that Judah writes about the Rechabites as biblical figures with resonances that associate them with contemporaneous, medieval Arabs who were guardians of the language but also quintessential outsiders. Descriptions of the Bedouins are not uniformly flattering: with respect to Bedouins in particular falling under the broad literary rubric of Arab, Ross Brann offers two examples of Andalusi writing, one adapted from another, in which Bedouins, designated as Arabs, are the subject of mockery. The first is an eleventh-century *maqāma* (a highly ornamented tale in rhymed prose, or *saj'*, of a rogue and his confederate, pl. *maqāmāt*) that survives in quotation in Abū Ḥasan ibn Bassam al-Shantarīnī's *Dhakhīra*, and the second is the adaptation of that story into Judah al-Ḥarīzī's *Taḥkemoni*. In both stories, a figure designated as an Arab is portrayed as coming out of the hinterlands and failing to adapt quickly to the norms of urban life, thus becoming an object of derision and dishonest dealings.[51] Yet in other cases, as we shall see below, Bedouins were viewed, as they were in the Islamic east, as guardians of the Arabic language and worthy of deep respect.

The image of the Bedouin was, for better or for worse, still a current one for Judaeo-Arabic readers; and within their own biblicizing historical narratives, it was a common feature within that literary universe to ascribe Rechabite heritage to the Bedouins. One particularly common Judaeo-Arabic association between historical Bedouins and biblical Rechabites comes in the form of discussions about the lineage of the Jews of the Arabian cities of Tayma and Khaybar, two communities regarded as ancient and with particular connections to pre-Islamic and early Islamic-period Arab communities in the region.[52] In sources that span the range from documentary to literary, the Khaybar and Tayma Jews are frequently both noted and praised for their close association and confederacy with the Bedouin tribes, and, like the Bedouins, are referred to simply as "Arabs."[53] They remain connected, in reputation, to the city of Medina, thereby asserting their protected status within the Islamic world; the number of individuals attempting to draw on protection and privilege they believed would be accorded to them if they were firmly identified as Khaybarī Jews[54] was sufficiently large that Goitein identifies records in which tax collectors were forced to adjudicate between individuals with real roots in the Arabian Peninsula and those who were Iraqi but had adopted the *nisba* (onomastic adjective denoting heritage) of al-Khaybarī.[55] They were also regularly and closely identified within both Jewish and Muslim sources as Yehonadav's descendants.[56] A co-identification of Rechabites and Bedouins is misattributed to Qirqisānī as early as the middle of the twelfth century in *Eshkol ha-Kofer*, a rhymed-prose work of *kalām* written by the Karaite scholar and pietist Judah Hadassi,[57] which is to say that by the twelfth century, at least Karaite authors and their readers were laboring under the belief that this co-identification was already more than two hundred years in its antiquity. It is a case in which what readers thought they knew is more important than the historical reality of the textual situation. Thus, for Judah to invoke the Rechabites in his missive to Samuel is to make them serve as an easily recognizable metaphor with two complementary faces.[58] They serve as a model of sons who follow the example of a good life set by their ancestors, but they also would have been an immediately recognizable, tangible connection to the Arabian Peninsula and its Arabic linguistic and grammatical tradition that Judah was also attempting to impart to Samuel and encourage him to value highly. The image of an Arabizing people—and Arabizing in a way that evokes their guardianship of a pure language—who don't assimilate must have been awfully attractive to the Arabizing Judah ibn Tibbon, who was struggling to keep his remembered Andalusi culture.[59]

Examples of conflations between the Rechabites and the Jews and Bedouins of Arabia abound in both Karaite and Rabbanite and sacred and secular sources. Another example of the latter in each pairing is found in the mid-twelfth-century *Itineraries* of Benjamin of Tudela.[60] This is a text to be treated with some caution: where we as modern scholars treat pieces of the travel account as a historical document, it is still built on a background that presumes a certain and distinct value of the Bible for historical writing in later periods. The manuscripts are late and have a variety of variants, some that bear directly on the question of the association between the Khaybar Jews of the Arabian Peninsula and the Rechabites in the mind of medieval readers. Adler largely (though not as much as some of his contemporaries) holds the view that even pieces of the travelogue do not represent a chronicle of places the author visited; rather "it is no longer, for the most part, a record of personal travel, it is rather an attempt to supplement the first part 'of things seen' by a second 'of things heard.'"[61] Yet it is on the grounds of manuscript inconsistencies rather than of implausibility that he rejects the possibility that Benjamin of Tudela might have met people he identified as Rechabites.[62] While Adler's contemporary, S. L. Rapoport, went to great lengths to demonstrate why these manuscript inconsistencies were of little consequence, it is in fact those very inconsistencies that prove the point.[63] Even a late introduction of Rechabites into Benjamin of Tudela's account demonstrates that late medieval and early modern readers co-identified Rechabites with Arabians, even if Benjamin himself might have not. Nonetheless, if we read with all manuscript exemplars but for the British Library manuscript[64] of the *Itineraries*, the text tells us that the Khaybar Jews might be descendants of the biblical tribes of Reuben, Gad, and Manasseh, and then comments on the "descendants of Rechab, who are the people of Tayma,"[65] observing that they do not own homes or property, but instead dwell in tents and forage and tend livestock for a living. Indeed, the image of the Rechabite community as it is represented in the Hebrew Bible serves as a model for a medieval Jewish community clinging equally to its faith and its Arabized acculturation.

In the realm of lexicography, too, the cultural patterns of the Bedouins as the guardians of the sacred language are imported into Jewish contexts. Nehemiah Allony identified the anecdotal opening to the grammatical reference written by 'Eli ben Judah ha-Nazir as utilizing the descriptive tropes usually applied to Bedouins leveraged in the service of explaining the role of the local Tiberian population in preserving the privileged register of Hebrew.[66] Ha-Nazir explains in his preface that he could verify his linguistic theories when he "used to spend much time sitting in the squares and streets of Tiberias, listening to the speech of the marketplace and the simple people. I would observe their language and its grammar in order to see whether something in my grammar was lacking or there was something incorrect in my understanding."[67] Yet, as Marina Rustow observes, this account is one that deploys the literary tropes associated with Bedouins in an anachronistic way to cement the status of Hebrew through a central locus inhabited by grammatical authorities, in much the same way that Bedouins in the Arabian desert were the authorities to whom Arabic grammarians spoke as the prime source for Arabic. She comments:

> The suggestion that Hebrew was spoken in Tiberias in the tenth century seems far-fetched, especially given ha-Nazir's contention that it was "simple people" who spoke it. . . . Aramaic is more plausible. But the truth of ha-Nazir's statement is not the point. Rather, it is his belief that Tiberian Hebrew was superior to all the others and the terms in which he casts that belief: terms borrowed directly from the literary ideology surrounding the Qur'ān. Just as Muslims had developed ideals about the purity of Bedouin Arabic and mustered them in debates about the inimitability of the Qur'ān and its language, Jews now reclaimed the language of their sacred text and claimed for it a locus of production in its purest state.[68]

'Eli's grammar was known in the Islamic West and northern Europe, cited in, among other works, the *Mikhlol*, the grammatical work composed in Provence by David Qimḥi, the son of Judah's contemporary and fellow Andalusi exile, Joseph Qimḥi, and, possibly, too, in Abraham ibn 'Ezra''s preface to his own biblical commentary.[69] It is also important to note that the image of the Tiberian as the Bedouin-like guardian of the language was current in the Maghreb, including more specifically in al-Andalus. In furthering her argument for the parallel statuses of Hebrew and Arabic, Masoretes and Bedouins, Rustow goes on to cite David al-Fāsī, a Karaite lexicographer and grammarian whose work was deeply influential in Spain and the wider Maghreb, and Dunash ibn Tamīm, a scholar and grammarian whose proximity to the Iberian Peninsula makes his opinion particularly salient, holding similar, if somewhat less explicitly analogic opinions.[70] And so, while these examples do not tie the Bedouins to the Rechabites, they do demonstrate the sway that Bedouin imagery had over discussion of questions of language and sacred text and the willingness of Jewish authors to draw analogies and even stronger comparisons between Bedouin and Jewish keepers of the language.

The image of Bedouins, thus co-identified with the biblical Rechabites in the minds of Andalusi readers and acknowledged as keepers of the sacred tongue, is further developed as a specifically Andalusi trope by Jewish and Muslim[71] writers of both prose and poetry. Within Andalusi writing, the Bedouin serves as a conduit for Arabic language and literature, and through emphasis on the Arabness of the Bedouins and their traditionally strong familial ties, this trope helps shore up the nostalgia and claims of legitimacy that hearken back to the Umayyad period in a way that did not represent a present or immediate cultural threat to Andalusi Jews by offering Arabic a context that did not encroach on their own culture or faith.[72] In his monograph on literary nostalgia for al-Andalus written from various kinds and points of exile, Alexander Elinson demonstrates the extent to which Bedouin imagery and Arabian toponymy serve an Andalusi audience: Through the replacement of Andalusi images and places with older and better ones, various Andalusi literary writers became able to speak with two voices, preserving the Arabic background of their work by portraying it as something that was at once familiar and new. And although Drory,[73] arguing even more forcefully than Blau,[74] shows that courtly poetry is the predominant mode of poetic expression among the Jews of al-Andalus, Elinson and others have demonstrated that this kind of literary knowledge of pre-Islamic poetry and its tropes was readily available and, indeed, expected of cultured, urbane, Andalusi readers, especially those at court, where images of the Bedouin habitus serve as an extra evocation of a lost, almost paradisiacal homeland, complementing poetic recourse to the Andalusi *hortus conclusus*.[75]

All told, then, when Judah tells Samuel to read about the Rechabites, he is using the common technique of employing biblical figures to speak metonymically about other aspects of his own contemporaneous culture, using imagery that speaks through the metaphors of a literary past to the realia of the present day. By evoking the biblical Rechabites, a group tied literarily to the likewise literary Bedouins, Judah uses the Hebrew Bible to tell Samuel not just to be a faithful son but to remain faithful to the dictates and history of the Arabic language, its grammar, and its poetry while grounding that linguistic, literary, and textual tradition firmly within a Jewish sphere. His recourse to biblical tropes made relevant through their connection to the Arabizing culture of al-Andalus is just one part of his engagement with the Hebrew Bible specifically from his position as an Arabophone Jewish reader.

NOTES

Chapter title from Judah ibn Tibbon, "Musar Av," 17a.

1. Rina Drory, *Models and Contacts* (Leiden: Brill, 2000), 134–37.
2. An excellent survey work that, as a monograph dedicated to the subject, rather than a section in a chapter of one, necessarily covers much more ground both in content and bibliography is Sidney Griffith's *The Bible in Arabic* (Princeton, NJ: Princeton University Press, 2012). A more specialized overview may be found in the first half of Ronny Vollandt's *Arabic Versions of the Pentateuch* (Leiden: Brill, 2015).
3. Griffith, *The Bible in Arabic*, 121–32.
4. Robert Hoyland, "Mount Nebo, Jabal Ramm, and the Status of Christian Palestinian Aramaic and Old Arabic in Late Roman Palestine and Arabia," in *The Development of Arabic as a Written Language*, ed. M. MacDonald (Oxford: Archaeopress, 2010), 35.

5. Vollandt, *Arabic Versions*, 73.

6. On the Arabic question, see Meira Polliack, *The Karaite Tradition of Arabic Bible Translation* (Leiden: Brill, 1997), esp. 30–31. On the question of Hebrew superseding Aramaic in imitation of the work of Muslim counterparts, see Marina Rustow, *Heresy and the Politics of Community* (Ithaca, NY: Cornell University Press, 2008), 40.

7. Griffith, *The Bible in Arabic*, 159; and Miriam Goldstein, "Arabic Composition 101 and Early Development of Judaeo-Arabic Bible Exegesis," *Journal of Semitic Studies* 55, no. 2 (2010): 452.

8. See, among other works, Geoffrey Khan, "Al-Qirqisānī's Opinions Concerning the Text of the Bible and Parallel Muslim Attitudes towards the Text of the Quran," *Jewish Quarterly Review* 81 (1990): 59–73.

9. Griffith, *The Bible in Arabic*, 160, following Wechsler.

10. Bruno Chiesa disagrees with both Hirschfeld (1918) and Nemoy (1952), considering these principles to be a part of Qirqisānī's Kitāb al-Riyāḍ.

11. Although quite old at this point and rendered outdated by more recent discoveries in the Cairo Genizah, one of the classic scholarly biographies of Saʿadya is Henry Malter's *Saadia Gaon: His Life and Works* (Philadelphia: Jewish Publication Society, 1921). More recently, see part 3 of Robert Brody's *The Geonim of Babylonia and the Shaping of Medieval Jewish Culture* (New Haven, CT: Yale University Press, 1998).

12. For more on this connection within Saʿadya's introduction to the thesaurus, see Robert Brody, "Linguistics and Poetry," in his *The Geonim of Babylonia*, 316–29; and Aaron Hughes, *The Invention of Jewish Identity: Bible, Philosophy, and the Art of Translation* (Bloomington: Indiana University Press, 2010), 35, in which he discusses Saʿadya's recourse to biblical models of multilingualism to condemn the forgetting of Hebrew within an Arabophone context.

13. Hughes, *The Invention of Jewish Identity*, 51–53; and Vollandt, *The Arabic Versions of the Pentateuch*, 82–83.

14. By far the best and most thorough discussion of the relationship between Arabic and Hebrew exegetical categories within the Judaeo-Arabic environment, beginning with Saʿadya and covering the work of a variety of other geonic and Andalusi figures, including Ibn Janāḥ and Ibn Naghrīla, Ibn Balʿam, and both Ibn ʿEzra's, may be found in Mordechai Z. Cohen's *Opening the Gates of Interpretation* (Leiden: Brill, 2011), 31–85. On Islamic sources in the *Tafsīr*, see David Freidenreich, "The Use of Islamic Sources," *Jewish Quarterly Review* 93, no. 3 (2003): 353–95. See also Hughes, *The Invention of Jewish Identity*, 51–53.

15. The Arabic translation provokes these questions, but the text itself is also the source of controversy among scholars, specifically the relationship between the translation and commentary and whether they were originally two versions of the same work or conceived of as two separate works. Most recently, Richard Steiner has argued for pattern of transmission that includes much adaptation over two distinct versions; for perhaps a more cautious assessment of the state of the question, see Brody, *The Geonim of Babylonia*, 301–4. See also Joshua Blau, "Saadya Gaon's Pentateuch Translation and the Stabilization of Medieval Judaeo-Arabic Culture," *The Interpretation of the Bible*, ed. J. Krašovec (Sheffield: Academic Press, 1998), 393–97.

16. Vollandt, *The Arabic Versions*, 80.

17. Hughes, *The Invention of Jewish Identity*, 33. Although a balance between embrace of Arabic and ambivalence toward it is a feature of the work of most Judaeo-Arabic

writers, it is worth cautioning that Hughes's reading of Sa'adya is very much through the lens of the modern German translator of the Bible Franz Rosenzweig; as a consequence, he writes more about a nationalism that is informed by the modern nation than about the difficult-to-define cultural nationalism of the Jewish communities of the Middle Ages.

18. Rustow, *Heresy and the Politics of Community*, 39–40.

19. Goldstein, "Arabic Composition"; Marzena Zawanowska, "Was Moses the Mudawwin of the Torah? The Question of the Authorship of the Pentateuch According to Yefet ben 'Eli," in *Studies in Judaeo-Arabic Culture: Proceedings of the Fourteenth Conference of the Society for Judaeo-Arabic Studies*, ed. Haggai Ben-Shammai et al. (Tel Aviv: Tel Aviv University Press, 2014), 7–36; Griffith, *The Bible in Arabic*, 169–70.

20. Angel Sáenz-Badillos and Judit Tarragona Borras, *Los Judíos de Sefarad ante la Biblia* (Córdoba: Ediciones El Almendro), 1996.

21. Sáenz-Badillos and Tarragona, *Los judíos de Sefarad*, 56–104.

22. In his *Comparative Semitic Philology in the Middle Ages* (Leiden: Brill, 2004), Maman observes that despite approaching translation from a different perspective, Judah ibn Tibbon seems to have relied upon Ibn Chiquitilla's original compositions on Hebrew grammar.

23. Cohen, *Opening the Gates*, 21–23; Maman, *Comparative Semitic Philology*, 288, 384–85.

24. Cohen, *Opening the Gates*, 15–18, 83–85.

25. Sánez-Badillos and Tarragona, *Los judíos de Sefarad*, 159–72.

26. Aharon Maman, "Medieval Grammatical Thought: Karaites versus Rabbanites," *Meḥqarim be-lashon* 7 (1995): 79–96; Polliack, *The Karaite Tradition*, chap. 3; Rustow, *Heresy and the Politics of Community*, 41–42.

27. Polliack, "The Spanish Legacy," 86; Mordechai Z. Cohen, *Three Approaches to Biblical Metaphor* (Leiden: Brill, 2004), 24–26. See also several relevant studies in Fernando Díaz Esteban, ed., *Abraham ibn Ezra and His Age* (Madrid: Asociación Española de Orientalistas, 1990).

28. Sa'adya ibn Danān was a fifteenth-century grammarian and exegete who authored an important late dictionary of biblical terminology; see Sáenz-Badillos and Tarragona, *Los judíos de Sefarad*, 248–56.

29. Maman, *Comparative Semitic Philology*, 140.

30. Ibid., 143.

31. Ibid., 88.

32. Trans. Steven Harvey in his "Did Maimonides' Letter to Samuel ibn Tibbon Determine Which Philosophers Would Be Studied By Later Jewish Thinkers?," *Jewish Quarterly Review* 83, no. 1 (1992): 51.

33. Ibid., 51–70.

34. *Seder Rav 'Amram ha-Shalem* (Warsaw, 1865; Jerusalem, 1921).

35. Trans. Haggai Ben-Shammai in his "The Tension between Literal Interpretation and Exegetical Freedom: Comparative Observations on Saadia's Method," in *With Reverence for the Word*, ed. Jane Dammen McAuliffe et al. (Oxford: Oxford University Press, 2003), 152–54.

36. Lit., "with the words in Arabic books."

37. Ibn Tibbon, "Musar Av," 17a.

38. Ibid.

39. See Vollandt, *The Arabic Versions* (74), for discussion of Karaite debates over whether reading anything written in letters other than those of the Hebrew alphabet, regardless of the language of the text, was permissible on the Sabbath.

40. Despite Judah's extensive assertions that Samuel never listened to his advice and did not familiarize himself with the contents of his library or listen to his considerations about what to read, the textual record offers a forceful rebuttal of these complaints. In this instance, we know Samuel to have been a dedicated reader of Sa'adya's *Tafsīr*, who applied that reading to both his religious and his professional life. In several places in his *Perush ha-Millot ha-Zarot*, or the *Explanation of Foreign Terms*, an appendix to Samuel's second version of his Hebrew translation of Moses Maimonides' *Guide of the Perplexed*, Samuel defines terms that he has coined in the process of translating the *Guide* and, in places, describes his lexicographic process, including his sources and models. Among those that Robinson has identified is Samuel's explanation of how he came to employ the Hebrew term *ḥoq* in an unconventional way, to mean *description* rather than the usual *law*, in his translation of the *Guide*: Samuel's definition of this term comes as a subsection of the definition of *ekhut*, or quality, the first entry in the work and the only one to comprise a multipartite definition. Thirteen of the seventeen parts of this definition are word-perfect translations from al-Farābī's versions of the *Eisagoge* and the *Categories*, and included in the thirteen are the sub-definitions for the terms *ḥoq* and *geder*. The other four sections are paraphrases from those two works. Yet we see that Samuel goes to some length to sublimate the accessibility to the reader of his reliance on al-Farābī, instead choosing to highlight how these terms relate to the Judaeo-Arabic biblical tradition. After defining the five predictables, he continues to write: "Having explained the meaning of those words I will attach to them the explanation of two additional terms, namely, *geder*, 'definition,' and *ḥoq*, 'description.' . . . As for the term *ḥoq*, I do not remember having seen this term used in this way by any previous translator, but I have seen that Rabbenu Saadia translated the biblical term *ḥoq*, as in the phrase *ḥoq u-mishpat*, 'a statute and an ordinance' [see, e.g., Exod. 15:25], as *rasm*; and similarly he translated *ḥuqqay* as *rusûmî* [see, e.g., Ps. 50:16]. Because of this, I have translated the Arabic term *rasm* into Hebrew as *ḥoq*." Trans. Robinson, in Samuel ibn Tibbon's Commentary on Ecclesiastes (Tübingen: Mohr Siebeck, 2007).

41. Ephraim Kanarfogel, "Compensation for the Study of Torah in Medieval Rabbinic Thought," in *Of Scholars, Savants and Their Texts*, ed. Ruth Link-Salinger (New York: Peter Lang Press, 1989), 135–48; and Menachem Kellner, "Maimonides' Disputed Legacy," in *Traditions of Maimonideanism*, ed. Carlos Fraenkel (Leiden: Brill, 2009), 245–76.

42. Particularly as it had a specific impact upon my thinking about this issue, I would like to acknowledge James T. Robinson's suggestion that I reconsider the use of the term *professional* to describe Judah's work as a translator; this was one place in the argument where the full range of English denotations and connotations of the word originally led my argument astray and in a very different direction. And so, while I have continued to choose to use the term in line with Twersky, Robinson's questioning of it has led me to be more mindful and precise about the nature of Judah's activity as a translator and how that might have borne upon his day-to-day and sacral lives.

43. It is also worth noting that in an ethical will falsely attributed to Moses Maimonides, the trope of the Rechabites are used to impute filial piety; the text may be found in *The Path of Good Men*, ed. Hirsch Edelman (London: A. P. Shaw, 1852), 17–18, and in Abrahams's *Hebrew Ethical Wills*, 101–17.

44. This figure's name is rendered in several different ways in the text of the Bible; I have transliterated it in all instances following the most common spelling that occurs in Jeremiah 35.

45. Ibn Tibbon, "Musar Av," 19b.

46. Jeremiah 35:5–10.

47. I find no concrete reason to read the refusal to assimilate into what is specifically identified in the Hebrew Bible as a Judahite context (Jeremiah 35 begins: "This is the discourse that Jeremiah received from Yahweh in the days of Joachim ben Josiah, the king of Judah") as an additional way for Judah to engage in plays-on-words, riffing on his own name; such an interpretation would require thinking that through all of his cajoling and educating and supplicating and insisting, Judah was giving Samuel a knowing wink and a nod and permission to go his own way, to refuse to assimilate to his own personal "Judahite" culture, and that seems unlikely. However, it remains an attractive possibility both because of Judah's own tendency toward puns and because other roughly contemporaneous Andalusi writers, those called Judah and those with characters in their tales called Judah, would often evoke the biblical figure or tribe of Judah in some form.

48. The question of whether or not drinking alcohol would evoke the image of Bedouins for medieval readers would seem, on the surface, to rely upon popular and puritanical misconceptions about the place of alcohol in the Arabophone and Islamicate world, a readerly culture that not only admits drinking but indeed has a whole genre of poetry dedicated to the subject, the *khamriyya* (wine poem). However, several caveats allow the characteristic of alcohol abstention to be sustained as part of a wider description of Bedouins that would be recognizable to Andalusi readers. First, across both Arabic and Hebrew Andalusi wine poetry, wine drinking is depicted as a courtly, urban activity rather than as a desert activity as it is sometimes represented in eastern *'udhrī* poetry. Second, Roger Allen has shown that the poetics of the *khamriyya* rely upon the poet divorcing literary representations of wine consumption from the act of consumption in reality and an insistence (however disingenuous) that this is a theme for poetry rather than a practical activity; see his summary of this discussion in *The Arabic Literary Heritage: The Development of Its Genres and Criticism* (Cambridge: Cambridge University Press, 1998), 187–89. Furthermore, see the discussion of voice and irony in wine poetry in Andras Hamori, *On the Art of Medieval Arabic Literature* (Princeton, NJ: Princeton University Press, 1974), chap. 2, and of the representation of Christians and Jews as tavern keepers and wine pourers in Arie Schippers, "Wine Poetry," in *Spanish Hebrew Poetry and the Arabic Literary Tradition: Arabic Themes in Hebrew Andalusian Poetry* (Leiden: Brill, 1994), 105–43 (see also for more on the development of the wine song in Andalusi Arabizing Hebrew poetry). And so, as surely as we see wine-drinking evoked and praised in poetry, we also see readers reminded of the prohibitions against it and the virtues of abstaining. It is also worth noting that in the *maqāma* in the *Taḥkemoni* that mocks the Bedouin, he and the urban trickster Ḥever the Kenite specifically drink water and not wine (*Tahkemoni, maqāma* 21/9).

49. Israel Friedlander, "The Jews of Arabia and the Rechabites," *Jewish Quarterly Review* 1 (1910): 252–57.

50. A considerable amount of scholarship on the relevant terminology derived from biblical onomastica has been carried out. For the development of these terms, Ishmaelite and Hagarite, in biblical and ancient texts, and particularly for a consideration of whether the two terms refer to the same group of people in those texts, see Israel Eph'al,

"Ishmael and the Arab(s): A Transformation of Ethnological Terms," *Journal of Near Eastern Studies* 35, no. 4 (1976): 225–35. For an overview of this terminology in rabbinic literature, consult Carol Bakhos, *Ishmael on the Border: Rabbinic Portrayals of the First Arab* (Albany: State University of New York Press, 2006). Nehemiah Allony considers the linguistic-terminological function of the biblical figure of Hagar, Ishmael's mother, in "Sarah and Hagar in the Poetry of Spain," in *Studies in the Bible and the History of Israel* (Jerusalem: Kiryat Sefer, 1979), 168–85. John Tolan, "The Muslim in the Ideologies of Spain," in his *Saracens: Islam in the Medieval European Imagination* (New York: Columbia University Press, 2002), 174–93, assesses the representation of Muslims in the Iberian Latin and early Romance literature of the twelfth- and thirteenth-centuries, though his terminological interests run more toward the uses of the epithet *moro*. Ross Brann reviews the terminological question over a wider temporal and national-literary span in "The Moors?" *Medieval Encounters* 15, no. 2 (2009): 307–18.

51. Ross Brann, *Power in the Portrayal* (Princeton, NJ: Princeton University Press, 2002), 146–47.

52. Shari Lowin, "Khaybar," *Encyclopedia of Jews in the Islamic World*, ed. Norman Stillman (Leiden: Brill, 2010), http://referenceworks.brillonline.com/entries/encyclopedia-of-jews-in-the-islamic-world/khaybar-COM_0012910, accessed February 21, 2016.

53. Joseph Sadan, "An Admirable and Ridiculous Hero: Some Notes on the Bedouin in Medieval Arabic Belles-Lettres," *Poetics Today* 10, no. 3 (1989): 472–73, 478, 483.

54. Hartwig Hirschfeld, "The Arabic Portion of the Cairo Genizah at Cambridge," *Jewish Quarterly Review* 16, no. 1 (1903): 112. See further discussion in Phillip I. Ackerman-Lieberman, "The Muḥammadan Stipulations: Dhimmī Versions of the Pact of 'Umar," in *Jews, Christians and Muslims in Medieval and Early Modern Times*, ed. Arnold Franklin et al. (Leiden: Brill, 2014), 198–99.

55. S. D. Goitein, *A Mediterranean Society*, vol. 2 (Berkeley: University of California Press, 1967), 386–87.

56. In a polemical context, Samawa'l al-Maghribī also asserts a connection between desert Arabs, the Khaybar "Judaizing Arabs," and the rise of Islam (see in Moshe Perelman's edition of *Ifḥām al-yahūd*, in *Proceedings of the American Academy for Jewish Research* 32 (1964): 56).

57. Judah Hadassi, *Eshkol ha-Kofer*, ed. Wilhelm Bacher and Sandor Scheiber, *Jewish Quarterly Review* (o.s.) 8 (1863).

58. It is also worth making mention of the fact that a variety of medieval Arabic texts written by Muslim authors for Muslim audiences connected their own community heritage with the biblical Rechabites. In his study on asceticism and purity, *Virtues of the Flesh: Passion and Purity in Early Islam* (Leiden: Brill, 2004), 6, Ze'ev Magen identifies the use of variants of the term "Rechabite" in Arabo-Muslim sources to identify monks in the pre- and early Islamic periods.

59. It is interesting to note that immediately following the discussion of the Rechabites is the episode in which Baruch ben Neriah writes down Jeremiah's prophecy and reads out from the book. I do not wish to push the interpretation too far, but the juxtaposition of a laudatory portrait of the imagined guardians of Arabic that is immediately followed by an image of reading from books is evocative in the context of the present study, an extended metaphor that connects the Arabic literary tradition to a book culture.

60. Benjamin of Tudela, *Itinerary*, ed. and trans. Marcus Nathan Adler (Oxford: Oxford University Press, 1907). A full list of manuscripts, editions, and translations may

be found in Abraham David, "Benjamin ben Jonah of Tudela," *Encyclopaedia of Jews in Islamic Lands*, http://ezproxy.library.nyu.edu:2447/entries/encyclopedia-of-jews-in-the-islamic-world/benjamin-ben-jonah-of-tudela-COM_0003980, accessed February 15, 2016.

61. Adler, introduction to Benjamin of Tudela, *Itinerary*, 49.

62. Ibid.

63. S. L. Rapoport, "On the Independent Jews of Arabia," *Bikkurei ha-'ittim* 4 (1824): 51–77.

64. Other manuscripts survive in Rome (Biblioteca Casanatense MS 216, a miscellany copied by a named scribe that also includes a copy of the account of Eldad ha-Dani), Oxford (Bodl. Opp. Add. 8° 36), Ferrara, and Vienna (a manuscript that was, at the time of Adler's publication, in the private collection of a certain Herr Epstein).

65. Benjamin of Tudela, *Itinerary*, 46.

66. Nehemiah Allony, "Eli ben Yehudah ha-Nazir and His Composition of the *Foundations of the Hebrew Language*," *Leshonenu* 34, no. 1 (1970): 84.

67. Trans. in Rustow, *Heresy and the Politics of Community*, 50.

68. Ibid., 50–51.

69. Allony follows Geiger and Pinsker in suggesting Eli ben Judah uses the phrase "me'or 'eynayim" in his preface as an allusion to Abraham ibn 'Ezra''s commentary.

70. Rustow, *Heresy and the Politics of Community*, 51.

71. Among the Andalusi Muslim writers who evoked the Bedouins to various literary effect are Ibn Hazm, in his *Tawq al-Ḥamama* (Neck-Ring of the Dove), and al-Ṣaraqustī, in the so-called "Qairowan Maqāmā." Discussion of both of these may be found in Alexander Elinson, *Looking Back at al-Andalus* (Leiden: Brill, 2009), and Ross Brann, "Andalusi Exceptionalism," in *A Sea of Languages: Rethinking the Arabic Role in Medieval Literary History* (Toronto: University of Toronto Press, 2013), 119–34.

72. Elinson, *Looking Back*, 56; Esperanza Alfonso, *Islamic Culture through Jewish Eyes* (Routledge: New York, 2008), 20–21.

73. Drory, *Models and Contacts*, 173–75.

74. Joshua Blau, "On the Status of Hebrew and Arabic amongst Arabophone Jews," *Leshonenu* 26 (1962): 281–84.

75. Elinson, *Looking Back*, 30, 137. Elinson also draws upon the work of Iḥsān 'Abbās as another scholar who argues for this kind of contiguity.

4 "THE WORDS OF THE ANCIENT POETS"

Poetics between Jewish and Islamic Scripture

THE PREVIOUS CHAPTER dealt with the topic of the Hebrew Bible in Arabic as a cultural touchstone and as a literary text rather than as exclusively a theological one, but there I omitted discussion of one of the most significant and signal uses of the Hebrew Bible in the literature of Jews in Islamic lands: as a medium, reagent, and catalyst for poetry. Instead, such a topic belongs within a more holistic discussion of poetry and poetics that casts it as an integral part of those types of writing rather than making them a side consideration to a theological and professional discussion. To be sure, Judah ibn Tibbon treats the Hebrew Bible as a foundational religious text and source of moral guidance, but at the same time he also acknowledges it as a literary and cultural work by making the Hebrew Bible part of the discussion of poetry rather than making poetry part of the broader discussion of the Hebrew Bible. Hebrew poetry, particularly through its complex relationship both to Arabic poetry and the Hebrew Bible, is a form of "culturally national" self-expression; it provides a way for culturally Judaeo-Arabic authors to negotiate literary commitments in a textual world that could not conceive of a full separation between the secular and the sacred. Perhaps most paradoxically, it is ultimately the Hebrew Bible that highlights the unique and inimitable place of poetry within the canon.

As noted in the previous chapter, the Qur'ān is a self-conscious text, aware of itself as an Arabic book and as one written in *saj*ʿ, or rhymed prose; the text makes a sharp distinction between Scripture and poetry by telling its adherents, regarding Muḥammad and his prophetic proclamations: "We have not taught him poetry and it does not become him. It is but a reminder and a clear text."[1] And so Jewish responses, both those that implicate the Arabic language and those that implicate the Hebrew Bible as a work of Scripture, must also grapple with and then move beyond the question of poetics. The three critical elements—language, Scripture, and poetry—are thus not construed as identical or co-terminal but rather as components of a single, coherent literary-theological discussion that occurs in the Islamic world, first among Muslims and then among other groups of people in significant cultural contact with them and with long and complex literary heritages and sacred Scriptures of their own.

Muslim theologians and literary critics alike recognized certain rhetorical elements in common between the text of the Qur'ān and the verse of pre-Islamic and early Muslim poets and grappled with how to reconcile their formal similarities with the important differences in their functions. The relationship between poetry and Scripture became a central focus of Arabic literary theory and poetics, as in this crucial passage of the foundational work known simply as *Iʿjāz al-Qur'ān* (the Inimitability of the Qur'ān), by the eastern Ashʿarī thinker and Mālikī *qāḍī*, Muḥammad ibn al-Ṭayyib al-Bāqillānī:

> There is no approach to the understanding of *iʿjāz al-Qur'ān* by way of the rhetorical figures (*badīʿ*) such as they find and describe in poetry. This holds because this branch of knowledge in no way disrupts the habit nor transcends the sphere of common experience. On the contrary, it can be improved upon by study, training and application, just as the composition of poetry, the making of prose addresses, the writing of epistles, and the skill in eloquence. And toward this skill, there exists a trodden path, a traditional approach, a ladder which can be ascended step by step, and a pattern which the student may follow.[2]

This is a canonical and important statement on the relationship between poetry and Scripture. Yet in spite of the sharp distinction between the forms—poetry is not only distinct from an Arabic Scripture, it is unbecoming in relation to it and cannot be at all helpful in interpreting it—nonetheless poetry became an important way in which to glorify Arabic, the language in which God revealed the Qur'ān.[3] However, very quickly such ideas became more integrated and were no longer an external challenge but represented, rather, an integral, if conflictive, part of a unitary system of poetics with the tensions between Scripture and poetics in Islamic writing pulling the edges from the center for Jewish writers. Scripture and poetry were distinguished from one another, with one being the store of content and the other a store of style, at once mutually incompatible and completely aligned; and although we have reviewed implications of *iʿjāz* in certain contexts for Arabophone Jews, the composition and reception of poetry is so distinct in the minds of both Muslim and Jewish writers, thinkers, and theologians that it is worth revisiting that discussion for this specific context. Even while acknowledging the initial dependency of Judaeo-Arabic poetics on its classical Arabic counterpart, it is the Judaeo-Arabic cultural and literary framework into which Judah's archly conservative, archaizing poetics must be set.

THE ORCHARD OF DUNASH AS A METAPHOR FOR AL-ANDALUS

Just as we saw in the previous chapter that grammatical study and lexicography were important in biblical exegesis, so, too, are they an important part of the elaboration of an Arabized poetry and poetics native to the Andalusi Jewish intellectual elite. Dunash ben Labraṭ (d. ca. 990) was the figure most responsible for adapting both the grammatical and the poetic to that cultural context; consequently, it is hardly surprising that he became a powerful figure to whom Judah could refer in delineating his own Arabizing cultural program.[4] While much of what we believe we know about Dunash's biography relies heavily on the intuition and informed speculation of Ezra Fleischer,[5] Dunash's professional life and his roles as a grammarian, theorist, and poet are more securely documented. Born in Baghdad, raised in Fez, and educated at the feet of Sa'adya Ga'on back in Baghdad, Dunash returned to the western Mediterranean after his teacher's death and made a place for himself, and fast friends and enemies, in the circle of Ḥasdai ibn Shapruṭ at the court of the newly self-proclaimed neo-Umayyad caliph, 'Abd al-Raḥmān III.

Dunash's grammatical innovations came first in the course of developing the rivalry that would define and ultimately end his life at the court at Córdoba.[6] By taking on the foundations of Hebrew morphology laid out in the newly completed dictionary of Ḥasdai's chief courtier, Menaḥem ibn Saruq, and arguing that they were both linguistically and theologically unsound, Dunash fired the opening shots of what would become a long-running rhetorical battle between those two men,[7] their students after them,[8] and subsequent generations of Judaeo-Arab grammarians, linguists, and lexicographers. Menaḥem is sometimes incorrectly described as being opposed to comparative Semitics and being reluctant to admit the validity of linguistic comparison between Arabic and Hebrew; however, the reality of the situation is somewhat more complex, and both Menaḥem and Dunash might effectively be described as comparatists. While Menaḥem's comparatist tendencies were not articulated as such in his work and were subsequently obscured deliberately by his students who sought to impute to his work a more pure rabbinic and Hebrew character,

Dunash drew more explicitly on his teacher Saʿadya's understanding of the relationship between Arabic and Hebrew.[9] Yet Dunash was not the only one to volley charges of both linguistic and theological impropriety at linguistic and literary advances being made: when he himself moved on from the Arabization of grammatical study to the Arabization of poetic meter, he would find himself facing charges of a similar nature.[10]

Ḥasdai's partisans did not manage to carry the day; Dunash's comparative approach to both language and literary theory came to dominate poetic discourse among the Arabic-speaking Jews of Spain. Ultimately Joseph Tobi goes so far as to characterize him within the mold of a "cultural hero" for the way in which he was able to draw poetry to the fore in many aspects of the Judaeo-Arabic culture of al-Andalus rather than leaving it limited to liturgical contexts.[11] Competing systems of poetics grew up, but all at least acknowledging Dunash's basic framework: Abraham ibn 'Ezra' would go on to criticize the grammar of the *payetanim* (pietistic poets) harshly while still giving them their place in his own lineage of Spanish poets.[12] Judah Halevi wrote about the history of the Hebrew language in his major work of religious philosophy, the *Kuzari*, and wrote about quantitative poetic meter in a dedicated treatise that exposes his conflictive attitude toward the secular poetic tradition in which he made his name. As an author whose work Judah ibn Tibbon would eventually translate, his opinions are particularly salient.[13]

Among the revolutionary aspects of the new Spanish poetry was the way in which it incorporated the text of the Hebrew Bible as a kind of ornamentation in secular works rather than as a semantic signifier. In other words, the use of quotations from the Hebrew Bible within the work of these poets was significant because it was the foundational national text and because it suited the poetry aesthetically; but in most cases it was not important in a traditional source-critical way in that the sense of the biblical text could be read into the medieval poem. This was a way of responding, again, to the notion of the divinity of the Arabic language and the perfection of the Qur'ān and the theological challenge those twin ideas posed to the Jews of al-Andalus while nonetheless participating fully and with varying degrees of self-awareness in the wider literary culture.[14] As the work of the new Hebrew poets developed, it is natural that a poetics should have grown up alongside the body of their work, and these ideas were also addressed more explicitly in such works. As was discussed in chapter 3, Saʿadya played a crucial role in the normalization of Arabic in Jewish liturgical contexts. So, too, did he conceive of his lexicographic work as creating a poetic toolkit through his major dictionary, commonly known in the Hebrew translation by Judah ibn Tibbon according to its Hebrew title, *Sefer ha-Egron* (The Thesaurus), properly entitled *Kitāb uṣūl al-sh'ir al-'ibrānī* (The Book of Fundamentals of Hebrew Poetry). And so despite the naysayers who found Arabizing poetry to be everything from unnecessary to religiously impertinent, its principles and foundations became the norm. In a work of apologetic, rather than prescriptive, poetics that will be discussed in greater detail toward the end of this chapter, Moses ibn 'Ezra' essentially reworked and amplified Ibn Rashīq's *Kitāb al-'Umda*, drawing in the works of additional Arabic poeticists such as Ibn al-Mu'tazz and Qudāma ibn Ja'far, creating a work that is part memoir, part literary history, and part treatise on poetics. Ultimately he offered up a text that wades tentatively into an alternative discussion of *'arabiyya*, the "Arabicness" of literature, that developed uniquely within the Maghreb and, more specifically, among culturally Arabized Jews.[15]

Despite all of the medieval historians and their readers who regularly made note that his origins were outside of the Iberian Peninsula—born in Fez and educated in Baghdad—they also made him to be foundational and firmly within the Andalusi poetic tradition. Moses ibn 'Ezra', although he does not go into the same kind of detail about Dunash's poetic or grammatical career as he does with some of the other Andalusi poets, nonetheless places him at the head of that poetic tradition: "One among the writers and poets is Dunash ben Labraṭ ha-Halevi, Baghdadi by birth and Fez-educated; Ibn Sheshet was his student. Menaḥem ibn Sarūq from Tortosa, later, from Córdoba, was among those who appreciated his work but diminished its value and did not ever turn to it as a topic of special interest."[16] Solomon ibn Gabirol, in a lament written for Samuel ibn Naghrīla, would laud him by cementing his poetic lineage, placing him in succession of Dunash's poetic mantle and describing him as Dunash's very son.[17] Moses ibn Taqāna writes, also in verse, about Dunash as the benchmark against whom he measures himself when boasting about his own poetic prowess. When he writes: "I say! Who is this Dunash? And who Menaḥem? . . . Are they not lacking and worthless before me?"[18] he demonstrates that the way to make sure that his readers knew him to be a great poet is to claim that he has exceeded Dunash, even as he haughtily feigns ignorance and diminution of his predecessor's accomplishments. In the *maqāmāt* in his *Sefer Taḥkemoni*, Judah al-Ḥarīzī makes only brief and not overwhelmingly laudatory mention of Dunash, but, again, acknowledges his place at the head of the line of Andalusi poets. In the third *maqāma* in the collection, he writes about the superlative excellence of Dunash's poems, calling him Adonim, the Hebrew name by which he is also known: "There are none like [the poems of]

Adonim, embraced by his beautiful hand."[19] And in the so-called "*maqāma* of the poets," he writes about the origins of Arabizing Hebrew poetry in Spain, he specifically mentions Ḥasdai's patronage and his large coterie of poets and *udabā'*, but does not refer specifically to any of them;[20] the first named poet in this *maqāma* is Isaac ibn Khalfūn.[21] Despite his lukewarm reception in the historians of Andalusi poetry, and despite one curious total omission—from Abraham ibn Daud's *Sefer ha-Qabbalah*[22]—the poetic diwān of Dunash ben Labraṭ is, in the mind of the medieval reader, firmly an Andalusi work.[23]

One of the most significant ways by which Judah transmitted an Andalusi curriculum (and one that is discussed in greater detail in the following chapter) was through quoting a variety of Andalusi writers and other Arabic-language writers in particular and demonstrating interest in al-Andalus to readers of his ethical will and providing Samuel and other readers with a broad sampling of Andalusi texts; and poetry was no exception. Thus Dunash's poetic *diwān* becomes an important metaphor that Judah uses both to communicate his nostalgia to readers who shared his longing and loss and who would know to read between the lines[24] while still promoting the cause of reading from the Andalusi Arabic canon for readers for whom those texts did not have immediate emotional or intellectual purchase. By adapting Dunash's work for this later and more remote audience, Judah was able to make the beginnings of Arabizing Andalusi Hebrew serve these twin purposes. In what is necessarily the ethical will's most poetic expressions of the idea of Arabic as a language of value, Judah writes, "My son, make your books your companions, and your shelves and bookcases your paradise and orchard."[25] The poetic character of this quotation and its implicit argument for the prestige of Arabic are both owed to the remark's clear, direct, and unattributed allusion to an epigram found in Dūnash's *diwān*. His version reads: "Your Garden of Eden will be your holy books, and your orchard the Arabs' books."[26] Both versions of the quotation ask their readers to compare books with verdant, almost heavenly, paradisiacal landscapes. Some differences exist between the two versions; some of these are insignificant choices in diction, while others show Judah to have been a shrewd cultural translator in spite of himself and in spite of his strong preference for the literal translation of texts.

Both Dunash's quotation and Judah's reworking of it have the same bipartite construction that consists of two hortative-equational phrases. There are some differences in the structure of the formulation, but these are largely insignificant. Where Dunash exhorts his reader to let the physical books take on a metaphorical dimension and the books themselves are the subject, Judah exhorts Samuel to take a more active role, namely to make the literal figurative; Dunash asks his reader to allow the books to become paradise where Judah tells Samuel to go and to make the books his paradise. With respect to the Elysian-horticultural terminology, Dunash modifies his garden as specifically *Gan 'Eden*, the Garden of Eden, where Judah, as noted earlier, just uses the word *gan*; however, the idyllic connotations of *gan* render the image practicably the same. In fact, in *Sefer ha-Shorashim*, the definition of *gan* makes an explicit equation between *gan* and *gan eden*. The entry opens by spelling out the letters of the lemma, and then moves on to give its definition by prooftext: "*Gimel* and *nun*. Garden. The Garden of Eden (Gen. 2:8). To feed in the gardens (Cant. 6:2). Like gardens along the river (Num. 24:6). This is known."[27]

However, other changes and differences are more significant and it is through these that we may begin to adduce a deeper cultural meaning. While the imagery is the same and created from shared terminology, the distinctive phrasing does not represent a variant that we find in Yehudi's compilation of the *diwān*, and so it can be reasonably attributed to Judah as a textual variant he himself developed as he incorporated Dunash's verse into his work. And so it is this second set of differences that allows us a window onto what was important to Judah as both a reader and a cultural conservator. Most significant is his adaptation of the description of the books themselves. While Dunash writes about "holy books" and "the Arabs' books" as the two literary forms of paradise, Judah writes about books generally and the collections of books on shelves as his two literary forms of paradise. Where Dunash distinguishes holy books from Arabs' books, he is separating what we modern readers might call the sacred from the secular. Secular poetry, while occupying a privileged place within and in between that dichotomy as secular poetry that could not exist without the Hebrew Bible, must fall into the other category: Poetic *dawawīn* were Arabs' books even when they contained Hebrew poetry, and no one knew that better than Dunash. Thus, in addition to all of the other productive similarities between the two versions of the epigram, Dunash has left yet another analogy between Hebrew poetry and the Arabic language, one ripe to be read in between the lines of Judah's version.

While the differences between the two versions of the epigram serve to call attention to their shared cultural context, it is also worth addressing the similarities between the two. These seem clear enough, beginning with their shared use of gardening terminology.[28] Both use the term *gan*, a Hebrew word for garden that often carries otherworldly connotations,[29] in the first half of the quotation. Both use the term *pardes*, orchard, in the second half of the quotation, a choice that strengthens its association both with scientific learning and, ultimately, with that kind of learning in al-Andalus itself. And both make essentially the same claim: books are a paradise for readers. But not only is it that, it is also a granadine paradise. Jonathan Decter notes that "the enclosed garden (*hortus conclusus*), which became a synecdochic icon of Andalusian culture, emerged as a subject of sustained engagement in literary texts,"[30] and, further, that "when the Andalusian context began to break down, the garden remained a persistent symbol of the cosmopolitan culture that poets recognized as their own."[31] First, Judah fortifies the connection to al-Andalus through the specifics of the type of orchard. And in this case, the evocation of the *pardes*, specifically, a kind of orchard that is consistently identified with groves of pomegranate trees (*pardes-rimon*),[32] takes the general allusion to al-Andalus suggested by the *hortus conclusus* imagery and makes it more specific to the city of Granada (*Rimon-Sefarad* lit.: the pomegranate of Sefarad) itself. It is a connection that could not have escaped Judah ibn Tibbon: The definition of *pardes* in *Sefer ha-Shorashim* is brief, beginning with a citation that must have appealed to the Granadine exile translating it into Hebrew. The definition consists of a list of prooftexts and a comparison with the Arabic term: "*Pardes*. Pomegranate orchard (Cant. 4:13). Guard the orchard (Neh. 2:8). Gardens and orchards (Eccl. 2:5). In Arabic, it is *firdaus* and *farādis*."[33] *Pardes-rimon* is the first definition, building, it seems, on the inherence of pomegranate trees in the definition of a true orchard. Dunash's quotation, through its explicit parallelism, equates gardens with holy books and orchards with Arabs' books; but through his choice to describe the lush landscape of the Arabs' books with the type of landscape that by all accounts must include the kind of tree by which the city of Granada was and is also known, he is also equating the pleasure garden of Arabic books with the heart of al-Andalus, a nostalgic turn that cannot have been lost on his later exilic readers. When Judah reworks the quotation, then, he does so with two parallel sets: gardens, holy books, and the Edenic paradise itself, parallel to orchards, Arabs' books, and his city of Granada.

Then, Judah both reinforces the notion of translation as an activity grounded in a book culture and reasserts that book culture as an Andalusi one. He further draws the connection between book culture and gardens even closer by both extending the garden metaphor with specific plants and then going on to use a verb most closely associated with the act of translating (*le-ʿateq*, to translate, imperative *heʿeteq*) to suggest to Samuel the nearly infinite possibilities for finding matters of interest in these paradise libraries: "My son, make your books your companions, and your shelves and bookcases your paradise and heavenly garden. Revel in their verdancy, pick their roses, and gather up their fruits, spices, and myrrh. If you come to dread all of this, transpose yourself from garden to garden (*he'eteq mi-gan el-gan*), from flowerbed to flowerbed, and from *mirador* to *mirador*; and in doing so you will renew your interest and pleasure."[34] Although the term *mar'ah* (vista point) might not merit special attention on its own, in the context of the enclosed garden imagery it evokes the architecture of the Andalusi garden palaces and their *miradores*, the patio bay windows that look out onto the gardens. The passage as a whole is set in an Andalusi *hortus conclusus* made up of verdant plants and pleasurable and informative books.[35] The instruction, then, to "translate" or transpose oneself from garden to garden in this case is to peruse the bookshelves and even different libraries in search of new reading material, always grounded in the activity at hand, namely translating both literatures and cultures.

The confusion between the poets that so calls attention to this cited poem, then, does not appear to have been on Judah ibn Tibbon's part, and so it is worth considering the inclusion of this poem as part of the creation of his Andalusi literary environment within the text. This poem by Halevi also makes use of garden imagery to write about the act of writing and draws on the same image of books as a garden:

> How could I fear any man when I have a soul
> through which lions are terrified of their cubs?
> How could I worry about poverty when it contains the wisdom
> from whose hills I can cut rubies?
> If I am hungry, here are her [wisdom's] choicest fruits,
> and if I am thirsty, here are her streams.
> How could I sit alone when her lyre
> delights me with her songs?
> How could I seek a friend to speak with me
> when I hear the wisdom of her words?
> My lute and my lyre are at the nib of her pen (*nivli ve-khinori befi 'eṭah*).
> My gardens and my orchards are her books (*gani u-fardesi sefareha*).[36]

Thus we see that in his ethical will, Judah ibn Tibbon both draws on the trope of the garden as a library that occurred commonly in Andalusi poetry as well as on Dunash's particular use of it. In doing so, he connects the book culture that he so dearly wishes to impart to his sons and to his readers to the literary production of al-Andalus and its representations.

Ultimately there can have been no medieval Andalusi or Andalusi-exile reader of the ethical will who would not have recognized the resonance with the words originally written by the first of their poets.[37] Even with the omission of the direct reference to the Arab authors of the books, the force of the silence still conveys the sense that Samuel's shelves and cases would be full of Arabic books. Judah takes a reference to Arabic books and makes it more universal, transmitting Dunash for a non-Arabophone audience while, at the same time, saying something slightly different with the selfsame phrase to those who could more easily recognize its source. He advocates for Arabic books among those who could read them and, subtly, among those who could not.

This instance of cribbing and adapting the work of an earlier writer is particularly interesting because it subjects Jewish literary writing to the same kit of tools that is most often called on by writers incorporating Arabo-Islamic texts of a religious character when they want to obviate the theological problems that those texts and their claims about religious authority might have posed, and that Judah himself uses elsewhere in the oeuvre. For example, the translator of a philosophical text that called on verses of the Qur'ān in creating its argument might have either substituted the citation with a similar biblical one or, alternatively, might have in effect "cleansed" the text by translating the quotation but omitting any explicitly Islamicizing references and as the nature of the original source; and in other types of texts, *udabā'* would engage in a systematic program of substitutions of biblical toponyms and personal names as they adapted Arabic collections of *maqāmāt* written by Muslim authors into Hebrew for a Jewish audience.[38] This practice of omitting references to Islamic and even Arabic material of a religiously neutral or Jewish character is even documented elsewhere in Judah ibn Tibbon's own work. In translating Jonah ibn Janāḥ's dictionaries, he systematically omits Arabic prooftexts and declines to translate Arabic terms that help define various lemmata, and also omits grammatical discussion that is not directly related to the definition of the Hebrew terms; he often replaces a more involved discussion of Arabic language or grammar with the one-word explanation in Hebrew: *yadu'a* (it is known).[39] The combination of the cleansing of sources with the very simple, subtle, between-the-lines appeal to the authority of the Arabic language and linguistic tradition as arbiter of correct definitions is a tidy illustration of Judah ibn Tibbon's position: Arabic was, at once, an authoritative and important source of knowledge, but one that had to be transmitted carefully and unobtrusively to non-Arabophone audiences.

In this case Judah does that very same thing but to a completely different effect. He does not name his source and eliminates the reference to the "Arabs' books," offering a kind of literary knowing nod to the reader who knows, without alienating the one who does not have a familiar point of reference within the world of Arabic books. The allusion transmits a famous epigram of perhaps the most important Arabizing Hebrew poet, the one who, in effect, single-handedly Arabized Hebrew poetry. But it does so in a way that does not limit its reach. Although Samuel is nominally the recipient of the ethical will, its audience was much wider than that. And by not limiting his advice to the pleasures that Arabic books could bring, Judah is able to transmit that very Arabizing advice to an audience that would not have derived pleasure or benefit from Arabic books for not having been able to read them.

A scribal error in the complete surviving manuscript copy of the ethical will has the side effect of calling attention to Judah's more-than-passing familiarity with the image of the library as a garden. Following the above-cited passage in which Judah adapts Dunash's epigram, he cites some poetry, which he introduces with the phrase: "Remember what the poet said in verse."[40] This phrase is then followed by the words "Ben Mishlei," although the poem itself is a composition not of Samuel ibn Naghrīla, but of another Andalusi poet, namely Judah Halevi. First, a word on this misidentification: The poem is attributed in modern scholarship to Judah Halevi, an identification made by Hirsch Edelman and Leopold Dukes on the basis of Bodleian MS Mich. 354.[41] It does not appear in the printed edition of the *diwān* edited by Brody, although he considers the identification to be genuine; Israel Davidson, too, attributes the poem to Halevi.[42] Furthermore, it bears some striking similarities to other poems by Halevi, including poems in Brody's edition of the *diwān*. At first blush it is shocking that Ibn Tibbon, an Andalusi reader through and through and a devotee of Ibn Naghrīla's poetry, could make such an error; however, the misidentification appears to have been introduced by the scribe and not by the author. The annotation "Ben Mishlei" that follows the phrase "remember what the poet said in verse" does not fit in with the flow of the text; nor, in fact, do most of the other annotations that read "Ben Mishlei" that precede the poetry throughout, annotations that mostly do not fit into sentences but sit apart from them. Furthermore, the author of the text makes a clear distinction between the composer of these lines of poetry and Ibn Naghrīla. This is the only text that is attributed to "the poet"; in other words, Judah himself seems to be distinguishing between the poetry of "the nagid," that is, Samuel ibn Naghrīla, and that of "the poet," that is, Judah Halevi. Because Judah ibn Tibbon consistently identifies Ibn Naghrīla in one way and the author of this poem in another way, and because the frequent announcements that the quoted poetry comes from *After Proverbs* are incongruous with the flow of the prose, it is reasonable to conclude that the misidentification of the Halevi poem as one by Ibn Naghrīla is the scribe's rather than the author's. With the manuscript copied in the early 1340s, it is also reasonable to conclude that the poet might have been less familiar with the Hebrew poetry of al-Andalus and might also have sought to help his readers, similarly unfamiliar, by identifying (however infelicitously) the poet.[43]

A POETICS OF THE UNTRANSLATABLE

In the previous section, we looked at the extent to which Judah, following Dunash, made a distinction between sacred and secular texts. That cleavage becomes greater when viewed through the broad notion of the sacral untranslatability of Arabic; however, at a point at which the doctrine of *iʿjāz* was no longer understood to be a direct theological threat to Jewish readers, it becomes a more playful literary notion that readers, and especially translators, can mold to serve their own cultural rather than communal religious needs. Across the body of Judah's work, this freedom manifests itself through the treatment of Arabic and Arabizing poetry as untranslatable without, as we already saw in chapter 2, contesting the inherent translatability of Scripture.

The notion of the untranslatability of a text was popularized in modern literary theory by Walter Benjamin's essay "The Task of the Translator," in which he asserted that the ability to be translated is a quality inherent in some texts but absent from others.[44] While the notion of "untranslatability" has gained traction in recent years, particularly in critiques of the discipline of comparative literature,[45] it is, as we saw in the previous chapter, a far more entrenched idea. Benjamin's ideas about translation alternately resonate and clash with the Tibbonid project, making them an interpretive cipher to be used with some caution. The central challenge of reading Arabic and Arabizing literature through the lens of Benjamin and his successors is reconciling the notion of untranslatability that is an inherent characteristic of the doctrine of *iʿjāz* with Benjamin's assertion that it is Scripture that is uniquely translatable.[46] With respect to Judah,[47] despite Benjamin's implicit criticism of word-for-word translation,[48] in the "Task of the Translator" he hews along the same lines as Judah's poetics. Scripture is, as we saw in the previous chapter, the uniquely translatable thing, the thing that is so translatable that concessions can be made to sense-for-sense translation. In Judah's universe, *iʿjāz* is no longer a prime theological assault and it is poetry that is elevated to the level of the untouchably untranslatable.

Judah never authored a single text in which he delineates a system of poetics; however, several of his prefaces and letters, including the ethical will itself, contain lengthy discussions that, all together, form a coherent poetics. One of those texts is his letter from Judah to Asher ben Meshullam of Lunel, a text that came to stand as the translator's preface to *Sefer Tiqqun Middot ha-Nefesh*, his Hebrew translation of Solomon ibn Gabirol's *Kitāb iṣlāḥ al-akhlāq* (Improvement of Moral Qualities); in that text, he draws clear distinctions between prose and poetry on the basis of the relative ease with which each mode can or cannot be rendered in translation. After observing in the letter that it was the experience of studying Ibn Gabirol with Meshullam and Asher that interested him in translating the whole of *Kitāb iṣlāḥ al-akhlāq*, Judah praises Ibn Gabirol's text for its wisdom and then proceeds to describe the kinds of sources that are incorporated into that text, and the special challenges that this poses to the translator. He writes that Ibn Gabirol's words

> move in the ways of wisdom and are supported by the Bible (*ve-semukhim 'al ha-miqra*), they are based on the sayings of the sages (*divrei ha-ḥakhamim*), the proverbs of the ancients (*mishlei ha-qadmonim*),[49] and the maxims of the philosophers (*musrei ha-filosofim*). The organization of all the chapters is straightforward, and he arrives at his stated goal with concision, his dicta (*'imarot*) are refined, and he introduces riddles (*ḥiddot*) for the benefit they offer. . . . This chapter alone would be enough for us. . . . It would free us from the burden of verbosity so that we could remember its contents. . . . I have translated it for you to the best of my ability, and I was able to translate all of it—all of the words (*devarav*), its figurative expressions (*meliẓotav*), its proverbs (*mishlav*), its maxims (*muserav*), and its riddles (*ḥiddot*). But in the place of the poetry that is brought into the text, I have not yet incorporated it, following the suggestion of our master and teacher, your father, that I complete it [the rest of the translation] before turning my attention to translating the occurrences of poetry as they are [i.e., in verse]. If I should encounter the words of the ancient poets as I encountered the words of the present author and the words of the Nagid, others who conducted themselves in similar manners, and still others who were close to them, I will write them down with their names attached. What I am unable to find I will make anew to the best of my ability and based on my own understanding, and I will write every poetic excerpt down in its place in the treatise.[50]

In this passage, Judah distinguishes between established prose genres and modes and poetry. By describing one process for translating all prose types and another wholly different one for poetry that he holds aside and continues developing for use after the completion of other work and the exhaustion of all other possibilities, he holds poetry as the thing apart, the type of writing that is incapable of being related to or described by the others. It is not the Bible that is untranslatable or inimitable; rather, it is that Scripture and a variety of biblical genres and commentaries, both rabbinic and medieval, that can be fully integrated into a literary system, and an Arabizing one at that. Conversely, it is poetry that can be neither imitated nor translated.[51]

Through this passage, Judah defines the kit of rhetorical strategies that occur in the text he is translating. The uncompleted draft of the translation is, he tells Asher, a Hebrew-language version of an Arabic-language text that is "supported" by biblical quotations and all other manner of tidbits of wisdom expressed in prose. Not only is the text of the scriptural citations relatively unimportant as an element of composition and of translation, the two lists of kinds of texts that are quoted within the original text and that are thereby incorporated into Judah's Hebrew translation go a long way to demoting the text of the Hebrew Bible from any exalted place in the canon. In the introduction to his 1902 edition of the Arabic text, Stephen S. Wise went as far as to understand the description of the Ethics as "supported" by these *shibbuẓim* to mean that the Scriptural citations were "mere mnemonics."[52] We saw in the previous chapter that, theologically speaking, Judah did not distinguish between the Bible and other texts either in their ability to be translated or in their implication in a professional program of translation. Here, again, the Bible is just one kind of text among many that may be translated: proverbs, sayings, other wisdom literature, dicta, enigmas, and figurative or metaphorical textual ornament. Even without the explicit comparison it reflects the very poetic tendency to "transform the Hebrew Bible into a source"[53] for poetry and verse. Translating, adapting, or incorporating—because, of course, he did not translate the quotations from the Hebrew Bible and Hebrew-language rabbinic literature back from Ibn Gabirol's Arabic but rather incorporated them anew from the original Hebrew text, a process, nevertheless, of transposition, adaptation, and interpretation—any of these kinds of texts do not pose any more special challenge than any of the others, according to Judah's estimation of his task, and by the time of his writing the letter to Asher, he has accounted for them all.

Within this passage, in addition to offering some insight into his process as a translator, Judah divides his source material along the lines of generic categories that occur elsewhere in the canon. Within this hierarchic taxonomy of genres, poetry comes out on top. His sources include, he tells us, dicta, maxims, proverbs, and excerpts from the biblical text, and he places all of these into a single category of easily translatable sources. Poetry is another matter entirely and belongs in its own category. When Judah tells Asher that he is leaving the translation of the poetic quotations aside until the end, he in effect characterizes poetry not exactly in Benjaminesque terms as uniquely untranslatable, but certainly as being a far greater challenge to translate than any kind of prose text—divine, sacred, or otherwise—and more deserving of careful attention and even of meticulous research and preparatory work; and he would have his reader believe that this was also Meshullam's position on the matter. It is only something that he would attempt to translate on his own if he could not find existing translations that he could use to render the poetic interpolations. Judah's devotion to the poetic tradition and the specificity with which he distinguishes his sources as belonging to different genres of writing is highly evocative of the formalization of Arabic poetics and the ways in which lines of verse are necessarily frozen by all of those formal requirements.

Already from the very beginning of the letter to Asher, we see deeply embedded evidence of Judah's attitude toward the literary status of Arabic. Though written in the highly stylized form of epistolary composition, the formal introductory address of the letter nonetheless contains a clever play on words that hints to the reader that this letter will materially concern the role of the Arabic language for its translators and that the author considers Arabic to be an extremely valuable component, even as he is working to transpose texts out of that language. This rhymed-prose salutation reads: "*Ha-ḥever he-ʿarev, ve-ha-'aḥ ha-qarev asher divro 'or le-darki*" (My dear interlocutor, my close brother, whose words light my path).[54] The particularly salient element in that flowery list of epithets is "*ha-ḥever he-ʿarev*" (my dear interlocutor). The phrase must, on the grounds of both context and rhyme, be read with this pattern of vocalization and understood primarily to mean "dear interlocutor"; however, it is impossible to escape the double entendre. The adjective *ʿarev*, meaning *nice* or *pleasing*, is built from the same consonantal root, ʿ-R-B, that yields the word *ʿarav*, or *Arab*, and its related semantic range; thus, in the unvocalized consonantal skeleton of the letter, this term "*ha-ḥever he-ʿarav / ha-ʿarav*" (the dear/ Arab interlocutor), reads at a minimum with an understanding of and appreciation for the homophony at play. In some way, the reader of this letter (whether that be Asher, the specific, intended recipient, or a wider audience for the translation of Ibn Gabirol's treatise) is Judah's companion in his Arabic translation. Plays on this word,[55] simultaneously reflecting both the "Arabness" or "Arabicness" of his interlocutors and sources as well as esteem in which he held them, occur elsewhere in Judah's writing. The word is a "dual sign" that "works like a pun" but is "the lexical equivalent of two simultaneous, synchronized expansions generated parallel to each other, but separately."[56] Even though Asher, like most but not all of his contemporaries in Provence, could not read these texts in Arabic, he nonetheless becomes Judah's companion in reading the Arabs' books; as with Dunash, what is absent and allusive in a formulation is as important as what is present within it. And furthermore, as we saw in the introduction, Provence was not yet uniformly an Arabic desert; and so again this represents yet another instance of Judah speaking to multiple audiences. Returning to the ethical will, we see Judah commenting on the need for all words in poetry to be pleasant (*va-yehiyu ha-millot ʿarvot*).[57] Even as Judah insists that all the words within a poem be natively Hebrew, he nods to the Arabizing character of the secular Hebrew poetry of al-Andalus through the way he chooses to play on the root ʿ-R-B to describe good poetic style and diction. By hinting at a connection between *ʿarav* and *ʿarev*, a phenomenon that can be seen quite commonly in the work of the culturally Judaeo-Arabic writers,[58] Judah establishes an Arabizing linguistic ground against which ornament, elegance, rhetoric, and poetry can indeed come out ahead of Scripture, just as we saw Scripture sublimated to the act of translation itself in the previous chapter.

Muslim writers writing in Arabic, too, had begun to seize on the notion of untranslatability as a more fruitful way of articulating the relationship between Scripture and poetry and discuss the contours of their own human, literary heritage. Another example of an almost dogmatic insistence on the untranslatability of poetry is found in *Kitāb al-Ḥayawān* of the eighth-century Baṣran writer al-Jāḥiẓ, whose work was available in al-Andalus as early as the middle of the ninth century and influenced subsequent work of Andalusi writers even including, as we shall see in the next chapter, Judah ibn Tibbon himself. Influential among medieval writers in both the Islamic East and West, he has also proven to be of considerable interest to modern literary theorists, particularly following the creation of new editions and translations of the texts by James Montgomery that have made accessible sections of Jāḥiẓ's literary theory to scholars working past the material turn in book history,[59] and has attracted particular attention in both theoretical and scholarly writing. Among those with a renewed interest in Jāḥiẓ as a theorist of translation is the critic Abdelfattaḥ Killito, who is attracted by Jāḥiẓ's question regarding the blameworthiness of poor translations of poetry and philosophy; in reading his work, Killito arrives at the conclusion that it is precisely the distinction in where to place the blame that defines the special characteristic of poetry: "However skillful the translator, poetry refuses translation, and if it is transferred from its original language into another one, it loses its value and becomes a distorted, disfigured text."[60]

Killito identifies the central distinction Jāḥiẓ makes between poetry and prose texts on philosophy and theology. Both are untranslatable, but this characteristic inheres in the one form because of the nature of the text while being accidental to the other, which might in and of itself be translatable but for the inherent human flaws of translators. But he also wrote that both poetry and religious texts are fundamentally not fully translatable out of Arabic. Religious prose texts, he writes, are untranslatable because of the difficulty of the subject matter as well as the inimitability of the language, while poetry poses special linguistic challenges that a translator must be able to surmount in two languages:

> How should a translator be made aware of the workings of the rhetorical devices, simile and paronomasia? How will he be made to know what divine revelation is? What about metonymy? Will he know the dividing line between pernicious and deliberately doubt-inducing prattle and that which is more innocent, even comical in its nature? And what about the differences between restricted, unrestricted, and abridged speech? How do we induce him to know the syntactical structure of the language, the habits and customs of the people and their means and methods of reaching accord? These are but a few of many things to be considered. And whenever the translator is ignorant of or insensitive to any one of these things, he will commit errors in interpreting religious texts. . . . Suppose one well versed in Greek were to forward to one well versed in Arabic a piece rendered into Arabic via some translator. Then suppose the targeted Arab recipient was not versed in the area of Greek rhetoric. He would consequently find no deficiency or shortcoming in either the intermediate translator nor the semantic content of the rendered work. The Greek, unsatisfied with his level of proficiency with respect to Arabic, would find no other choice than to pardon and excuse the two parties involved.[61]

He continues to develop the particulars of poetry as an untranslatable form when he writes that it is a phenomenon owed to the miraculous character of the language in which it is written: "Through this process some of these works have increased in excellence and some had forfeited a portion for their original quality. And had the genius of the Arabs been converted, that miracle which is meter would have been rendered null and void. . . . It has been confirmed that books and poetry are superior to the monuments in their ability to preserve the grand achievements of civilization."[62] Thus we see that when Judah goes on to argue for the untranslatability of poetry, he does so well within the framework of the Arabic literary tradition as it was received and spread in al-Andalus.

PROSE AND POETRY SEPARATE IN PRACTICE

A distinction between prose and poetry is something that is consistently manifest throughout Judah's oeuvre when he writes about poetry; he observes differences not only in the way that the two modes must be approached by translators, but also by those composing new texts. One of the clearest and most practical elements of Judah's poetics is, in effect, a style guide that offers advice on how to write clearly by drawing a contrast between the specific requirements of good style imposed for prose and poetry. He first addresses prose composition, reminding Samuel that all prose writing must be grammatically correct, with particular attention to agreement in gender between verb and subject:

> My son, when you write any document, return to it and read it aloud because there is no man who[se writing] is completely error-free. . . . Be on your guard against errors in language: in verbal forms, in grammar, and in gender agreement. Sometimes errors in these areas creep in from the vernacular. Mistakes that a man makes are seized on and he is remembered by them for the rest of his life. . . . Be careful with conjunctions and particles and with how you use them, and with verbs and how you conjugate them. . . . In your writing, try to be elegant, brief, and concise. Do not try to make your writing rhyme unless you can do so perfectly and avoid heaviness.

He also explains to him that everyone makes mistakes when they write first drafts quickly and that this is the reason for careful editing and review. He holds up concision, elegance, and fluidity as the highest virtues in writing prose texts. He then goes on to address the set of stylistic requirements that he considers applicable to poetry: "You should also do the same thing when writing poetry. Avoid drawing in heavy expressions and excess verbiage. Let your words be pleasant and light on the tongue. Verbal forms should be ones that are attested in the language; do not incorporate any foreign ones, nor any other foreign lexical items. Even if you can explain them by analogy, such words are unnatural."[63] Even as he admits some contiguity of style between prose and prosodic writing, Judah nonetheless, and just as he does in the letter to Asher, separates out poetry from all other types of writing. This example takes that principle to a new extreme, wherein Judah actively contravenes one of the most central practices of his work as a translator of prose texts, namely the coining of new terminology and the adaptation of foreign words for use in technical discourses on philosophy and science in Hebrew.[64] Yet here in the ethical will, in the section on prosody, he tells Samuel to avoid doing that very thing: No coining new terms or using foreign ones.[65] Even though Hebrew poetry was stylistically Arabizing, the lexical content was ideally to be purely and exclusively Hebrew. Among all the types of writing Judah could undertake or translate or contemplate or write about, poetry would always be distinct in its underpinnings, its composition and reception.

Judah is not principally recognized as a poet himself, and perhaps not without reason. As we have seen over the course of this chapter, Judah was well versed in the poetry and the poetics of the Hebrew poets of Spain; but his poetry found at the openings and closings of his prefaces and ethical will shows him to have been less proficient, by the measure of the standards that he himself knew so well, as a practitioner of that art. While he adheres to the basics of his own statement of poetic style, using verbs attested in the biblical corpus and a "light" style (although this could be the subject of some debate), for the most part he does not conform to the principles of poetics that otherwise governed the craft by the middle of the twelfth century. His diction is repetitive in ways that are anathema to good style as defined by concision and inventiveness. For example, in lines 7, 9, and 10 of the opening poem, which is monorhyme in—*me'/—meh*, he achieves that rhyme by repeating the word *yegame'*, each time with the same sense; as did Ibn Rashiq before him, Ibn 'Ezra' notes this as a poetic failing.[66] Furthermore, Judah makes neither the expected nor any kind of unexpected, innovative use of figurative language, and his metrical sense requires some unusual reformulation of the rules of Hebrew syllabification, even by the relaxed standards of his poetic contemporaries, who took full advantage of the influence of Arabic syllabification on Hebrew.[67] The poems that bookend the prose body of the ethical will are composed roughly in one of the meters that is not imported from Arabic poetics but is, instead, native to Arabizing Hebrew poetry: *mishqal ha-tenu'ot*.[68] This is a meter that is characterized by lines consisting of two feet, each with four pairs of long syllables, with the feet separated by a caesura;[69] Judah's syllabification, however, includes a variety of syllables that in only the most creative way of counting might be construed as long ones.[70] The body of Judah's work itself shows a clear practical distinction between the theory of poetry, expounded on expertly in prose, and the practice of poetry, with the composition of verse so strikingly out of line with its author's understanding of the theory that it cannot but invite the kind of qualitative assessment that scholars of literature are mostly trained to avoid rendering; in other words, Judah was a terrible if historically important poet.[71]

Nevertheless, in spite of its full complement of technical and aesthetic gaffes, Judah's poetry provides a bespoke proving ground for assessing his poetics. It is on that proving ground that we discover the depth of the separation that he makes between prose and poetry. It is only through Judah's poetry that he is able to address certain themes, both through substance and rhetoric, that are left aside in the prose body of the text of the ethical will. Specifically with respect to his insistence on the firm and total distinction between prose and poetry, we find that particularly manifest in the ethical will and in the way that it blends and fails to blend the two modes of writing; furthermore, the particular balance that he strikes impels further forward his broader cultural argument about the particular cultural value of Arabic and its literary and other textual forms. And so even where he makes a hash of it, his use of *mishqal ha-tenu'ot* makes an argument that is equal measures Hebrew poetry and Arabic poetry. Additionally, the kind of content that he consigns to poetry, contrasted with what is covered in the prose body of the work, highlights the distinctions that he saw between prose and poetry and what they could do, and even marshals them to support his cultural convictions.

In the general introduction to this work, I referred to the distinction that James T. Robinson has identified between the biblically inflected *ẓeva'ah* form and the Arabic *waṣīya* documentary form that finds its origins in the early years of Islam;[72] in the context of the present discussion, I would like to examine the ways in which distinctions between prose and poetry in the ethical will further open up the cleavage between the two formal models that inform the structure of the text. The concluding poem in particular represents a superficial articulation of the genre of the Hebrew ethical will and echoes the rhetoric and literary character of its model, Deuteronomy 32, and throws into sharp relief the contrast in content with that which the prose body of the text cannot do as it more closely resembles Arabo-Muslim *waṣīya* documents, fulfilling the functions of curriculum, community document, and cultural-intellectual legacy.[73] The concluding poem touches only briefly on the intellectual and professional matters that are of such central concern in the prose section of the text; and even when it does address those topics it does so without the characteristic sophistication and simultaneous, encapsulated address to multiple audiences that characterizes the prose body of the ethical will. A mere 12 of the 144 lines of the concluding poem deal with the topic of writing that, as we have seen and shall continue to see, forms such an important part of the content of the prose section of the text:

Be careful of mistakes in your writing
  lest they disgrace you when it is time to be read
It garners shame from the audience
  and is seen as a defect and error.

Return to your books once you have written them
so that you won't leave out letters or phrases from them.
Know that a man's words and books
indicate the rectitude of his intellect and character.
From afar, men will praise him for his writing
or write him off and mock him for his writing.
Through his wisdom he will be the best of the flock
and though his understanding, honored among his cohort.[74]

Other instructions about work and professional commitments are sparing and general:

Give no due to play or happiness
Do not choose recreation or relaxation
And do not let your heart tend towards rest
lest you be left in the lurch afterwards.
Engage yourself but do not take on too much.
Do not take your ancestors' inheritance as a surety.
Work until you have fulfilled your needs.[75]

Aside from these two sections of the poem, its overwhelming interest is in the correct treatment of family and friends[76] and in steadfast religious practice and belief in God.[77] Its form is more like the aphoristic ethical will that we saw in the general introduction and the aphoristic poetry in Judah's model, *After Proverbs*, than the narrative type of ethical bequest that follows in prose; the poetic sections allow Judah to walk the line between Hebrew and Arabic models and to speak to a distinct set of concerns.

Where Judah does attempt to make poetically effective poetry, it is very much in the service of the familial and personal rather than the professional.[78] The poems and the beginning and the end of the ethical will themselves touch on issues of both personal and national separation, of family and of exile. The prose body of the text, composed beginning in or around 1172, is something to which Judah returned to and revised at different moments in Samuel's life; it was not considered complete until Judah's death in 1190. This continual history of redaction leaves the text with chronological strata, in places addressing an adolescent just beginning to develop the skills that will afford him entrée into the vaunted and venerable family profession of translation, and in others admonishing the groom about to marry and start a family, and in still others reproaching the man who has begun to stand on his own two feet in his mercantile business and make decisions that are not the ones his father would have made. These strata in the text do not always run chronologically, but the opening paragraphs do appear to be among the first composed. At the outset of the prose composition, Judah addresses a twelve-year-old Samuel:

> You know, my son, that I nurtured and embraced you and that I raised you to be wise and well mannered. I set you out down the path of wisdom and into the realm of integrity. I kept you in food, drink, and clothes. I went to great trouble so you could study. I protected you from fear. I sacrificed sleep to make you wiser, better educated, and better mannered than all of your peers. Over these past twelve years I have abstained from every nicety and worldly pleasure that a man could enjoy; and I am still working to build up your inheritance.[79]

Juxtaposed against this address to the youngest Samuel we will meet, the poetic preamble that immediately precedes it is an anachronistic, wistful, out-of-order coda written after Samuel had achieved many of Judah's goals for him, having gone into business and begun to travel:

> Take this father's advice, given from his broken heart as you set out like the ebbing tide.
> With great, unending grief his eyes are emptied out as never before.
> God has tested him through the wanderings of his children, unequal to other fathers;
> and time has provoked the heart within him, enticing and inveigling him.
> It sent him into the chasm of separation and cast him onto a sea of grief.
> It impoverished him through their wandering and his yearning as though he were clothed in their robes.
> With sound and fury it shall come to perturb him and then envelop him,
> perturb him with absinth and poison on his plate and in his cup.
> His eyes drooped, full of tears, almost as though he could see as little light as a blind man.
> They did not fall to the desolate earth, but made reeds and shrubs grow.
> He eats the bread of tears and drinks, thirsty and deep, of the tears.
> His soul abhorred all food because he saw all as unclean.
> My God, my God, why and how has all of this bad come to me?
> And until when will this separation be in force?[80]

Bolstered, as was stylistically appropriate, by citations of and allusions to the biblical books of Job, Lamentations, and Psalms, Judah utilizes an extended metaphor to describe a literal wave of pain that surges in proportion to the scale of his longing for his son.[81] He begins by speaking of the sea of grief when he describes Samuel setting out by that same sea to travel and trade, using a motif that is typical for *ʿaṭlāl* (lamenting over the ruins of the beloved's encampment) and *nasib* (elegy) sections of Arabic poetry;[82] by the time he progresses to describe the more internal ramifications of the pain of his separation, the water in the poem is on the scale of drops of poison and tears. The motif of crying tears into another body of water (though usually a river that is portrayed as a messenger, conveying the tears downstream) is catalogued thoroughly in *Kitāb al-Muḥāḍara*[83] and exists across the Arabic poetic corpus and in its indigenous works of poetic theory. Despite his apparent awareness of how to use the motif of tears turning into a sea after the departure of a beloved,[84] Judah fails to utilize other related techniques. Both Montgomery and Sperl identify seafaring references that are coupled with carefully selected epithets of God that relate divine power to the separating power of the sea; any kind of literary connection between the divine and the ocean is absent in spite of several appeals to God within the poem and even though such a connection is regularly made in Andalusi Hebrew sea poetry, including that of Judah's very literary role model, Samuel ibn Naghrīla. Whereas the overwhelming concern of the prose section of the text deals with Judah's day-to-day contact with Samuel and opinions about his life, the poetic introduction is entirely concerned with Judah's longing for his only son and the loneliness he felt in his absence. Even as the poem itself is somewhat one-dimensional, its presence within the integral textual unit of the ethical will demonstrates Judah's ability to use the poetic form to serve a variety of different purposes and to address various audiences from within a single text.

The thematic content of the poetry, on top of its technical failings, mean that it is the poetry rather than the prose that fulfills the stated purpose of the ethical will to be a kind of deuteronomic bequest. Whereas the subtle complexities of the rhetoric and content in the prose body of the text make those sections about Arabic literature and literacy, about community formation and identity, about reading, and about al-Andalus and Judah's fading memory of his glistening pomegranate of a homeland, it is as much (if not more so) about a father's guidance to his son wherein the poetry speaks a plainer, simpler truth in a specific form. Judah's lesser skill as a poet than as a writer of prose does not allow him to layer meaning on top of meaning and instead limits him to the single dimension of his stated purpose, to write a deuteronomic *ẓeva'ah* or *musar av*. It is in the wholly different world of prose composition that he can more deftly use the available literary forms to engage with the totality of the textual possibilities for communicating to Samuel and to his adopted and natal communities.

Across the board, medieval poetic thinking makes all kinds of distinctions between prose and poetry. At times these distinctions were made along generic lines, protecting the "inviolate tradition which formally excluded the meterless rhymed-prose narrative from the category of poetry."[85] In other instances, the boundaries between prose and poetry served to reinforce national ideals in a universe that could not yet truly accommodate the idea of nation: "The borders of that national territory are projected onto the borders of the language."[86] But despite these real and significant generic distinctions, the same authors wrote prose and poetry that could comfortably inhabit a single textual space.[87]

We can even see how clear this distinction was to later medieval and early modern readers of the ethical will and how predominant it became in their reading. The single surviving complete manuscript of the ethical will reflects an understanding of the separateness of the prefatory poems from the rest of the text on the part of a later medieval or early modern reader. This reader is the copyist, known to us only as Yo'av. We meet him in the colophon of the Bodleian manuscript, which reads:[88]

> Completed—praise God!—by the hand of Yo'av [in 1341]; please, God, redeem my soul. May God give His good refuge to all of Israel; let all of them be amongst those inscribed for eternal life in the world to come. Amen, amen, amen. For the sake of Your name, God, renew my life through Your justice, free my soul from its straits, through Your mercy repress my enemies, and dismiss my troubles; because I am your servant. Lord, honored be your name.

The supplication that follows the declaration of the completion of the manuscript, *ana adonai, malṭa nafshi*[89] (please, God, redeem my soul), appears in the *Hallel* cycle of Psalms recited during the pilgrimage and other festivals; that phrase is rendered as acronym, with only the first letter of each word given: *aleph*, *yud*, *mem*, *nun*, each letter with a single point above it to indicate the first letter of an omitted word (see Plate 12). Such acronyms, when found in colophons, often represent chronograms, the encoding of dates within abbreviated liturgical or scriptural phrases. The numerical value of this abbreviation, based upon the numerical value of each letter within the system that assigns such a value to each Hebrew letter, equals 101. Chronograms often omit the initial indication of 5,000 years since the creation of the world in the reckoning of the Jewish calendar, with readers knowing to supply it.[90] Thus, the chronogram in this colophon refers to the year 5101, or 1340/1341 of the Common Era; this specific date comports with older catalogue descriptions of this manuscript that, on the basis of the scribal hand, place its origins in France sometime between the mid-fourteenth and mid-fifteenth centuries. The phrase with which Yo'av indicates the date is an unusual one to find in a colophon, and so it is possible that he is indicating completion of the manuscript shortly before one of the three major pilgrimage festivals when this psalm was used in a liturgical setting; thus we can suggest at least tentatively that the manuscript was copied sometime between the first and last of the pilgrimage festivals of the Jewish calendar, namely Sukkot and Shavuot, of 5101, that is, between the fifteenth day of the month of Tishrei, or October 7, 1340, and the beginning of Shavuot in that same year on the Jewish calendar, the sixth day of the month of Sivan, or May 23, 1341. Yo'av was copying the manuscript, then, at a considerable remove in both space and time from the Andalusi context that the text's author, Judah ibn Tibbon, so emphasizes throughout the work.

One of the most striking decisions that Yo'av made as scribe was to separate the prefatory poem out into an otherwise unmarked margin on the leading edge of the page (see Plate 1). This margin is a visual manifestation of the boundaries and tensions between poetry and prose in medieval text that resonates with modern readers' and editors' own tendency and quickness to read over and around and past the poetry that is an integral, if conflictive, part of many medieval prose texts.[91] Viewed through the eyes of the modern medievalist, the poetry on the edge of this manuscript's pages is a concrete illustration of the facility with which medieval historiography and criticism marginalize verse.[92] What was once preface becomes marginal ornamentation, turning against each other the two modes of text that had coexisted unitarily: "Once the manuscript page becomes a matrix of visual signs and is no longer one of flowing linear speech, the stage is set not only for supplementation and annotation but also for disagreement and juxtaposition—what the scholastics called *disputation*."[93] In this case, the disputation is between the poetry and the prose, shouted across the gulf of white space that separates the text block from the margin peopled in verse, its meaning "perched between [the] grace" of the poetry and the "garrulousness" of the prose.[94]

The location of the poetry in the outer margin of the text obviously and literally marginalizes it. It also relegates the poetry to the physical position and thus to the function of commentary on the text. Borrowed into Hebrew scribal and codicological practice from Latin glossed manuscripts, the main body of a Hebrew text, especially if a biblical or talmudic one, was often copied into the center of the page with commentaries copied into the side and top margins.[95] Yo'av, the copyist of Bodleian Mich. MS 50.3, was working within this framework but also, in keeping with changing norms, was beginning to transgress what had been an inviolate boundary. Vertically scored lines that mark the bounds of columns and margins are an "integral" feature of the page destined to be filled with Hebrew text, and "until the fourteenth century, the ruled line was treated with absolute respect."[96] In the ethical will, the lines were transgressed and a margin imagined onto the page with poetry rather than with rules. On the one hand, the thematic sweep of the verse is as much a father's lament as it is an invitation for the later scribe to cast it across a space, in a margin, by being the unique locus for the discussion of separation. The poetry interacts with the prose by separating itself from it temporally, tonally, and thematically and invites and amplifies the reaction of the later scribe and later readers who would already be uncomfortable with the presence of poetry in a prose epistle: uncomfortable poetry of separation separated—simultaneously uncomfortably and naturally—into a margin. But on the other hand, when we read this or other historical texts without the poetry included within them, we lose a valuable medieval commentary on the prose; by placing the poetry in the margin, the scribe paradoxically converted it into a cipher integral to the interpretation of the text as a whole, separating it from a text from which it was never meant to be apart while simultaneously making it a part inseparable from the text.

Through his diffuse poetics and his bad poetry, Judah ibn Tibbon continues to convey the notion of Arabic as a source of cultural prestige. By turning to the Hebrew versions of a form that is taken to so essentially demonstrate the merit of the Arabic language and the skills of its best masters, Judah speaks to a fully Hebrew audience quietly and subtly about the Arabic underpinnings of the literature to which they so desired access. Judah's poetics and poetry manifest a kind of secularizing Andalusi cultural nationalism cloaked for a European Jewish audience. This is not to say that Judah's poetics is an inauthentic one; rather, simply, it is one that shrewdly knows its audience and itself and plays to both.

NOTES

Chapter title from Judah ibn Tibbon, "Letter to Asher ben Meshullam of Lunel."

1. Qur'ān 36:69, trans. N. J. Dawood (reprint, New York: Penguin, 2005).

2. Muḥammad ibn al-Ṭayyib al-Bāqillānī, *A Tenth-Century Document of Arabic Literary Theory and Criticism: The Sections on Poetry of I'jāz al-Qur'ān. Ed. Gustave von Grunebaum* (Chicago: University of Chicago Press, 1950), 53–54. The Arabic text appears in an edition published in Cairo in 1930. Other foundational tenth-century texts that deal with the notion of *i'jāz al-Qur'ān* and its reconciliation with poetic writing and culture include those written by 'Abd al-Qāhir al-Jurjānī (*Al-Nukat fī i'jāz al-Qur'ān* [Samplings of the Inimitability of the Qur'ān]) and al-Khattabī (*Bayān i'jāz al-Qur'ān* [Proof of the Inimitatbility of the Qur'ān]).

3. Kh in particular, see Geert van Gelder's discussion of the development of metaphoric language (*majāz*) in relationship to this concept in *Beyond the Line: Classical Arabic Literary Critics on the Coherence and Unity of the Poem* (Leiden: Brill, 1982), 5–7.

Particularly in cases such as that of the Ibn Tibbon family, where we are dealing with texts that are firmly part of some canons (most significantly, the canon of medieval Jewish philosophy and even medieval philosophy more general) while remaining on the margins of other canons (as in the case of classical Arabic poetics, which is both materially and artificially differentiated from Judaeo-Arabic poetics), it is important to assert a point to which we return several times in this chapter: Regardless of the dependency of middle Arabic poetics on classical Arabic poetics, the latter cannot be an absolute benchmark in assessing the former, which continued to develop its own conventions and practices.

4. David Yellin, *Spanish Poetic Theory* (Jerusalem: Magnes Press, 1972). See also two articles by Federico Corriente, "La métrica hebrea cuantitativa," *Sefarad* 46 (1986): 123–32; and "Again on the Metrical System of the Muwaššaḥ and Zajal," *Journal of Arabic Literature* 17 (1985): 34–49.

5. Ezra Fleischer, "On Dunash ben Labraṭ, His Wife and His Son," *Jerusalem Studies in Hebrew Literature* 5 (1984). It is perhaps interesting to note that the poetic voice described as Dunash's refers to his wife in a poem as *maskelet*, that is, cultured or wise: "How could I betray a wise woman (*maskelet*) like you?" Judah uses the same term, not a typical adjective used to describe women in texts from this period, to apply it to his daughter-in-law as he urges Samuel to treat his wife well to the best of his ability: "My son, I also order you to honor your wife to the best of your ability because she is a wise (*maskelet*) and modest woman" (78).

6. Of course, this holds only if we take Fleischer's interpretation of the poem at face value.

7. Editions of the writings between Dunash and Menahem are listed in the bibliography. Aharon Maman, in his *Comparative Semitics*, (Leiden: Brill, 2004) compiles these references and creates a meta-study that incorporates the secondary analyses of Dunash's linguistic work; see esp. 289–95. Another overview of Dunash's work as a grammarian may be found in Angel Saénz-Badillos. "Early Hebraists in Spain." A classic, if now somewhat outdated, source on the dispute between Dunash and Menahem and their partisans remains Eliahu Ashtor's *The Jews of Moslem Spain* (reprint, Philadelphia: Jewish Publication Society, 1992).

8. See the discussion in chapter 3. See also Maman, *Comparative Semitic Philology in the Middle Ages* (Leiden: Brill, 2004), chapter 7 and, additionally, pp. 384–92.

9. On the question of Menaḥem as a comparatist, and the extent to which later readers, both medieval and modern, have shaped that question to suit their own linguistic and cultural agendas, see Maman, *Comparative Semitics*, 276.

10. Fleischer, "Towards a History of Secular Hebrew Poetry," in *Culture and Community in the History of the Jews of the Middle Ages*, Ed. Reuven Bonfil and Menahem Ben-Sasson (Jerusalem: Zalman Shazar Center, 1989).

11. Joseph Tobi, *Between Hebrew and Arabic Poetry: Studies in Spanish Medieval Hebrew Poetry* (Leiden: Brill, 2010), 31, 39–43. While I disagree with Tobi's assessment of the moralizing character of much of the corpus, I find his formulation of the secular poet as cultural hero (in line with, if a bit more exaggerated than, Freudenthal's figure of the cultural intermediary referenced in the first chapter) to be a useful one in this context.

12. Abraham ibn 'Ezra', *Commentary on Ecclesiastes*, chap. 5. Compare with Samuel ibn Tibbon's discussion of poetry in his *Commentary on Ecclesiastes*.

13. Judah Halevi, *Kuzari*, II.63–80; and his *Treatise on Poetic Meters*, ed. and trans. Tova Rosen, in *Israel Levine Jubilee Volume*, ed. Reuven Tzur and Tova Rosen (Tel Aviv: Tel Aviv University Press, 1994), 324–28.

14. Ross Brann, *The Compunctious Poet: Cultural Ambiguity and Hebrew Poetry in Muslim Spain* (Baltimore: The Johns Hopkins University Press, 1991), 23–26.

15. I am using the term *'arabiyya* here to refer specifically to the linguistic and cultural Arabization of Jews in Spain and the particular cultural and religious responses that this acculturation provoked, local and concomitant to it specifically; it should not be understood in this usage to invite a reading in the traditional binary framework of *'arabiyya* (Arabness) and *shu'ūbiyya* (other people-ness). At its inception, the cultural movement known as *'arabiyya* refers to the privileged position of Arabs within early Islamic society, as contrasted with *shu'ūbiyya* as the cultural response to it, spearheaded by Persian political and intellectual elites who sought to bolster the cultural position and prestige of non-Arabs within the Islamic world. One true incident of *shu'ūbiyya* occurred in al-Andalus in the middle of the eleventh century, when Abū Amīr Aḥmad ibn Gharsiyya, a vizier at the court of Mujāhid al-Amirī at Denia who had been born to a Christian family, kidnapped as a child and raised as a Muslim, wrote an explicitly *shu'ūbī* epistle defending himself and his non-Arab patrons against claims of Arab supremacy from the court of the rival party kingdom at Almería. The existing dichotomy between *'arabiyya* and *shu'ūbiyya* makes for an attractive framework in which to understand the response of culturally Judaeo-Arabic writers to the advent and normalization of Arabic literature and its implication for their Judaeo-Arabic- and Hebrew-language production. However, the implication of active competition and polemic within that dichotomy means that it cannot precisely reflect the attitudes of these writers to the languages, literatures, and audience identities implicated in their work and its reception. On the question of *'arabiyya* within the wider Judaeo-Arabic cultural world, see Nehemiah Allony, "The Hebrew *Egron* as a Response to the 'Arabiyya," in *The Zalman Shazar Jubilee Volume*, ed. B. Luria (Jerusalem: Qiryat Sefer, 1973), 465–74; and "The Reaction of Moses ibn 'Ezra' to 'Arabiyya," *Bulletin of Jewish Studies* 3 (1975): 19–40. For a general discussion of the rise of the *shu'ūbī* movement, see H. A. R. Gibb, "The Social Significance of the Shu'ūbiyya," in *Studies in the Civilization of Islam* (reprint, Princeton, NJ: Princeton University Press, 1982), 62–73; Ignaz Goldziher, "'Arab and 'Ajam," and "Shu'ūbiyya," in *Muslim Studies*, vol. 1 (reprint, Chicago: Aldine, 1968), 98–168. For the specific application of *shu'ūbiyya* in al-Andalus, see James T. Monroe, *Shu'ubiyya in al-Andalus: The Risāla of Ibn García and Five Refutations* (Berkeley: University of California Press, 1970); Goran Larssen, *Ibn García's Shu'ūbiyya Letter: Ethnic and Theological Tensions in Medieval al-Andalus* (Leiden: Brill, 2003); and Goldziher, "Die Shu'ūbijja unter den Muhammedanern in Spanien," *Zeitschrift der Deutschen Morgenländischen Gesellschaft* 53 (1899): 601–20.

16. Moses ibn 'Ezra', *Kitāb al-Muḥāḍara wa-l-muḏākara*, f. 31r.

17. *Shemuel met, beno Labraṭ* (Samuel, son of Labrat, has died). Hayyim Schirman, *Hebrew Poetry in Spain and Provence* (Jerusalem: Mosad Biyalik, 1957), 1:204.

18. "*Mi Dunash, emor, u-mi Menaḥem . . . halo ein ve-efes hem lenegdi?*" in Schirman, *Hebrew Poetry*, 1:145.

19. *Taḥkemoni*, 107.

20. *Taḥkemoni*, 209–33 (please note that in Yahalom and Katsumata's edition, this is *maqāma* 12).

21. On Ibn Khalfūn, see Ann Brener, *Isaac ibn Khalfun: A Wandering Hebrew Poet of the Eleventh Century* (Leiden: Brill, 2003).

22. Abraham ibn Daūd, *Sefer ha-Qabbalah*, ed. and trans. Gerson D. Cohen (Philadelphia: Jewish Publication Society, 1967), 46–74(H). Ibn Daūd's drive to demonstrate and perpetuate the superiority of the Jewish community of Córdoba over that of Baghdad could be one of the factors that led to this otherwise curious omission; by eliminating Dūnash, whose formation occurred at the hands of Sa'adya, from his nationalistic accounting of the Hebrew poets, Ibn Daūd diminishes the direct influence of the Babylonian geonate on the development of Andalusi literary culture. However, it is also important to note that Ibn Daūd's own aesthetic preferences also factored heavily into his categorization and typology (for further discussion of this phenomenon, see Cohen's notes to the text, 267–68).

23. See Ángel Sáenz-Badillos, "La obra de Abraham ibn Ezra sobre las críticas contra Se'adyah," *Abraham ibn Ezra and His Age*, ed. Fernando Díaz Esteban (Madrid: Asociación Española de Orientalistas, 1990), 287–88, for further discussion on whether a reference to a certain 'Adonim ha-Levi, a Hebrew name by which Dunash is also known, is, in fact, also a reference to him or a conflation with or reference to another writer.

24. Leo Strauss, *Persecution and the Art of Writing* (Chicago: University of Chicago Press, 1952). Despite the caveats delineated by Dimitri Gutas in his "The Study of Arabic Philosophy in the Twentieth Century: An Essay on the Historiography of Arabic Philosophy," *BJMES* 29 (2002): 16–19, Strauss is perhaps one of the most productive founts of theoretical modeling through which to consider Judaeo-Arabic writing in general and Judah ibn Tibbon in particular. Because of his academic interest in classical and Jewish philosophy, his work is well calibrated to the issues at play here and specifically to their exploration within this textual corpus. His theory of writing between the lines, developed specifically to address the question of Maimonides' rhetoric and the seeming lack of subtlety in the exoterica in the *Guide of the Perplexed*, speaks very clearly to the issue of Judaeo-Arabic authors needing to address different audiences from within the same text, particularly as they turned from the Arab world to a non-Arabophone, Christian Europe.

25. "*Beni, sim sefarekha ḥavereikha ve-ganotekha, ve-'argazekha pardesekha*," in "Musar Av," 16b.

26. "*Ve-gan 'ednakh yihyu sifrei qodshim/u-fardeskha yihyu sifrei 'aravim*," in *Teshuvot Yehudi ibn Seshet*, 37; Dunash ben Labrat, Shirim, ed. Nehemiah Allony (Jerusalem, 1948). 93.

27. *Sefer ha-Shorashim*, ed. Wilhelm Bacher (Berlin: Defus Itzikovsky, 1896), 96.

28. Often times when we see poetry quoted within prose texts, the prose texts become our single source for the preservation of poetry that is otherwise lost, such as Samuel ibn Naghrīla's lost ode to his pen, which is preserved partially, quoted only in a few lines, in an adoring Judah ibn Tibbon's ethical will. This epigram of Dunash is often regarded as the opening line of a longer poem, the rest of which is thought lost. However, to have it quoted in Yehudi's edition of the *diwān* and then to have the same line referenced within a prose work raises the question of whether this was only ever an epigram. It is quite probable that the rest of the poem was lost by the time it got to Judah, but to have two citations of the same line does raise at least the possibility of whether it was only ever an epigram.

29. As shall be noted in greater detail below, there is a direct association in the field of medieval lexicography with the simple word *gan* and the paradise of the Garden of

Eden. For Andalusi readers this also has many other, equally pleasurable, sometimes heavenly, and sometimes quite the opposite connotations. In fact, Jonathan Decter, in his *Iberian Jewish Literature* (Bloomington: Indiana University Press, 2007), has recognized the extent to which garden imagery is a kind of linchpin motif for the literary "culture of transition" of the poets moving out of al-Andalus while attempting to maintain ties to their literary grounding. In particular, he observes that when foreign visitors write about Granada, they exclusively make note of the garden landscapes there (21), and when local poets, including Ibn Shuhayd and Ibn Naghrīla, write laments over their lost cities, they often do so by extolling the gardens that had been destroyed or left behind (24–25). See the discussion on the pages following in Decter's book for further detail on the specific use of the Andalusi garden as a motif in Hebrew poetry in Christian Spain and a particularly incisive analysis of Moses ibn 'Ezra''s attempt to grapple with and replace that favored set of images.

30. Decter, *Iberian Jewish Literature*, x; and Yaseen Noorani, "The Lost Garden of al-Andalus: Islamic Spain and the Poetic Inversion of Colonialism," *International Journal of Middle East Studies* 31, no. 2 (1999): 237–54.

31. Decter, *Iberian Jewish Literature*, 24.

32. The identification of orchards with specific groves of pomegranate seeds is a deep-seated one in classical Jewish texts. The depth of this connection is illustrated in, among other places, BT Baba Meẓi'a 104a, which contains a discussion about the definition of what constitutes a *pardes* for the purpose of determining whether a sale of one has been legal. The text concludes that while a *pardes* definitionally includes stands of pomegranate trees, if the seller discloses that his *pardes* lacks them, then the sale is still valid and has not been concluded under false pretenses; this demonstrates that the term *pardes* by default refers to a plot of land that includes pomegranate trees.

33. *Sefer ha-Shorashim*, 419. The etymology of the Arabic term is, of course, Persian. In his *Spanish Hebrew Poetry,* Arie Schippers makes much of the Persian etymons of many of the flower terms that appear in Arabic and Arabized Hebrew garden and nature poetry, arguing that this reflects a Persian origin for the poetic form (181–82); this seems somewhat overdetermined.

34. Judah ibn Tibbon, "Musar Av," 16b.

35. For an example that would come later in time of the juxtaposition of books, gardens, and architecture in Granada, see Juan Carlos Ruiz Souza, "El Palacio de los leones de la Alhambra: ¿Madrasa, zāwiya, y tumba de Muḥammad V?," *Al-Qantara* 22 (2001): 77–120.

36. Judah Halevi, cited in Judah ibn Tibbon, "Musar Av," 16b.

37. Although the edition of Yehudi survives in a single manuscript that offers up many difficulties in terms of its state of preservation and the skill of the scribe, there is no reason to doubt the wide dissemination of Dunash's work among medieval readers. In addition to the culturally Arabized writers referred to in the previous pages, recent scholarship has shown his impact on non-Arabophone readers. See, for example, Judith Olszowy-Schlanger, "Bilingual Hebrew-Latin Manuscripts," in *Hebrew Scholarship and the Medieval World*, ed. Nicholas de Lange (Cambridge: Cambridge University Press, 2001), 107–28; and Wout van Bekkum, "The Hebrew Grammatical Tradition in the Exegesis of Rashi," *Rashi, 1040–1990*, ed. Gabriel Sed-Rajna (Paris, 1993), 427–35. Both of these works demonstrate the influence of his work in Jewish and Christian grammatical and exegetical thinking in Europe.

38. This type of emendation through cultural translation of religious texts is detailed in Jonathan Decter, "The Rendering of Quranic Quotations in Hebrew Translations of Islamic Texts," *Jewish Quarterly Review* 96 (2006): 336–58. The same phenomenon, as it applies to literary toponyms, is studied in Abraham Lavi, "A Comparative Study of al-Ḥarīrī's Maqāmāt and the Hebrew Translations" (PhD diss., University of Michigan, 1979). The continuation of that phenomenon in the modern period, with explicitly cultural-nationalist goals, is discussed in Meron Benvenisti, *Sacred Landscapes* (Berkeley: University of California Press, 2002).

39. Maman, *Comparative Semitics*, 140–46.

40. Judah ibn Tibbon, "Musar Av," 16b.

41. Hirsch Edelman and Judah Lieb Dukes, *Ginzei Oxford: An Anthology of Piyyutim and Other Poems by the Beloved Poets of Old Spain* (London, 1850), 67.

42. Israel Davidson, *Thesaurus of Medieval Hebrew Poetry*, vol. 1, entry 2761 (New York: Ktav, 1970), 130. Davidson observes that in some places that the poem appears in print, modern editors have adopted Yo'av the scribe's misidentification of the source.

43. The scribe's general discomfort with the poetry cited throughout the text is the subject of the final section of this chapter.

44. Walter Benjamin, "The Task of the Translator," in *Illuminations* (New York: Schocken Books, 1969), 70–71.

45. See, for example, Emily Apter, *Against World Literature* (New York: Verso Books, 2013); Jacques Lezra, "This Untranslatability Which Is Not One," *Paragraph* 38, no. 2 (2015): 174–88, and "On Contingency in Translation," in *Early Modern Cultures in Translation*, ed. Karen Newman and Jane Tylus (Philadelphia: University of Pennsylvania Press, 2015), 153–74; and Zrinka Stahuliak, "Medieval Fixers: The Politics of Interpreting in Western Historiography," in *Rethinking Medieval Translation*, ed. Emma Campbell and Robert Mills (Woodbridge, UK: Boydell and Brewer, 2012), 14–63.

46. Benjamin, "Task of the Translator," 78–79.

47. Beyond the scope of the present discussion but equally fascinating is the mediation between the two notions of untranslatability with respect to Sa'adya's *Tafsīr*, a question that I hope to address in a subsequent project on the poetics of translation.

48. "Translation is so far removed from being the sterile equation of two dead languages that of all literary forms it is the one charged with the special mission of watching over the maturing process of the original language and the birth pangs of its own" (73). One wonders what Benjamin might have made of Tibbonid Hebrew, a new language born of translation of precisely the sort that Benjamin suggests cannot do such a thing.

49. Without wishing to dwell on the issue, since it is not directly related to questions of genre, I think it is nonetheless quite apropos to put some pressure on Judah's use of the term *qadmonim* here as it, too, speaks directly to his Arabic literary heritage. This remark cannot help but call up associations to the *qudamā'* of Arabic poetics. The *qudamā'*, also referred to as *mutaqaddimūn*, are "the ancients" or "ancient poets" of a predominant medieval Arabic poetic schema that, among other things, categorizes some poets as ancients and some as moderns, representing an observed break in the corpus, thematically and stylistically, between old and new as absolute categories that do not correspond simply with the rise of Islam. That is to say that the *jāhilī*, or pre-Islamic, poets do not represent the totality of the ancients; some Muslim writers are included in that category as well. For a good overview of the category of *qudamā'*, see Ignaz Goldziher's foundational study, "Alte und neue Poesie im Urtheile der arabische

Kritiker," in *Abhandlungen zur arabischer Philologie*, vol. 1 (Leiden: Brill, 1896), 122–76. More recently, the discussion of the ancient-modern distinction in classical Arabic poetry in Wolfhart Heinrichs's seminal article, "Prosimetrical Genres in Arabic Literature," in *Prosimetrum*, ed. Joseph Harris and Karl Reichl (Cambridge: Brewer, 1997), 249–76, is of particular interest because of the acknowledged interplay between poetry and history. This technique of appealing to the ancients and reading through a framework that distinguishes between what happened literarily from the historical reality around the mid-second through eighth centuries and onward is not unique to Judah among the Jewish writers. (It is also worth mentioning that this question of the *jāhiliya* as a metaphor in the construction of the Arabic identity of Arabophone Muslim and Jewish writers was a topic that Rina Drory was beginning to investigate at the time of her premature death in 2000.) It is a ready trope in the writing of the Judaeo-Arabic thinkers. In the surviving letter from Maimonides to Samuel, he expresses surprise at Samuel's very existence. In praising Samuel, Maimonides employs the rhetorical device of the "ancient poets," subsuming the work of the poet and theorist Moses ibn 'Ezra'—who himself develops a category of ancient poets in his own Judaeo-Arabic poetics—into that category of *qudamā'*. In response to Samuel's queries about terminology in the *Guide of the Perplexed* Maimonides praises their acuity: "I quoted an ancient poem: The father's excellence has passed to the son. Blessed is the one who compensated your father for his wisdom by giving him a son like this."

50. Judah ibn Tibbon, "Letter to Asher ben Meshullam of Lunel." The manuscript, like that of the ethical will, was owned by Joseph Michael Heimann and can now be found at the Bodleian Library as MS Mich. 240 and in the Neubauer catalogue as item 1402.

51. And, in fact, he never returned to translate the poetry interspersed through this work into Hebrew (see the notes in Wise's edition and translation of the Arabic text). The migration of Ibn Gabirol's poetry and poetic citations within that work is, therefore, one of reception history, the preliminary results of which are the subject of current work in progress.

52. Stephen S. Wise, ed., *The Improvement of Moral Qualities*, 106.

53. Brann, *The Compunctious Poet*, 23.

54. Judah ibn Tibbon, "Letter to Asher ben Meshullam of Lunel," 366.

55. That the author also plays on the personal name of the recipient in the opening formulae seems to confirm his willingness to pun. Judah engages in other instances of punning in the opening of his letter, making fruitful use, for example, of the homonymy of the recipient's name, Asher, with the Hebrew relative pronoun *asher*. For example, the opening salutations might also be understood as "My dear interlocutor, my close brother, Asher; his words light my path." Later, the letter also makes puns on Asher's name and its homophony with the verb *le-asher* (to authorize).

56. Michael Riffaterre, *Text Production* (New York: Columbia University Press, 1983), 64–65. For a discussion of this phenomenon in Jewish texts written within a non-Jewish cultural context, see Daniel Boyarin, *Intertextuality and the Reading of Midrash* (Bloomington: Indiana Univeristy Press, 1994), 57.

57. Ibn Tibbon, "Musar Av," 17b.

58. Judah is not unusual in using words built from this root in order to make a subtle association between certain literary characteristics and their Arabic context.

See, for example Brann's discussion (*The Compunctious Poet*, 36–37) of the use of Psalm 106:35 ("they mingled [*va-yit'arvu*] among the nations and learned their ways") as a way to comment on Jewish acculturation in the Arab world in the work of Halevi, al-Ḥarīzī, and Moses ibn 'Ezra'.

59. Both the Edinburgh University Press and the Library of Arabic Literature are publishing new editions and translations of various texts from Jāḥiẓ's ouvre; these are listed in the bibliography. For further discussion of the implication of Jāḥiẓ's writing in literary (and especially translation) theory and book history, see Peter Webb, "Foreign Books in Arabic Literature: Discourses on Books, Knowledge, and Ethnicity in the Writings of al-Jāḥiẓ," in *Journal of Arabic and Islamic Studies* 12 (2012): 16–55. Additional bibliography on this subject appear in the next chapter in the course of the more involved discussion of Judah as a reader of Jāḥiẓ. See also the discussion on Jāḥiẓ as a literary theorist, which includes a discussion in Wolfhart Heinrichs, "Isti'āra and Badī' and Their Terminological Relationship in Early Arabic Literary Criticism," *Zeitschrift für Geschichte der Arabisch Islamischen Wissenschaften* 1 (1984): 80–111; and Lara Harb, "Poetic Marvels: Wonder and Experience in Medieval Arabic Literary Theory" (PhD diss., New York University, 2013), 92–100.

60. Abdelfattah Killito, *Thou Shalt Not Speak My Language* (Syracuse: Syracuse University Press, 2008), 28.

61. Al-Jāḥiẓ, *Kitāb al-Ḥayawān*, ed. 'Abd al-Salam Muhammad Hārūn. Beirut: Dar al-Jīl, 1996. 75–76. Trans. Sherman Jackson, "Al-Jāḥiẓ on Translation," *Alif: Journal of Comparative Poetics* 4 (1984): 104–6.

62. Al-Jāḥiẓ, *Kitāb al-Ḥayawān*, 75. Trans. Sherman Jackson, "Al-Jāḥiẓ on Translation," 102.

63. Ibn Tibbon, "Musar Av," 17b.

64. Again, where Judah leads in his preface to *Sefer ha-Riqmah*, Samuel follows in his *Perush ha-Millot ha-Zarot*, once again demonstrating that in lexicographic matters, he falls closely into line.

65. It is also worth mentioning that Schirman ties Judah's younger contemporary Meshullam Depiera's poetic-morphological innovations directly to the wider Tibbonid project of Hebrew vocabulary coinage (*History of Hebrew Poetry in Christian Spain*, 321–29); and so even if Samuel did not situate himself in a literarily Provençal framework, that does not imply that such a framework did not draw on his presence within it.

66. Moses ibn 'Ezra', *Kitāb al-Muḥāḍara*, folios 125b–126b.

67. As noted, the early fights over the use of Arabic meter in Hebrew poetry were largely to do with the ability of the Hebrew vowel system to accommodate the kind of quantitative meter that is naturally concordant with Arabic. Even as the form reached its apogee, some liberties were inevitably taken with syllabification.

68. While it is not a meter that is found in Judah's favorite *After Proverbs*, it appears frequently elsewhere in the work of Samuel ibn Naghrīla and other Andalusi poets, who often make a habit of taking liberties with weighing syllable length.

69. In other words: — — — — — — — — || — — — — — — — —.

70. Judah uses long and short *a* and *e* vowels interchangeably and also uses the shewa as a long or short vowel with no regard for consistent application of the rules, biblical or medieval, for syllabifying quiescent and mobile *shewas*. This might raise the question about whether he is in fact using a different meter that I have not identified

here; however, an exhaustive consideration of the metrical possibilities has determined that *mishqal ha-tenu'ot* is, despite the places where it needs to be fudged, the best fit for this poem; even though this solution requires some creative syllabification, the other possibilities require total disregard for syllable length. And again, although Judah's case is extreme, the idea of taking some liberties with syllabification is not unheard of.

71. I would argue that there are quite a number of Arabizing Hebrew poets we could include in this category of historically important poetasters, which I label as "terrible" only with the deepest sense of affection for these poets and their poetry. Nevertheless, Judah's poetry is not solely a historical document; its aesthetic and communicative values, specifically the depth that the specifically bad poetry adds to the ethical will's double voice, are delineated below.

72. Please refer back to the discussion in the general introduction.

73. See the general introduction for discussion of the similarities and differences between Judaeo-Hebrew and Arabo-Muslim advice and ethical will documents. Because of the content differences between the prose body of the ethical will, which clearly plays a curricular (although I am loathe to use the word didactic) function, and the poetry that envelopes it, which deals more with moral guidance, it would not be appropriate to refer to this as didactic poetry, a category unto itself that exists in all the classical poetic traditions. For more on that separate category within the Arabic and Islamicate cultural contexts, see Geert van Gelder, "Arabic Didactic Verse," in *Centers of Learning*, ed. Jan Willem Drijvers and Alisdair MacDonald (Leiden: Brill, 1995), 103–17; and Rosa Kuhne Brabant, "Algunos aspectos de la literature didáctica entre los medicos árabes," in *Actas de las II Jornadas de Cultura Árabe e Islámica* (Madrid: Instituto Hispáno-Arabe, 1985), 273–80. See also Maud Kozody, "Medieval Hebrew Medical Poetry: Uses and Contexts," *Aleph* 11, no. 2 (2011): 213–88, which offers an overview of didactic poetry in Greek and Latin before discussing specifically medically didactic poetry written in Hebrew.

74. Ibn Tibbon, "Musar Av," 20b.

75. Ibid., 20a.

76. Ibid., 20b.

77. Ibid., 20a–b.

78. In fact, as Rina Drory points out in her *Models and Contacts* (Leiden: Brill, 2000), classical Arabic poetics typically leaves very little room for autobiographic disclosure, and it is the great innovation of the culturally Judaeo-Arabic prose writers that they were able to accommodate that kind of disclosure within a framework that would otherwise not accommodate it (although, for a challenge to this conventional interpretation of the literary landscape, see Dwight F. Reynolds et al., *Interpreting the Self: Autobiography in the Arabic Literary Tradition* (Berkeley: University of California Press, 2001). Eleazar Gutwirth further explores the role of autobiographical writing and poetry in the creation of a historical narrative for Spain and its exiles in his "History and Intertextuality in Late Medieval Spain," in *Christians, Muslims, and Jews in Medieval and Early Modern Spain; Interaction and Cultural Change*, ed. Mark D. Meyerson and Edward D. English (Notre Dame, IN: University of Notre Dame Press, 2000); there, he writes this reflection on the historical work of Isaac Baer: "Even Baer was not entirely consistent on this point. Years later he could emphasize the value of brief fragmentary narratives which belonged to an 'ancient tradition' of history writing. Elsewhere he could argue that although 'the centuries old tradition closed the doors to

the development of secular historiography and autobiography Todros [the thirteenth-century Hebrew poet] left us in his poems a more complete autobiography than his Jewish predecessors.' In this view, poetry takes the place of history and biography in medieval Jewish culture, even though poetry is at least as strongly marked by biblical allusion as historiography" (162). Perhaps, then, it is part of the innovation of Judah's poetic composition that even though it fails in so many respects, it succeeds in challenging the boundaries of a generic gauntlet that later writers would continue to pick up and push forward and outward.

79. Ibn Tibbon "Musar Av," 15b.

80. Ibid. I have preserved the line breaks in the poetry despite translating it into prose. For more notes on the text and translation, see the text appendix.

81. In this thematic concern, too, he very obviously echoes Samuel the Nagid's writing about his longing for his son, Yehosef, continuing the various stylistc, formal, and substantial allusions to the Nagid's work, allusions that I have pointed to throughout.

82. James Montgomery, "Salvation at Sea? Seafaring in Early Arabic Poetry," in *Representations of the Divine in Arabic Poetry*, ed. Geert Borg (Atlanta: Rodopi, 2001), 25–47.

83. Angel Sáenz-Badillos identifies later instances in which the sea is a metaphor for poetry itself in "Hebrew Invective Poetry: The Debate Between Todros Abulafia and Phineas Halevi," *Prooftexts* 16, no. 1 (1996): 49–73.

84. Andras Hamori, in his *Medieval Arabic Literature*, documents that this motif usually uses the sea as a metaphor for a female beloved, 92.

85. Brann, *The Compunctious Poet*, 137–38.

86. Esperanza Alfonso, *Islamic Culture through Jewish Eyes* (New York: Routledge, 2008), 13.

87. See the introduction to Drory, *Models and Contacts*.

88. Colophon to Bodleian MS Mich. 50.3, 21a.

89. Ps. 116:4.

90. Colette Sirat, *Hebrew Manuscripts of the Middle Ages*, (Cambridge: Cambridge University Press, 2002), 217–20.

91. It seems that the scribe Yo'av was generally uncertain about how to treat the poetry in his copy of the text; even lines of poetry cited within the text are often run straight into the prose (Plates 7 and 8) or broken up into three-part lines that do not conform to sensible breaks in meter or meaning (Plate 3). Additionally, it appears that it was his election to add the annotation "After Proverbs" before most of the citations of Samuel ibn Naghrīla's poetry, an annotation that does not fit into the flow of the text and is, in one case, utterly incorrect. In the incomplete manuscripts where the beginning of the text is preserved, we see scribes handling things differently. In the Bibliotheca Lorenzana manuscript, the poetry is copied in two columns that fill the page, preserving the line and hemistich breaks; the Frankfurt manuscript omits the opening verse.

92. This final discussion within this section of this chapter, namely that of the layout of the manuscript pages and the treatment of poetry by the scribe, was initially written as part of a critical engagement with the late Michael Camille's seminal work on medieval book history, *Image on the Edge*, for a 2015 special issue of the journal *Postmedieval* that centered around the theme "contemporary poetics and the medieval muse." It appeared as S. J. Pearce, "Poetry on the Margins: Medieval Historiography's Marginal Verse," *Postmedival* 6, no. 2 (2015): 223–39. Both that piece and its repurposing here in

this present discussion represent, for me, the beginnings of a larger ongoing project on the poetics of historiography and the uses of poetry in contemporary historical writing about medieval history.

93. Michael Camille, *Image on the Edge* (reprint, London: Reaktion Books, 2012), 21.

94. Ibid., 53.

95. Colette Sirat, *Hebrew Manuscripts of the Middle Ages* (Cambridge: Cambridge University Press, 2000).

96. Ibid., 129.

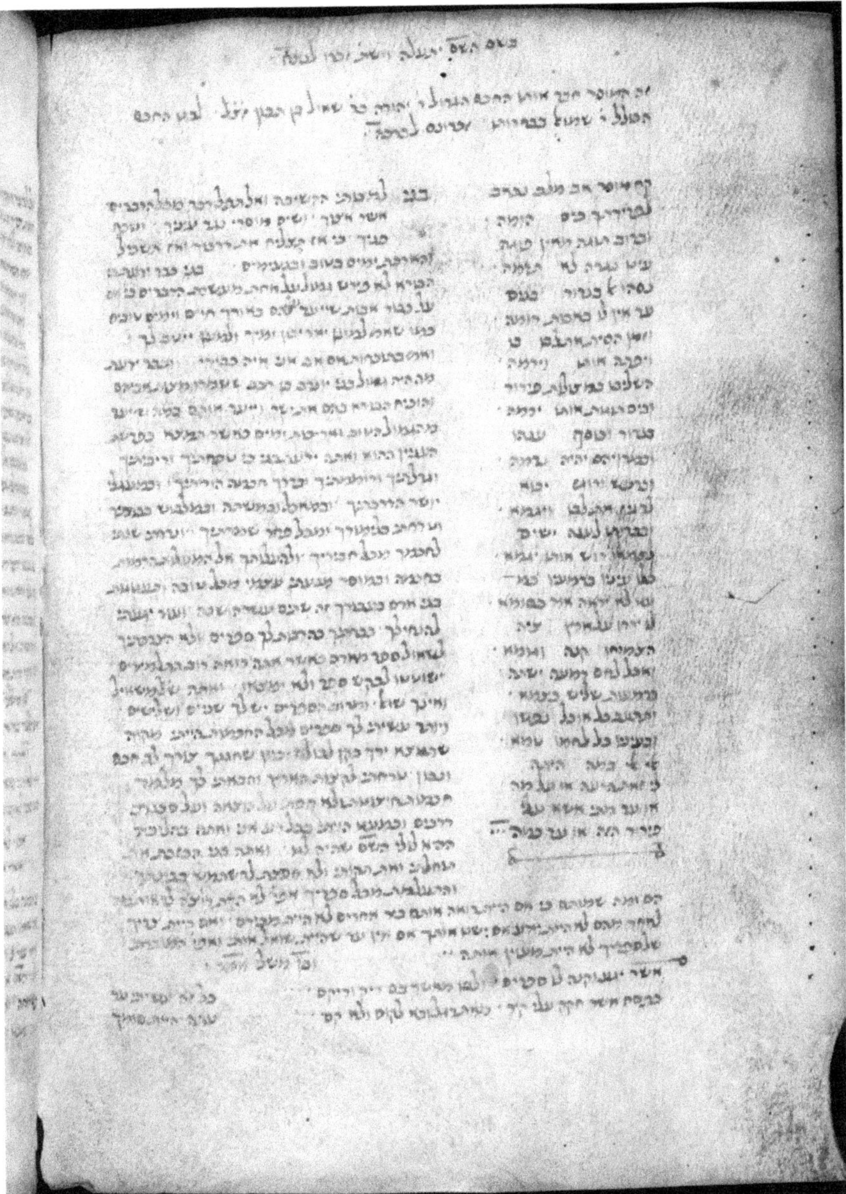

Plate 1. The Bodleian Libraries, University of Oxford, MS Mich. 50.3, folio 15b

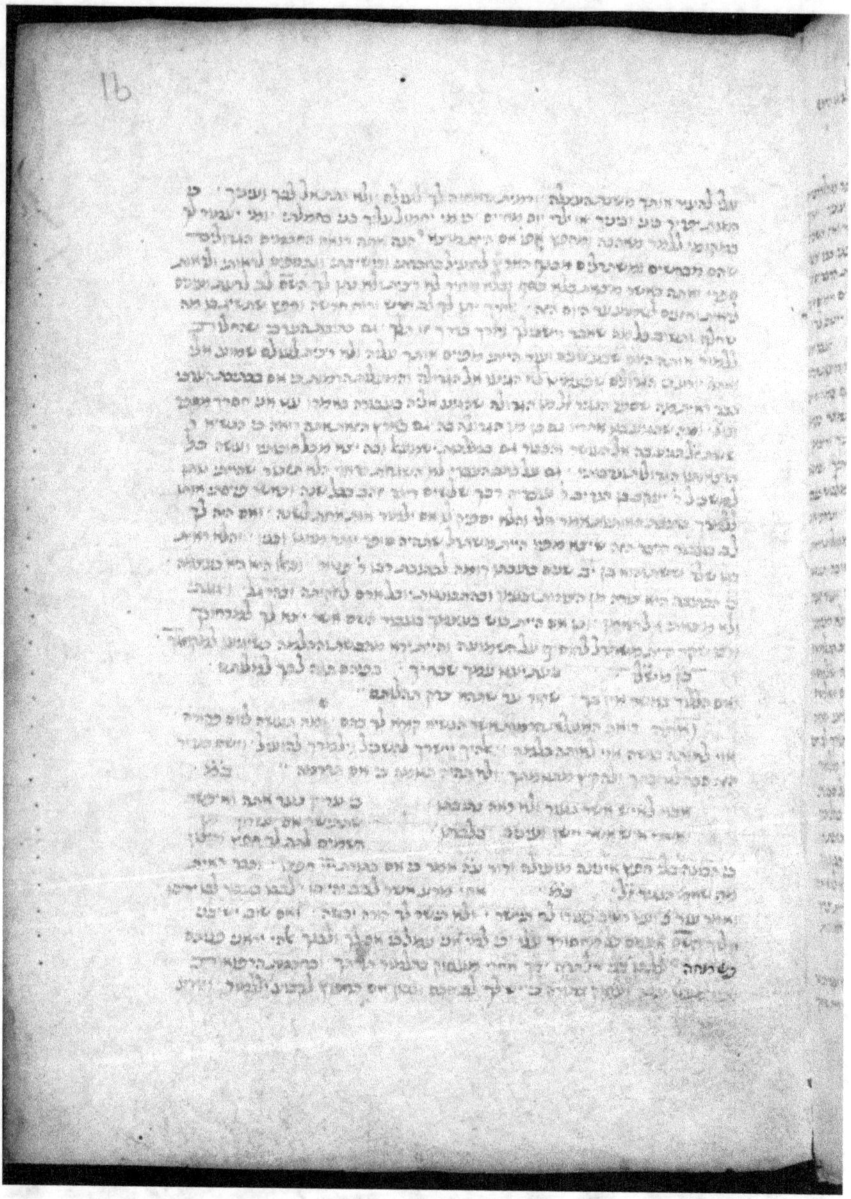

Plate 2. The Bodleian Libraries, University of Oxford, MS Mich. 50.3, folio 16a

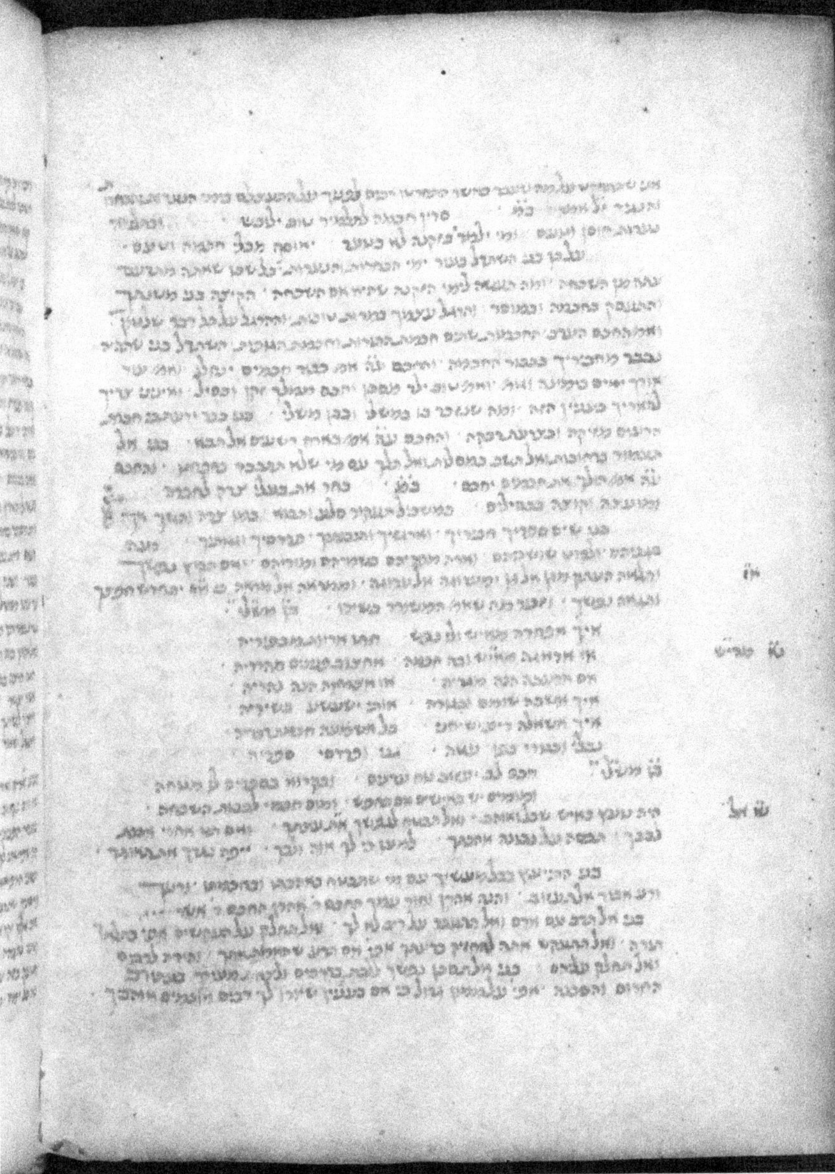

Plate 3. The Bodleian Libraries, University of Oxford, MS Mich. 50.3, folio 16b

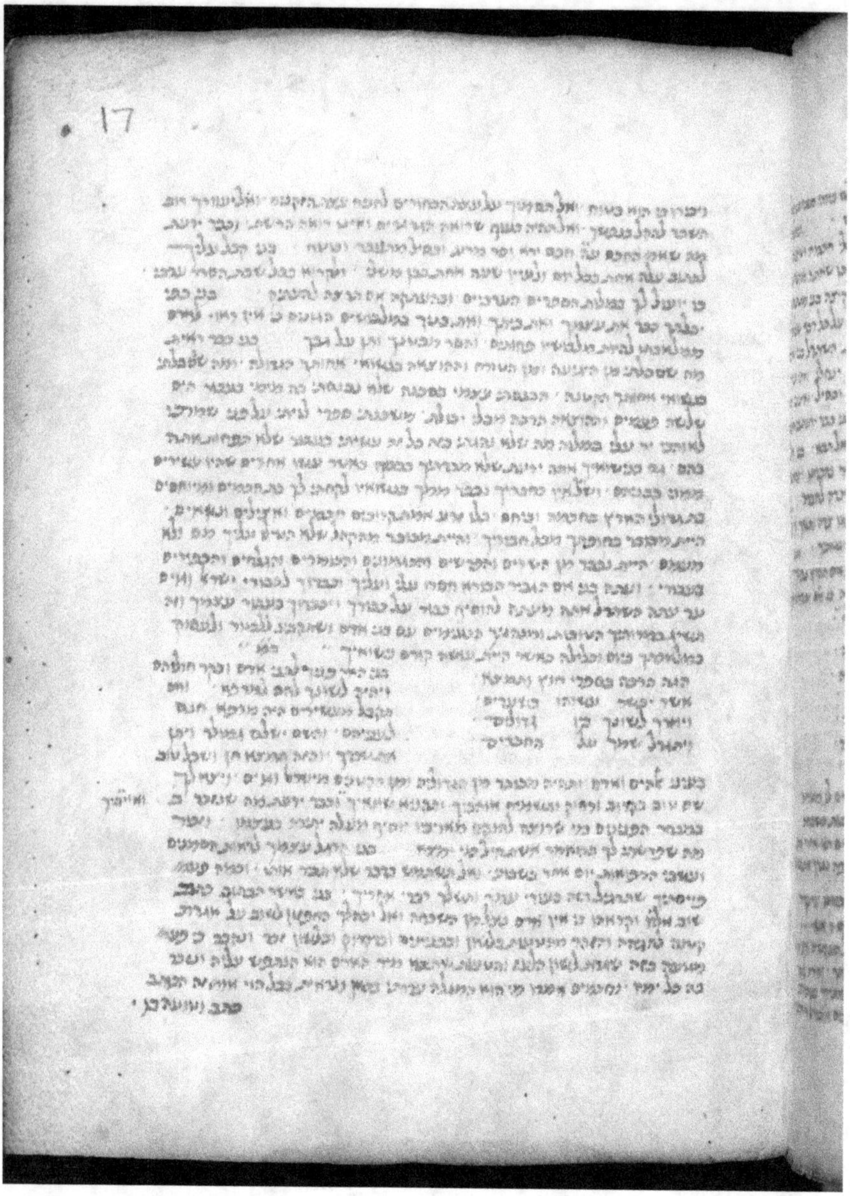

Plate 4. The Bodleian Libraries, University of Oxford, MS Mich. 50.3, folio 17a

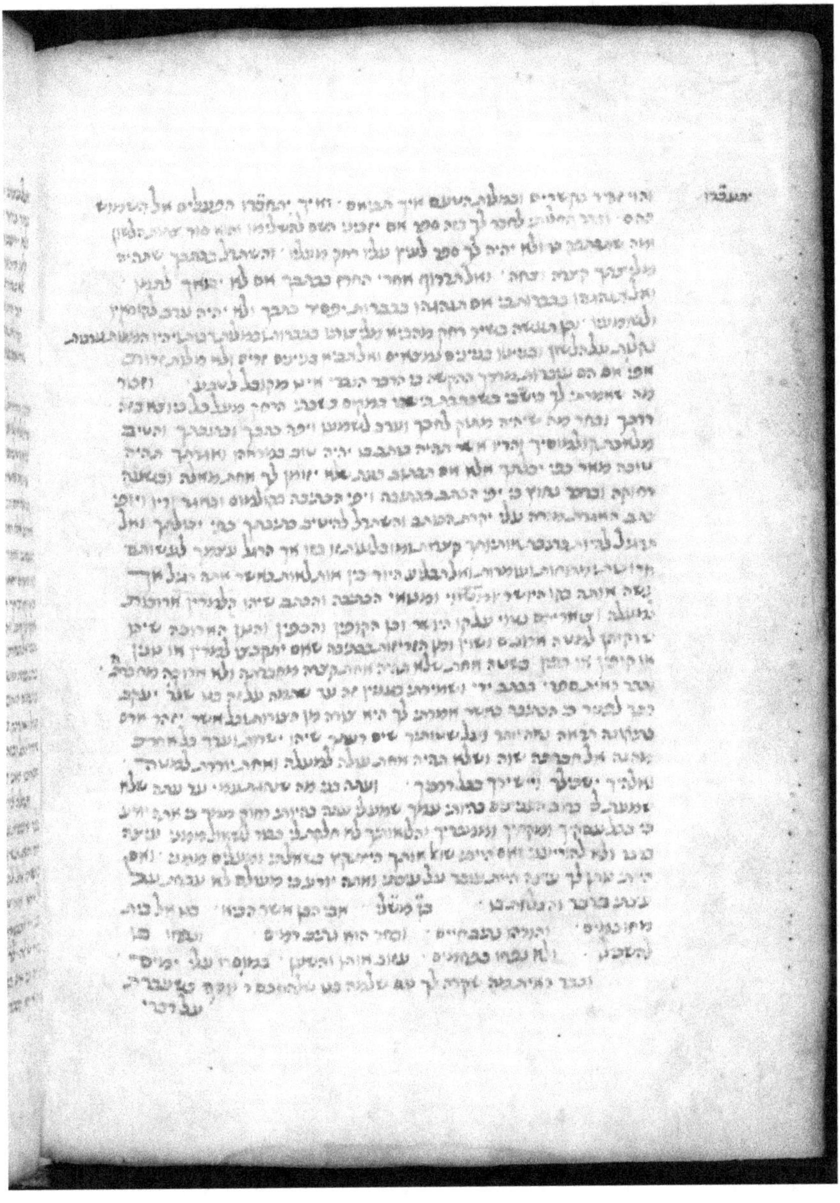

Plate 5. The Bodleian Libraries, University of Oxford, MS Mich. 50.3, folio 17b

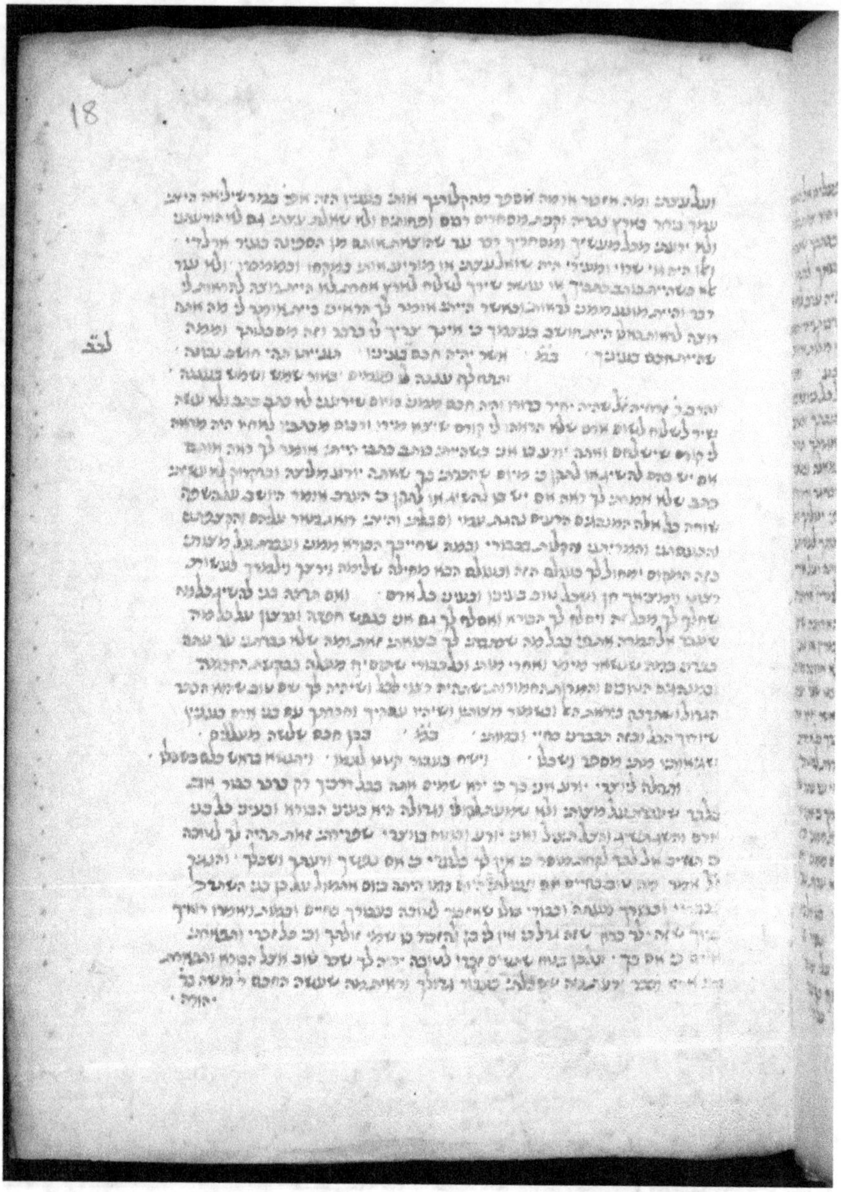

Plate 6. The Bodleian Libraries, University of Oxford, MS Mich. 50.3, folio 18a

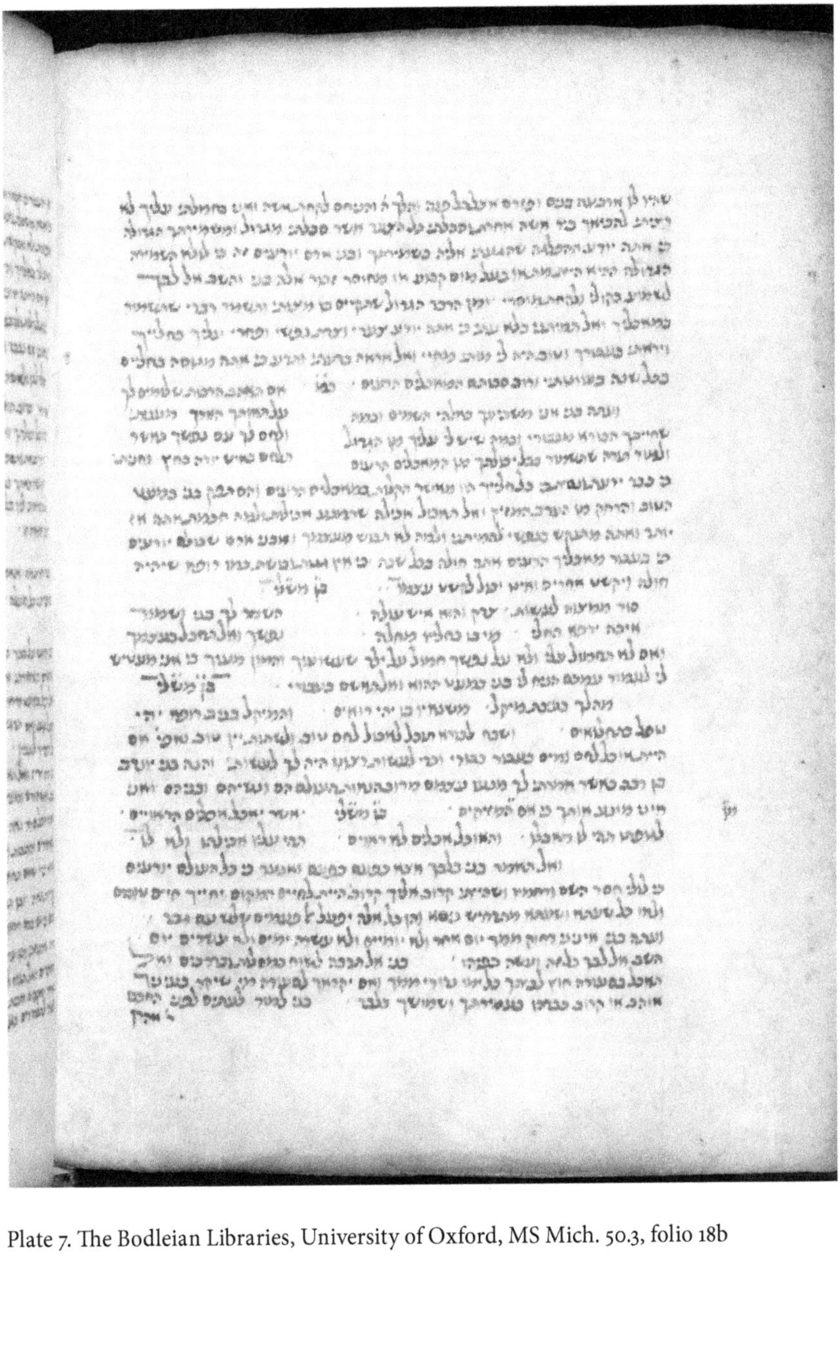

Plate 7. The Bodleian Libraries, University of Oxford, MS Mich. 50.3, folio 18b

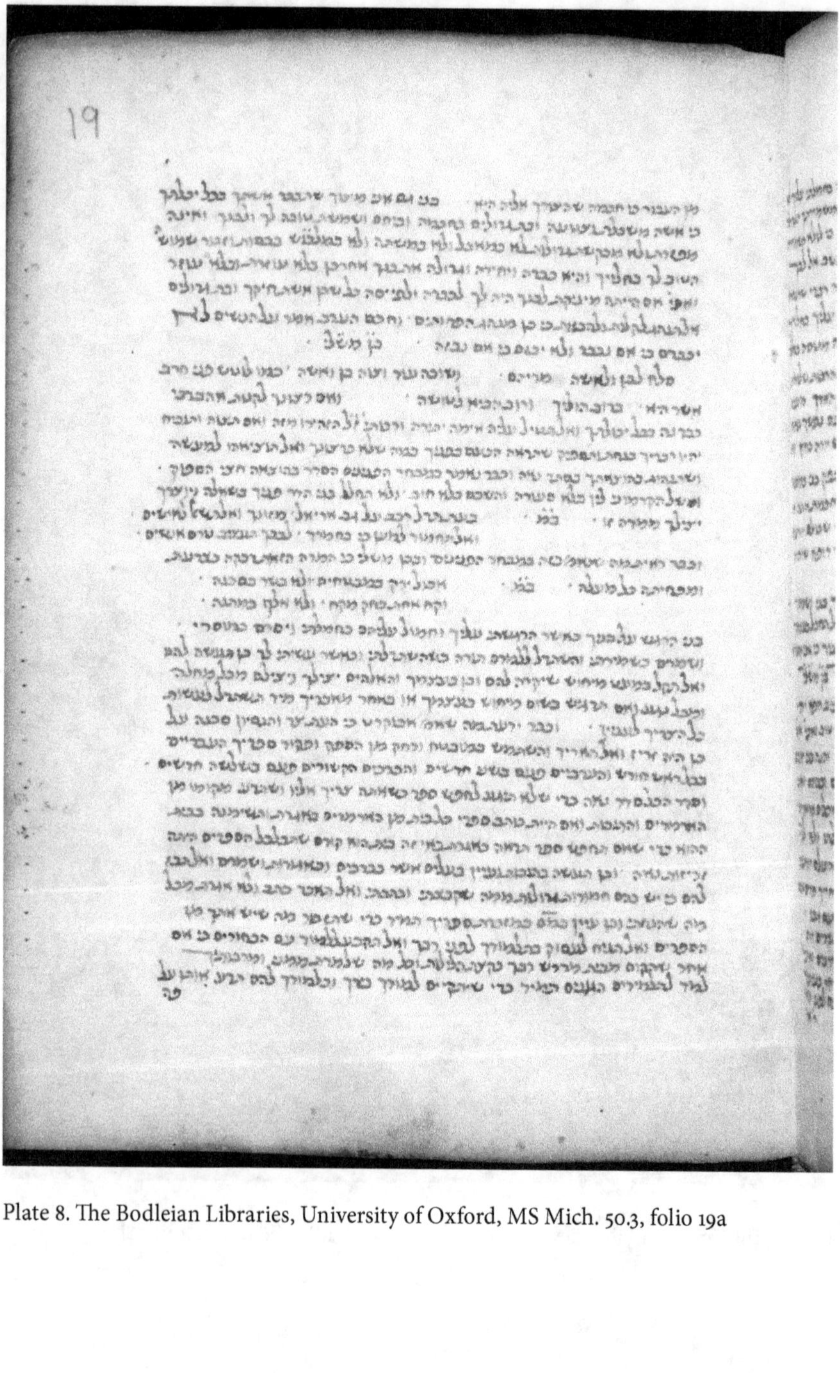

Plate 8. The Bodleian Libraries, University of Oxford, MS Mich. 50.3, folio 19a

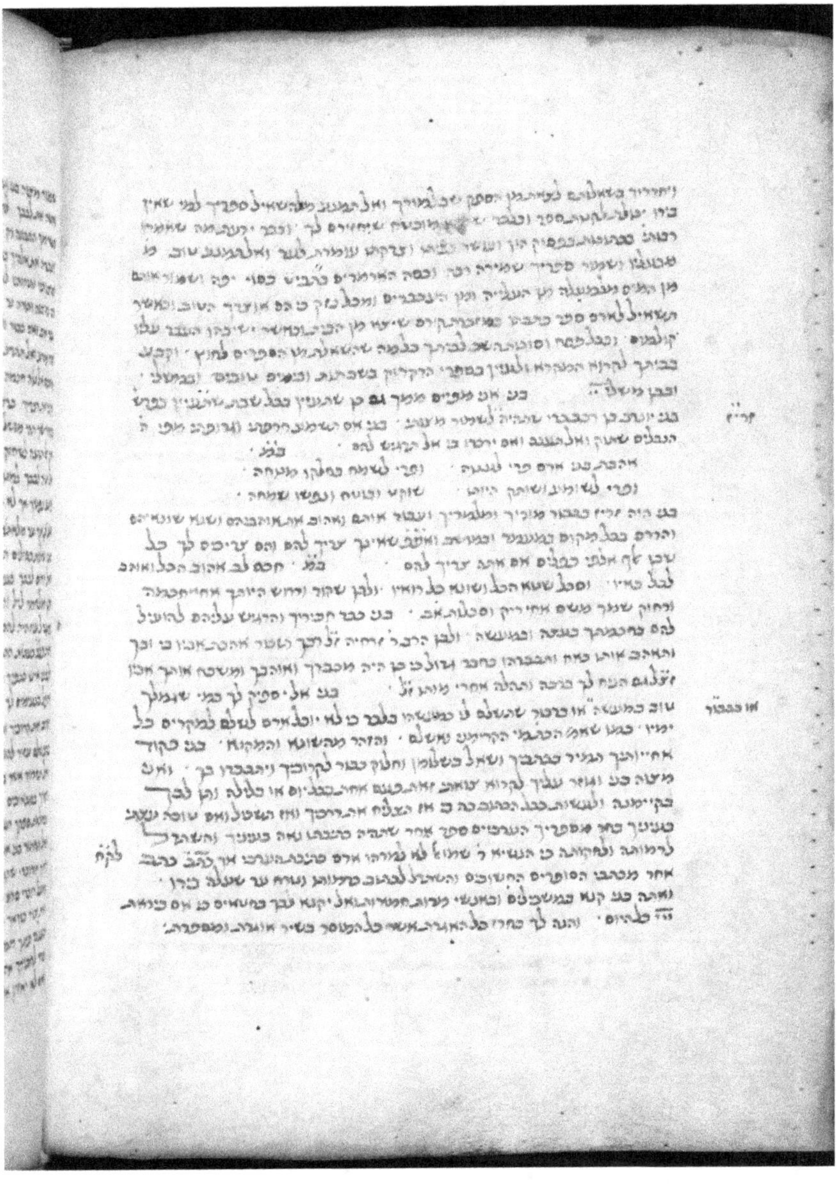

Plate 9. The Bodleian Libraries, University of Oxford, MS Mich. 50.3, folio 19b

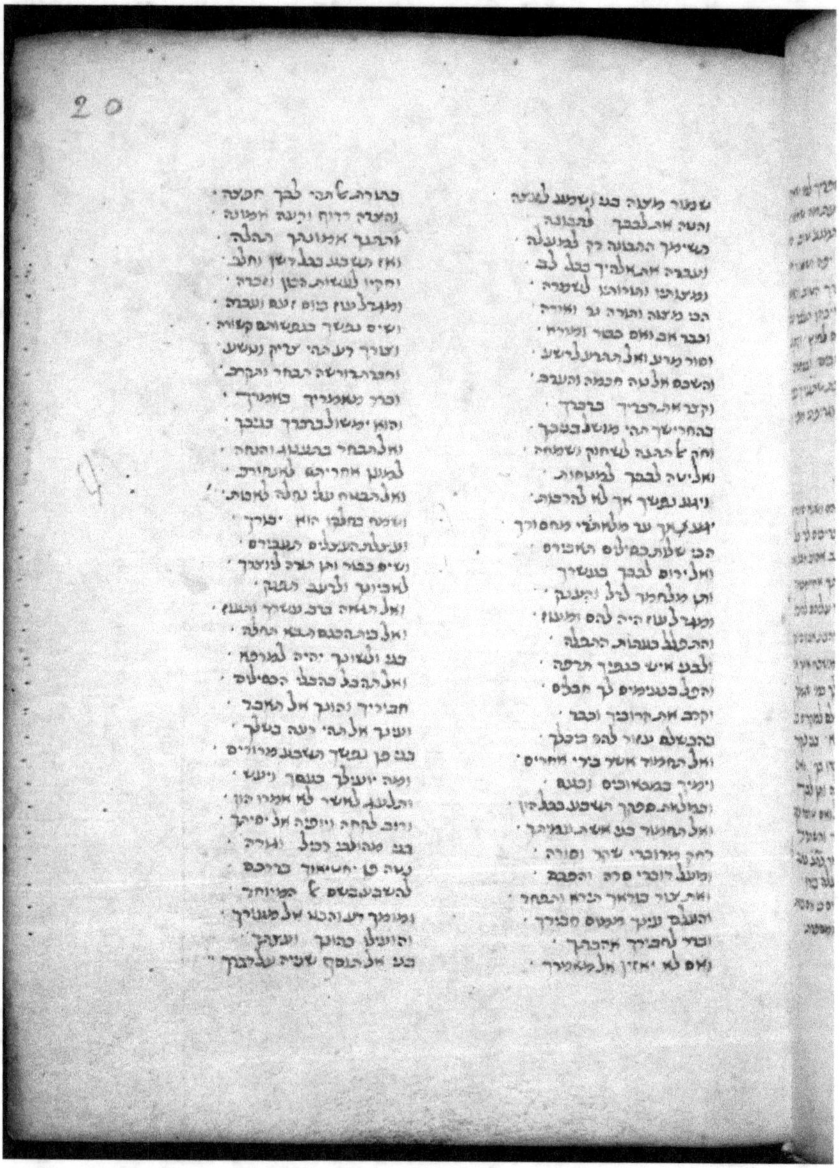

Plate 10. The Bodleian Libraries, University of Oxford, MS Mich. 50.3, folio 20a

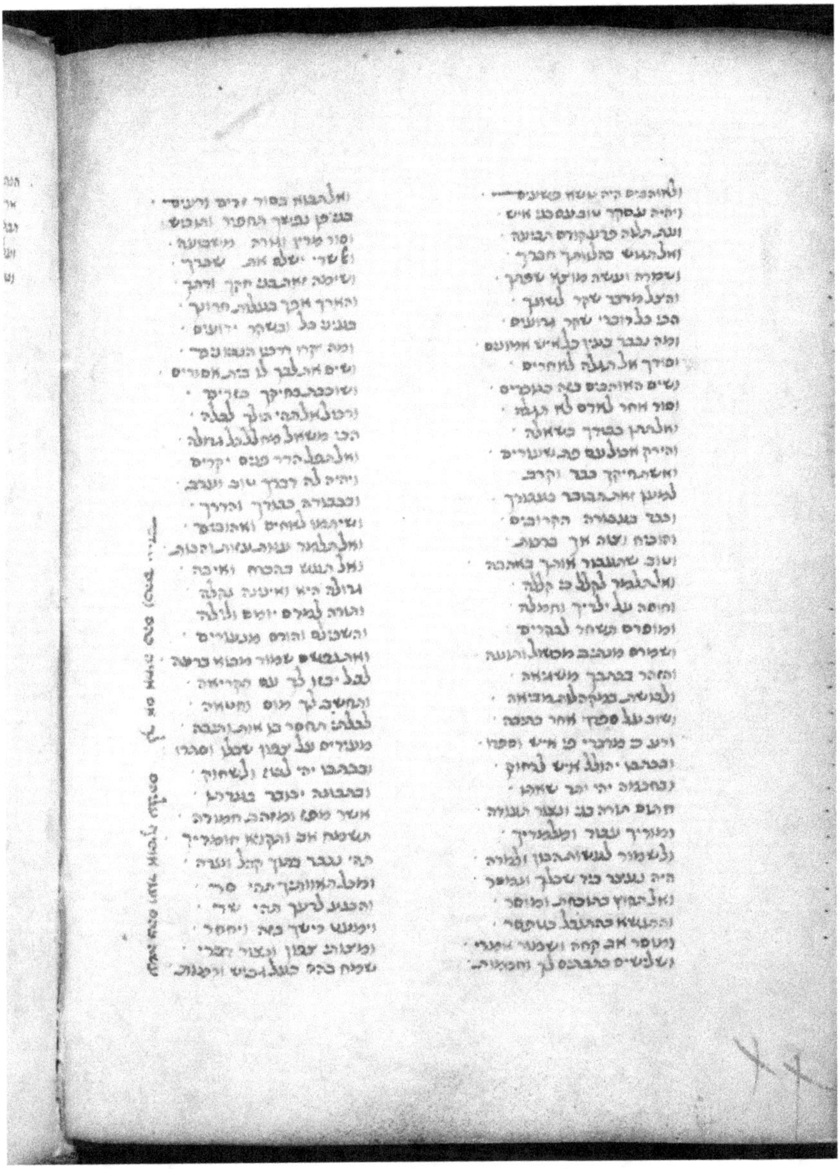

Plate 11. The Bodleian Libraries, University of Oxford, MS Mich. 50.3, folio 20b

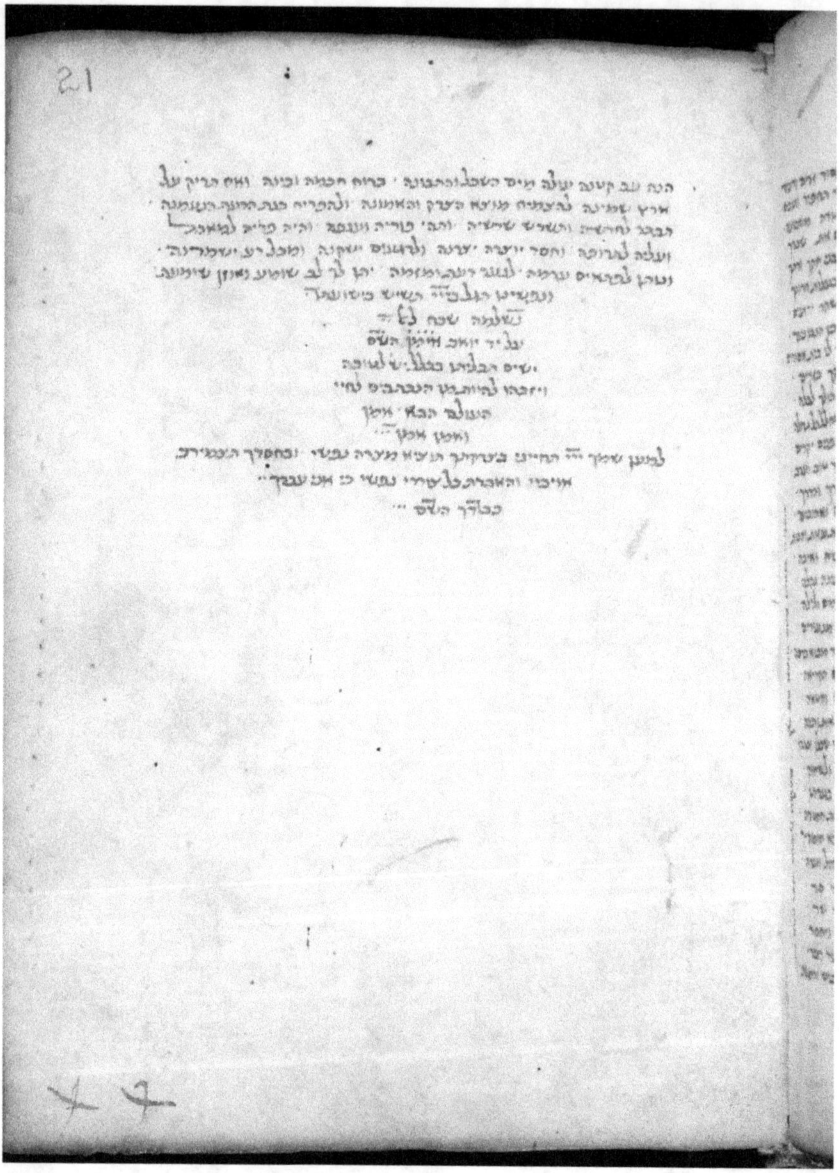

Plate 12. The Bodleian Libraries, University of Oxford, MS Mich. 50.3, folio 21a

5 "THE ARAB SAGE SAID"

Transmitting Arabic Philosophy in Translation

The figure of the sage is present in many of Judah ibn Tibbon's prefaces as well as in the ethical will. These "*ḥakhamim*" are often the biblical tradents, talmudists, geonim, and other religious authorities, as well as rationalist philosophers. Judah's use of the sage trope, usually unremarkable, serves to lend credence to Judah's claims or to lend weighty authority to textual traditions. One variant on this trope—the Arab sage (*ha-ḥakham ha-ʿaravi*), as Judah specifies—functions somewhat differently. The estimable Arab sages of Judah's whole oeuvre stand in contrast to those who appear in other corners of medieval Andalusi and Andalusi-exilic Hebrew literature. For example, the group of "Ishmaelite sages" who feature in Jacob ben Elʿazar's collection of *maqāmāt* (rhymed prose tales), *Sefer ha-meshalim* (*Book of Exempla*), praise the Arabic language while serving as exaggerated straw men who expound on the superiority of Arabic. While Ḥayyim Schirman has described these sages simply as an anonymous archetypal group of Muslims who serve as an abstract foil against which the protagonist can defend the Hebrew language and expound on views that are the author's own,[1] Joseph Sadan, by contrast, identifies them closely with the theologian al-Qurṭubī and the defenses of Arabic that he mounted in the course of writing anti-Christian polemics.[2] Either way, the Ishmaelite sages in the *Book of Exempla* function as a literary device that allows the author to respond to a perceived challenge from the Arabic language and to exalt and advocate for the superiority of the Hebrew language in a way that is organic to the text. Both Jacob ben Elʿazar and Judah ibn Tibbon wrote about Arabic in Christian Spain and Provence; that is, they were writing as Arabized Jews in a non-Arabized environment. Although each of them handles the role of Arabic and treats the proponents and expounders of its wisdom in very distinct ways, they both participate in a debate, grounded in al-Andalus and North Africa, that had become as irrelevant, in practical terms, as it was exponentially intensified. Just as Sadan identified the Arab sages from *Sefer ha-Meshalim* with al-Qurṭubī, it is possible to identify the Arab sage of Judah's ethical will as the Persian-born philosopher-turned-mystic Abū Ḥāmid al-Ghazālī (d. 1111). Yet while Jacob ben El'azar used the Ishmaelite sages to assail the primacy of Arabic, Judah's Arab sage helps to ground his proposed Andalusi curriculum even more firmly within the Arabic textual tradition.

ADAPTING THE *IḤYĀ' 'ULŪM AL-DĪN*

Credit for first identifying the sage as al-Ghazālī belongs to the editor of the modern standard edition of the text, Israel Abrahams. In a single footnote in the critical apparatus, Abrahams simply indicates his opinion that the Arab sage in question is al-Ghazālī, leaving no further indication of why he believed that to be the case or the sources for the quotations.[3] Further investigation indicates that both come from al-Ghazālī's theological summa, *Iḥyā' 'ulūm al-dīn* (Revival of the Religious Sciences). Judah quotes his "Arab sage" in two places in the ethical will. The first quotation is rather straightforward, while the second offers more detailed insight into Judah's process of working as a translator, the relationship between translation and lexicography within the Tibbonid project, and Judah's cultivation of Arabic as a source of cultural prestige.

One of the two quotations attributed to the Arab sage is introduced with the phrase: "Regarding women, the Arab sage said: 'None respects them except he who is himself respectable; and none disrespects them except he who is himself disrespectable' (*ve-ha-ḥakham ha-'arav 'amar 'al ha-nashim: lo yikhabdem ki 'im nikhbad ve-lo yevazem ki 'im nivzeh*)."[4] The same phrase appears in Arabic in the *Iḥyā'*, in the third chapter of the second section of the second book, the section on the obligations within marriage.[5] The ultimate source of this quotation is the sound ḥadīth collection of al-Tirmidhī, where it is attributed to Abū Daūd. This collection of sayings attributed to the prophet Muḥammad was available in al-Andalus as early as the fourth/tenth century.[6] Tirmidhī's collection of ḥadīth was an extremely popular source for *shamā'il*, that is, aphorisms or wisdom sayings, and so it is possible that Judah knew this phrase having heard it from neighbors or confederates; however, the precision with which Judah quotes directly from text that appears in the *Iḥyā'* not once but twice, and in both cases giving its source the epithet of sage that he otherwise applies to authors of other written texts, seems to suggest that Judah's source was written and textual rather than oral and folkloric.

The second quotation attributed to an Arab sage yields much more in terms of Judah's process of translation. It reads: "The Arab sage said: 'The types of wisdom are two in number: Knowledge of laws and knowledge of bodies' (*ve-'amar ha-ḥakham ha-'aravi: ha-ḥokhmot shetayim: ḥokhmat ha-torot ve-ḥokhmat ha-gufot*)."[7] An investigation into all the instances in which al-Ghazālī uses the term *ḥikmah* (wisdom),[8] which is the most plausible word that might be rendered by the Hebrew term *ḥokhmah* (the unbound form of *ḥokhmat*), the term that Judah utilized to describe the two types of knowledge within his letter, points to a sentence in the third subsection of the fourth chapter of the second book of the *Iḥyā'* (a treatise entitled *Kitāb qawā'id al-'aqā'id* [Foundations of the Credos]): "*li-l-imān wa-islām ḥikmāni: al-ukhrawī wa-l-dunyawī*" (within faith and within Islam [particularly], there are two types of wisdom: the otherworldly and the worldly).[9] A careful examination of this sentence reveals that it is an almost exact syntactic and lexical calque of the sentence from the *Iḥyā'*. Judah ibn Tibbon was, as Abrahams suggested, quoting directly from al-Ghazālī when he incorporated this sentence into his work, attributed to "the Arab sage."

The first similarity between the two sentences is syntactic. Each begins by asserting the existence of two types of wisdom; al-Ghazālī writes "*li-l-imān wa-islām ḥikmāni*" (within faith and within Islam [particularly], there are two types of wisdom), while Judah writes "*ha-ḥokhmot shetayim*" (the types of wisdom are two in number). The only difference between the two comes in Judah's failure to render the terms that al-Ghazālī uses to define those parameters (*imān* and *islām*), predictably altering the reference to Islam present in the original quotation to make it more relevant to his Jewish audience. Rather than substituting the reference with a more religiously palatable and meaningful one or simply removing the reference to Islam while leaving the reference to religion intact, Judah eliminates it entirely. Whereas Ghazālī's two types of wisdom exist within a religious framework and within Islam in particular, Judah's two types of wisdom simply exist. This procedure for altering a text is consistent with other Jewish translators' methods of handling Islamic texts, especially but not limited to quotations from the Qur'ān and ḥadīth, where the divine status of the language and revelatory status of the respective scriptures were at stake: "In translating philosophical and ethical literatures, in which quranic verses are introduced as prooftexts for arguments, translators make efforts to de-Islamicize texts lest the Qur'ān appear as a valid source of truth.

Even still, quranic verses are often preserved in Hebrew garb, though usually with an omission of attribution."[10] In a case in which the Jewish author of an ethical will seeks to quote from an extra-quranic but explicitly Islamicizing text, the quotation that results is very much, as shown below, "preserved in Hebrew garb." And although Judah does not fully omit the attribution, he does nonetheless obscure it by attributing it simply to "an Arab sage," and, moreover, he completely omits the explicit reference to Islam. While the two phrases are similar enough in both structure and content that the one is clearly a translation from the other, this ideologically motivated departure from the literal word-for-word translation does call into question the limits of Judah's program of literal translation; it reflects a broader understanding of the practices and function of translation as a mode of cultural as well as linguistic mediation.

The terms that are included within those parallel structures likewise correspond directly. Just as the syntactic similarity is self-evident, the lexicographic similarities between the two pairs of Hebrew and Arabic terms used to define and describe each type of wisdom are similarly inescapable: Judah's *ḥokhmat ha-torot* (knowledge of laws) corresponds with al-Ghazālī's *ukhrawī* (otherworldly knowledge); and the former's *ḥokhmat ha-gufot* (knowledge of bodies) corresponds with al-Ghazālī's *dunyawī* (worldly knowledge). Each of the Hebrew terms draws on images, ideas, and metaphors that were current among Jewish theologians, philosophers, grammarians, and exegetes in such a way that they made for a clean equation with the corresponding Arabic term.

Broadly speaking, within various modes of Islamic religious and philosophical thinking, the concepts of *ākhira* and *dunyā*, the two nouns that yield the adjectives *ukhrawī* and *dunyawī*, respectively, refer to *the world to come* and *this world*. Literally, *ākhira* means *last*; and early Muslim commentators designated the term as a reference to "the final abode." *Dunyā*, literally meaning *nearest*, refers to the world and particularly to material possessions.[11] The terms occur in opposition to one another in the Qur'ān[12] and can be used metonymically within theological and philosophical texts to refer to more narrow aspects of those two broad concepts. Frequently, consistently, and across a broad range of types of theological and philosophical writing, the terms occur together as a frozen pair of opposed concepts. The *Iḥyā'* is notably preoccupied with both of these concepts: in the *Kitāb Qawā'id al-'aqā'id* al-Ghazālī utilizes these two concepts as they occur within his outline of Islam to distinguish between faith more generally and Islam in particular. He further addresses the role of these concepts in the lives of believers even more directly in a section in the fourth treatise of the summa, the *Kitāb al-tawba* (Book of Repentance), in which he writes: "This life (*dunyā*) is of the material world while the hereafter is of the transcendent world. By 'this life' I refer to your state before death, and by the 'hereafter' to your condition after death. For your [temporal] existence and afterlife are your attributes and states; [that] which is near is called 'this life' and that which follows later is called the hereafter (*ākhira*). We speak now while being in this life of the next."[13] These are well-known concepts within the Islamic ambit that al-Ghazālī deploys and discusses to articulate his principles of faith.

Widely known, these concepts make their way into culturally Judaeo-Arabic discourses in both Arabic and Hebrew, as in the present example where they are translated linguistically and culturally into Hebrew by Judah in his lexicographically informed use of the quotation from the *Iḥyā'* in his letter to Samuel. The lexicons that were available to and utilized by Judaeo-Arabic thinkers during Judah's lifetime, and especially the lexicons that he himself had a hand in translating from Arabic into Hebrew, define the terms *gufot* and *torot*, as well as the semantic ranges covered by the words built from the same two triliteral roots as these specific lexemes, by employing examples that show them to be conceptually similar to the corresponding Arabic terms from al-Ghazālī's sentence. Lexicographic evidence is particularly important in this context because of the close ties in the Judaeo-Islamic world during much of the medieval period between scriptural exegesis, rationalist philosophy, and lexicography. Among Jewish rationalists, as among their Muslim counterparts, the creation of linguistic reference works including grammars, lexicons, and guides to style was considered an integral part of the pursuit of religious truths, as was the use of the Greek-derived tools of rhetoric and logic. The tools of philosophical rationalism and of grammatical study were crucial building blocks for exegesis, and as such can be treated both as sources for and reflections of the ways in which medieval Jewish and Muslim rationalists wrote about religious concerns.

While late-antique Jewish texts such as the Mishnah frequently defined terms as part of their exegeses, lexicography as a formal and separate field of study among Jewish thinkers and writers came about in the Islamic world concomitant to the social, religious, and linguistic pressures and considerations that are enumerated and described in the first section of this paper. Medieval Jewish Hebrew-language lexicography as its own entity, then, dates to the beginning of the tenth century with the composition of two Hebrew-Arabic lexicons by Sa'adya Ga'on, the *Egron* (Thesaurus) and the *Kitāb al-Sab'īn Lafẓa al-Mufrada* (The Book of Seventy Hapax Legomena). Lexicographical study flourished both among the *ge'onim* (academy heads) and their disciples in Mesopotamia and the Levant and especially in the western Mediterranean, where fierce debates erupted over the nature of the triliteral root in Semitic languages and the value and appropriateness of comparing Hebrew and Aramaic to Arabic; the term "geonic-Andalusian" has even been coined in modernity to describe the setting that allowed for the development of philological exegesis among Jews in the Muslim West.[14] One of the methods that the lexicographers utilized to create definitions for terms was to use biblical prooftexts and to define the terms through the contextual example of those biblical citations. In addition to reflecting the knowledge of the intended readership, which did not require definitions to be set out explicitly for them, this method of writing definitions played an important role in one of the major tasks of the lexicographers, which was to reconcile medieval theological concepts with an ancient and human language. José Martínez Delgado explains that "medieval Andalusian dictionaries, unlike modern ones, were not just reference works. They were meant to be read from cover to cover, so that, at the end, readers would be able to understand and interpret the Bible. Dictionaries allowed users to accrue the knowledge needed to understand the Bible in its original form, to engage in exegesis, and to express themselves in Hebrew. . . . The goal of biblical lexicography was, then, to increase knowledge about the language of the Bible as a means of understanding its message."[15] The dictionaries tie the pursuits of language and exegesis together, and the prooftexts that are used in the definitions in question demonstrate a close connection between the theological concepts pointed to by *gufot* and *dunyawī* and between *torot* and *ukhrawī*.

Medieval Jewish lexicographic studies of the trilateral root G-W-F, and particularly the word *guf*, or body, which is formed from that root, yield an overall picture that both argues for and sheds light on the notion that *gufot* is the term calquing the Arabic adjective *dunyawī*. In his seminal Arabic lexicon of the Hebrew Bible, known as *Kitāb Jāmiʿ al-Alfāẓ* (The Book of Collected Meanings), the late-tenth-century Karaite lexicographer Daūd ibn Abraham al-Fāsī employs two biblical citations in support of his definition of the word *guf*.[16] The first comes from a passage in First Chronicles that concerns the corpses of King Saul and his sons and compatriots, which reads: "Once every soldier arose they ferried the body of Saul (*gufat Shaul*) and the bodies of his sons (*gufot benav*), bringing them toward Yavesh and burying them under a tree."[17] The second concerns the rights of the freed slave to agency over his body: "If he arrives possessed of sound body, then he should leave possessed of sound body (*'im be-gufo yavo' be-gufo yetze'*)."[18] This definition was self-evidently current for Judah since the quotation from I Chronicles is also the one that appears in Judah's *Sefer ha-Shorashim*,[19] drawing on its occurrence in the work it translates, Jonah ibn Janāḥ's *Kitāb al-Usūl*. Both of these examples assert the materiality, the "objectness," and the worldliness of the body, making plain the correspondence between the two terms. For those charged with seeing to the disposition of Saul's and his sons' remains, and for the medieval readers whose understanding of the word *body* was formed through that image, the body was something to be lugged about and returned ultimately and unceremoniously to the very earth itself. For the slave, his body was his only material possession, the only thing he owned in this world. The medieval lexicographers make the human body emblematic of the chief characteristics of this world, of the *dunya*.

The contemporaneous commentaries on these verses *qua* verses (rather than purely as sources of lexemes) bear out a perception of the body as a worldly, even an earthy, entity. In his commentary on Exodus, Abraham ibn 'Ezra' employs the verse about Saul's body as a prooftext in remarks on the verse about slaves' bodies. But he also sets Exodus 21:3 against the backdrop of Psalm 129, in which the enemies of a national Israel are described in metaphorical terms as vicious agriculturists who will themselves ultimately be mowed down.[20] Excerpts from that psalm cited by Ibn 'Ezra' read: "They have oppressed me much since my youth but could not overcome me; ploughmen plowed across my back, digging their furrows. . . . Let them be like rooftop grass that dries out before it has grown."[21] Although the word *guf* does not appear in Psalm 129 as it does in the linked citation from the book of Exodus, it uses terminology to name specific body parts, specifically the back, such that it is obviously connected in the mind of the commentator to a verse that does explicitly use that word and other clear images of the human body. Furthermore, it paints a very clear image in which the bodies of conquered peoples are being tamed and beaten back specifically with agricultural equipment as though they were untidy plots of earth in need of tilling and plowing; when the poetic voice wishes ill on his tormentors, he again does it in terms that link their bodies with the earth. This psalm and the image that it paints of the use of agricultural equipment as a way to tame the unruly bodies of a conquered people appears as a means of explicating a verse on the possession and disposition of the human body, thereby suggesting the commentators' appreciation of the materiality of the body by drawing a one-to-one correspondence between parts of the human body and the earth itself.

Similarly, the lexicographic sources and commentaries define the notion of *torot* as laws or as guidance in such a way as to clarify its connection with the otherworldly. Returning again to *Sefer ha-Shorashim*, that text offers a definition of the root Y-R-H (which generates the word *torot* encountered in Judah's phrase *ḥokhmat ha-torot*) that draws particularly on exegesis of a passage from the Hebrew Bible, namely Isaiah 30:19–26, a passage that uses "your Guide" (*morekha*) as the epithet for God and casts the God-as-Guide figure as the creator of rain, provider of food, and source of moral and practical instruction. The definition turns repeatedly to verse 20, which emphasizes the role of God as a divine guide or *moreh*, a word connected at its root to the term in question, *torot*: "God will give you scant bread and meager water. Then your Guide will no longer be turned away; rather your eyes will turn toward your Guide." Thus (along with several other references to the wider passage from Isaiah), the definition cements the congruity of the word *torot* with the concept of the otherworldly, making the Hebrew word a loan translation of the Arabic.

Through his commentary on selections from the above-mentioned passage, Judah ibn Tibbon himself illustrates the divine or otherworldly aspect that he saw in guiding systems of laws (described with words like *moreh* and *torot* that are built from the root Y-R-H). Phrases from verses 23–25 are paraphrased, abridged, and commented on (although in the Arabic original, those verses are quoted directly and completely) in order to argue that the ontology of rain is proof of the existence of a divine guide and his divine guidance. Ibn Tibbon's commentary on those verses reads: "Just as it was said to them that the Guide would not be ignored further, and He will not keep the rain from you nor will he make it cease; but rather you will regard him. Aren't you aware? It says: He will make rain for your land so that you can sow the land . . . and the cattle that work the land . . . and on every tall hill."[22] The inclusion of this phrase highlights the otherworldliness of God as guide, and thus of divine law as guidance, just as do the aforementioned multiple references to verse 20. It serves another function as well, by cementing the connection between the terminology devised for the worldly-otherworldly pairing of concepts within the Tibbonids' vocabularistic construction of the universe. This is made clear by the use of agricultural tropes and imagery to illustrate the lexicographical source material for both the words *gufot* and *torot*. One places emphasis on the worldly aspect of those images, such as people tilling the land, and the other emphasizing the divine aspects, such as the ontology of the creation of rain. The thematic consistency of the imagery and the highlighting of its distinct aspects demonstrate Judah's selection of a pair of Hebrew words that is as logical, static, and consistent as the common and virtually frozen pairing of the words *ukhrawī* and *dunyawī* and the concepts they represent.

Particularly in Judah's case, where we are witness to his lexicographic work through his translations of much earlier lexical and grammatical works, some of the early false starts in understanding the relationship between groups of Hebrew and Arabic words are preserved in these later medieval texts in spite of the fact that Judah and his contemporaries already had a far better understanding of Hebrew grammar and its relationship to Arabic than their predecessors did. Yet in spite of this more advanced state of knowledge, it is not inconceivable that the presence of these earlier grammatical strata in their own work should have borne on the later medieval grammarians and lexicographers in their thinking, at least in the background. Both the beginning and the end of Judah's definition (as well, of course, as the Arabic original from which it was translated) are concerned with the weak letters that appear in various places in words formed from the root Y-R-H, their grammatical functions and contextual meanings. The entry in *Sefer ha-Shorashim* for the root Y-R-H begins by acknowledging and then dismissing definitions of two completely different words that come from the same root, connected to the words *moreh* and *torot* by virtue of homophony: *yarah*, or "flung," as in Exodus 15:4—"[God] flung Pharaoh's soldiers and chariots and soldiers into the sea"—and *va-yor'u*, or "shot," as in II Samuel 11:24—"The archers shot your men from atop your walls." The inclusion of this second lexeme is particularly problematic because the root is not Y-R-H, but rather Y-R-', reflecting a preservation of some of the tenth- and eleventh-century ambiguities of the analysis of triliteral roots within *Sefer ha-Shorashim* by virtue of its being a translation of a much earlier work. After presenting these alternatives, the entry for the root Y-R-H then directs its reader to the tenth-century grammarian Ḥayyūj's[23] treatise on words formed from roots with weak radical letters to clear up any remaining difficulty. The end of the entry, however, draws the problem of weak consonants firmly into the metaphysical realm. In this instance, the dictionary entry refers to the fact that the plurals of words formed with the weak Hebrew consonant *hey* as their third root letter can substitute the letter *yud*, a letter that would mark the formation of a plural noun in other circumstances; it reminds the readers that the presence of this letter does not always indicate a plural and ought not be taken to supersede theological truth. One example of this type of explanation reads: "The *yud* in [the word] *morekha* is not a maker of the plural . . . as it is written in plene orthography. And aren't you aware that it says 'your guide will no longer be ignored' in the singular?"[24] The entry in the lexicon goes on to provide several other caveats about weak letters not representing the pluralization of nouns. Defining the semantic range of the root Y-R-H becomes an exercise in affirming the central tenet of Judaism, namely, the oneness of God, the *moreh*, or *guide* of the dictionary entry. Even through the signaling of grammatical irregularities, the concomitant, lexicographically linked divine law, the *torah*, is thus made to conform to the very definition of the Arabic *ukhrawī* in its usage within the *Iḥyā'*.

The contrast between the human body and divine law occurs elsewhere in Judah ibn Tibbon's translated oeuvre. Although it is beyond the realm of the purely lexicographic and therefore, strictly speaking, beyond the methodological scope of this chapter, it is nonetheless instructive to observe this pairing of concepts and terms as it occurs in Judah's Hebrew translation of the *Kuzari*. In that text, a fictional central Asian king seeks advice from a philosopher and from Muslim, Christian, and Jewish sages after intuiting that "his intentions were pleasing to God but his actions were displeasing."[25] At the beginning of the first of the five treatises, the king dispatches the first three wise men after hearing their arguments for their respective visions of God before cottoning on to the approach of his Jewish interlocutor. In establishing the framework for the discussion he will have with the king, the philosopher explains the concepts of First Cause and of Active and Passive Intellects and how these relate to human inquiry and activity. In the text, he says: "This degree is the ultimate end for which the perfect individual hopes after his soul has been purified of doubts and acquired mastery of the sciences according to their true character, so that it may come to be like an angel. It thus attains the lowest level of the divine kingdom (*al-malkhutiya*), which is separate from bodies (*al-ajsād*)."[26] Judah translates the terms *al-malkhutiya* and *al-ajsād* into Hebrew as *malakhutiyah* (angelic) and *gufot* (bodies). While Judah ibn Tibbon emphasizes the angelic aspect by capitalizing on the near homophony of the terms for kingdom and angel, in the notes to their new English translation of this text, Barry Kogan and Lawrence Berman seek to diminish that connection and the introduction of the angels in this passage by arguing that the philosophical parameters of the philosopher's discourse do not actually serve "to introduce a new species between the divine and the human."[27] Regardless, this is a very clear opposition between the divine kingdom and the human body with which Judah was familiar and with which he clearly grappled.

Despite Judah being a proponent of literal translation, here we have an example of Judah using the technique known as loan translation, which, at a minimum, seems to depart from that, and at a maximum "potentially invites . . . exegetical anarchy."[28] But again, it is Judah's background as a lexicographer, and especially his interface with Jonah ibn Janāḥ's work, mediating between the Arabic original and its potential Hebrew readers, that sheds light on the genesis of this practice and sets it into its context. So, while Judah's treatment of al-Ghazālī's words may seem to depart from his typical techniques as a translator, it is nonetheless deeply rooted in his work as a lexicographer and requires a return to considering additional ways in which the source texts he translated had an impact on his own thinking about language and translation.

In chapter 27 of *Kitāb al-Lumʿa*, Ibn Janāḥ establishes the principle of loan translation on the basis of the quranic hermeneutical practice of *taqdīr* (supposition), in which the exegete or reader himself reconstructs the sense that is missing from an elliptical phrasing.[29] At the start of that chapter, Ibn Janāḥ observes that "occasionally one thing is put in place of another, even though it's not associated with it in any way, and this is based on their view on this, other than what we have mentioned. If it is sought, it will be found."[30] In other words, Ibn Janāḥ describes the explanation or translation of terminology by a process of drawing one-to-one equivalences with terms that are not literal representations of the terms or concepts in question.[31] In most of his own translations, Judah uses his own process, as does Samuel; however, in the case of the Ghazālī calque, he falls back on the whole of the Judaeo-Arabic Hebrew lexicographic and linguistic tradition to create the terminology to reflect those ideas. He uses lexicographical background to make an association between the Arabic terms and terms that he finds suitable in Hebrew, and uses a process that is deeply grounded in his familiarity with the lexicographical materials to create the Hebrew loan translation of those Arabic terms.[32]

Judah indubitably established his own program of translation and criteria for what constituted sufficient translation and, in the process, broke with the tradition out of which he grew. Nevertheless, his engagement with that Andalusi tradition, even in his Provençal exile, bore on the extent to which he was willing to break from it. His own statements about translation depart radically from those made by Ibn Janāḥ, whose work he translated; yet his work itself reflects both his own process and elements of what he had learned from or observed in the course of his work on the *Maḥbarot ha-diqduq*.

AL-GHAZĀLĪ AMONG THE ANDALUSIS

The specific channels through which Judah came to know and to have access to the text of the *Iḥyāʾ ʿulūm al-dīn* are not clear, though the notion that he did is in no way surprising. Many of his coreligionists were familiar with the text, and it led a wild and extensive afterlife in the Muslim West, both in North

Africa and the Iberian Peninsula. Although the text was widely accessible, Jewish readers in particular had very circumscribed techniques that they used to treat it, by and large different from their treatment of works by other Muslim philosophers. Al-Ghazālī is typically not quoted directly within Jewish *kalām* (rationalist dialectical theology) texts while other Muslim philosophers are, at least in a limited fashion, and in this respect, by quoting directly from al-Ghazālī's work, Judah differed from other Judaeo-Arabic thinkers. As noted, although Judah's method of incorporating the quotation from the *Iḥyā'* into his own writing was unique with respect to other Judaeo-Andalusi readers, he was not alone in consulting with al-Ghazālī's work, drawing on it or finding his own thinking influenced by it; al-Ghazālī formed a part of the Andalusi canon, despite the well-known (if largely invented) narrative connecting al-Ghazālī's work with the Almohad movement, one that drove Judah into exile and was generally unfriendly to members of the various Jewish Andalusi communities who remained. Nevertheless, that very same corpus of Ghazālī-authored texts was an integral component of Jewish *kalām* and Jewish intellectual-literary self-identification.

In the Muslim west, the most famous component of that textual afterlife enjoyed by al-Ghazālī was the use of his work to undergird the revisionist-revolutionary Berber Almohad dynasty founded by Ibn Tūmart; and it is this afterlife, the one that would drive the seat of the Tibbonid workshop to the city of Lunel in Provence, that carries the potential to complicate Judah's reading of the *Iḥyā'*. An elaborate, finely wrought, and largely apocryphal Almohad history with al-Ghazālī and his teachings at its center is asserted by both primary and secondary-primary sources for the life of Ibn Tūmart,[33] a man who proclaimed himself to be the messianic, divinely guided figure known as the *mahdī*. The later and more easterly of these sources themselves begin to express doubt over the veracity of such an encounter.[34] While it has been suggested that the skepticism with which the claim of an intellectual filiation between al-Ghazālī and Ibn Tūmart is treated is in fact unwarranted,[35] this line of thinking ignores sources that directly contradict a call for greater guile to be applied to the legend.[36]

This history, fabricated though it is, ties the work of al-Ghazālī to the Almohads and necessarily colored the reception of the work in al-Andalus and by Andalusis. Furthermore, although the details of a supposed meeting of the Ibn Tūmart's and al-Ghazālī's minds are unreal, there is sound reason to consider the former to have been a student of the latter, *grosso modo*: "Although Ibn Tūmart could not have met with al-Ghazālī, he should still be regarded as one of his students, albeit not an immediate one."[37] The two thinkers are in line with each other, and, more importantly, Andalusi readers largely understood them to be in line with each other and perpetuated the connection even when they doubted the specifics.

Nevertheless, the apocryphal details of an encounter between the two men are powerful and persistent. Ibn Tūmart's history within the West is said to have included a period of study with Ibn Ḥamdīn (d. 1114), the Cordoban *qāḍī* known for instigating the burning of al-Ghazālī's books under the Almoravids, who ruled prior to the Almohads in spite of a version of the story that at the same time he is claimed to have studied with al-Ghazālī himself. Neither of these anecdotes is likely true, but particularly with respect to the latter, "the story has a clear emblematic value and tells us something about Ibn Tūmart's desire, or that of his followers, to stake a claim to ghazalian teaching and about the reverential prestige which then attached to the figure of al-Ghazālī in the Maghreb."[38] A variant legend reports that the impetus for Ibn Tūmart's move westward was a desire to defend al-Ghazālī's work on his behalf in the Maghreb.[39] In spite of the spurious nature of its origins, the link between al-Ghazālī's thought and the Almohads was thus solidified and the reception of both was likewise highly nuanced and even conflictive and self-contradictory with the rise of Almohad governance in the Iberian Peninsula. While there was some mistrust of aspects of his thinking, in certain circles it did flourish and become popular. Other refutations and even *fatāwa* were written against both Ghazālī and the use of his work in the development of western Sufism.[40] In spite of the campaign during the earlier Almoravid period against al-Ghazālī's work, especially the *Iḥyā'*, other contemporaneous groups of thinkers and religious adherents found tremendous benefit in reading, commenting on, and extrapolating from it. Sufis known as the *ghazāliyya* seem to have been "united by doctrine derived mainly from the *Iḥyā'*."[41] By the height of Judah ibn Tibbon's career, then, al-Ghazālī was received by Muslim readers not only as an intellectual father of the Almohad movement but also as a supremely Andalusi source among his followers and for the rousing dissension his work provoked within al-Andalus.

The same was true for Andalusi Jewish thinkers and their reception of al-Ghazālī. Like its Islamic counterpart, the Jewish *kalām* of the Maghreb naturally did not follow a single, totally coherent, or established textual curriculum. Even so, none of the practitioners of this type of thinking worked in isolation, and as a consequence many drew from a common pool of Arabo-Islamic texts; in this particular time and place, that common pool included al-Ghazālī.

Judah ibn Tibbon, then, is not the only—or even the earliest—Jewish intellectual whose work clearly manifests traces of al-Ghazālī's writing. There are two main, established ways of treating such a canonical source within Jewish writing: unspecified influence and large-scale paraphrastic translation and commentary. Prior to Judah ibn Tibbon, the poet and philosopher Judah Halevi (1075–1141) utilized some of the modes of reasoning that are particular to Ghazālī's *Tahāfut al-Falāsifa* (*Incoherence of the Philosophers*). D. Z. Baneth largely upended previous scholarship when he argued compellingly that the careful reader may find what is, in effect, a negative relief of the *Incoherence* impressed on Judah Halevi's major work of theological dogma, *The Kuzari* (which was, again, a work translated into Hebrew by Judah ibn Tibbon). While noting several important differences in the views of the two thinkers, Baneth writes, nonetheless, it seems "as if [Halevi] deliberately avoided repeating the other thinker's arguments" and also that "several differences in their conceptions of the points in dispute seem to indicate that Judah Halevi, when he wrote his work, no longer had Ghazālī's treatise actually before him, but merely recalled a general outline."[42] Likewise, Moses Maimonides (1138–1204) seems to have been influenced by broad trends particular to al-Ghazālī's thinking. He did not quote directly from many Islamic sources, and his use of Ghazālī's work is that much more discreet. Shlomo Pines noted in the introduction to his translation of the *Guide of the Perplexed* that "the question whether Maimonides was acquainted with al-Ghazālī's *Tahāfut* presents considerable interest. No absolutely certain answer can be given to it; however, the probabilities are that at the time of the writing of the *Guide* Maimonides had read the celebrated work. No philosopher who wished to keep abreast of the intellectual debate of this period could have afforded not to have done so; and such a lacuna in Maimonides' knowledge of Arabic theological literature would have been most uncharacteristic."[43] Steven Harvey has also argued that Maimonides' *Mishneh Torah* owes a debt to the *Iḥyā'*,[44] and Franz Rosenthal[45] and Avner Giladi[46] have argued the same with respect to the *Guide of the Perplexed*. Additionally, Hava Lazarus-Yafeh has written about the parallels between Maimonides' treatment of religious law and al-Ghazālī's.[47] Both Maimonides and Halevi seem, then, to have been influenced by al-Ghazālī at the same time as they concealed this influence, an intellectual transaction that Judah ibn Tibbon would later upend completely by quoting directly from his work.

Other Jewish thinkers borrowed more concrete elements from al-Ghazālī's work and would ultimately go on to paraphrase, comment on, and translate long tracts of his work. The *Emunah Ramah* (*The Exalted Faith*), a text originally written in a now-lost Arabic version by Abraham ibn Daūd (ca. 1110–1180), borrows tropes from al-Ghazālī's *Incoherence of the Philosophers*. Hasdai Crescas (ca. 1340–1410) borrowed similarly in his attempts to lessen the role of Aristotelianism in Jewish thought. Many of Ghazālī's texts were translated fully into Hebrew beginning in the mid-thirteenth century with the *Sefer Moznei ẓedek*, a paraphrastic translation of and commentary on al-Ghazālī's *Mizān al-'amal* rendered by Abraham ibn Ḥasdai (1165–1215), and picking up pace toward the beginning of the fifteenth century, by which point many of Ghazālī's texts were translated fully into Hebrew. These included Isaac Albag's commentary on the *Intentions of the Philosophers* and the translations of and commentaries on both the *Intentions* and the *Incoherence of the Philosophers* by Moses Narboni (d. 1362).[48] The most interesting of these, in the context of a discussion of Tibbonid translation, is the translation of the *Intentions* entitled *Sefer Moznei ha-'iyyunim* made by Jacob ben Makhir, an Ibn Tibbon cousin. Another interesting example is a Judaeo-Arabic poem, written anonymously before 1384 and spuriously attributed to al-Ghazālī.[49] Jewish *mutakallimūn* from al-Andalus and later from the Christian north and in Provence saw al-Ghazālī as an important component of their canon of Arabic-language sources; they consulted with his writing even when they had access to what might have been considered superior texts, commentaries, and sources.[50] To write as an Andalusi or as an Andalusi exile meant to recourse to al-Ghazālī.

Al-Ghazālī's work continued to be utilized by Andalusi exiles in similar ways up through early modernity. Esperanza Alfonso describes and analyzes a particular Hebrew translation of a poem attributed to al-Ghazālī that Cairo Genizah evidence suggests was in wide circulation in Jewish communities in the Muslim world at least as early as the thirteenth century. That translation appears appended to a commentary on the Book of Proverbs authored by Abraham Gavison (d. 1605), an Algerian Jew whose family, like the Ibn Tibbons, traced its lineage back to Granada. Gavison took an approach to the questions of authorship, quotation, and appropriation that was very different from the one adopted centuries earlier by Judah ibn Tibbon. Alfonso observes that after asserting his own exilic status, Gavison creates an Andalusi identity for himself through a compositional strategy in which he draws work attributed to al-Ghazālī, whether correctly or otherwise, into a very pointedly Andalusi intellectual conjunction. This is accomplished in part by the presentation of Gavison's translation of this poem along with both the work of an Algerian Jewish poet who was a slightly older contemporary of Abraham, and with that of Solomon ibn Gabirol:

> Abraham Gavison places al-Ghazzālī within a Jewish context, firstly by enumerating the texts attributed to him by Jewish sources and then by pointing out the existence of a tradition of reliance on al-Ghazzālī's works among recognized Jewish authorities. Overall, one might argue, this introduction is intended to translate al-Ghazzālī from an Arabic to a Hebrew cultural context. . . . By affiliating his translation of al-Ghazzālī's poem with the work of a renowned Algerian poet close to his own family and also with that of a widely acknowledged poet from al-Andalus who was actually influenced by al-Ghazzālī, the translator achieves a double effect. Firstly, this strategy contributes to the location of the Arabo-Islamic source in a Hebrew-Jewish target milieu; by the same token, it turns Abraham Gavison himself into an author situated at the end of a continuum of classic writers which runs from 11th-century al-Andalus to 16th-century Algeria.[51]

In sixteenth-century Algeria, just as in twelfth-century Provence, appeal and recourse to the work of al-Ghazālī proved to be a powerful statement of an Andalusi intellectual identity. The persistence of this rhetorical strategy for so many centuries is testament to the strength of al-Ghazālī's position in the canon of Arabic learning and writing idealized by Jewish exiles of al-Andalus.

In sum, as Israel Abrahams originally claimed in his extremely succinct footnote, Judah ibn Tibbon did indeed quote one sentence directly from al-Ghazālī's work—the *Iḥyā' 'ulūm al-dīn*—in his ethical will. He drew from an Islamic[52] theological summa that was widely available to and consulted by many and various Andalusi thinkers, including Jewish thinkers in the Iberian Peninsula and Andalusi Jewish thinkers who had departed from there but continued to affirm an intellectual and religious provenance for themselves that was locally Iberian, and, more specifically, Andalusi. Judah treated the *Iḥyā'* differently than his coreligionists in that he quoted from it directly, utilizing it as a literary source for wisdom to transmit to his son and treating it simply as one wisdom source among many others. This differs from the more typical way that other Andalusi Jewish *mutakallimūn* (practitioners of *kalām*) treated al-Ghazālī's work: by paraphrasing; by absorbing influence of new and refigured ideas; and by writing full translations, some with running commentaries. In spite of the stylistic and technical difference, the fact of his recourse to the *Iḥyā'* was very much in keeping with Andalusi Jewish use of Arabo-Islamic sources and of al-Ghazālī's work in particular. Judah used his background as a lexicographer to craft terms for the knowledge of this world and knowledge of the next world that would have resonated with a Jewish audience and with his son, Samuel, in particular. And while this kind of translation was part and parcel of a translation project on a much vaster scale, this microcosm offers insight into the ways in which Judah navigated the practical challenges of translating in the face of a dogmatically asserted protocol for how to move text from Arabic into Hebrew, and of a longstanding heritage of earlier translators who assigned textual value very differently than he did. In spite of what the Tibbonid translators themselves said about their process, there was some flexibility there, occasionally allowing them to transmit not just the language they had left behind but also units of their former Andalusi Judaeo-Arabic culture. Even as they set themselves apart from it through their approach to translation (and more specifically through their approach to al-Ghazālī), they nonetheless participated fully in the Andalusi lexicographic and translatorial world, drawing equivalencies based on investigation of many types of texts, through including Greek philosophy, and through Judaizing the Islamic texts that they found to be valuable. The turn to the *Iḥyā'*, too, places them on a par with their Andalusi counterparts, utilizing the full spectrum of texts and ideas that they had used in al-Andalus, including al-Ghazālī's work, even as one of the major byproducts of that work, namely the Almohadism born across the Strait of Gibraltar, had driven their seat north.

A footnote in the history of scholarship conceals all of this. A brief sentence in a twelfth-century ethical will and an even briefer footnote in the twentieth-century edition of the text open a window into a long series of contradictions within the Tibbonid approach to text. There we find an exile from Granada departing from his usual and stridently asserted techniques as a translator in favor of techniques reflective of an Andalusi lexicographical and grammatical heritage, and applying them to the text that was the intellectual, religious, and philosophical underpinning of the North African regime that that drove him into that very exile. As a result, he was able to preserve and perpetuate what he believed to be the Andalusi textual canon and curriculum.

NOTES

Chapter title from Judah ibn Tibbon, "Musar Av," 16b.

1. Ḥayim Schirman, *Studies in the History of Hebrew Poetry and Drama* (Jerusalem: Mosad Bialik, 1979), 377.

2. Joseph Sadan, "Identity and Inimitability: The Contexts of Inter-Religious Polemics and Solidarity in Medieval Spain, in Light of Two Passages by Moše ibn 'Ezra' and Ya'qov ben El'azar," *Israel Oriental Studies* 14 (1994): 339–41. In conjunction with Judah's use of the "Arab sage" epithets, this additional reference begins to suggest a pattern of Jewish authors using "Arab sage" terminology as an established way to signal to the reader that the work of a specific Muslim author is being referenced without naming him, that is, that it is one of the kit of cloaking devices, discussed above, used by Jewish writers incorporated Arabo-Islamic ideas into their work.

3. Historians of the work of Abrahams's younger contemporary and denizen of the Cairo Genizah, S. D. Goitein, have made similar observations about Goitein's footnotes, e.g., Jessica Goldberg, "Goitein, Free Trade Zones, and the Writing of Economic History," paper delivered at the annual meeting of the Medieval Academy of America, New Haven, CT, March 18, 2010. A published version of that talk, which focuses less on the footnote aspect of history writing, appears as "On Reading Goitein's *A Mediterranean Society:* A View from Economic History," *Mediterranean Historical Review* 26, no. 2 (2011): 171–86.

4. Judah ibn Tibbon, "Musar Av," 19a.

5. Iḥyā' II:2:3. For the preparation of this paper, I used the edition published in 1933 in Cairo.

6. Peter C. Scales, *The Fall of the Caliphate of Córdoba: Berbers and Andalusis in Conflict* (Leiden: Brill, 1993), 13.

7. Judah ibn Tibbon, "Musar Av," 16b.

8. Farid Jabre's *Essai sur le lexique de Ghazali* (Beirut: Publications de L'Université Libanaise, 1970) was especially useful in identifying instances of this term.

9. *Iḥyā' ulūm al-dīn* II:4.3.

10. Jonathan Decter, "The Rendering of Quranic Quotations in Hebrew Translations of Islamic Texts." *Jewish Quarterly Review* 96 (2006): 338. Decter also specifically addresses the question of how the Hebrew translator Abraham ibn Ḥasdai rendered quranic quotations within his Hebrew translation of al-Ghazālī's *Mizān al-ʿamal*, though not how Ibn Ḥasdai handles the translation of non-quranic but nonetheless explicitly Islamic material and references within al-Ghazālī's original writing (343–48). His discussion (356–57) of Moshe Narboni's translation of explicitly Islamic material within Ibn Rushd's *Epistle on the Possibility of Conjunction with Active Intellect* is also particularly interesting insofar as Narboni was, like Ibn Ḥasdai, a Hebrew translator of al-Ghazālī.

11. A. S. Tritton in *Encyclopedia of Islam*, 2nd ed. (2012): "Ākhira," http://referenceworks.brillonline.com/entries/encyclopaedia-of-islam-2/akhira-SIM_0469; and "Dunyā," http://referenceworks.brillonline.com/entries/encyclopaedia-of-islam-2/dunya-SIM_2155.

12. Examples of this contrastive pairing in the Qur'ān include *sūra* 2:86: "Such are they who buy the life of this world (*al-ḥiyāwa al-dunyā*) at the price of the life to come (*al-āẖira*). Their punishment shall not be mitigated nor shall they be helped"; and *sūra* 87:16–17: "Yet you prefer this life (*ḥiyāwa al-dunyā*), although the life to come (*al-āẖira*) is better and more lasting"; trans. N. J. Dawood (reprint, New York: Penguin, 2005).

13. *Al-Ghazzali on Repentance*, trans. Marc S. Stern (New Delhi: Sterling Publishers, 1990), 66–67.

14. Mordechai Cohen, *Opening the Gates of Interpretation* (Leiden: Brill, 2011), 60.

15. José Martínez Delgado, "Maimonides in the Context of Andalusian Hebrew Lexicography," *Aleph* 8 (2008): 22. This article offers an excellent description of the dictionaries and encapsulation of the history of Andalusi Hebrew grammatical and lexicographical study with particular attention to the ways in which it bore on late twelfth-century lexicography and exegesis.

16. Daūd ben Abraham al-Fāsī, *Kitāb Jāmiʿ al-Alfāẓ*.

17. I Chron. 10:12.

18. Exod. 21:3a.

19. Judah ibn Tibbon, *Sefer ha-Shorashim*, 33.

20. Abraham ibn 'Ezra', *The Short Commentary on Exodus*, 2–3.

21. Ps. 129:2–3, 6.

22. Judah ibn Tibbon, *Sefer ha-Shorashim*, 204–5.

23. Judah ben David al-Fāsī, known as Ḥayyūj (ca. 940–ca.1013), was a Cordoba-based grammarian and devotee of Ḥasdai ibn Shapruṭ responsible for establishing that the principle of triliteralism that governs Arabic morphology also obtains in Hebrew.

24. Judah ibn Tibbon, *Sefer ha-Shorashim*, 204–5.

25. Judah Halevi, *Kitāb al-radd wa-l-dalīl fī-l-dīn al-ḏalīl*, ed. David Zvi Baneth and Haggai Ben-Shammai (Jerusalem: Magnes Press, 1977), 3.

26. Judah Halevi, *The Kuzari*, trans. Barry Kogan and Lawrence Berman (New Haven, CT: Yale University Press, forthcoming), 2.

27. Kogan and Berman, trans., notes to Treatise 1 of Halevi, *Kuzari*, 4–5.

28. Cohen, *Opening the Gates*, 60.

29. Ibid., 57–59.

30. Ibid., 59. The original citation is found in *Sefer ha-Riqmah*, 345.

31. For more on the use of loan translation in the Hebrew-language grammatical and exegetical traditions, see Ma'aravi Peretz, "Substitution of One Word for Another as an Exegetical Method," in *Studies in the Bible and Its Exegesis*, vol. 2, ed. Uriel Simon (Ramat-Gan: Bar Ilan University Press, 1986), 207–28.

32. There are other indications throughout the Tibbonid corpus that Judah was willing to depart quite radically from word-for-word translation, going beyond making concessions to intelligibility in texts otherwise translated according to that method and instead wholesale adopting techniques of sense-for-sense translation. His translator's preface to his Hebrew version of Baḥya ibn Paqūda's *Ḥidāya li-farā'id al-qulūb* bears some striking thematic similarities to the discourse on translation in the encyclopaedic work *Kitāb al-Ḥayawān* by the classical Arabic writer, *adīb*, and theologian Abū 'Uthmān 'Amr ibn Baḥr al-Baṣrī (d. 869), best known by his sobriquet al-Jāḥiẓ ("the bug-eyed one"). The philological evidence is somewhat less clear-cut and so this is a possible textual nexus to which I intend to return in future studies, but an overview of the thematic similarities between the two texts is in order here.

In this case, rather than translation through lexical calquing, Judah translates by omission, another practice that appears in the toolkit of culturally Judaeo-Arabic translators and literati. In a departure from Judah's usual technique, an author cites an earlier text by omission when he mirrors certain structural and thematic affinities in such a way as to make clear that the new text bears a relationship, structural and thematic, to the source text. It is a type of citation that is especially apt in situations where authors and books are in motion and writers may not have direct access to the texts that have formed their intellectual bases but instead draw on their memories of those texts or settings in which authors wish to speak to multiple audiences, citing texts that will add meaning for one group while concealing their origins from the other. One particularly notable example of citation by omission is identified by David Zvi Baneth and sees Judah Halevi drawing, unacknowledged and in broad strokes, on the structure of yet another work by al-Ghazālī, namely *The Incoherence of the Philosophers*. Particularly interesting, though, is the procedure identified Baneth by which Halevi drew on that text, quietly and with minimal attribution. Baneth largely upended previous scholarship, which argued that Jewish writers generally and Halevi in particular failed to engage with al-Ghazālī's work despite its prominence in philosophical and religious discourse, arguing instead that the careful reader may find what is, in effect, a negative relief of *The Incoherence of the Philosophers* impressed on Halevi's major theological-philosophical work, the *Book of the Kuzari*. While noting several important differences in the views of the two thinkers, Baneth writes, it seems nonetheless "as if [Halevi] deliberately avoided repeating the other thinker's arguments" and also that "several differences in their conceptions of the points in dispute seem to indicate that Judah Halevi, when he wrote his work, no longer had Ghazali's treatise actually before him, but merely recalled a general outline" (D. Z. Baneth, "Judah Halevi and al-Ghazali," *Studies in Jewish Thought*, ed. Alfred Jospe [Detroit: Wayne State University Press, 1981], 183–84). By examining both similarities and key glaring differences between the two texts, Baneth argues that the *Kuzari* reflects Halevi's knowledge of the text, his engagement with that text and reluctance to sign onto it wholeheartedly, and the fact that at some point he had direct access to the text but later no longer did and was writing on the basis of his memory of having read the book earlier. Likewise, this method of citation by omission also seems to account for traces of al-Ghazālī's work in Moses Maimonides' *Guide of the Perplexed*, as noted in the body of this chapter.

Judah ibn Tibbon seems to have treated *Kitāb al-Ḥayawān* in the same way, borrowing the structure of the discourse on translation in a way that allowed him to engage with debates over translation within the Arabophone Islamicate world without alienating his European readers, whose concerns were somewhat different and more ephemeral. Where he cites the *Iḥyā'* through lexical adaptation, in his preface to his Hebrew translation of Baḥya's *Duties of the Heart*, he seems to adopt another mode of translation for sense, that is, this well-documented phenomenon of translating a text by omission and reflecting a memory of reading rather than the act of reading itself. Like the works of al-Ghazālī, those of al-Jāḥiz enjoyed considerable popularity among Andalusi readers long after the death of the author. For example, Ross Brann counts "an abundance of quotations from al-Jāḥiẓ's work in Andalusi letters" (*Power in the Portrayal*, [Princeton, NJ: Princeton University Press, 2002], 60). Shari Lowin goes farther in identifying several instances in which Ibn Hazm's usages of literary and cultural terms evoke those of al-Jāḥiẓ (*Arabic and Hebrew Love Poems in al-Andalus* [New York: Routledge, 2014]); through Lowin's work, we begin to see an Andalusi writer treating al-Jāḥiẓ's work as a source to be transmitted in Baneth's "negative relief." In the context of the wider Arabized Jewish world, Richard Steiner (*A Biblical Translation in the Making: The Evolution and Impact of Saadia Gaon's Tafsīr* [Cambridge, MA: Harvard University Press, 2010], 109–17) argues that Sa'adya Ga'on's *Kitāb al-amanāt* shows both structural and thematic affinities with al-Jāḥiẓ's *Radd 'alā al-naṣāra* (*Polemic against the Christians*). Thus, in a cultural and readerly context in which authors are comfortable adapting the structure of earlier texts as much as translating their content, both literally and culturally, and in a particular time and place where we find much reading of the works of al-Jāḥiẓ, it is perhaps not at all surprising that we should find his magnum opus, *Kitāb al-Ḥayawān*, cited obliquely in this way in Judah's work.

In this case, the evidence of the skeleton of *Kitāb al-Ḥayawān* (*Book of Animals*) in the preface to *Ḥovot ha-Levavot* comes in the thematic structure of the two texts. Four themes emerge that are also present in Judah's discussion of translation in his preface to that work. These themes are: the corruption of texts by translators who do not have equal facility in the source and target languages, the usefulness of translation in the affirmation of divine unity, the possibility of translating technical texts that include a wide range of terms of art, and, finally, who is blamed and who should be blamed for bad translations. The presence of these same themes within Judah's preface in the same order in which they appear in Jāḥiẓ's original gives the preface the appearance of the kind of mental image that Baneth defined as a characteristic of this type of adaptation and reuse of text. If we assign a letter to each theme—"A" for translations becoming corrupt by translators who are unskilled in either the source language or the target language, "B" for translation and *tawḥīd* (the affirmation of the oneness of God), "C" for technical texts, and "D" for blame and responsibility—it is easier to visualize the structural parallels between the two texts. In *Kitāb al-Ḥayawān*, the pattern A-B-A-C-D occurs, and in Judah's preface to *Duties of the Heart*, these themes occur in the pattern B-A-C-D. In other words, after al-Jāḥiẓ begins with a bit of extra attention to the relationship of divine unity to textual translation, Judah follows his progression through these specific common themes exactly. Although these themes are not unique, both the details of their articulation and the similarities in the order of the argument strongly suggest that Judah wrote his preface consulting or recalling Jāḥiẓ's work on translation. As noted earlier, there are significant conceptual and lexical differences between the two texts, and so it is too early to be able to say definitively that Judah certainly read *Kitāb al-Ḥayawān* and then quoted from his memory of it; but so, too, are the similarities too great to dismiss the possibility.

33. These include Ibn Tūmart himself and his companion al-Baydhaq in the first category and later writers such as Ibn Ṣāḥib al-Ṣalāt, Ibn Qaṭṭān, al-Marrākūshī, and even Ibn Khaldūn in the second.

34. Frank Griffel, "Ibn Tūmart's Rational Proof for God's Existence and Unity, and His Connection to the Niẓamiyya Madrasa in Baghdad," *Los almohades: problemas y perspectivas*, ed. Maribel Fierro et al. (Madrid: CSIC, 2005), 754.

35. Madeleine Fletcher, "Ibn Tūmart's Teachers: The Relationship with al-Ghazālī," *Al-Qantara* 18 (1997): 305–30.

36. Griffel, "Ibn Tūmart's Rational Proof," 755.

37. Ibid., 756ff.

38. Mercedes García-Arenal, *Messianism and Puritanical Reform: Mahdis of the Muslim West* (Leiden: Brill, 2006), 163.

39. Griffel, "Ibn Tūmart's Rational Proof," 753.

40. References to these, as well as an in-depth consideration of the earlier *fatwā* issued by Ibn Rushd al-Jadd in 1126, may be found in Delfina Serrano Ruano, "Why Did the Scholars of al-Andalus Distrust al-Ghazālī?," *Der Islam* 83, no. 1 (2006): 137–56; Kenneth Garden, "Al-Ghazālī's Contested Revival: Iḥyā' 'ulūm al-dīn and Its Critics in Khrasan and the Maghrib" (PhD diss., University of Chicago, 2005), 141–84, also delineates both the opposition to and support for al-Ghazālī's work in the Muslim West. See also the introduction to Vincent Cornell, *The Realm of the Saint* (Austin: University of Texas Press, 1998).

41. Garden, "Al-Ghazālī's Contested Revival," 166.

42. Baneth, "Judah Halevi and al-Ghazali." This article first appeared in German and later in Hebrew translation; the notes and sources are somewhat different in each of the three versions and as such it is advisable to consult with all three in conjunction with each other: "Jehuda Hallewi und Ghazali," *Korrespondenzblatt des Vereins zur Gründung und Erhaltung einer Akademie für die Wissenschaft des Judentums* 5 (1924): 27–45; and "Yehudah Halevi ve-Alghazali," *Kenesset* 7 (1941): 311–29.

43. Shlomo Pines, "Translator's Introduction," *Guide of the Perplexed* (Chicago: University of Chicago Press, 1974), cxxvii.

44. Steven Harvey, "Alghazali and Maimonides and Their Books of Knowledge," *Be'erot Yitzhak*, ed. Jay M. Harris (Cambridge, MA: Harvard University Press, 2005), 99–117.

45. Franz Rosenthal, *Knowledge Triumphant*, ed. Dimitri Gutas (Leiden: Brill, 2006), chap. 5.

46. Avner Giladi, "A Short Note on the Possible Origin of the Title *Moreh ha-Nevukhim*," *Tarbiẓ* 48 (1979): 346–47.

47. Hava Lazarus-Yafeh, "Was Maimonides Influenced by Al-Ghazālī?," in *Tehilah le-Moshe: Biblical and Judaic Studies in Honor of Moshe Greenberg*, ed. M. Cogan et al. (Winona Lake, IN: Eisenbrauns, 1997), 163–69.

48. Alfred Ivry, "Moses of Narbonne's 'Treatise on the Perfection of the Soul,'" *Jewish Quarterly Review* 57, no. 4 (1967): 271–99.

49. Tzvi Langermann, "A Judaeo-Arabic Poem Attributed to Abu Hamid al-Ghazali," *Miscelánea de estudios árabes y hebraicos* 52 (2003): 183–200.

50. Steven Harvey, "Why Did Fourteenth-Century Jews Turn to Alghazali's Account of Natural Science?" *Jewish Quarterly Review*, 91, no. 3/4 (2001): 359–76.

51. Esperanza Alfonso, "A Poem Attributed to al-Ghazzālī," *Mi-Kan* 11 (2012): 90–91.

52. I am not describing it in a more narrow way because of the dissension in the scholarship over how to precisely classify the type of theology that is represented in the work, and furthermore because a finer designation is not germane to this discussion.

6 "FROM VESSEL TO VESSEL"

The Reception and Reimagining of the Tibbonid Project

An appeal to the modern is not always out of line for the medievalist. Particularly when reading with something of an anthropological approach and particularly when arriving at the section of a project that examines the subsequent reception of medieval ideas and praxes, drawing on modern points of comparison is never probative but can often be instructive. In that vein, I begin this chapter with an anecdote from the present day, that of an observant Jewish acquaintance who is also an Arabist. Every Saturday, he learns with a *ḥevruta*, a reading partner, who is an emigrant from an Arabic-speaking country with a now-dwindling Jewish population. When they were reading the *Guide of the Perplexed*, the main text that they consulted was Samuel ibn Tibbon's Hebrew version because that is the one that has been elevated to canonical, sacral status within their community; but as an interpretive aid, they always had Maimonides' Arabic original open on the table. The scene is remarkable: the original has been made to take the role of commentary on or cipher for the translation, and the translated version has become the text itself.[1] It an illustrative microcosm of the wider world in which the translations proceeding from the Tibbonid workshop, as illegible as they may be, have become the authoritative versions of much of Judaeo-Arabic philosophy, theology, and science. But it also raises a provocative question. This translation was ostensibly created for an audience that could not consult closely with the original as my colleague does, but rather for an audience that did not have the ability to recourse to the Arabic as a way of making sense of the Arabizing Tibbonid Hebrew. How, then, could that intended audience have made use of such a translation-turned-text? Or, in other words, of what use is a word-for-word translation to such a reader? This is the main question of this chapter, which also examines the ways in which the translation functions as commentary, as surrogate, and ultimately as something canonized, authorized, and sacred for non-Arabophone Jewish communities in Europe. As a coda to a study of the literary forms through which the cultural prestige of Andalusi Arabic was preserved and transmitted in Europe, this will not be a traditional reception history as such, but rather a study of the way in which prose fiction, in particular, served as an apt vehicle for readers to grapple with difficult texts in difficult translations.

Judah himself was aware of his audiences and of the ramifications for his readers of his choice to translate *ad litteram*; he even made some concessions for places where sense-for-sense translation might be an acceptable alternative to his preferred word-for-word method. His preface to Baḥya ibn Paqūda's *Duties of the Heart* posits a relationship between original and translation in the more conventional, expected manner—that is, the translation in this case stands as the interpretive aid for the original text—but still requires that original and translation coexist at the moment of reading. This is one of the instances in which Judah asserts his belief that word-for-word translation does not represent an intervention in the text: "If it were possible for the translator to confine his interference to translating word for word without addition or subtraction he could save himself from that kind of failure and guilt."[2] However, he also acknowledges the difficulty of the texts produced this way and that to read them requires access to teachers, to books, and especially to the original source material. As he continues to delineate his argument in the preface, he acknowledges the limitations of the platonic form of a translation ad litteram: "Translation according to this method will be difficult to understand except for great sages who understand the ways of the holy tongue. This language is not pleasant or even especially acceptable, and it may even make the subject matter more difficult to understand."[3] The solution that he proposes for working around this difficulty requires consultation with both the original and the translation. He writes that changes made between the Hebrew Bible and the Babylonian Aramaic version known as Targum Onkelos, changes that in the Tibbonid schema would represent inappropriate interference on the part of the translator, were acceptable because readers had access to both the Hebrew original and the Aramaic translation:

> As such, the ancient translators who translated the Torah and the Bible, our masters the authors of the Targum tried to change examples and expressions. For example, Onkelos translated "brought them out with a raised hand" [Exod. 14:8] as ". . . with a bare head" because that was how 'someone who

> does not flee' is said in the target language. We can see here that many exegetes and translators commented and translated the books of the bible and the tractates of the Mishnah and the Talmud into other languages, and how many of the authors' opinions they have altered from their original compositions, that is to say that it says one thing but they say it says another. But because these books and their contents are available to us, themselves, without additions or deletions, and [so are] the commentaries accompanying the texts, then the matter is available and [their books] will reach many and their opinions will become widespread.[4]

In this preface, Judah makes allowances for culturally informed, sense-for-sense translation that uses metaphors that would make sense to the reader in the target language rather than retaining the ones that are operative in the source language; however, he does not wish for this kind of translation to be made available to anyone who cannot also consult the original text and observe the kinds of changes a sense-for-sense translator made in the text.

It is counterintuitive: the harder-to-read version of the text is destined for the reader less able to read it. Judah envisions the difficult-to-parse word-for-word translation as a substitute for the text because it ostensibly transmits the text wholesale without the translator's intervention,[5] whereas by contrast, an easier-to-read sense-for-sense translation can be used only in circumstances in which the reader has access to the original and can assess the degree of the translator's interventions himself. Neither vision of reading praxis allows for a reader wholly independent from the source language. The recipient of the sense-for-sense version must have access to the text in the original while the reader of the word-for-word translation must be able to navigate the grammar and syntax of the source text even in its absence. Neither option represents a way for a reader to approach these texts fully disconnected from the Arabic language. And so ultimately, where Tibbonid translations seem a bit useless on their own, that is a characteristic that is neither by chance nor by accident nor a byproduct of dogmatic adherence to a program of word-for-word translation, but is rather a deliberate consequence of specific ideas about the relationship between text and translation and the value of the original.

A complete readership history of Tibbonid texts and appreciation of the extent to which Tibbonid Hebrew was a usable form of language—that is, one that sought to offer a complete and definitive answer to the question *Of what use are the word-for-word translations that come out of the Ibn Tibbon family workshop?*—is desirable but, unfortunately, well beyond the scope of the present study. Such a reception history would follow several lines of development:

linguistic, material, and cultural-historical. Along linguistic lines, a reception history would need to trace new vocabulary coinages and track the extent to which those lexemes altered the landscape of the Hebrew language; it would treat Arabizing syntactic elements similarly and trace them through the later development of Hebrew writing by readers of the Tibbonid texts. Along material and numerical lines, a full reception history would have to study the surviving manuscripts and early print editions of the Hebrew translations of the texts that Judah and Samuel tackled—nearly one hundred manuscripts of Judah's translations survive, as do close to 150 surviving manuscript copies of Samuel's translation of the *Guide* alone[6]—and would compare the distribution of their literal translations for more literary Hebrew translations of the same texts. Transitioning from the material into the cultural-historical realm, a full reception history would have to assess the attitudes toward these texts expressed in various types of informal commentaries, including readers' notes in the margins of the manuscripts and letters requesting the purchase of books from distant booksellers; it would also survey later Hebrew literature for quotations and allusions that can be tied directly to Tibbonid translations. Ideally, all these elements would be considered in both Arabophone environments, as in Yemen, Syria, and Egypt, and in non-Arabophone ones like France and Germany. It would be a study of considerable heft. Even Adam Shear's recent history of the reception of a single work, Judah Halevi's *Kuzari* in Judah ibn Tibbon's Hebrew translation, represents a lengthy monographic study.[7] And so in the final chapter of this project I focus on one particular mode of reception history that is both in keeping with my own interest as a reader of Judah's work and is one that seems to have been a particularly fruitful way for later medieval and early modern readers to grapple with texts that were linguistically difficult and foreign to them. The end of this literary-historical study, fittingly, focuses on fiction as a mode through which later readers could make sense of the Tibbonid corpus.

FICTION AS A RESPONSE TO RATIONALISM

Diana Lobel opens *A Sufi-Jewish Dialogue*, her monograph on the Sufi influence on Andalusi Jewish philosophers and writers, and on the work of Baḥya ibn Paquda in particular, with a version of an anecdote told about one of the founders of the modern Ashkenazi (northern and central European Jewish) pietist movement known as *Ḥasidut*. An eighteenth-century *ḥasid* tells some soldiers that, having won the battle they had just fought, they now had to prepare for a greater, internal struggle. Lobel then comments:

> The source of this anecdote is the Hebrew translation of Baḥya ibn Paqūda's *Duties of the Heart*, written in Arabic—more precisely, in Judeo-Arabic—in eleventh-century Spain, but translated in 1161 into Hebrew and a favorite of Jewish devotion down to this day. What the eighteenth-century Hasidic master no doubt did not realize is that the origin of the anecdote is the Islamic tradition of *ḥadīth* and that the *ḥasid* about whom it is told is the founder of Islam, the prophet Muḥammad. . . . Readers of the work in Hebrew translation might also be surprised that Baḥya's term for both the external battle and the greater, internal struggle is *jihād*.[8]

What Lobel signals here as important and, perhaps, surprising, is the notion of early modern Ashkenazi Jews not only subscribing to, but building their entire pietistic mythology around, a worldview circumscribed by an Islamicate notion of greater *jihād*, or personal struggle, preserved in an Andalusi text written by a Jewish author not at all troubled by the Arabic terminology that was his native philosophical language and that Judah ibn Tibbon had translated out of Arabic and into Hebrew. Yet this phenomenon is less unusual than this registered note of surprise would seem to indicate. Both knowingly and unwittingly, early modern Ashkenazi readers accessed and valued Arabo-Islamicate Andalusi literary traditions through their textual canon, their intellectual debates, and the persistent memories that they adopted to give shape to their historical narrative. Philosophy-turned-fiction becomes one of the most important ways that Judah ibn Tibbon's translations and the cultural ethos that they embody are preserved for the European audiences he imagined.

The pietistic movements grouped under the heading *ḥasidei Ashkenaz* (the pietists of the Ashkenaz region) grew up in northern Europe beginning around the start of the thirteenth century, shortly after the death of Judah ibn Tibbon.[9] These spiritualist movements and their adherents often sought to engage with what they already viewed as some of the most canonical of Jewish texts, but they had difficulty reconciling their own approach to systems of religious belief and observance with the rationalism underpinned texts by Maimonides, Baḥya, and Halevi. Ashkenazi pietism was aware of Maimonides' work and the controversies it engendered from its earliest days; there have been connections between them from at least as early as the end of Samuel ibn Tibbon's life and the Maimonidean controversies of 1230–32,[10] largely those apparently designed, if unsuccessfully, to quell tensions between rationalists and kabbalists.[11] In one notable case, it was the absence of the Tibbonid text, and the presence, instead, of general knowledge about the text, that allowed it to be accepted into pietistic circles. Joseph Dan writes about the extent to which Sa'adya Ga'on was accepted into anti-rationalist kabbalistic tradition because such a tradition, explicitly in the absence of access to Judah ibn Tibbon's word-for-word translation and related lexicographic study, could accept Sa'adya as a compiler of tradition rather than as the author of Greek-style "dialectics," a term used pejoratively to refer to philosophical reasoning.[12] However, other previous scholarly studies have demonstrated that ignoring the text in favor of the prestige of the author was only one approach. Another was fantastical writing,[13] which served as a mode through which adherents to the Ashkenazi pietists could comfortably engage with the rationalism of Andalusi philosophers and theologians that might have otherwise challenged the spiritual focus that characterized their movement's approach to text.

Ashkenazi reception of the Judaeo-Arabic philosophical corpus was, necessarily and from the outset, colored by the types of translations available to readers and their awareness and knowledge of other translations; much of that came through the Tibbonid project.[14] A work such as the *Kuzari*, which already places its philosophical-theological discourse within a fictional frame, particularly invites further fictional treatment. That is precisely how the work is approached in the thirteenth-century reworking of the text by one of the founders of the pietist movement, Judah of Regensburg. The *Kuzari*, as mentioned above, is a philosophically informed dialogue in which a central Asian king consults a philosopher and Christian and Muslim clerics; when those three fail to satisfy the king's curiosity about how he might behave in a way that is pleasing to God, he deigns to consult with a Jewish interlocutor and is ultimately so compelled by the interlocutor's answers that he and all of his subjects convert to Judaism. In Judah of Regensburg's version, three Jewish scholars present their theological perspectives—one Saadyanic, one Maimonidean, and one based in the thinking of Abraham ibn 'Ezra'—to an individual described as an Arab king of Spain who, by the end, converts to Judaism; it is the adaptation of the *Kuzari* by an author familiar with its premise but unfamiliar with the text itself.[15] The reading practice is familiar. As discussed in chapter 5, it was not out of the realm of possibility for later readers to adapt and respond to texts even without the text in front of them, in effect creating an image of the original in negative. I would even venture to suggest that this approach to the *Kuzari* reflects the pietists' interest in Judah Halevi's work that was great but also hampered by their inability to make their way through a Hebrew text that read as Arabic. Only one direct citation of the *Kuzari* in Judah ibn Tibbon's Hebrew translation has as yet been uncovered.[16] However, this does not mean that readers among *ḥasidei Ashkenaz* were uninterested in Judah Halevi's work or the *Kuzari* in particular. An alternative Hebrew translation of the *Kuzari*, one created by Joseph ibn Kardinal, circulated widely in Provence during the same time period that the German pietists flourished, and proved much more popular than the Ibn Tibbon translation even if that version was easier to obtain.[17] Furthermore, where the Ashkenazi pietists largely ignore the text of the *Kuzari* despite their interest in its framework and transmission of Andalusi ideas, they made extensive use of Judah Halevi's liturgical poetry, and in particular his *ofanim*[18] (strophic poems that describe the biblical creation story and especially the role of angels in it).[19] They were clearly interested in both the *Kuzari* and the liturgical poetry, but could only engage with the texts that came to them in readable Hebrew, in this case the poetry. And furthermore, this shows that fiction was comfortably one of the textual modes through which contemporaneous Ashkenazi thinkers reckoned with the Maimonidean controversies, and through which even the usually anti-rationalist pietists could assimilate philosophical thinking. As we see, only shortly after Samuel ibn Tibbon and Judah al-Ḥarīzī created their respective translations of the *Guide*, Ashkenazi thinkers were participating in the debates over how best to understand and transmit Maimonides' work on completely different terms, ones that were ambivalent, at best, in their approach to philosophy and that did not yet account for differences in translation style but that did utilize fiction as a means to do so.

Error also sometimes crept in through these reading practices to add extra, inadvertent layers to these fictionalized treatments of philosophical ideas. Gershom Scholem offers a related example with a crucial difference that raises some interesting questions about the nature of fiction itself. Scholem notes that in one of the print editions of a commentary on *Sefer Yeẓirah* (*The Book of Creation*) by the author identified as a pseudo-Sa'adya, the work claims to cite from a certain esoteric work known as *Sefer Ẓaḥ ve-Ashur* (*The Clear and Authorized Book*) where more correctly transcribed editions cite the work of Abraham bar Ḥiyaa, a scientist and philosopher who was active in mid-twelfth-century Barcelona. Although no such work exists, the unusual coinage of the spurious title nonetheless refers to the work of Abraham bar Ḥiyya; the invented Hebrew title of the book represents a kind of echolalic corruption of Bar Ḥiyya's honorific Arabic title, *ṣāḥib al-shurṭā'* (chief of police). And so we see that the movement of Spanish works of philosophy into Ashkenazi realms in ways that they could be acceptable to Ashkenazi readers happens along a continuum that runs from error to fiction and raises interesting questions about the relationship between those two termini. The juxtaposition of error against fiction and the way in which an erroneous transcription makes its way into an edition of the text, thereby accidentally creating what becomes a fictional transmission history, is quite striking.[20]

The interface between Maimonideanism and *ḥasidut* had largely died down by the end of the period that we identify in Europe as the Middle Ages but was then renewed and continued to develop in early modernity. Elchanan Reiner has documented a variety of sixteenth-century debates and disputations about Maimonideanism, the dissemination of esoteric ideas, and the methods of understanding the *Guide* in Hebrew. For example, he describes two related disagreements over Maimonideanism that took place in the Polish city of Poznan in the latter half of the 1550s. Those two debates staked out terrain that will be immediately recognizable to students of twelfth-century debates over the role of rationalism in religion and the thirteenth-century ones that followed, having to do with the dissemination of esoterica: in the first instance, one young yeshiva student argued that philosophical pursuits were tantamount to heresy, but the defenders of Maimonides among the student's peer group prevailed to the point that he was ultimately gagged and prohibited from expressing his view. In the second instance a rabbi delivered sermons to defend himself against charges made by his son-in-law in mishnaic terms that he, the rabbi, was reliant on "Homeric books"—yet another derogatory term for works of Greek philosophical reasoning—in explicating text and extrapolating theological positions.[21] Reiner distinguishes between the thirteenth- and sixteenth-century iterations of these debates: "I am not arguing that nothing happened in Ashkenazi Jews' intellectual world in the sixteenth century, or that their culture was a direct continuation of that of medieval tradition, without change. Far from it."[22] Nevertheless, the terms of these debates, and the subject matter up for discussion, bear a striking resemblance, despite the discontinuity, between their medieval and modern iterations.

This was the environment that ensured that it was ultimately Samuel's work, marked by that extreme devotion to literalness, that defied the limited interest in Tibbonid Hebrew texts as texts going forward. Where Sa'adya was popular in Europe because European readers did not have access to his texts, and where the *Kuzari* was popular only insofar as the translators of culture could work around the text and transmit the story and the general framework, the *Guide of the Perplexed* was wildly popular, in and of itself (or rather, of its Hebrew version produced by the Tibbonid workshop). Defying the conventions that seem to have governed the circulation of other Tibbonid texts, it is a better testing ground for the viability of Arabizing Hebrew than any of Judah's own works. And so when later medieval and early modern writers in Europe turn to fiction as their mode of engaging with the Tibbonid texts, it is ultimately Judah's son Samuel who becomes their preferred protagonist. However, he stands as a literary figure as the face of the workshop and a bit of a metonym for his father and the wider cultural program: the heir, the first reader, and the representative. Two additional examples of late medieval/early modern texts that remained in the Mediterranean universe, from which the medieval intellectual and literary environment that had been al-Andalus at its apex was fading, are even fuller developments of the fictional form of Tibbonid reception and are the focus of the remainder of this chapter.

A COLOPHON AS THE SITE OF A POLEMIC ON TRANSLATION

The first example of a fantasy text through which readers could grapple with the problems posed by word-for-word translation even as the Tibbonid Hebrew versions of texts were becoming the standard and authoritative ones is itself found appended to a Hebrew-language biography of Alexander the Great (now known by the shelfmark Beinecke Hebrew Supplemental MS 103 and prior to the year 2000 by the shelfmark Jews' College London MS 145). This version of the life of Alexander is based on a now-lost Arabic translation of *Historia de Proeliis*, the Latin translation of the authoritative Greek-language biography written by the author identified as Psuedo-Callisthenes, with other Alexander source material drawn in throughout.[23] It was adapted to eliminate some, though not all, of its protagonist's attributes and practices that would mark him as pagan; he is also explicitly Judaized in the narrative of his visit to Jerusalem through various turns of phrase, through mentions of Jewish practice in Alexander's realm, and through the representation of Alexander's prostration before the *kohen* in the Jerusalem temple, which is explained away as an adoration of the divine name and not of the *kohen* himself, so as not to make Alexander seem too much like a pagan. It also pays particular attention to astronomical knowledge, tying it in with rabbinic ideas about that set of practices.[24]

What makes the work particularly significant and gives it a reach beyond the historiography of the Alexanderroman is the colophon, which falsely attributes the Hebrew translation to Samuel ibn Tibbon, adding itself as an additional work to the list of those commonly and (for the most part)[25] more securely attributed to Samuel ibn Tibbon; it furthermore implicates the text in debates over word-for-word and sense-for-sense translation and whose translation of the *Guide* should be considered the best. The colophon reads:

> This book was completed, having been translated by the sage and the true investigator of the secrets of life and wisdom, R. Samuel bar Judah ibn Tibbon (of blessed memory) of Rimon-Sefarad [Granada]; he translated it at the same time as he translated the *Guide*, which cannot even be valued by the gold of Ofir. This book is found in the hands of few people in the translation of al-Ḥarīzī, which is very error-ridden because *he adapted it from its language*, but the excellent above-mentioned translator (let his recompense be complete!) translated it from Arabic[26] into Hebrew. Perfected and completed, praise the Lord of the Worlds. He alone is God and there is no other.[27]

Despite the unreliability of the colophon's statements about its own creation, the Arabizing features of the Alexander romance's Hebrew make it quite likely that this text was in fact translated from a now-lost Arabic version, as the text itself claims. It is not as rigidly Arabizing as we would expect properly Tibbonid Hebrew to be, though. And furthermore, the chronology of texts on which this version draws makes it all but impossible for Samuel ibn Tibbon to have been the translator.[28] The reader is faced with an invented account of the text's creation that attempts to accrete some of the prestige of a famous translator to itself; this counterfactual colophon also makes the Hebrew Alexander romance a site for continued debate over who created the best translation of the *Guide* and how. This section of the discussion examines the imaginative character of the colophon and its implications for interpreting the text as a whole, as well as various scholarly responses to what is, on the face of it, a puzzling bit of paratext.

While one particular infelicity in the phrasing of the colophon has typically been interpreted as some kind of scribal error, I intend to argue that it is not an error at all but rather a subtle salvo into the debate over which translation of the *Guide* is superior. The colophon explains that Judah's version is "meshubash me'od" (very error-ridden) because al-Ḥarīzī "*he'etiqo me-lashon*," whereas Samuel "*he'etiqo me-lashon hagari*"—apparently distinguishing between "translation from [lacuna?] language" and "translation from the Arabic language." This is unexpected and initially points to a copyist's omission of an additional adjective. However, a more detailed linguistic and historicizing reading of this colophon begins to suggest that this phrase represents, rather than a mistake, a clear assertion of the stylistic stakes of the question about the transmission of the *Guide* in Hebrew. The sense of this phrase, which has fortuitously been the subject of a variety of attempts to parse it, hangs on the multivalent sense of the verb *he'etiq*[29] and reveals a very sensitive understanding of the distinctions between Samuel and Judah's versions of the *Guide*.

Moritz Steinschneider initially dismissed the value of this brief paratext: "This confusing epigraph appears completely worthless."[30] Subsequently Adolf Neubauer grappled more purposefully and seriously with the phrasing of the colophon as he catalogued the original Jews' College manuscript collection,[31] suggesting in subsequent publications that the first instance of the word *lashon* (tongue/language) was a mis-rendering of *laṭin* (Latin).[32] This interpretation was rejected almost immediately by Israel Levi on the grounds that al-Ḥarīzī was working from the same Arabic as Ibn Tibbon and because Levi could not establish that al-Ḥarīzī knew enough Latin to give the author of the colophon any idea that this might have been plausible,[33] regardless of how plausible a scribal error it might be (particularly given the similarities between the *ṭ* and the *š* in the scribal hand). Linguistic evidence further troubles Neubauer's reading, with *laṭin* appearing in Hebrew to describe Latin or the Romance vernaculars only very uncommonly prior to the copying of this manuscript. We shall see below that later medieval and early modern readers have no problem inventing and accepting highly convoluted transmission histories between unexpected pairs of languages, in unexpected directions, and along roundabout and back-and-forth paths, and so while a version of events in which al-Ḥarīzī was translating from Latin rather than from Hebrew might represent yet another twist in an invented narrative of the colophon, it seems as unlikely as it is inelegant.

The most common explanation for this infelicity has been the assumption that this awkwardness is the result of the scribal omission of an adjective that would distinguish the language from which Samuel translated the *Guide* from the language from which Judah translated it, despite the usual care of the scribe to correct his own few errors. We do not know at what point in time the colophon was added to this text. It is not included in a related but not identical Hebrew translation of *Historia de Proeliis* that also came through a now-lost Arabic version, nor do we yet know of a Vorglage from which the scribe might have been working or where the error might have been introduced if it was not our scribe's. However, because both Judah and Samuel were translating from the same Arabic version of the *Guide*, as Levi noted, there is no word that could sensibly fill the lacuna and distinguish between the text from which Samuel translated and the identical text from which Judah translated because both men worked from the same source. A solution that proposes a dropped word would have to presume a certain degree of ignorance or willful confusion on the part of the colophon's author about the Maimonidean sources from which Samuel ibn Tibbon and Judah al-Ḥarizī worked.

The editor of the text, Wout van Bekkum, moved generally if tentatively toward a different solution that could explain the text as it is received, without any emendation, writing in the notes to the text: "A deliberate omission?"[34] In other words, while van Bekkum does not propose an alternative reading, he opens the door to the possibility that such an alternative ought to come from the page rather than from an addition to it, and it is on the foundation of his suggestion that I build my reading of the colophon. As noted above, the verb *heʿetiq* has an unusually wide and flexible semantic range and is sometimes even used with different meanings within the same text or even the same paragraph. It is this suggestion that I would like to draw out further in my own reading of the colophon, resolving (at least to a great extent) the apparent awkwardness in the language and also explaining the colophon author's choice not only to implicate Samuel ibn Tibbon in the creation of the Alexanderroman but also to stand him in sharp contrast to Judah al-Ḥarīzī.

Bearing the flexibility of the word and its multifarious definitions in mind, it is possible to understand the first occurrence of the word, the one that describes Samuel's work, as meaning "he translated," while simultaneously understanding the second occurrence of the word, the one used with respect to Judah's, to mean "he adapted." This contrast draws on the distinctions between the task of the translator and the task of the author that were current in discussions about the translation of Maimonides' work and that the Ibn Tibbon family members themselves set out. In other words, the sense of the colophon takes advantage of the many possibilities of a single lexical item in order to create a salient and realistic distinction between the two translators of the *Guide*, to articulate the terms of the existing debate over the two modes of translation, and to take sides in that debate by claiming that Samuel ibn Tibbon's method of translation (that is, word-for-word translation) is better than Judah al-Ḥarizī's method of adaptation (that is, sense-for-sense translation). This solution retains the slight awkwardness of the phrasing but keeps the meaning of the text in line with the rest of the details drawn into this made-up history of the text.

The relationship between the colophon and the text fortifies reading of the colophon as a referendum on the two different styles of translation. Connections exist between the text and the colophon in two major categories: first, the fact that both Alexander and Maimonides bore a close intellectual relationship to the work of Aristotle, and second, through the question of this Alexander's interest in esoterica and Samuel's insistence on literal translation as the best way to translate the esoterica in the *Guide*. Shamma Boyarin, the scholar to have most recently contended with this codex, has delineated these connections in some detail:

> The colophon places the work of perhaps the most influential Jewish medieval neo-Aristotelian, Maimonides, next to the ostensible biography of a man whom many considered one of the greatest students of Aristotle: Alexander the Great. Samuel ibn Tibbon's translation project might be described as the importation of Aristotelian and neo-Aristotelian works into Hebrew, and some, obviously including the colophon's author, might have viewed the Alexander Romance as a natural component of such a project.
>
> The colophon describes Ibn Tibbon as the 'learned investigator into the true secrets of existence' because of his inquiry into, and exposition of, Maimonides' esoteric teachings. The colophon's author is simply making an easy connection between Maimonides' (neo)-Aristotelian esoteric writings and another group of esoteric teachings that present themselves and were accepted by some as written by Aristotle. . . . And studying the Alexander Romance 'at the same time as' the *Guide* makes sense if one views Alexander's relationship to the knowledge transmitted via this relationship, as part of 'the enhancement and intensification' of the philosophical inquiry that led both to the original writing of, and Ibn Tibbon's deciphering of, the *Guide*. . . . Even the incidental information contained in the colophon of Beinecke Heb. Suppl. 103 is important to its meaning.[35]

The Alexander romance as a genre can be all things to all people: his administration of a large empire was emphasized in Victorian English versions, while a sixteenth-century version from a persecuted crypto-Muslim community in Spain chooses to highlight his contact with and protection of persecuted peoples. The colophon of Beineicke Hebrew Suppl. 103 argues, in effect, that an Alexander romance is the appropriate place for an Arabized Jew to expound on Maimonideanism because of the Aristotelian substrates in both, a connection that is amplified by this Alexander's interest in the pursuit of scientific and philosophical knowledge;[36] and Alexander's interest in esoterica demands Samuel ibn Tibbon's literal approach to translation in the same way that Maimonides' work does. By disregarding Maimonides' own ideas about the superiority of sense-for-sense translation in the interest of Samuel ibn Tibbon's Maimonideanism and word-for-word translation, the colophon goes farther than commenting on the text and places it firmly in the realm of its readership history.[37]

A *TREATISE*, A PREFACE, AND A FICTIVE RECEPTION HISTORY

The debate over how best to translate Maimonides came in the course of a series of intellectual disputes that have collectively come to be known as the Maimonidean controversies, which dealt largely with questions of how to understand the esoterica found within the Maimonidean corpus and how to transmit it so as not to confuse or taint the lay populace. However, these questions were beginning to be raised even in the years before Maimonides' death, such that he himself had the chance to respond to charges that his works were more rational than they were pious. Kicking off those controversies,[38] the ga'on of Baghdad, Samuel ben 'Elī ibn al-Dastūr (d. after 1197), charged that the rationalist undercurrent of Maimonides' legal compendium, the *Mishneh Torah*, and the distinction that it made between different types of reward in the afterlife, some of which would be suitable to corporeal beings and some not, showed that its author did not believe literally in the central Jewish tenet that the dead would be resurrected in the eventual and forthcoming messianic age; and similar claims were made against Maimonides across the Near East, from Damascus to the Yemen.[39] Because of the seriousness of such a charge of heresy both within the Jewish community as well as for Muslim authorities in Cairo who were no great proponents of rationalist thinking and who, had they become aware of this "heresy," could easily have taken action, Maimonides found it necessary to defend himself.[40] In order to do so he wrote an essay bilingually entitled *Maqāla fī teḥiyyat ha-metim* (Treatise on the Doctrine of Resurrection),[41] a work in which he reconciles rationalist philosophy and metaphorical interpretation of Scripture with literal adherence to the tenet of the bodily resurrection of the dead.[42] Like the *Guide*, it was translated into Hebrew by both Samuel ibn Tibbon and Judah al-Ḥarīzī (although the existence of al-Ḥarīzī's version was not confirmed until its rediscovery toward the end of the 1970s and its publication in 1980).[43]

A fourteenth-century reader of the *Treatise* chose to respond to the text by writing a preface for it that draws an analogy between translation and retranslation, and death and resurrection. The preface—a unicum that precedes a copy of Samuel ibn Tibbon's Hebrew translation of the *Treatise* made no earlier than 1348[44]—contains a baffling, brief story about one branch of the reception history of Maimonides' *Treatise*. The preface opens with four lines of poetry from al-Ḥarīzī's *Taḥkemoni* in praise of Maimonides. The prose body of the text is written in the voice of a narrator, a certain Joseph ben Joel, who introduces the text that will follow as Maimonides' *Treatise on the Doctrine of Resurrection*. He observes that it was translated into Hebrew, describing it as a process of "emptying it [the text] from vessel to vessel" that ultimately drove the text into a kind of "exile, until someone could redeem it." Already from the outset, he sets the Arabic original as the home of the text, and Hebrew as the locus of its exile. After another four lines of poetry, the narrator first introduces himself to us by name. Some of the previous scholarship on this preface has taken this introduction in media res to indicate a change of author or narrative voice, but that seems to be a needless complication unwarranted by an already complicated text. I read it, instead, as a précis of what is to follow. We see that the narrator is speaking to a friend, an interlocutor who has asked him to translate the *Treatise*—and we shall see momentarily that the question of the language into which the friend wishes to see the *Treatise* translated and the language into which the narrator can translate is not a straightforward one. Joseph praises Maimonides; and he viciously criticizes a certain group of talmudists "who see themselves as wise and fit to speak, regardless of the subject matter" for being uncouth, disrespectful to Maimonides himself, and for interpreting his text in ways that constituted a stumbling block rather than a clear path to an explanation. Joseph notes that although Maimonides sent the treatise to "every nation and every community,"[45] somehow a copy did not make its way to him and he did not have access to the Arabic original. Instead, he has a copy of Samuel ibn Tibbon's translation; but he would really like to have a copy in Arabic. He goes on to explain that with the collaboration of his friend, he will translate it back into Arabic, and then explains his own principles as a translator, which are delineated in much greater detail below. This confused and confusing preface contains many difficult points and raises many questions about its own nature, character, and veracity; ultimately, though, I argue that it is, like the Alexander colophon, a shrewd literary work that uses the mode of imaginative prose to highlight favored aspects of the Tibbonid program of translation.

The name of the picaresque literary persona of the narrator, Joseph ben Joel, is apparently unattested in documentary sources but is perhaps the literary alter-ego of the anonymous author.[46] The preface and the translation that should ostensibly follow it are dedicated to an equally unknown, if not also entirely fictional, patron whose name evokes those of the grandees of Provençal Jewry: Meir ben Sheshet. By using the preface to serve as a kind of frame for the *Treatise*; through deploying the tropes of the lost-and-found manuscript and the curious, bookish friend (as well as the *maqāma*-esque dynamic between the two figures of the narrator-hero and the friend); and through a narrative that sees the fortunes of its hero change rapidly and frequently, the text shows all the narrative and stylistic signs of being a work of fiction rather than of historical reporting. The possible fictional character of this text has, however, long troubled the scholars who have approached it. In his storied *Hebraische Ubersetzungen*, Moritz Steinschneider concludes that the text was simply "something that perplexes us completely," writing it off in a manner similar to his dismissal of the Alexander colophon.[47] However, in the preface to his study of the main text of the *Treatise on the Doctrine of Resurrection*, Joshua Finkel seeks to consider all of the manuscript evidence for the *Treatise*, including this strange preface, in a serious and engaged manner. A long section of his analysis of the preface is composed of bewildered-sounding but pointedly accurate rhetorical questions about its character, origins, and purpose, ultimately allowing Finkel to shed light on the sheer volume of inexplicable, strange, and deeply contradictory features of the text.[48] Nevertheless, unlike Steinschneider, who considered the text to be a factual, if deeply flawed, accounting of events surrounding the production, dissemination, and translation of the *Treatise on the Doctrine of Resurrection*, Finkel recognized the preface for what it is: a work of fiction. Following the interrogative section of his introduction to the text, Finkel comments:

> What motives could have prompted our Anonymous to invent such an involved account of the translation of the Treatise, it is hard to discover. I am inclined to think that the writer drew inspiration for this theme from the accounts of mishaps and changes of fortune befalling the heroes of fiction. If so, we must say that his introduction is a highly original and fanciful piece of belles-lettres. . . . The background for all these assertions seems to be anything but real. We have seen how the writer has twice telescoped his personalities. Now he is also juggling with their works. Bearing all these inconsistencies in mind as well as the basic fact that the pattern of the account is that of the familiar ups and downs of a hero's career in fiction, we can do nothing better than maintain that the account is a whimsical Maqāma . . . a sort of composition which, from suggestive analogy to the Historical Romance, I would venture to characterize as a 'Scholarly Romance.'[49]

While later scholars have largely tended to continue to read with Steinschneider,[50] it is rather important to distinguish between a text that draws in details of a real situation and a historical accounting of that situation; in other words, even if the Arabic were available, the claim that five translations had been executed back and forth within the space of well under a century makes this out to be a work of fiction, even if it is grounded in reality and even if some of the details jibe. When Sarah Stroumsa writes, "Its peculiarity, however, is recognized also by those who do not question its authenticity,"[51] she is speaking of the *Treatise* itself (the authenticity and authorial attribution of which have also been questioned)[52] but might as easily be speaking of this preface. In the case of the preface the situation is almost reversed: one need not create or believe the fairly incredible backstory that allows this text to be a genuine one; recognizing it as a legitimate, authentic work of fiction with its own set of parameters also allows for a discussion of peculiarities that signal quite a lot about culture, religion, and readership.

The text is a challenging one because it is not always totally linear; because it hedges, almost as if trying to avoid coming down firmly on one side or the other of the series of debates over Maimonides, Maimonideanism, and translation that were roiling the Jewish communities of medieval Provence; and because it so obviously disregards the implausibility of the chain of events described therein and the contradictions posed to it by the material record of its own existence. Even the manuscript evidence proves to be a problem. The preface is, ostensibly, to accompany this final translation back into Arabic; however, as noted above, the only copy that exists is appended to a copy of Samuel ibn Tibbon's Hebrew version of the *Treatise*; there is no reason to believe that an Arabic retranslation ever existed. Nevertheless, a careful reading of the preface and all of its quirks reveals it to be an artifact of cultural memory of the Tibbonid workshop: a text that employs that same prominent Andalusi cast of characters as the Alexander colophon—Samuel ibn Tibbon, Judah al-Ḥarīzī, and Moses Maimonides—to opine not only on the process of translation from Arabic into Hebrew but on the linguistic, literary, and cultural value of the Arabic language itself. In doing so, it serves as yet another demonstration of the ways in which the Tibbonid workshop, in both cases with the ultimately more famous and widely read Samuel standing in for the Andalusi values of his father, came best to serve as touchstone of Judaeo-Arabic cultural and literary heritage.

The narrator, Joseph, introduces his readers to both of the Hebrew translators of the *Treatise*. He opens by praising Maimonides with four lines of poetry borrowed, uncredited, from al-Ḥarīzī's *Sefer ha-Taḥkemoni*. Also without naming the translator, he criticizes Samuel ibn Tibbon as "the one who translated it to the sacred language added depth to its content but did not clear away the stones from the path."[53] The attitude of this preface toward the two approaches to translation is decidedly ambivalent. Time and again, the narrator aligns himself with the culturally prestigious Tibbonid school of translation, all the while critiquing its methodology. On the one hand, he describes Samuel as his "learned, honored interlocutor" who is "knowledgeable in every field"; on the other hand, he returns to his original assessment of Samuel ibn Tibbon as creating translations that do not really clear things up for the Hebrew reader. While he pays lip service to word-for-word translation, declaring it to be the best in the abstract and writing that "if it is possible to continue every action like this, to translate word for word, then the expressions poured out will be clear, and this is the fulfillment of all the goals of this effort. In this vein, it is incorrect for the translator to pursue words according to his own reasoning," he ultimately concludes that if the translator were to "focus on the words and turn his eyes away from the subject matter . . . there would be a loss of the subject matter but a preservation of its accidental qualities"; as such, he tells us, he himself is choosing to translate the text back into Arabic and that

> I have chosen, for this translation of mine, to privilege the words so that they are bound in clarity and approximate their order . . . and I am disinclined to the ones that are not based on a solid foundation. However, I did not pay attention to preserving changes in conjunctions and verbal forms. This is because my main goal is that no word should be separated from from its subject matter; and so you will find that I explain a word in a number of places in the language that is suitable for it. In some places I will choose a certain word and I won't leave it stuck in the original language. One example of this is the word "matter": Sometimes I will render it as "matter" and sometimes as "goal" and sometimes as "principle" and sometimes as "thing." So, too, the word "body": I can render it as body, as "corpse," "skeleton," "being," or "body," and so on and so forth. It is all according to what I see as fitting for the place. The main concern is to clarify and open up. In general, my main goal is to choose what the subject matter demands so that the reader will understand it.[54]

He even goes as far as to make an explicit statement of the importance of the sense of the subject matter over the style of the words: "From time immemorial, we have known that the first goal of every translator in his translation is the subject matter, which is the pillar on which the whole building will stand."[55] In other words, Joseph wishes and tries to abide by the principles of his "learned, honored interlocutor," but finds that when he himself translates, it is more important to create a text that is easily readable in the target language, Hebrew. He does not wish to preserve the "accidental qualities" of a text—the order of the words, the grammatical gender of nouns, and other particular features of the language—at the expense of the holistic, conceptual meaning of the text. When necessary, he translates sense-for-sense, rendering "a word in language that is suitable." While espousing Tibbonid principles, trying to "privilege the words . . . keeping them together," the fictional translator–persona of Joseph ultimately prefers translations that are of greater communicative value to his non-Arabophone community.

Ultimately, though, it is the narrator's unwavering and clear-eyed (if anachronistic) attitude toward the Arabic language itself that is the most compelling testament to the perdurance of aspects of the Tibbonid project. He comments on the relative utility of Arabic compared with Hebrew for expressing complex philosophical ideas in a turn of phrase that is remarkably reminiscent of what we have already seen in Judah ibn Tibbon's work and that may also be found in echoes of that in Samuel's: "As the boundaries of Arabic widened, the footsteps of Hebrew came too close together to keep up with it."[56] It is the narrator's obsession with the Arabic language and his desire to read the *Treatise* in Arabic—and as we shall see shortly, it need not be Maimonides' Arabic; any Arabic will do—that fuels the plot (paltry though it may be) of this prefatory anecdote. Joseph, who articulates a very clear view that a good translation ought to be an interpretation of the text, begins his praise of the Arabic language and the *Treatise* as an Arabic text with his harshest critique of Samuel ibn Tibbon's translation. In it he explains that Samuel's translation uses Hebrew words that are not suitable to the subject matter, all the while not really helping to clarify, explain, or interpret the subject of the text through his translation: "None of it [the text] remains in our hands, not even a little bit. But rather, this translation has come down to us, complex and enigmatic, and the forms of its subject matter were foolish, and they were held up in the marshes of their words and caught up in their corruptness." In one of the most literary flourishes of the preface, he tells his readers that as a consequence, a "cultured" friend of his who was a great lover of Arabic literature asked him to translate the preface back into Arabic: "So a literary *amateur* and cultured friend asked me to return it to its origins in the Arabic language and so I set myself to translating it in order to fulfill the request of this seeker and to get it to him in some semblance of the language of its author."[57] At this point it no longer mattered that the text be in Maimonides' Arabic; any Arabic would be better than any Hebrew at expressing his ideas.

This attitude is manifest between the lines, too. The narrator playfully calques Arabic words in way that uncharacteristically escaped Steinschneider's notice but that Finkel would later identify in the course of attempting to parse the way in which the preface renders the title of the *Treatise*, not as *Ma'amar fī teḥiyyat ha-metim* (*Treatise on the Doctrine of Resurrection*) but rather as *Megillat sod teḥiyyat ha-metim* (*The Scroll Containing the Secrets of Resurrection*). Commenting on this discrepancy, Finkel almost apologetically tries to explain that the narrator is still talking about Maimonides' *Treatise* even if the title is not exactly the same: "The word *sod* [secret], nowhere else used as a substitute for *ma'amar* [treatise] or *iggeret* [epistle], should not invalidate the identification. The Anonymous made a mystery of everything, including the title of the Treatise."[58] More than a mere error, though, the discrepancies between the phrasing in the preface on the one hand and the title and content of the text on the other represent a series of sophisticated bilingual plays on words that highlight central aspects of the Maimonidean controversies, including the debate over the value of esotericism and the persistent tensions between Arabic and Hebrew as languages of intellectual and religious investigation. Finkel goes on to point out that the word *megillah* (scroll) in this case should be read as a calque of the Arabic term *maqāla* (treatise);[59] the description of the text in this preface is Arabizing rather than mistaken. The text also deploys a sophisticated play on words to comment slyly about the inferior value of Hebrew despite its status as a sacred language and to complicate the religious dimension of Joseph's preference for Arabic. In the course of describing the series of translations and retranslations between Arabic and Hebrew that the preface asks us to believe the text underwent, he writes, on the one hand that translation of the text into Hebrew would represent its redemption from his exile: "But then they translated it from our tongue to the Arabic language with lovely expressions and nice words, emptying it from vessel to vessel; and thus it proceeded in exile until someone would redeem it."[60] However, he describes that ultimate retranslation with an inescapable double entendre: the sense of the text being returned to its beginnings when it "comes around again" is rendered with the Hebrew phrase *ḥazar ḥallilah*, which, through a pernicious homophony, may also be read to mean "turned into a sacrilege." The Hebrew language as both redemption and sacrilege stands in sharp contrast with the unqualified good, secular and religious, that is the Arabic language in the eyes of the narrator of this text.

Ultimately this fictive preface to the *Treatise on the Doctrine of Resurrection* articulates two relationships, one in which the Arabic language is crucial to a sense of religious-national identity for Andalusi Jews, and the other in which acts of translation and retranslation are made parallel to vivification and revivification. As in much of the literature to emerge from al-Andalus and influenced by its literary trends, Hebrew never cleanly or simply signifies *Judaism*, while Arabic, even more so, is never wholly correlated to *Islam*; rather, authors—Arabophone Andalusi Jewish authors, in this instance—navigated a complex palette of religion and religious principles and the language in which those might be delineated. The preface reflects the evolving and resolving tensions between Jewish readers and the sacral status of Arabic and Hebrew within Islam and Judaism. As narrator, Joseph's allegiance is to the Arabic language, no matter whether it was Maimonides' Arabic or that of a translator. A careful close reading of the preface reveals the importance of fidelity to the language for the narrator. By the dawn of the fourteenth century, building on the work of those who came before him and writing exactly contemporaneously to the copying of the Bodleian manuscript of Judah ibn Tibbon's ethical will, Joseph has wholly inverted the relationship between language and religion that emerged at the origins of Islam and the early Jewish responses to it. For Jewish readers and writers, that relationship and their relationship to the Arabic language began to elide very early on, with Jewish readers initially reacting forcefully against the claims that Arabic was not only a sacred language but the one divine one, moving toward adopting Arabic as a liturgical language as early as the ninth century, lowering the hackles that were raised at the initially perceived challenge to their sacred tongue, and wholly embracing the range of possibilities, sacred and secular, of Arabic.

This preface and the other works of Ibn Tibbon–related imaginative texts surveyed in this chapter reflect a tendency, from the late Middle Ages moving forward, of its readers to use fiction, imagination, fantasy, and paratext as a way of grappling with a whole host of narrative, historical, cultural, and linguistic complexities. Nevertheless, these accounts reflect the state of affairs in many Ashkenazi yeshivot around the time when these texts were copied in the sixteenth century, which saw renewed interest in the *Guide* and a revisiting of many of the issues surrounding Maimonides' work that cropped up as it was being written and in the thirteenth century, in the wake of Maimonides' death, including those surrounding translation and transmission as well as those that attempted to reconcile religious belief and philosophical reason. In *The Historian's Craft*, the founder of the Annales school, Marc Bloch, writes: "Above all, a fraud is, in its way, a piece of evidence. Merely to prove that [it] . . . is not authentic is to avoid error, but not to acquire knowledge."[61] These fantasies of Maimonideanism are more than error or even fraud, representing a medium through which Provençal readers and Ashkenazi pietists could puzzle through knowledge to a broader historical and spiritual truth. To recognize them as fictions rather than as erroneous chronicles or frauds allows us a more accurate window into the literary reception of the Tibbonid cultural project.

NOTES

Chapter title from Joseph ben Joel, "Preface to the Treatise on the Doctrine of Resurrection."

1. While remarkable in every iteration, the conception of an original serving as a commentary, faithful or not, on the translation is hardly a new one. See Ryan Szpiech, "The Original Is Unfaithful to the Translation: Conversion and Authenticity in Abner of Burgos and Anselm of Turmeda," *eHumanista* 14 (2010): 155, http://www.ehumanista.ucsb.edu/sites/secure.lsit.ucsb.edu.span.d7_eh/files/sitefiles/ehumanista/volume14/Szpiech.pdf, accessed October 10, 2012.

2. Judah ibn Tibbon, preface to *Ḥovot ha-Levavot*, 3. The assignation of responsibility for garbled meaning to either author or translator is a concern that Judah addresses similarly in the preface to *Sefer ha-Riqmah*.

3. Judah ibn Tibbon, preface to *Ḥovot ha-Levavot*, 4.

4. Judah ibn Tibbon, preface to *Sefer ha-Riqmah*, 2–3.

5. Of course, the notion that a word-for-word translation also does not represent an intervention in the text does not, ultimately, hold up.

6. These estimates are derived through consultation with the catalogue of the Institute for Microfilmed Hebrew Manuscripts of the National Library of Israel, which records approximately ninety percent of the Hebrew manuscripts that had survived through the year 1950.

7. Adam Shear, *The Kuzari and the Shaping of Jewish Identity, 1167–1900* (Cambridge: Cambridge University Press, 2008).

8. Diana Lobel, *A Sufi-Jewish Dialogue: Philosophy and Mysticism in Bahya ibn Paquda's Duties of the Heart* (Philadelphia: University of Pennsylvania Press, 2007), ix–x.

9. A classic study of medieval Jewish history that includes sections on *ḥasidei Ashkenaz* is Israel Abrahams's *Jewish Life in the Middle Ages* (reprint, Philadelphia: Jewish Publication Society, 1962). More recently, see Ivan Marcus, *Piety and Society: The Jewish Pietists of Medieval Germany* (Leiden: Brill, 1997); and Ephraim Kanarfogel, "Pietistic Tendencies in Prayer and Ritual" and "Between Tosafists and German Pietists," in *Peering through the Lattices: Mystical, Magical, and Pietistic Dimensions in the Tosafist Period* (Detroit: Wayne State University Press, 2000), chaps. 2 and 4. On popular pietism, see Elisheva Baumgarten, *Practicing Piety in Medieval Ashkenaz: Men, Women, and Everyday Religious Observance* (Philadelphia: University of Pennsylvania Press, 2014).

10. Daniel Jeremy Silver, *Maimonidean Criticism and the Maimonidean Controversies* (Leiden: Brill, 1965).

11. Joseph Dan, "Ashkenazi Hasidism and the Maimonidean Controversy," *Maimonidean Studies* 3 (1995): 180–81.

12. Ibid., 187.

13. I have adopted the notion of fantasy here from the volume *Rabbinic Fantasies*, edited by David Stern and Mark Jay Mirsky, that anthologizes "imaginative" Hebrew literary texts from both the Sefardi and Ashkenazi worlds. For Stern and Mirsky (2–3), fantasy drives toward a recognizable notion of fiction without necessarily forming a distinct, coherent category of writing. It is a useful term here because it mediates between outright fiction, which is a reasonable way to describe the prologue to Maimonides' *Treatise on the Doctrine of Resurrection*, and something more like fabrication, which is a more suitable description of the colophon. The two texts relate to their historical and textual realities in different terms and function differently as literary texts, but each is a kind of imaginative counterfactual subsumed under this useful category of fantasy writing.

14. Steven Harvey, "Did Maimonides' Letter to Samuel ibn Tibbon Determine Which Philosophers Would Be Studied by Later Jewish Thinkers?" *Jewish Quarterly Review* 83, no. 1 (1992): 51–70.

15. An edition of the text appears in Joseph Dan, *Studies in the Literature of the Ashkenazi Pietists* (Ramat Gan, 1975), 159–60. For a discussion, see Dan, "Ashkenazi Hasidism," 190–93. For more on the relationship between the Ashkenazi pietists and other types of Spanish texts, see Ephraim Kanarfogel, *The Intellectual History and*

Rabbinic Culture of Medieval Ashkenaz (Detroit: Wayne State University Press, 2012), especially chap. 3. Finally, for a thorough and erudite treatment of the reception of Judah ibn Tibbon's Hebrew translation of the *Kuzari*, see Shear, *The Kuzari*.

16. Israel Ta-Shma, *Rabbi Zerahya ha-Levi Ba'al ha-Me'or and His Circle: Towards a History of Rabbinic Literature in Provence* (Jerusalem: Magnes Press, 1992), 49.

17. Shear, *The Kuzari*, 38.

18. Schirman, *Hebrew Poetry in Spain and Provence*, vol. 2, 700–701.

19. Ephraim Kanarfogel, "The Impact of Halevi in Medieval Ashkenaz," presentation given at the Annual Conference of the Association for Jewish Studies, Baltimore, December 14–16, 2014.

20. Gershom Scholem, "Reste neuplatonischer Spekulation in der Mystik der deutschen Chassidim und ihre Vermittlung durch Abraham bar Chija," *Monatsschrift für Geschichte und Wissenschaft des Judentums* 75, no. 5 (1931): 172–91.

21. Elchanan Reiner, "The Attitude of Ashkenazi Society to the New Science in the Sixteenth Century," *Science in Context* 10, no. 4 (1997): 589–91.

22. Ibid., 598.

23. This Hebrew text draws, more specifically, on the Latin recensions of *Historia de Proeliis*, usually called I2 and I3 in the standard scholarly stemma. For more on the relationship between versions and sub-versions, the textual stemmata and Alexander bibliography, see Wout van Bekkum, *A Hebrew Alexander Romance according to MS London, Jews College 145*, esp. 16–21; and Saskia Doenitz, "Alexander the Great in Medieval Hebrew Traditions," in *A Companion to Alexander Literature in the Middle Ages*, ed. Z. David Zuwiyya (Leiden: Brill, 2011), 21–39, where the relationship between one of the source texts, *Sefer Yossifon*, and the Alexanderroman under discussion is reassessed. Two new studies of Hebrew Alexander romances appeared in print the very week that I submitted the final version of this manuscript to Indiana University Press, and so all I can do is note their existence here and look forward to engaging with them more deeply in future work: Shamma Boyarin, "Hebrew Alexander Romance and Astrological Questions: Aleander, Aristotle, and the Medieval Jewish Audience," in *Alexander the Great in the Middle Ages: Transcultural Perspectives*, ed. Marcus Stock (Toronto: University of Toronto Press, 2016), 88–102; and, in the same volume, Ruth Nisse, "Diaspora as Empire in the Hebrew Deeds of Alexander," 76–87.

24. Van Bekkum, *Hebrew Alexander Romance* [JCL] 145, 25–26.

25. A variety of other texts in translation are falsely attributed to Samuel. Notable among these include Maimonides' introduction to the tenth chapter of Mishnah Sanhedrin and 'Alī ibn Ridwan's commentary on Galen's *Ars Parva*.

26. Lit., "from the Hagarite language." Please see the note in chapter 3 that discusses terminology referring to Arabs and Muslims in Judaeo-Arabic literature for more on the role of the biblical figure of Hagar in defining Arabs and Muslims in medieval rhetoric.

27. Beinecke Heb. Suppl. MS 103. 35v. The phrase in italics represents a significant departure in reading and translation from the work of previous scholars. This is discussed thoroughly in the following pages.

28. In the interest of space I refrain here from listing the well-documented intertextual dependencies that make up this version of the Alexander romance and complement the major source, namely the *Historia Proeliis*. These connections and dependencies are discussed in detail in van Bekkum, *Hebrew Alexander Romance*, and Doenitz, "Alexander the Great in Medieval Hebrew Traditions." Moritz Steinschneider's contention in his

discussion of the text in the *Hebraische Uebersetzungen* that Samuel ibn Tibbon could not have been the translator because such a text was beneath his dignity is a less compelling argument against his involvement. Steinschneider, *Die hebraeischen Uebersetzungen des Mittelalters* (Berlin: Kommisionverlag des bibliographischen Bureaus, 1893). The work has recently been made available in English translation: *The Hebrew Translations of the Middle Ages and the Jews as Transmitters*, ed. and trans. Charles Manekin et al. (New York: Springer, 2014).

29. For a discussion of this word, see Steven Bowman, review of van Bekkum, *Hebrew Alexander Romance*, *Journal of Jewish Studies* 48, no. 1 (1997): 166–68. Esperanza Alfonso identifies an instance of extreme multivalence of the sense of the term in the commentary on the biblical book of Proverbs written by Jacob Gavison, the father of the Abraham Gavison discussed in the previous chapter, in which the commentator moves from discussing the term as a word that refers to the translation or copying of written texts to exploring a definition in which the term might mean "an oral account which they had translated from a foreign language" (cited in Esperanza Alfonso, "From al-Andalus to North Africa: The Lineage and Scholarly Genealogy of a Jewish Family," in *The Jew in Medieval Iberia*, ed. Jonathan Ray (Brighton, MA: Academic Studies Press, 2012), 414–15.

30. Steinschneider, *Hebraische Uebersentzungen*, 899.

31. Adolf Neubauer, *Catalogue of the Hebrew Manuscripts in Jews' College, London* (Oxford: Oxford University Press, 1886).

32. Adolf Neubauer, "An Inedited Version of the Legend of Alexander the Great," *Jewish Quarterly Review* 4, no. 4 (1892), 687.

33. Israel Levi, "Sefer Toledot Alexander," *Sammelband kleiner Beiträge aus Handschriften*, vol. 2 (Berlin: Mekitzei Nedarim, 1886), xi. See also Levi's "Les traductions hébraiques de l'histoire légendaire d'Alexandre," *Revue des études juives* 7 (1883): 238–65.

34. Van Bekkum, *Hebrew Alexander Romance JCL* 145, 23.

35. Shamma Boyarin, "Diasporic Culture and the Makings of Alexander Romances" (PhD diss., University of California, Berkeley, 2008), 96–102.

36. For a discussion of the extent to which later medieval readers, both Jewish and Christian, associated Maimonides with Aristotle, see Angel Sáenz-Badillos, "Late Medieval Jewish Writers on Maimonides," in *Traditions of Maimonideanism*, ed. Carlos Fraenkel (Leiden: Brill, 2009), 223–43.

37. I have written more extensively about the specific ownership and readership history of this codex in "Matter, Meaning and Maimonides: The Material Text as an Early Modern Map of Thirteenth-Century Debates on Translation," in *Entangled Histories: Authority and Knowledge in the Long Thirteenth Century*, ed. Elisheva Baumgarten, Ruth Mazo Karras, and Katelyn Mesler (Philadelphia: University of Pennsylvania Press, 2016), 376–412.

38. For an overview of these, please refer back to the general introduction of the present book. I read with Stroumsa and Kraemer when they include the controversy surrounding Maimonides' ideas about the vivification of the dead that erupted during his lifetime with the broader collection of disputes known as the Maimonidean controversies; it is worth noting, though, that many other scholars only mark the beginning of the controversies after Maimonides' death and include only the posthumous reception of his work.

39. Tzvi Langermann, "Samuel ben 'Eli's Epistle on Resurrection," *Kovetz al-Yad* 15 (2001): 39–94.

40. See David Hartman's "Background of the Accusation," in *Crisis and Leadership: Epistles of Maimonides*, ed. and trans. David Hartman and Hillel Halkin (Philadelphia: Jewish Publication Society, 1994), 249–64. See also Joel Kraemer, *Maimonides: The Life and World of One of Civilization's Greatest Mind* (New York: Doubleday, 2010), 412, and Kraemer's notes to this section.

41. See the edition by Kafih (1971), as well as the much earlier edition of Finkel (1938), which is discussed in greater detail at the end of this chapter. The text was written in Arabic and the title uses the Arabic words for "treatise on" but then names the doctrine that will be treated therein, namely the doctrine on bodily resurrection, with the Hebrew phrase that designates it. It might, thus, also be rendered in English as the *Epistle on "Teḥiyyat ha-Metim."* And so, while it is typically referred to in English simply as the *Treatise on Resurrection*, I prefer to render the title as *Treatise on the Doctrine of Resurrection* to better reflect the function of the two languages in the title.

42. Sarah Stroumsa offers a detailed and nuanced account of this controversy, setting Maimondies' treatise into its cultural context and also reading it in the light of two other treatises on resurrection as well as private letters that were composed contemporaneously as a part of the affair in *A Portrait of Maimonides as a Mediterranean Thinker* (Princeton, NJ: Princeton University Press, 2008), 165–83.

43. A. David, 1980.

44. Bodl. MS Opp. Add. 4to 163 (Neubauer 2496). The scribe of the Bodleian manuscript placed a dot following each rhyming unit of text; Finkel follows this as the basis for the punctuation of his edition even though it sometimes represents an interruption in the flow of a single idea. The last few lines of the preface also appear in a miscellany, National Library of Israel MS Heb. Octavo 3941, before a Hebrew translation identified as al-Ḥarīzī's. However, the identification is questionable. Although Baneth makes certain stylistic arguments about it, a large part of the identification hinges on a belief that al-Ḥarīzī is the author of the preface (as in David's 1980 article) and that the translation must, therefore, be his.

45. Here the author of the preface borrows this phrase from Maimonides' own description of his distribution of his *Iggeret Teiman* (*Epistle to Yemen*) that appears in the concluding paragraph of that text.

46. On the phenomenon of the picaresque narrator in Arabic and Arabizing literature in al-Andalus, see James Monroe, *The Art of Badī'al-Zamān al-Ḥamadhānī as Picaresque* (Beirut: American University in Beirut Press, 1984).

47. Moritz Steinschneider, *The Hebrew Translations of the Middle Ages and the Jews as Transmitters*, ed. and trans. Charles Manekin et al. (New York: Springer, 2014). Steinschneider was responsible for the *editio princeps* of the text, which appears in *Israelitische Letterbode* 8 (1882): 99; he further references it in *Die Arabishe Literatur Der Juden* (Kaufmann: Frankfurt-am-Maim, 1902), 210.

48. Joshua Finkel, "Maimonides' Treatise on Resurrection." On 80–82, this interrogative section reads, in part, "The account provokes a multitude of questions. Without exhausting them all, it may be asked: Did Maimonides really send his treatise to (the Jews of) all nations and to every Jewish community? Did Ḥarīzī really write the beginning of the account? If he did, would he quote his Taḥkemoni poem, or conversely, as indeed the case might be, would he transplant the poem into his diwan? Are the phrases *he'emiq ha- 'inyan ve-lo sikel ha-mesillah* and *mi-klei el-klei* borrowed—all expressions employed by Ḥarīzī in his introduction to the Moreh? If so, were they thus utilized by

a skillful forger in order to lend the document an air of verisimilitude? Furthermore, are not *mi-rov asher herḥivah lashon ʿarav gevuleiha . . .* and *ki mimenah bi-yadeinu lo nish'ar ki im meʿat* reminiscent of numerous phrases in Judah ibn Tibbon's introduction to *Ḥobot ha-Lebabot*, that of Samuel ibn Tibbon's to the *Moreh*, and those of Ḥarizi to *Zeraʿim* and the *Diwan*? Should not, therefore, this additional array of resemblances further strengthens the supposition that our writer sought to fit out his report with the familiar trimmings of translators' introductions so as to cloak the more adroitly the spuriousness of his own? Is a secondary Arabic and a tertiary Hebrew translation of our Treatise probable? What accounts for the abrupt change of writers in the Introduction? If Maimonides sent his treatise to (the Jews of) every nation and to every Jewish community, how is it that Yosef ben Yoel could not find a copy of it? Would Maimonides ask Ibn Tibbon to pass on to Yosef the Treatise he had sent him? Would Ibn Tibbon dare to act contrary to Maimonides' wish? If he did, how would Yosef get wind of it and how would he still call Ibn Tibbon 'loyal friend'? Does *ki yesh 'et efareshnah ʿinyan ve-ʿetim kavvanah ve-paʿa moʿamad ve-paʿam davar* really mean 'Sometimes I render it by (Arabic equivalents to) *ʿinyan*, sometimes by (equivalents to) *kavvanah* or *moʿamad* or *davar*' or does the phrase mean, as it naturally should: 'Sometimes I render it *ʿinyan*, sometimes *kavvanah*, or *moʿamad* or *davar*, etc.,' whereby the Arabic translator (presumably Yosef) is suddenly transformed into the Hebrew translator (presumably Ḥarīzī)? A transformation, though in the reverse direction (from that of Hebrew into Arabic translator) in the transition from the first to the second paragraph. Should we therefore conclude that the writer rather than dealing with facts prefers to indulge in fancies, and should his whole account thus be discredited? . . . The Nasi R. Meir ben Sheshet and the translator Yosef ben Yoel are otherwise unknown personalities. Are we therefore justified in assuming that they are fictitious characters? Obviously some of these questions most decidedly undermine the veracity of the account, while others at least make matters doubtful. For some perhaps satisfactory answers may be dug up, but I am not going to subject any of these questions to a minute examination. The questions in their aggregate eloquently testify to the confusion and inconsistencies of the report, and such a general evaluation, I think, is sufficient for our purpose."

49. Finkel, "Maimonides' Treatise on Resurrection," 83–84.

50. In his article "Judah al-Ḥarīzī and the Chain of Translations," *Tarbiẓ* 10 (1942): 135–54, David Zvi Baneth comes down in favor of the text as a flawed work of historiography, and goes as far as to attribute the text to al-Ḥarīzī, as part of an effort to vindicate himself as a translator. The feasibility of al-Ḥarīzī as the author of this text will be discussed below. Bernard Septimus, in his *Hispano-Jewish Culture in Transition* (Cambridge, MA: Harvard University Press, 1982), also ultimately reads with the factual school of thought regarding Joseph ben Joel's preface, not only on the basis of the argument made by Baneth but also because the preface "tallies nicely with what we know from Ramah's Sanhedrin commentary" (54). Despite these later arguments, I maintain that it is Finkel's assessment of this text as a work of fiction composed by an anonymous author whose name has been lost or was deliberately obscured remains the correct one.

51. Stroumsa, *Maimonides in His World*, 165.

52. On this, see J. L. Teicher, "A Literary Forgery in the Thirteenth Century," *Melilah* 1 (1944): 81–92; and Lea Naomi Goldfield, *Moses Maimonides' Treatise on Resurrection: An Inquiry into Its Authenticity* (Jerusalem: Ktav Publishing, 1986). The *Treatise* itself has also been treated as having something of a fictional character—see Robert

Kirchner, "Maimonides Fiction of Resurrection," *HUCA* 52 (1981): 163–93—although this article treats the concept of fiction somewhat differently from my usage here. In any event, Sarah Stroumsa roundly quells this speculation through her discussion of the intertextuality of the *Treatise* and other related epistles written contemporaneously, all of which would need to have been an elaborate and wide-ranging forgery in order for the *Treatise* to have been so, as well, in *Maimonides in His World*, 166–67.

53. Finkel, "Maimonides' *Treatise on Resurrection*," Appendix B, 102.

54. Ibid., 103.

55. Ibid.

56. Ibid., 102.

57. Ibid.

58. Ibid., 83.

59. Ibid., 101. One might also argue that the presence of the word *megillah* and its homography with the word *megaleh* (reveals), juxtaposed against the word *sod* (secret) that is introduced into the title, alerts the reader that the text that follows will represent an intervention in the debates over the spread of the secret or esoteric contents of Maimonides' work.

60. Ibid. This phrase, which appears in the brief prose précis between the two sections of verse, almost seems, especially by virtue of the metaphor about pouring the text from vessel to vessel, to point to at least two additional translations between Arabic and Hebrew; perhaps the principle of preferring the *lectio dificilior* should even demand that we read this to mean that there were five translations back and forth rather than three; however, because I read the text to have a single narrator with these few sentences as a précis, I think I must also read this as a preview of what is to follow rather than as additional information.

61. Marc Bloch, *The Historian's Craft* (New York: Vintage, 1964), 77.

CONCLUSION

"This Book Has Been Completed": Looking Back and Ahead at al-Andalus in Translation

I should like to begin the final reflection on the work done here and summation thereof with a meditation on a single Arabic lexeme: the noun *tarjamah*. This is a word that appears in medieval texts, including those produced in al-Andalus and the greater Maghreb, with a very wide semantic range that includes many connotations relating to denomination, transfer, conversion, adaptation, and transmission—suggesting in this case the translation of a translator's life onto paper. Dwight Reynolds seeks to unify the different valences of the word[1] by casting this particular type of biographical writing as the translation of a man's life into writing:

> The *tarjama* as a biographical notice may be taken to be a representation of a person, to be distinguished from the physical being; it is an inexact, imperfect copy of a life, just as a commentary cannot represent the original text, or a translation represent the Qur'ān. But it is a key to the person, a clarification, an attempt to label and explain his or her actions and accomplishments and make them comprehensible to posterity and accessible to the student. To reach the original person in a more direct fashion can only be accomplished by reading the original text, that is, his or her works, or by receiving his or her teachings through oral transmission, passed down through generations of teachers. The biography may therefore be seen as a commentary on an original, a key to a great thinker, past or present.[2]

However, he further identifies the components of *tarjamah*-type biography,[3] elements that closer reading reveals to be precisely the same as the key elements of Judah's ethical will: ancestry and information about birth; roster of teachers; bibliography and examples of the subject's work in prose and verse; travelogue;

biographical anecdotes; and personal virtues. As noted earlier, the ethical will functions much more as Judah's intellectual biography than anything else; it details his travels, the community elders whom he holds in esteem, personal values, biographical anecdotes, and also bibliography and library catalogue. If a *tarjamah* is the translation of a man's life onto paper, then how much more so is this text—this Arabizing, Hebrew-language *waṣīya* that both prescribes and describes the translation of words, text, philosophy, literature, and culture—the translation of a translator's life into writing?

Judah's program of translation was enthusiastically Andalusi-Arabizing, particularly through his use of literary forms and his ability to adapt, shape, and cloak their shapes to speak to an audience that had little access to the wide array of templates from which they came. Adapting secular prose and poetry allowed Judah to transmit the prestige of the culture that produced it; even the Hebrew Bible and other sacred texts he reads with an eye toward the Arabic literary tradition that he left behind. But perhaps even more crucially, it is the silent, almost subconscious, operation of the Andalusi background of that project, within the frame of Judah's program of word-for-word translation, that makes even that piece of it a cultural artifact. It was the decisions that Judah had already made on the basis of his Andalusi intellectual formation that produced the word-for-word translations that he believed in no way interfered in the transmission of the text except to give it a wider audience. The literary heritage of al-Andalus is what is infused in the non-intervention of Judah ibn Tibbon's translations just as it runs parallel to it in another stratum of the corpus.

Despite the inclination to view it as the purest way to transmit a text, and despite Judah's own articulation of the idea that his kind of translation was completely separate from the authorial act, it is as much an intervention as sense-for-sense translation; even translating word-for-word is not the "sterile equation of two dead languages."[4] Despite himself, and despite the unsustainability of his venture, Judah's program of literal translation was also a program of cultural translation. It was a fleeting one, to be sure, one that faded along with the Andalus that it recalled, but all the same it was a laudatory and nostalgic tribute to the cultural prestige that the Arabic language had always afforded him in tracing out with the fingertip sensitivity the language and culture of people struggling to hang on. I have not explicitly drawn on Mary Louise Pratt's influential theory of the contact zone[5] earlier in this work; in the ways in which Andalusi literary scholarship has developed within the orbit of the Tel Aviv poststructuralists' literary polysystems, the notion of a contact zone is virtually taken for granted.[6] In concluding the study, though, I am finding it useful to do what I have not done throughout and to draw more explicitly on her terminology and thinking: translation is a cultural practice that is constituted by and constitutive of zones of cultural contact.[7] It produces texts that are never completely for monolingual readers—not at first, anyway. As translations are created and disseminated, and as they increasingly move out into a monolingual world external to the contact zone that created them, they confer a kind of multilingualism on their readers through the cultural mediation they execute. Not only is the target language changed through contact with the source language—as in the extreme case of the birth of an identifiably different new variety such as "Tibbonid Hebrew"—but also more subtly and integrally through contact with the source culture. Genre by genre, type by type, and mode by mode, Judah ibn Tibbon renders Europe's Hebrew the Arabic heritage of al-Andalus.

BACK AND AHEAD

In his letter to Asher ben Meshullam, Judah uses the phrase "I have freed myself from the burden of translating it" to describe the end of his work on Solomon ibn Gabirol's *Improvement of Moral Qualities*. It is a feeling that I, now at the end of writing this book, can fully understand and embrace. At the end of his letter to Asher, Judah reflects on what he had left undone in translating Ibn Gabirol—in this case grappling with poetic citations—and made the calculus that we all do: that if he didn't have time to come back to it in the end, that might be all right. This book, this burden from which I have just freed myself, is one that was written in a serious time crunch, within the confines of a system of merit and evaluation that seems—except in a few rare cases—to privilege *Sitzfleisch* and speed over the kind of meditative, slow scholarship that produced the magisterial masterworks of half a century ago or more that are still the classics in our medieval fields. The intellectual demands of the work are too often subjugated to the practical demands of the profession. It is devastatingly tempting to think that in a different era, this might have been a very different book even though, as a medievalist living in this modern world, I know well enough to be on guard against the romanticization of an imagined past. And perhaps this is such a rich text and corpus that no one book, no matter how slowly written, could ever have encompassed everything. Yet there is some comfort and some intellectual satisfaction in having written this first, rushed, book, about an individual who left behind similar contemplations about the shortness of time, the extent of the work, the demands of the taskmaster, and on what still remains to be done. In doing so, he beckons me to do the same.

The obvious question that remains for me comes in the very first chapter. To what extent do Judah's ideas about the relative authority of translators and authors develop with some kind of awareness of or filiation to the context of the Romance-language literatures that also saw, in the twelfth and thirteenth centuries, a blossoming awareness of the authority of all the hands that participated in their creation? A second question is that of translating poetry and to which later readers returned to complete the tasks that Judah left unfinished. These two are questions that were raised by the completion of this work that I intend to address in future work. The second of those two questions is suggestive of a broader project that is a major desideratum, namely a wider reception history of the Tibbonid translations more based on the filiations of the manuscript tradition. The texts that are the subject of chapter 6—the fictive colophon and prologue—ought perhaps to be reconsidered as part of a wider reconceptualization of the nature, role, and place of fiction in the Arabophone Middle Ages. A study that focused on the stratigraphy and compositional chronology of the text could also be both interesting and intellectually profitable. Another pressing theme still outstanding for some readers might be that of how to situate Judah's writing to his son in a wider context of Andalusi and Andalusi-exiled fathers writing to their sons, among these David and Joseph Qimḥi, Moses and Abraham Maimoindes, Abraham and Isaac ibn 'Ezra'. And, furthermore, where I have treated this text as an artifact of literary, intellectual, and cultural history, it is ripe for a similar close reading and contextualization from social, medical, and economic historians, for whom this text should also yield much.

The ethical will is a text that invites reflection, both backward and forward on the literature of al-Andalus, but also on what remains undone, what remains to be done. This comes not only through its admonitions to lazy students and poor writers, by which we all might find ourselves spurred on from time to time, and not only from Judah's own reflections on what he found himself unable to finish while also siring the dynasty that would carry on his work, but also by teasing its reader with tantalizing hints of the still-lost texts that may be out there yet to be found. Perhaps that in and of itself is a consolation of sorts. Even if all the other work that could possibly be imagined for the Tibbonid corpus as it exists today, even if all the other work to be done were finally done, there is still much left to be discovered. The work is never done, but this little sliver of it is now completed.

Tam ve-nishlam, as the medieval colophonists might have had it; *shevaḥ la-'el bore' 'olam.*

NOTES

Chapter title from Colophon, Beinecke MS Heb. Suppl. 103, f. 35b.

1. Of the medieval dictionaries, it is the *Taj al-ʿarūs* that documents the widest variety of definitions of the term and the gives the most attestations of *tarjamah* being used to indicate biographical notices. In the modern Orientalist dictionaries of classical Arabic, Lane, as expected, documents the relevant medieval sources and Dozy offers definitions that include both biography and epitaph. In Maghribi varieties of Arabic, the lexicographical tools offer a somewhat less clear-cut sense of the usage in this way: Corriente offers an attestation of the verb referring to the utterance of personal expression, although the documentation of this usage in dictionaries for the Arabophone West is somewhat less robust. Blau does not attest the form in his dictionary of Judaeo-Arabic, although the limitations of that meticulous and valuable volume are well known.

2. Dwight F. Reynolds, *Interpreting the Self: Autobiography in the Arabic Literary Tradition* (Berkeley: University of California Press, 2001), 42.

3. Ibid., 41–42.

4. Walter Benjamin, "The Task of the Translator," in *Illuminations* (New York: Schocken Books, 1969), 73.

5. Mary Louise Pratt, "Arts of the Contact Zone," *PMLA* 91 (1991): 33–40.

6. As noted in the work of Brann, Hamilton, and Wacks.

7. See also Itamar Even-Zohar, "The Position of Translated Literature within the Literary Polysystem," *Poetics Today* 11, no. 1 (1990): 45–51.

APPENDIX

Judah ibn Tibbon's Ethical Will: A New Translation

TRANSLATOR'S NOTE

Foremost in my mind while translating this text was Maimonides' description of the process of translation in his letter to Judah's son, Samuel. First, the translator must understand the text and then explain it to the reader in the target language. To treat the process as an interpretation or an explanation of the original text is the only way that the resulting text in translation will read in a lucid manner, and so that has been my approach here. The ethical will is not a difficult text but it is a complex one; having made it the focus of my intellectual endeavors these last many years, I hope that the specialist reader might benefit from my interpretation of the text even more than from an attempt to render it in Judah's style, word for word, or in a manner close to it, as one would do in a text seminar. And similarly, if there is anything in this book of value to the non-specialist it is this appendix; as noted in chapter 6, a more literal translation is virtually useless to the non-specialist or to the reader requiring a translation. Both audiences, then, are served best by a translation that privileges intelligibility in the target language over an exact representation of the grammar, syntax, and even style of the source. I have tried to walk a fine line in this translation in order to produce a text that would be readable and thoughtful about content and language in ways that produce a certain kind of fidelity to style, register, and readability, but still conservative enough to produce the different kind of fidelity expected in translation that accompanies an academic volume; outside of an academic framework this text might prove to accommodate yet another type, extent, or register of target text.

I briefly vacillated about whether to include this appendix in the volume at all, wondering whether it was necessary and whether it was worth potentially exposing myself to extra criticism for inclining toward translation for sense and readability. But the decision was made easy when, shortly before completing the manuscript, I read the text with students in my graduate seminar on translation in the Middle Ages; observing the interpretive struggles of the students who could not read the text in the original and had to grapple with Israel Abrahams's English version and some of the decisions that he made was what convinced me that the time was right for a new English translation of this text. Abrahams's translation is the artifact of a Victorian Orientalist sensibility that treated any medieval text as written in a high register of language on the basis of notions about writing, literacy, and the intellectual elite in that era. With regard to the register of the language in my own translation, I have tried to consider the context, author, and audience in order to make the translation more approachable and to more closely replicate a text that was once an intimate family exchange and always destined for a wider readership of fathers and sons. I am also cognizant that I am translating for a different modern audience, one that is simultaneously not exclusively immersed in some kind of Jewish learning, whether for secular or sacred purposes, and not concerned in the same way with assimilation and passing in a wider academic world. In this respect I have made some of the references to Jewish practices—references that are actually quite explicit in the original text—more explicit than Abrahams did. Finally, I have simply disagreed with him in some places in matters of interpretation, places where my study of the text and the literary context in which it was written have further illuminated troubling or obscure passages of the text. In fact, despite my priority for sense translation, the reader will find that in some places my English version hews more closely to the original than Abrahams's; these are places where a more literal rendering does not interfere with readability and conveys some important sense of a term of art. Nevertheless, the principal goal of this translation was to provide an up-to-date, readable English text more concerned with interpretation than with literal rendering.

Where Judah ibn Tibbon proposed two different poetics of translation, one for prose and the other for poetry, I have followed his lead. In the sections of the ethical will that are written in original verse, as well as those that quote earlier Andalusi poets, I have not translated for characteristics of the text other than the words themselves. While I have maintained the line breaks in the poetry, I have otherwise kept it in English prose. A poetic touch that I do not possess is necessary to translate poetry; to try to do so without such a gift yields goofy English renderings of even the most sublime Hebrew text. I have still not aimed for a literal rendering but have left many of the poetic characteristics alone.

For example, I have rendered images and metaphors more literally instead of substituting those that are common in contemporary English; in some cases, it was interesting for me to note that many images and metaphors were quite intelligible and expected because of the ways in which King James's English has pervaded our language, similar to the way in which the language of the Hebrew Bible pervaded that of the Andalusi Hebrew poets. Be that as it may, I have largely treated the poetry and prose in opposite fashions and have given more weight to a more literal rendering of the text than to one that preserves other qualities beyond the purely literal. The ultimate effect of this decision is that the translation of the poetic sections of the ethical will preserves the aphoristic character of some examples of this genre (as discussed in the general introduction) and also happens to emphasize the lack of poeticism in Judah's own verse (as discussed in chapter 4).

To translate texts about translation can be a head-spinning meta-literary exercise. In this case, more than once, it has provoked doubt about which type of translation would best serve the audience for this book. This translation is the final appendix in a book that is ultimately for a specialized academic audience that can recourse to the text themselves, either in the manuscript as reproduced here or in any of the text editions. A word-for-word translation is less useful to such readers. Further, I have kept the notes here to a minimum and have not repeated Abrahams's identifying of the biblical and talmudic sources to which Judah alludes and from which he quotes; those identifications, as well as the very minor manuscript variations that occur between the full copy and the few fragmentary additional ones, may all be found in the critical apparatus to his edition and translation of the text. Parenthetical numbers within the text indicate page references both to Abrahams's edition of the text (54–92) and to the folios of the Bodleian manuscript (15b–21a).

Judah himself writes that in a situation like this, when the original is readily available, accommodation can reasonably be made for intelligibility in the target language.[1] It is axiomatic that translation is always interpretation. My interpretation of the ethical will is what follows. *Ve-ha-maskilim yavinu.*

TRANSLATION OF JUDAH IBN TIBBON'S ETHICAL WILL, ACCORDING TO BODLEIAN MS MICH. 50.3, FOLIOS 15B–21A

In the name of God, may he be exalted, praised, and remembered eternally. This is the guidance (musar) *that the great sage, Judah ibn Tibbon, son of Saul, the memory of the righteous is a blessing, composed for his son, the wise and perfect Samuel, in his youth; their memories are as a blessing.*

Take this father's advice, given from his broken heart
  as you set out like the ebbing tide.[2]
With great, unending grief his eyes
  are emptied out as never before.
God has tested him through the wanderings of his children,
  unequal to other fathers;
and time has provoked the heart within him,
  enticing and inveigling him.
It sent him into the chasm of separation
  and cast him onto a sea of grief.
It impoverished him through their wandering
  and his yearning as though he were clothed in their robes.
With sound and fury it shall come
  to perturb him and then envelop him,
perturb him with absinthe and poison
  on his plate and in his cup.
His eyes drooped, full of tears, alm-
  ost as though he could see as little light as a blind man.
They did not fall to the desolate earth
  but made reeds and shrubs grow.
He eats the bread of tears and drinks,
  thirsty and deep, of the tears.
His soul abhorred all food
  because he saw all as unclean.
My God, my God, why and how
  has all of this bad come to me?
And until when
  will this separation be in force?

My son, pay attention to my admonitions and do not ignore a single one of my charges to you: Take my guidance into account—keep your eye on it—and you will succeed on your path in life and become wise; and your days will be full of goodness and gifts.

My son, you have long known that the Creator did not offer a reward for observance of any of the Ten Commandments except for the one about honoring one's parents, for which the reward is long life and good days. As it is said: "[Honor your father and mother as the Lord, your God, has commanded you] so that your days may be lengthened and so [life] will go well for you." And in a rebuke (*tokheḥa*): "If I am a father, then where is my honor?" You also know about the reward received by the descendants of Yehonadav ben Rekhab, who observed the customs of their ancestor: the Creator granted them good and long lives, and He used them [as a contrast by which] to rebuke Israel, as you can see in commentaries on the matter.

(57) You know, my son, that I nurtured and embraced you and that I raised you to be wise and well mannered. I set you down the path of wisdom and into the realm of integrity. I kept you in food, drink, and clothes. I went to great trouble so you could study. I protected you from fear. I sacrificed sleep to make you wiser, better educated, and better mannered than all of your peers. Over these past twelve years I have abstained from every nicety and worldly pleasure that a man could enjoy; and I am still working to build up your inheritance.

I have honored by [buying you] many books so that you would not have to borrow books from any other man, which you see most students doing: trudging about to borrow books and not always finding them. But you—praise God! —can lend and do not have to borrow since you have two or three copies of most of your books. And what's more, I have compiled anthologies for you in every discipline and I had hoped that your hand would be a cradle[3] to each of them. I took the trouble to go to the ends of the earth to bring back a teacher for you[r instruction in] secular subjects only because your Rock graced you with a wise, judicious mind. I paid no mind to the expense or the danger. We had many close calls on that trip, but God was with us.

But you, my son, belied my expectations and my hopes. You did not see fit to make use of your vision. You have separated yourself from your books, (58) and have shown no interest in them—not even in their titles or tables of contents. If you were to see them in someone else's hands you would not recognize them as your own. You would not know if you had one that you might need without asking me. You have not even looked at the catalogue of your books (*mazkeret shel sefearekha*); it is of no interest to you.

After Proverbs says:[4]

He who goes to great lengths to buy himself books
  but whose heart is empty of their contents and unfamiliar with them
is like a crippled man who graffitied the image of a leg onto a wall
  and when it came time to stand, he could not.

This is exactly as you have done. Even now you rely (16a) on me to wake you from your lazy slumber. You must imagine that I will always be here at your side but it has escaped your notice that death with eventually separate you from me. It will eventually occur to you: Who will care for you, my son, as I have cared for you? And who will stand in to take my place and teach you, willingly and out of love? Even if you could find [a substitute], you see that great sages seek *me* out and try to come here from the far corners of the earth to avail themselves of fellowship in *my* salon. They yearn to see me and my books; but you, despite finding yourself here at no cost, do not. God has not given you a heart with which to know, eyes through which to see, or ears through which to hear. May God give (59) you a new heart and spirit, and a desire to secure what is gone and recuperate what is lost. May He set you on the path you should walk and guide you along it.

You have not cultivated your Arabic writing as expected: You began to study it seven years ago when I forced you to do it, even though you did not want to. You know that the greatest men of our nation did not achieve their greatness or their lofty heights but through their Arabic writing. You know that the *Nagid* explained that the acclaim accorded to him—and to his son after him—was because of it: "Pen, I recount your favor! . . ." And so on. You can see that the *nasi*, Sheshet, achieved wealth and honor through his Arabic writing in this land as in a kingdom of Ishmael; through it he paid off all of his debts and met his extensive personal and philanthropic expenses.[5] Nor have you progressed as expected in your Hebrew writing. Do you not remember that I have been paying your wise teacher, Jacob, the son of the most magnanimous Ovadiah, [a salary of] thirty gold dinars per year? When I pressed him into service to teach you how to write the letters, he said to me: "Wouldn't it be enough for him to learn one letter per year?" If (60) you had been bothered by what he said, you might have tried to become a better scribe than he or his sons. Haven't you seen the handwriting of Sheshet's son, who is [also][6] only twelve, which so resembles the handwriting of his teacher, Patur, that it could be the same hand? Script is made up of shapes, like any others, and any man can copy it from a model with sufficient scrutiny and drive. Do not believe in [the saying]: "I sought but I could not find." If you were ashamed of yourself or the reputation you have earned in the wider world—even though it is mostly a lie—you would have tried harder to end those rumors, out of dismay at the shame and humiliation heaped upon you.

From *After Proverbs*:

When your nation sings, with your praises
  on their lips, pay careful attention to their words.
If they praise you for [an attribute] that is not yours
  endeavor to be worthy of their praise.

You know that the *nasi* [Sheshet] has praised you highly; but what good will that do you on your day of reckoning? Oh, the shame! Oh, the humiliation! May your God direct you toward wisdom and teach you to serve, give purpose to your digressions, and wake you from your sleep. May your sleep be nothing but the beginning of your awakening!

After Proverbs says:

(61) Woe to the man who is awake
  but cannot see his own path.
Blessed is the man who sleeps
  and whose eyes point inward to his heart.

You are still a young man and it is still possible to right yourself—Heaven help you!—through determination and will. Perception without determination is useless. [King] David, peace be upon him, said: "His delight is in the law of God." And you have read what the *nagid* [Samuel ibn Naghrīla] wrote in *After Proverbs*:

Let my most learned brother take heart:
  his heart will give heart for the fight.

And he further wrote:

Best to straighten the flowering tree branch while it is wet
and not to straighten it when it is dry, lest it break.

If God would only return me to you, I would bear [responsibility for] all of your needs.[7] Why do I work if not for your benefit and your children's? May God allow me to see all of their faces happy! My son, do not refrain from following in my footsteps in studying Torah and the medical sciences—but mostly occupy yourself with Torah. You have a wise and perceptive mind; if only you desired to learn (62) and comprehend! I know (16b) that you will come to regret your past just as many people before you have come to regret the laziness of their childhood and youth. The *nagid*, the memory of the righteous is a blessing, wrote in *After Proverbs*:

Wisdom's robe is the good student's to wear.
  Learning while young bears strength and sweetness.
But he who might study in old age without [having studied in his] youth
  will glean things, but without wisdom or taste.

And so, my son, strive during your youth. You complain now that you are forgetful; but what will you do in old age, which brings with it even more forgetfulness? Wake up, my son, from your sleep and occupy yourself with science and culture. Hold yourself to high standards as a matter of habit because habit becomes second nature.[8] As the Arab sage said: "The types of wisdom are two in number: Knowledge of laws and knowledge of bodies." Strive, my son, in both of them and you will be honored more than your friends for your wisdom. The sage, peace be upon him, said: "Wise men will inherit honor." He also said: "A long life is in her [wisdom's] right hand." And he added: "A wise but mesquin child is better than a simple elder statesman." But I do not need to perseverate on the matter, nor on what is written about it in Proverbs and *After Proverbs*.

(63) My son, you know that friendship with the wicked is harmful: as intractable as leprosy. The sage, peace be upon him, said: Do not start down the path of evil people. My son, do not loiter out on the street, standing or sitting; and do not associate[9] with someone whose friendship you do not value." The sage, peace be upon him, said: "If you walk with wise men you will become wise."

As it says in *After Proverbs*:

Choose righteous men as your friends
  and circle of advisers, and spurn fools.
With a wise man you can turn over stones and pass
  Through the straits with him and weather the rage of giants.

My son, make your books your companions, and your shelves and bookcases your paradise and orchard. Revel in their verdancy, pick their roses, and gather up their fruits, spices, and myrrh. If you come to dread all of this, transpose yourself from garden to garden, from flowerbed to flowerbed, and from *mirador* to *mirador*; and in doing so you will renew your interest and pleasure.

Remember what the poet said in verse:

How could I fear any man when my soul
  makes lions terrified of their cubs?[10]
How could I worry about poverty when it contains the wisdom
  (64) from whose hills I can cut rubies?
If should hunger, her [wisdom's] choicest fruits are here
  and if I should thirst, here are her streams.
How could I sit alone when her lyre
  delights me with her songs?
Why would I seek another friend to speak with me
  when I already hear the wisdom of her words?
My lute and my lyre are at the nib of her pen.
  My gardens and my orchards are her books.

In *After Proverbs* it also says:

A wise man leaves behind the ease of [material] comforts
  and finds respite through reading books.
If you look [you will find that] all men have flaws;
  the flaw of the wise man is forgetting.

Take consultations from wise, beloved men;
  do not be confident in your own opinions alone.
If you pursue your heart's desire,
  your desire will conceal what is right.
This is what you desire and your heart
  will embellish your desire before you.

(65) My son, be thoughtful about whose affection and wisdom you rely on. Never abandon your friends or mine. Aaron and Hur are on your side: The sage Aaron and the sage Asher.[11] My son, do not fight with other men and do not involve yourself in fights that are not your own. Do not try to win arguments against stubborn people, even in matters of Torah; and do not force your opinion on others even if you know that the truth is on your side. Defer to those in the majority without argument. My son, do not put yourself at risk by traveling in times of strife and danger, not even for a large financial gain. Travel only with a great many men who are wise, who care for you, and who have made your concerns their own, (17a) because your security will be in their hands. Do not rely on the advice of young men; defer to the advice of your elders. Do not allow a salary to blind or cosset you; do not be like the bird that sees the seeds but does not see the hunting net. You know what the sage, peace be upon him, said: "The wise man fears evil and turns away from it while the simple man is bullish and confident."

My son, take it upon yourself to copy out one page of *After Proverbs* and to consider its advice daily. On every Sabbath, (66) read the weekly portion [of the Bible] in Arabic because it will be useful to you in developing your Arabic vocabulary[12] and in translation, should you wish to become a translator.

My son, to the extent that you can, make your home respectable by [hanging up] proper drapery. Show that you respect yourself and your children by wearing proper clothing; it is not fitting for a man to dress more shabbily at home than he would at work. Let your stomach want and provision your back.

My son, you know how much I had to bear—the effort and the burden and the expense!—to arrange the marriage of your older sister, and how I suffered similarly to arrange your younger sister's marriage. I exposed myself to unprecedented danger to cross the sea three times. I spent more than I could afford: I mortgaged my books, I borrowed from friends, and I put my hand out to beg from my loved ones, which I am not accustomed to doing. I did all of this so that [the expenditures] would not diminish you[r inheritance]. At your wedding you know that I did not pay your bride price in silver even when others, richer than me, did so for their sons.[13] None of your peers was so honored at his wedding. I chose as your wife the daughter of a wise and learned family, well-connected grandees of this land, each relative a kernel of truth: wise, noble, lofty, and trustworthy. You were venerated more than all of your friends at your wedding when the community accorded you honor by not imposing any taxes or fees upon you. You were rewarded by (67) princes, cavaliers, bishops, rectors, priests, and warriors, all because of what I did. My son, Israel and the other nations continue to honor us both because the Creator has demonstrated his strength through his favor toward you and me. Try, from here on, to add to that honor so that they will respect you for yourself: through your good morals and courteous behavior toward other men as well and by studying consistently and working with determination and devotion, just as you did before your marriage.

In *After Proverbs* it says:

> Study much from secular books[14] and you will find that
> that doing so makes the one who does suitable at the gates of heaven.
> Your opinion will be valued[15] amongst the grandees
> and your name will be glorified amongst your friends.

My son! Be generous with your time and presence. Care for the sick and let your knowledge cure them. Since you receive [payment] from the rich, you can treat the poor for free. God will grant you your reward and your salary; and you will build a reputation for kindness and sensibility in the eyes of both God and man; and you will be respected by both great and small, and by Israel and the other nations. Your good name will reach near and far, (68) which will please your loved ones and inspire jealousy in your enemies and in those who hate you. You know what is mentioned in *Choice of Pearls*: Anyone who wishes to take vengeance on his enemies should increase his own finest qualities to excess. Remember how I explained this in my treatise on "Who Can Find a Strong Woman?"[16] My son, make it your habit to look over your pharmaceutical simples and medical herbs one day each week and do not use anything that is unfamiliar to you. How many times have I urged you to adopt this habit? Yet my words fall by the wayside.

My son, when you write a text, review it and reread it because no man is impervious to carelessness. Do not let haste keep you from returning to any letter to revise it—even a short one. Take care to avoid mistakes in [Hebrew and classical Arabic] language, in verb forms, in grammar, and in grammatical gender because sometimes familiarity with the vernacular language (*lashon ha-la'az*) can lead to mistakes in these areas. A man will be known his whole life by the mistakes written in his own hand.[17] The sages said: "Who flaunts himself nude as though he were already exposed? One who writes a document full of errors." (17b) Be attentive to how you include conjunctions and particles and to how they concord with the verbs that you use. I have begun to compose a book about all of this for you—if only God allows me to grow old enough to complete it!—called (69) *The Purity of Language*.[18] Even if you are satisfied [with an expression] but do not have a reference against which to review it, keep from using it. Try to make your writing mellifluous, short, and clear. Do not write rhymed prose if you cannot rhyme perfectly. Do not make your writing dense because if you do your writing will lose out and will not be pleasant (*'arev*) to your reader or listener.

You should also do the same thing when writing poetry. Avoid drawing in heavy expressions and excess verbiage. Let your words be pleasant and light on the tongue. Verbal forms should be ones that are attested in the language; do not incorporate any foreign ones, nor any other foreign lexical items. Even if you can explain them by analogy, such words are unnatural. Remember what I said to you when you wrote *during my seat* instead of *during my seating*: "Above all else, distance yourself from anything similar that might appear in your work." Choose what is sweet on the palate and pleasant (*'arev*) to the ear. Make your handwriting and calligraphy beautiful. Keep your pen sharp.[19] The ink that you use to write with should have a good visual aspect. Your letters should be well formed, to the best of your ability, unless you find yourself writing with a [poor quality] pen and do not have the chance to get a better one, as in an emergency or time of urgent need. The beauty of a written text is in the script and the beauty of the script is in the pen, in the ruling, and in the ink. The beauty of a written letter (70) demonstrates the worth of the scribe. Try to improve your handwriting as much as you can. Do not grow accustomed to letting the smaller letters get swallowed up by others; but instead, develop the habit of making them long, evenly spaced, and tall. Do not let the *yud* be swallowed up between other letters, as you are accustomed to doing; instead, write it with a full, straight line. A feature of [good] calligraphy and handwriting is that the *lamed*s should extend long above the lines and be tilted relative to the vertical. The *quf*s and the [final] *kaf*s and the *nun*s all have down-strokes that should be long and even. When *lamed*s or *nuns* or *quf*s or final *kaf*s descend below the line, some techniques can be employed with dexterity to make sure that one is not shorter than the next or longer than the next. You have seen that I have attended to this in the books I have copied in my own hand; your teacher, Jacob, even commented on it in your presence. A handwritten word, as I have told you, is just a shape like any other shape and it looks better the more care a man puts into it. Pay attention to your mistakes so you can straighten them out: Each one has a compounding effect on the next and soon enough one line is ascending and the next descending. Do not do that. And may God make you wise and set you straight on every path!

My son, you never heed (71) me when I am with you; listen to me now that I am far away. You must be aware that you have not done me the courtesy of seeking my counsel or keeping me informed about any matter relating to your sales and purchases; and when I asked you about it, you interrupted my questions and hid things from me. When I offered you counsel, you declined my advice, [even though] you know that you have never succeeded in any matter on which you have ignored my advice.

As *After Proverbs* says:

The father of the son who brought
  his son to the house of the sages
and guided him along the path of life,
  he chose the path of the eminent for him,
They breathed wisdom into him
  instead of breathing onto their own coals.
Leave him to rely
  on his education [for the rest of] his days.

You saw what happened to you [in your dealings] with Solomon, the son of Joseph the sage, when you departed from my methods (18a) and ignored my advice. I need not remind you of how you made light of me during that incident. In Marseilles, too: We were together in a strange land and you bought a lot of merchandise of little value without asking my counsel (72) or informing me. I did not find out anything about your activities or business until you offloaded the riverboat in the city of Arles. Even a non-Jew from my city would have kept me apprised of his purchases and sales. And even worse, when you write out texts or compose poetry to send off to foreign lands, you do not see fit to show me any of it; and you actively prevent me from looking at it. When I say: "Show me!" you say to me: "What? You want to see this?" as though you have decided for yourself that you do not need me for anything. It is hubris that you have deemed yourself so wise, as in *After Proverbs*:

Whoever sees himself as wise,
  his error is in thinking he is correct.
To him, sometimes a cloud will appear
  to turn into sunlight, and the sun into a cloud.

Whenever Rabbi Zeraḥya, who is the greatest of his generation and wiser than me, wrote text or composed poetry to send to anyone else, he never allowed it to leave his possession without showing it to me first. And you know that when I write out my own texts, I say to you: "Look at them to check (73) and correct them." From the day that I recognized that you had a sense of style and knowledge of grammar, I asked you to review, check, and correct everything I wrote. As the Arab said: "The one who sits on the edge falls off." But you have adopted all of these bad manners toward me; and I have suffered and been terribly pained by them. You fomented against me, raged at me, grew embittered toward me, and made light of my honor, which the Creator commanded you to respect. This is how you have transgressed the Commandments. May the Source[20] forgive you completely in this world and favor you in the next, teach you to do His will, and cause you to find favor in the eyes of God and man. If you have the will to recover what you have lost in all of this, the Creator will forgive you; and I, too, with my longing heart and through the force of my will, can forgive you for everything that has happened. Do not let what I have written here in my testament leave a bitter taste in your mouth. By the same measure that you have not honored me up to this point, honor me now in what is left of my life and after my death by continuing in your pursuit of wisdom, through your polite manners and good grace, and by being considerate to all. In this way you will gain a good reputation, which is the greatest crown of all. Be steadfast in your fear of God and your observance of the commandments. Show concern for your friends and for mankind and everyone will acknowledge you for it; and in doing so you will honor me during my life and after my death.

In *After Proverbs* one finds:

(74) A wise son has three traits:
He admits his errors and his follies.
In his humility he diminishes himself before his nation.
And he is raised up to its head because of his wisdom.

Praise my Creator! I know that in every path you pursue you fear the heavens, except in the matter of honoring your father; in this you have violated all of my orders to you and have not heard my voice. Greatness is in the eyes of the Creator and in the eyes of all mankind. I know—and have faith in my Creator—that my departure now will benefit you; when you see that you have nothing except for me, yourself, and your knowledge and education, you will have to come to your senses and accept my guidance.

The Nagid—the memory of the righteous is a blessing—said: What good is there in life if my work today is just like my work yesterday?

So, my son: From now on, work to earn respect for me and honor for yourself. I will only be remembered well in my life and after my death by my honor, through you. May those who see you say: "Blessed is the one who fathered him and blessed is the one who raised him!"[21] because I have no son but you by whom I might be remembered. So, make good on my memory and you will be recognized for it by the Creator and praised for it by man.

(75) You know what I went through while raising you. You saw what the sage Moses bar Judah did: (18b) He had four sons and sent them to the far corners of the earth, left, and let them find their own wives. I, in my grace toward you, did not wish to leave you in the hands of a strange woman.[22] I suffered through every possible predicament while raising and caring for you, and everyone knows that but for my care and upbringing you would have died or been permanently disabled or otherwise deficient. Remember this, my son, and take my advice to heart and accept my guidance.

Amongst the most important things that will come up in my admonitions and my instructions to you is that you should pay attention to what you eat. You are killing me before my time! I was in a crisis of fear for you when I cared for you while you were ill. Yet I would prefer to die than live seeing [the consequences of] my wrong actions. Every year—because of my own shortcomings—you experience illnesses, most of which are caused by bad food.

In *After Proverbs* it says:

If you wish to increase your fortunes
  cut long furrows through your desire
Fight for yourself with your soul just as
  you would fight against an archer with an arrow and a lance.

And now, my son, I adjure you—by the God of the Heavens (76) and by the requirements imposed upon you by the Creator—to honor me. By everything that I have done to raise and teach you, I adjure you: Keep yourself, to the best of your ability, from eating bad foods! You know from experience that you take ill because of your taste for bad foods. My son, satisfy yourself with a little bit of what is good and keep yourself from what is sweet but damaging [to your health]. Do not eat food that will prevent you from eating more. Why would you study so much only to let yourself be caught in a trap to die? Why are you not embarrassed that everyone knows that you get sick each and every year from bad food? There is no disgrace or shame like a doctor who has been ill. How could he heal others when he cannot heal himself?

Again, from *After Proverbs*:

Turn away from the man who orders [others] to do
justice while he himself is unjust.
How can he who is sick with an illness
cure others from that illness?

Take care, my son, and do not tie your own hands. Even if you have no consideration for me or for yourself, take pity upon your son who delights you and whom you so desired. I have little time remaining. My son, allow me to spend a little bit of it with you; and for my sake, do not be guilty [of these things].

After Proverbs says:

(77) One who follows the advice of a fool
will be seen [acting foolishly] by those who hate him.
The one who dismisses the advice of a doctor
will be the one who falls ill.

Praise the Creator! You can eat good bread and drink good wine. But even if I expected you to eat only bread and water you would have to do it. Keep in mind the descendants of Yehoadav ben Rechab, about whom I have told you: They, their wives, and their sons avoided most worldly pleasures [at their ancestor's instruction]. I myself do not keep you from them—except for the dangerous ones.

After Proverbs says:

Whoever eats the diet customary
for his own body, his food is on his side.
The one who eats unexpected foods,
his food will be on him and not on his side.

Never say: "I will stray from time to time and get away with it." Do not even think it! Everyone knows that but for God's kindness and mercy and my close attention to you would have no more than clung to life. May the Source renew your life for good! Miracles are infrequent, though, and God only performs them two or three times in a lifetime.

(78) Even now, my son, I am never far from you: not for a day, for two, and not for ten or twenty days. Take all of this to heart and act on it. My son, do not wander too far down [the wrong] roads and paths.[23] Do not eat any meal out of the house during the days that I am traveling and away from you. If you happen to be invited to a meal by someone who is dear, beloved, or close to you, honor him only by your presence and your company.

My son, study history from time to time with the sage Aaron [ben Meshullam]. (19a) It is a necessary science.

My son, I must also insist that you honor your wife to the best of your ability because she is a wise and modest woman, the daughter of a wise and prestigious family. She is a good companion to you and for your sons. She is not profligate nor does she make large requests for food or dress or outerwear.[24] Remember how well she cared for you when you were sick. She is honorable and unique. She has brought up your sons without a maidservant or a manservant. Even if she were only your sons'[25] wet-nurse she would be an honor and a credit to you, but she is all the more so because she, the daughter of a great family, is your soulmate. Do not (79) raise your voice to her or debase her; that is the behavior of lesser men. Regarding women, the Arab sage said: "None respects them except he who is himself respectable; and none disrespects them except he who is himself disrespectable."

After Proverbs says:

Forgive your son and wife their rebelliousness
  and return to admonishing your son and your wife
as you sharpen the edge of a sword as it should be,
  with much back and forth across the whetting stone.

If you have the will to earn my love and honor, then do not impose upon her excessively. Our sages, may the memory of the righteous be a blessing, cautioned against this: If you must demand or rebuke, speak calmly. It is enough that your anger show on your face when matters are not as you wish; do not let it come across in your actions.

Conduct yourself in such a way that your expenditures are in good order. It is said in *Choice of Pearls* that maintaining orderly finances is halfway to satisfaction. There is an ancient proverb: Go to bed without a meal and wake up without debt. Do not debase your reputation[26] by borrowing. May your Creator save you from that moral failing!

After Proverbs says:

At times when you are poor, ride on the back of a lion
  toward your food rather than asking for anything from anyone.
Do not yearn [for anything] lest in your desire
  your heart lament it ahead of [your fellow] man.

(80) You have read what is written on this subject in *The Choice of Pearls* and in *After Proverbs*. This moral failing clings like leprosy and diminishes everything it touches.

After Proverbs says:

Eat greens with confidence!
Do not eat meat [lest it put you] in danger.
Acquire one thing yourself through considered negotiation
rather than a thousand things as gifts.

My son, be attentive to your children as I was to you; be kind to them as I was to you; guide them as I guided you; and watch over them as I watched over you. Try to teach them Torah just as I tried. Just as I did for you, you should do for them. Do not ignore any of their maladies nor your own, no matter how small; and thus God can save you and them from every illness or plague. If you feel [symptoms of] any illness in any of your organs you should immediately try to do everything necessary to [cure] the thing. You know what Hippocrates (*Abuqeraṭ*) said: "When time is short, trial-and-error is dangerous." Therefore, be quick and do not delay! Utilize known [remedies] and distance yourself from the unknown [ones].

Examine your books: the Hebrew ones monthly on the first of the month, the Arabic ones bi-monthly, (81) and the codices and bound volumes once every three months. Put everything in good order so that you will not have to search for any book when you need it; but rather, you will know its location on the shelves and in the cases. If you were to write down the location of all the books on the shelf in a record (*iggeret*) that you would then put in that very shelf, you would then be able to find any book quickly by reviewing the memo that covers that shelf instead of rifling through all of them. Do the same thing for every book case. Conserve loose leaves in the bound volumes and those that are in the archival files with care; and do not lose them because there are great and wonderful things in them that I have compiled and written out for you. Don't lose any of the written documents or essays (*al-te'abed ketav ve-lo iggeret*) that I have collected for you. Review your book memorandum[27] (*mazkeret sefarekha*) regularly so that you will remember which books you own. Neither take your studies with your teacher for granted nor cease to study with the younger men, even if you do not leave your teacher's study until late at night. You should always share everything that you have learned from me and from your teachers with other worthy students to keep your knowledge fresh at hand; by teaching them, you will learn it by heart (19b) and by answering their questions you will remove any doubt. Nor should you refuse to lend books to anyone who does not have any or the (82) ability to buy them, as long as you are sure he will return them to you. You know what our sages wrote: "Wealth and happiness reside with him and his righteousness remains forever." So, do not keep the benefit of your possessions [from others] or guard your books closely." Cover your book cases with lovely tapestries and guard them against moisture, bookworms, and damage, because they are your treasure. When you lend a book to anyone, inscribe his name in the catalogue before it leaves your house; and when it is returned, cross it out with a pen. On Passover and Sukkot, recall all of the books that you have lent out.

On the Sabbath and the holidays, the members of your household should read the Bible and peruse books of grammar, the book of Proverbs, and *After Proverbs* as a matter of habit. My son, I also encourage you to peruse, on every Sabbath, the biblical portion concerning the descendants of Jonadab ben Rechab so that you will be fastidious in observing my admonitions to you.

My son, if you hear numbskulls criticizing or cursing me, keep quiet and do not respond. If they speak ill of me, do not let it affect you.

In *After Proverbs* it says:

The love of man is the fruit to humility
  and in his fruit, the happy man finds tranquility.
(83) And the fruit of the quiet listener
  is quiescence and confidence and happiness.

My son, be quick to honor your mentors and teachers. Serve and love them and those who love them and hate those who hate them. Glorify them everywhere, while sitting and while standing.[28] Even though you are expendable to them, they are indispensable to you—in a thousand ways they are indispensable to you.

From *After Proverbs*:

A wise man is loved by all
  and loves everyone who approaches him.
A fool is hated by all
  And hates everyone he sees.
And so, strive and seek
  to become wisdom's brother
And keep your name far from those
  of the brothers of vanity and great foolishness.

But, my son, honor your friends, too. Be attentive to them and avail them of your wisdom, advice, and actions. Remind the son of Zeḥaryah, the memory of the righteous is a blessing, of the affection that both you and I had for his father; love him as a brother and honor him as a great friend because his father, the memory of the righteous is a blessing, honored, loved, and praised you similarly. He also left prayer and praise for you [to be read] (84) after his death, the memory of the righteous is a blessing. My son, it is not enough that you repay one who has treated you so well through his actions, honor, and speech because it is not possible, even in a whole lifetime, for any man to repay those who came before him. As the Scripture says: How shall I repay him who comes before me? Be wary of haters and zealots. My son, write letters to your sisters regularly and inquire about their welfare; accord honor to your relatives and they will honor you.

I would impress upon you, my son, that you should read this testament of mine daily, either during the daytime or at night. Take care to effect and act upon everything that is written in it; that way you will have success on your every path and you will become wise. If you find my counsel to be worthwhile, then choose one of your Arabic books that is written in a hand that appeals to you aesthetically and try to learn from it by imitating it. No one taught the Arabic script to the *nasi*, Samuel; rather, he took one of the documents written by an important scribe and tried to write using it as a model. He kept at it until he exceeded it. Now, my son, zealously pursue the path of educated men and those with good moral qualities; do not envy sinners, and instead fear God always.

(85) And here, I have set this whole epistle (*iggeret*) for you in rhyme so that all of my guidance (*musar*) can be collected and recalled in verse:

(20a) Observe my admonitions and hear my advice:
  Let the law of God be your heart's delight
Turn your heart toward understanding.
  Pursue justice and make truth your companion.
May your understanding elevate you
  and may your faith be the source of your praise.
Serve God with your whole heart
  And thus you will be satisfied with every luxury and excess[29]
His commandments and laws are to be observed.
  Follow His rules, stay steadfast, and remember them.
Thus the commandments and law are a lighted candle
  and a fortress of aid in a time of wrath and transgression.
Honor your father, mother with reverent respect[30]
  and bind your soul tightly to theirs.
Turn from evil and do not befriend any evil person.
  Know your Rock, be righteous, and be saved.
Get up early to go to the oases of wisdom and stay late.
  Befriend and draw close the community of [wisdom's] seekers.
(86) Be brief in your words when you speak.
  Be clear in your discourse when you talk.

Be the lord of your tongue in your silence.
 And it will govern your words and your tongue.
Give no due to play or happiness
 Do not choose recreation or relaxation
And do not let your heart tend toward rest
 lest you be left in the lurch afterward.
Engage yourself but do not take on too much.
 Do not take your ancestors' inheritance as a surety.
Work until you have fulfilled your needs.
 The one who is happy with his lot will be glorified
But fools are lost through too much tranquility
 And the lazy are enslaved by sloth
Do not be proud of your wealth,
 but rather honor and give thanks to your Creator [for it].
Give your own bread to the weak
 and the destitute. Indulge the hungry.
Be a fortress of strength and help to them.
 Do not be proud of your wealth, but rather use it to help.
(87) Pray at prayer times,
 arriving early at the synagogue.
Let your wings protect the sons of other men.
 My son, let your [the words on your] tongue heal.
Cast lines to [catch] the things that please you
 and do not glory in the vanities of fools.
Draw close those close to you and honor
 your friends, and thus you will not lose your fortune.
Help them through their failings as much as you can
 and do not look kindly on your own.
Do not covet what is in the hands of others,
 my son, lest your soul be full of bitterness
and your days [full of] pain and anger.
 What use is anger or despair to you?
When your needs are filled you will be satisfied with your fill.
 Mock the one who has not yet said: "enough."
Do not long, my son, for your neighbor's wife
 Though her morals and beauty inflame your desire.
Distance yourself from liars and turn away,
 my son, from those who walk in the ways of slander and strife
and from those who advocate revolts; and away from their partisans
 (88) disincline, lest you err in their same ways.
Fear the Rock, your Creator and
 be cautious about swearing oaths in His unique name.
Hide your eyes from the faults of your friends.

Know your own faults, and see to their absence
Make your love clear to your friends
and avail them of your wealth and counsel.
If they will not hear what you have to say,
my son, do not add another word.
(20b) Bear the sins of those who love you
and do not join forces with foreign or evil people.
Let your business with all of mankind be good,
my son, lest your soul come to disgrace and shame
When you borrow, repay [the loan] before it is due.
Turn away from lawsuits and hedge against oath-swearing.
Do not stop the repayment of a friend.
God will assure your repayment.
Keep your word and act on it;
make this your law and your bond.
(89) Free your tongue of lies.
When you extend your anger, discover your patience.
Liars are the most derogated
in everyone's eyes; and they are known by their lies.
How honored are the truthful in the eyes of mankind
and how valued are the paths of the upright!
Do not reveal your secrets to others;
place it in your heart as in a prison.
Keep even those who love you as strangers in this respect
and the one who lies at your chest as a foreign.
Do not reveal your secrets to any other man
and do not accompany any gossip.
Do not loan out your honor;
that which is loaned out most freely is what most loses its glory
Eat your greens with barley bread
and do not cover up the splendor of your dear face.
Honor your soulmate and keep her close;
let the words you speak to her be kind and pleasant.
And because of this, she will be honored on your account,
and you will have honor and splendor because of her honor.
(90) For her, honor those closest to you
and make them as your brothers and beloveds
Be gentle when you demand or command
and do not employ harsh responses or violence.
It is good that this way she will treat you with love
and will not approach you with resentment and hostility.
Do not learn to curse because cursing
is a big deal, not a trifle.

Take pity and mercy on your children
  and teach them Torah every day and night.
Get up early to educate them,
  teach them, guide them, and keep them in line.
Keep them from stumbling blocks in their paths, from error,
  and from falling into evil.
Be careful of mistakes in your writing
  lest they disgrace you when it is time for them to be read.
[Mistakes] garner shame from the audience
  and are seen as a defect and error.
Return to your books once you have written them
  so that you won't leave out letters or phrases from them.
Know that a man's words and books
  (91) indicate the rectitude of his intellect and character.
From afar, men will praise him for his writing
  or write him off and mock him for his writing.
Through his wisdom he will be the best of the flock
  and though his understanding, honored among his cohort.
Seal the Torah and lock in its witness
  that are more precious than treasure or gold.
Serve your guides and teachers;
  bring joy to your father and vex those who are jealous of you.
Take care to observe my guidance and learning
  so that you will be honored in every community and congregation.
Let yourself be trapped in wisdom's hand and guided by it,
  and thus you will be a prince of all your pursuits.
Do not abhor your critics; instead be guided
  and humble, and you will be a prince amongst your friends.
You will be lifted up like a warrior-scribe
  and in this way your poverty will be diminished and disappear.
Take this father's guidance and observe my sayings
  Let my admonitions be your moral north and safeguard my words
I have written this wisdom out for you three times[31]
  (92) Take joy in it as you would in gemstones and coral.
Follow it and add to it.
  I will live on through it.

(21a) From here a small cloud ascends from the sea of knowledge and understanding on a wind of wisdom and vision. When that cloud rains down onto the fertile land, it seeds the source of justice and truth and allows pleasure and wisdom to flourish with contentment. Its [wisdom's] produce will ripen and its roots grow deep. It will branch out and flower, blooming with edible fruits and medicinal leaves. The favor of its Creator will protect it, water it as needed, and guard it from all evil. May the one who gives good judgment to the simple and wisdom and understanding to the youth give you a heart that listens and an ear that hears; then our souls will rejoice in God and exult in His salvation.

Completed—praise God!—by the hand of Yo'av [in 1341[32]*]; please, God, redeem my soul. May God give His good refuge to all of Israel; let all of them be amongst those inscribed for eternal life in the world to come. Amen, amen, amen. For the sake of Your name, God, renew my life through Your justice, free my soul from its straits, through Your mercy repress my enemies, and dismiss my troubles; because I am your servant. Lord, honored be your name.*

NOTES

1. See chapter 6.
2. This first paragraph is the English translation of fifteen lines of poetry that open the ethical will. I have preserved the line breaks but translated the poetry into prose.
3. Lit., "nest," as in Isa. 10:14.
4. The repeated, explicit indications that poetry introduced into the text come from *After Proverbs* and always occur without a verb—that is, the manuscript simply reads "Ben Mishlei." I have supplied the verb for the sake of the flow of the text. These indications appear to be a late scribal emendation, possibly to flag text that would not have been immediately recognizable. For a more detailed discussion of the indications that these are late scribal additions, see the discussion in chapter 4.
5. The beginning of this paragraph, up to this point, is omitted from the Koraḥ edition.
6. This section of the text appears to be among the earliest, written to Samuel when he was about twelve; we see this when Judah complains about the sleep he has lost and the toil he has undertaken for the last twelve years. This, then, seems to be a reproach to Samuel for not keeping up with an immediate peer, rather than for being an older man with the handwriting of a child.
7. Note the shift in the chronology here; whereas up to this point Judah had been writing as a very attentive and hands-on parent to a young Samuel whom he was raising, here we are introduced to an older Samuel, one with his own children and one from whom Judah is separated for lengthy periods of time because of both men's professional commitments.
8. Lit., "habit governs all."
9. Lit., "do not go out walking."
10. The image of a lion scared by a much smaller animal is a relatively common one in Arabizing Hebrew poetry.
11. Here, Judah identifies two of Meshullam of Lunel's son's, Aaron and Asher, by biblical names that evince the loyalty he wishes to highlight: Aaron, the brother of Moses, and his companion, Hur, a Judahite warrior.

12. Lit., "with the words in Arabic books."

13. On the payment of bride prices in gold rather than in silver, see S. D. Gotein, *A Mediterranean Society*, vol. 3 (reprint, Berkeley: University of California Press, 2000), sec. viii.B.4, 119–23.

14. Koraḥ lays his editorial agenda—already revealed in the omission of Judah's admonitions to Samuel regarding Arabic learning—even barer here when he substitutes *sifrei ḥoq* (law books) where the manuscript clearly reads *sifrei ḥuẓ* (secular books).

15. Lit., "your tongue will grow long."

16. Prov. 31:10–31.

17. For a similar concern stemming from a Castilian literary context, see the author's preface of the *Book of Count Lucanor and Patronio* in which its author, Juan Manuel, asks his readers not to hold him accountable for infelicities in the work unless they have seen an autograph copy and know that the mistakes were the product of his own hand, not those of a scribe's.

18. Lit., "Secrets of the Purity of Language." Israel Abrahams chose to render the title of this work *Principles of Style*. It is a euphonic, colloquial rendering with perhaps appropriate overtones of Strunk and White; but as the title of a lost work that has yet to be identified, and one that uses a term for purity (*ẓahut*) that is often implicated in medieval comparisons of Hebrew and Arabic, it seems the better choice to translate it somewhat more literally.

19. Lit., "improve the workings of your pen."

20. The Divine epithet *ha-makom*, literally "the place," is the one that appears here in the text; I have chosen to translate it as "Source" because "place" sounds less capacious and universal in the English and another common translation of this epithet, "Omnipresent," does not correspond directly. With "Source" I have tried to allude to the derivation of what is ultimately a rabbinic epithet, namely Mordechai telling Esther that the Jews' help will come from "another place" (Est. 4:14), effectively from another source, namely God.

21. This phrase is also cited in Maimonides' letter to Samuel.

22. Edelman understands this phrase to refer to Judah not wishing to leave Samuel to his own devices to find a wife, while Abrahams rejects this reading: "E. has misunderstood the whole of this passage. The author clearly refers to his disinclination to provide a stepmother for his son. E. takes it to refer to Samuel's marriage." While my tendency would be to read with Abrahams here, I am not convinced that the force of his conviction is warranted and wish to leave open the possibility of the other interpretation.

23. This marks a shift back to an earlier phase in the compositional history of the text; where Judah had been writing to an older Samuel from whom he spent much time apart, here he is once again writing to the younger Samuel whom he had not yet left alone while traveling.

24. Outerwear was dear and often shared between husbands and wives (see Goitien, *A Mediterranean Society*, vol. 4, 154–57); here Judah seems to be complimenting her for not asking for fancy clothes or for her own coat.

25. The text goes back and forth in its references to Samuel's son and his sons. It is impossible to determine with certainty whether the difference in number is an artifact of the compositional chronology (that is, whether Judah added to it between the birth of Samuel's first son and his subsequent sons) or whether it is a scribal error, though I am more inclined toward the latter possibility.

26. Lit., “the splendor of your countenance.”

27. Here I am translating with Israel Abrahams, who uses the term *memorandum* to indicate both the catalogue and aide-memoire functions of the document.

28. Abrahams translates this phrase (*ma‘amad u-moshav*, from Mishnah Megillah 4:3) in a particularly elegant way, as “under all circumstances.”

29. Both terms that form this dyad, *deshen* and *ḥelev*, have a literal meaning of visceral animal fat, but they can also be used metaphorically to express luxury; as a choice in diction, this stands in interesting contrast to Judah’s admonitions in the prose sections that Samuel should eat lots of vegetables and avoid meat, and contributes to the idea that the prose and poetic sections of the ethical will express very different viewpoints.

30. In general, Abrahams’s transcription of the text is more accurate than Koraḥ’s, but here, where the manuscript clearly reads (and Koraḥ follows) “ve-khabed ’av va-’em kavod u-mora’,” Abrahams gives “ve-khabed ’av va-’em kevod moreh” (accord your parents a teacher’s honor).

31. In terms of the chronological stratigraphy, there appear to be three major points at which Judah returned to the text to add to it, as mentioned in the notes above; perhaps this is a reference to that compositional history.

32. See chapter 4 for a discussion of the encoded chronogram.

BIBLIOGRAPHY

MEDIEVAL SOURCES

Allony, Nehemiah. *The Jewish Library in the Middle Ages: Booklists from the Cairo Genizah*. Ed. Miriam Frenkel and Haggai Ben-Shammai. Jerusalem: Ben-Zvi Institute, 2006.

Assaf, Simha. *Sources for the History of Education in Israel*. Ed. Shmuel Glick. New York: Jewish Theological Seminary of America, 2006.

Bāqillānī, Abū Bakr Muḥammad. *A Tenth-Century Document of Arabic Literary Theory and Criticism: The Sections on Poetry of* 'Ijāz al-Qur'ān. Ed. Gustave von Grunebaum. Chicago: University of Chicago Press, 1950.

Benjamin of Tudela. *Itinerary*. Ed. and trans. Marcus Nathan Adler. Oxford: University Press, 1907.

———. *Libro de viajes*. Ed. and trans. José Ramón Magdalena Nom de Déu. Barcelona: Riopiedras Ediciones, 1989.

Ben Labrat, Dunash. *The Book of Dunash's Responses to Menaḥem*. Ed. Herschell Filipowski. London, 1885.

———. *Dunash ben Labrat: Shirim*. Ed. Nehemiah Allony. Jerusalem, 1948.

———. *Dunash Halevi ben Labrat's Responses to Sa'adya Gaon*. Ed. Robert Schroeter. Breslau, 1886.

———. *Tesubot de Dunash ben Labrat*. Ed. and trans. Ángel Sáenz-Badillos. Granada: Universidad de Granada, 1980.

———. "Vorlaeufige Notiz ueber Dunasch ben Labrat." Ed. Leopold Dukes. *Literaturblatt des Orients* 4 (1843).

Ben Sheshet, Yehudi. *Teshuvot*. Ed. S. G. Stern. Vienna, 1870.

Al-Birrī, Muḥammad Ibn Abī Bakr al-Tilimsānī. *Pearls of the Lineage of the Imam 'Alī and His Family*, ed. Muḥammad al-Tūnaji. Beirut, 1994.

Cole, Peter. *The Dream of the Poem*. Princeton, NJ: Princeton University Press, 2007.

———. *Selected Poems of Shmuel Ha-Nagid*. Princeton, NJ: Princeton University Press, 1996.

Al-Fāsī, Daūd ben Abraham. *Kitāb Jāmi' al-Alfāẓ*. Vol. 1. Ed. Solomon L. Skoss. Yale Oriental Series: Researches, vol. 20. New Haven, CT: Yale University Press, 1936.

Al-Ghazālī. *Kitāb iḥyā' 'ulūm an-dīn*. 1898. Reprint. Cairo: Al-Maṭb'ah al-azhariyya, 1930.

———. *Letter to a Disciple*. Ed. and trans. Tobias Mayer. Cambridge: Islamic Text Society, 2005.

Hadassi, Judah. *Eskol ha-Kofer*. Ed. Wilhelm Bacher and Sandor Scheiber. *Jewish Quarterly Review* (o.s.) 8 (1863).

Halevi, Judah. *Kitāb al-radd wa-l-dalīl fī-l-dīn al-ḏalīl*. Ed. David Zvi Baneth and Haggai Ben-Shammai. Jerusalem: Magnes Press, 1977.

———. *The Kuzari*. Trans. Barry Kogan and Lawrence Berman. New Haven, CT: Yale University Press, forthcoming.

———. *Treatise on Poetic Meters*. Ed. and trans. Tova Rosen. Israel Levine Jubilee Volume. Ed. Reuven Tzur and Tova Rosen, 324–28. Tel Aviv: Tel Aviv University Press, 1994.

Harīzī, Judah. *Taḥkemoni*. Ed. Joseph Yahalom and Naoya Katzumata. Jerusalem: Ben-Zvi Institute, 2010.

Ibn 'Abbar, Muḥammad. *Kitāb al-takmila li-kitāb al-ṣila*. Ed. Francisco Codera y Zaidín. In *Bibliotheca Arabico-Hispana* 5–6 (1886).

Ibn Abī Usaybi'ah, Aḥmad ibn al-Qāsim. *Kitāb 'uyūn al-anbā' fī ṭabaqāt al-aṭibbā'*. Cairo: Egyptian Foundation for the Book, 2001.

Ibn Daūd, Abraham. *Libro de la Tradición*. Trans. Lola Ferre. Barcelona: Riopiedras, 1990.

———. *Sefer ha-Qabbalah*. Ed. and trans. Gerson D. Cohen. Philadelphia: Jewish Publication Society, 1967.

Ibn 'Ezra', Abraham. *Dos comentarios al Libro de Ester*. Ed. and trans. Mario Gómez Aranda. Madrid: Consejo Superior de Investigaciones Científicas, 2007.

———. *Ha-Safah ha-Berurah*. Ed. and trans. Enrique Ruiz González and Ángel Sáenz-Badillos. Córdoba: Ediciones Almendro, 2004.

———. *Short Commentary on Exodus*. In *Mikraot Gedeolot Ha-Keter*, vol. 2. Ed. Menachem Cohen. Ramat Gan: Bar Ilan University Press, 2008.

———. *Yalqut*. Ed. Israel Levin. New York: Keren Yisrael, 1985.

Ibn 'Ezra', Moses. *Kitāb al-Muḥāḍarah wa-l-Muḏākara*. Ed. A. S. Halkin. Jerusalem: Meqiẓe Nirdamim, 1975.

———. *Kitāb al-Muḥāḍarah wa-l-Muḏākara*. Ed. and trans. Montserrat Abumalham Mas. Madrid: Consejo Superior de Investigaciones Científicas, 1986.

Ibn Gabirol, Solomon. *The Improvement of Moral Qualities*. Trans. Stephen S. Wise. New York: Columbia University Press, 1902.

———. *Kitāb iṣlāḥ al-akhlāq*. Ed. Moritz Steinschneider. In *Oẓrot Ḥayim*. Hamburg: Halberstadt, 1848.

Ibn Ḥazm, 'Alī ibn Aḥmad. *Rasā'il*. Ed. Ihsan 'Abbās. Beirut, 1981.

Ibn Naghrila, Samuel. *Ben Mishlei*. Ed. Dov Yarden. Jerusalem: Libov School of Graphic Arts, 1982.

———. *Ben Mishlei*. Ed. Shraga Abramson. Tel Aviv: Mossad Harav Kook, 1947.

Ibn Shuhayd, Abū Amīr. *Diwān*. Ed. James Dickie. Cairo: Dar al-Kātib, 1969.

Ibn Shu'ba, Ḥasan Ibn 'Alī al-Ḥarranī. *Tuḥaf al-'uqūl min ahl al-rasūl*. Beirut: Al-Maṭba'ah al-ḥaydarīyah, 1963.

Ibn Tabbān, Levi. *The Poems of Levi Ibn Tabbān*. Ed. Dan Pagis. Jerusalem: Israel Academy of Arts and Sciences, 1967.

Ibn Tibbon, Judah. "A Father's Admonition." In *Hebrew Ethical Wills*, ed. Israel Abrahams, 51–92. Philadelphia: Jewish Publication Society, 1926.

———, trans. *Ḥovot ha-Levavot* by Baḥya ibn Paqūda. Ed. Joseph Kafiḥ. Reprint. New York: Feldheim, 1984.

———, trans. *Ḥovot ha-Levavot* by Baḥya ibn Paqūda. Ed. M. E. Stern. Lemberg: Balaban, 1837.

———, trans. *Ḥovot ha-Levavot* by Baḥya ibn Paqūda. Venice: Bomberg, 1548.

———. *Iggeret ha-Musar*. Ed. Pinhas Korah. Jerusalem: Machon Marah, 2006.

———. *Musar Av*. Bodleian Mich. 50.3 (Neubauer 2219).

———. *Musar Av*. Firenze, Biblioteca Laurenziana 45/7, folios 38–51. IMHMS Film #17806.

———. *Musar Av*. Frankfurt Heb. MS. 266/1, folios 7a–12a. IMHMS Film #26500.

———. *Musar Av*. Parma, Biblioteca Palatina MS 2461, folios 40–41. IMHMS Film #13465.

———, trans. *Sefer ha-Kuzari* by Judah Halevi. Ed. Hartwig Hirschfeld. Leipzig: Schulze, 1887.

———, trans. *Sefer ha-Riqmah* by Jonah ibn Janāḥ. Ed. Michael Wilensky. Jerusalem: Academy of the Hebrew Language Press, 1964.

———, trans. *Sefer ha-Shorashim* by Jonah ibn Janāḥ. Ed. Wilhelm Bacher. Berlin: Defus Itzikovsky, 1896.

———, trans. *Tikkun Middot ha-Nefesh* by Solomon ibn Gabirol. In *Sefer Goren Naḥon*, ed. Eliezer Lipman Zilberman. Lyck, 1859.

———. *Testament of the Sage*. Ed. Simon Iakerson. St. Petersburg: Institute of Oriental Studies, 2011.

Ibn Tibbon, Samuel. "Commentary on Ecclesiastes." Ed. and trans. James T. Robinson. PhD diss., Harvard University, 2002.

———. *Commentary on Ecclesiastes*. Trans. James T. Robinson. Tübingen: Mohr Siebeck, 2007.

———, trans. *Moreh ha-Nevukhim* by Moses Maimonides. Ed. Judah Even-Shemuel. Tel Aviv: Shevil, 1935.

———. *The Reason for the Table and the Showbread and the Candelabrum and the Pleasant Smell*. Ed. D. Abrams. Los Angeles, 1995.

Al-Jāḥiẓ. *Kitāb al-Ḥayawān*. Ed. ʿAbd al-Salam Muhammad Hārūn. Beirut: Dar al-Jīl, 1996.

———. *Kitāb al-Ḥayawān*. Trans. Sherman Jackson. *Alif: Journal of Comparative Poetics* 4 (1984): 99–107.

Maghribi, Samaw'al. *Ifham al-yahūd: The Early Recension*. Ed. Ibrahim Marazaka et al. Wiesbaden: Harrasowitz Verlag, 2008.

———. "The Silencing of the Jews." Ed. and trans. Moshe Perlman. *Proceedings of the American Academy of Jewish Research* 32 (1964): 5–136 (English section); 3–146 (Arabic section).

Maimonides, Moses. *Epistles of Maimonides*. Ed. Isaac Shailat. Maaleh Adumim: Shailat Publishing, 1995.

———. *The Guide of the Perplexed*. Ed. Solomon Munk. Reprint. Beirut: Manshurat al-Jamal, 2011.

———. *The Guide of the Perplexed*. Trans. Shlomo Pines. Chicago: University of Chicago Press, 1974.

———. "Letter to Samuel ibn Tibbon." In "Texts by and about Maimonides." Ed. Alexander Marx. *Jewish Quarterly Review* 25, no. 4 (1935): 371–428.

———. "Letter to Samuel Ibn Tibbon according to an Unknown Text in the Archives of the Jewish Community of Verona." Ed. Isaiah Sonne. *Tarbiẓ* 10 (1942): 135–54, 309–32.

———. *Treatise on the Doctrine of Resurrection*. Bodleian MS Opp. Add. 4to 163 (2496).

———. *Treatise on the Doctrine of Resurrection*. In *The Epistles of Maimonides*. Trans. A. S. Halkin. Philadelphia: Jewish Publication Society, 1994.

———. *Treatise on the Doctrine of Resurrection*. National Library of Israel MS Heb. Octavo 3194.

———. *Treatise on Resurrection*. Ed. Joshua Finkel. *Proceedings of the American Academy for Jewish Research* 9 (1939).

Maqqarī, Aḥmad. *Analectes sur l'histoire et la literature des arabes d'Espagne*. Ed. Reinhart Dozy. Leiden: Brill, 1855.

———. *History of the Mohammadan Dynasties of Spain*. Ed. and trans. Pascual Gayangos. Reprint. New York: Routledge, 2002.

———. *Nafḥ al-ṭīb*. Ed. Ihsan 'Abbas. Beirut: Dar Sadir, 2008.

Qimḥi, Joseph. *Sheqel ha-Qodesh*. Ed. Hermann Gollancz. Oxford: Oxford University Press, 1919.

Schirman, Ḥayim, ed. *Hebrew Poetry in Spain and Provence*. Jerusalem: Mossad Biyalik, 1957.

———. *The History of Hebrew Poetry and Drama*. Jerusalem: Mossad Biyalik, 1979.

Van Bekkum, Wout Jac, ed. *A Hebrew Alexander Romance according to MS Heb 671.5, Paris Bibliotheque Nationale*. Leiden: Brill, 1994.

———. *A Hebrew Alexander Romance according to MS London, Jews College 145*. Peeters: Leuven, 1992.

MODERN SOURCES

'Abbādī, Hossam Muḫtar. *Las artes del libro en al-Andalus y el Magreb*. Madrid: El Viso, 2005.

Abbas, Iḥsān. *The History of Andalusi Literature*. Reprint. Amman: Al-Shuruq, 2001.

Aberbach, David. *Jewish Cultural Nationalism: Origins and Influences*. New York: Routledge, 2007.

Abrahams, Israel. *Jewish Life in the Middle Ages*. Reprint. Philadelphia: Jewish Publication Society, 1962.

Abu-Zayd, Nasr. "The Dilemma of the Literary Approach to the Qur'ān." *Alif: Journal of Comparative Poetics* 23 (2003): 8–47.

Ackerman-Lieberman, Phillip. "The Disappearance of the Early Phonetic Judaeo-Arabic Spelling and Sa'adya Gaon's Translation of the Bible." *Jerusalem Studies in Arabic and Islam* 41 (2014): 137–72.

———. "Legal Writing in Medieval Cairo: 'Copy' or 'Likeness' in Jewish Documentary Formulae." In *From a Sacred Source: Genizah Studies in Honour of Professor Stefan C. Reif*, ed. Ben Outhwaite, 25–42. Leiden: Brill, 2010.

———. "The Muḥammadan Stipulations: Dhimmī Versions of the Pact of 'Umar." In *Jews, Christians and Muslims in Medieval and Early Modern Times*, ed. Arnold Franklin et al., 197–206. Leiden: Brill, 2014.

Akasoy, Anna. "Convivencia and Its Discontent: Interfaith Life in al-Andalus." *International Journal of Middle Eastern Studies* 42 (2010): 489–99.
Alba Cecilia, Amparo. "El *Debate del cálamo y la espada* de Jacob ben Eleazar de Toledo." *Sefarad* 68, no. 2 (2008): 291–314.
Alexander, Tamar. "Hagiography and Biography: Abraham Ibn Ezra as a Character in the Hebrew Folk Tale." In *Abraham Ibn Ezra and His Age*, ed. Fernando Díaz Esteban, 11–16. Madrid: Asociación Española de Orientalistas, 1990.
Alfonso, Esperanza. "From al-Andalus to North Africa: The Lineage and Scholarly Genealogy of a Jewish Family." In *The Jew in Medieval Iberia*, ed. Jonathan Ray, 395–425. Brighton, MA: Academic Studies Press, 2012.
———. *Islamic Culture through Jewish Eyes*. New York: Routledge, 2008.
———. "A Poem Attributed to al-Ghazzālī." *Mi-Kan* 11 (2012): 80–94.
Allen, Roger. *The Arabic Literary Heritage: The Development of Its Genres and Criticism*. Cambridge: Cambridge University Press, 1998.
Allony, Nehemiah. "'Elī ben Yehudah ha-Nazir and His Composition of the *Foundations of the Hebrew Language*." *Leshonenu* 34, no. 1 (1970): 76–105; 34, no. 3 (1971): 188–209.
———. "Four Book Lists from the Twelfth Century." *Qiryat Sefer* 43 (1968): 121–39.
———. "The Hebrew *Egron* as a Response to the 'Arabiyya." In *The Zalman Shazar Jubilee Volume*, ed. B. Luria, 465–74. Jerusalem: Qiryat Sefer, 1973.
———. "The Reaction of Moses ibn 'Ezra' to 'Arabiyya." *Bulletin of Jewish Studies* 3 (1975): 19–40.
———. "Sarah and Hagar in the Poetry of Spain." In *Studies in the Bible and the History of Israel*, 168–85. Jerusalem: Qiryat Sefer, 1979.
Anderson, Benedict. *Imagined Communities*. New York: Verso Books, 1983.
Apter, Emily. *Against World Literature: On the Politics of Untranslatability*. New York: Verso Books, 2013.
Arberry, A. J. "New Material on the Kitāb al-Fihrist of Ibn al-Nadīm." *Islamic Research Association Miscellany* 1 (1948): 34–45.
Asad, Talal. "The Concept of Cultural Translation in British Social Anthropology." In *Writing Culture*, ed. James Clifford and George Marcus, 141–64. Berkeley: University of California Press, 1986.
Ashtor, Eliahu. *The Jews of Moslem Spain*. Reprint. Philadelphia: Jewish Publication Society, 1992.
Assaf, Simcha. "Letters of Samuel b. 'Eli and His Contemporaries." *Tarbiẓ* 1 (1930): 102–30.
———. "Letters of Samuel b. 'Eli and His Contemporaries, cont'd." *Tarbiẓ* 2 (1931): 43–84.
———. "Letters of Samuel b. 'Eli and His Contemporaries, cont'd." *Tarbiẓ* 3 (1932): 15–80.
Assis, Yom Tov. "The Judaeo-Arabic Tradition in Christian Spain." In *The Jews of Medieval Islam: Community, Society and Identity*, ed. Daniel Frank, 111–12. Leiden: Brill, 1995.
Athamina, Khalil. "Lafẓ in Classical Arabic Poetry." *Israel Oriental Studies* 11 (1991): 47–55.
Atiyeh, George Nicholas. *The Book in the Islamic World: The Written Word and Communication in the Middle East*. Albany: State University of New York Press, 1995.
Bahr, Arthur. *Fragments and Assemblages: Forming Compilations of Medieval London*. Chicago: University of Chicago Press, 2013.
Bakhos, Carol. *Ishmael on the Border: Rabbinic Portrayals of the First Arab*. Albany: State University of New York Press, 2006.

Bakhtin, Mikhail. *The Dialogic Imagination.* Trans. Michael Holquist. Austin: University of Texas Press, 1981.

Baneth, David Zvi. "The Common Teleological Source of Baḥyā Ibn Paquda and al-Ghazālī." In *Sefer Magnes.* Ed. Fritz Baer. Jerusalem: Hebrew University of Jerusalem Press, 1938.

———. "Judah Halevi and al-Ghazali." In *Studies in Jewish Thought*, ed. Alfred Jospe, 181–99. Detroit: Wayne State University Press, 1981.

———. "Jehuda Hallewi und Ghazali." *Korrespondenzblatt des Vereins zur Gründung und Erhaltung einer Akademie für die Wissenschaft des Judentums* 5 (1924): 27–45.

———. "Judah al-Ḥarīzī and the Chain of Translations." *Tarbiẓ* 10 (1942): 135–54.

——— "Maimonides as His Own Translator." *Tarbiẓ* 23 (1942): 170–91.

———. "Yehudah Halevi ve-Alghazali." *Kenesset* 7 (1941): 311–29.

Bar-Levav, Avriel. "When I Was Alive: Jewish Ethical Wills as Egodocuments." In *Egodocuments and History: Autobiographical Writing in Its Social Context since the Middle Ages*, ed. Rudolf Dekker, 45–60. Rotterdam: Verloren Publishers, 2002.

Baron, Salo. "Ghetto and Emancipation: Shall We Revise the Traditional View?" *Menorah Journal* 16 (1928): 515–26.

———. "Newer Emphases in Jewish History." *Jewish Social Studies* 25, no. 4 (1963): 235–48.

———. *A Social and Religious History of the Jews.* Reprint. New York: Columbia University Press, 1993.

Barstone, Willis. *The Poetics of Translation: History, Theory and Practice.* New Haven, CT: Yale University Press, 1993.

Bassiouney, Reem. *Arabic Sociolinguistics.* Edinburgh: Edinburgh University Press, 2009.

Baumgarten, Elisheva. *Practicing Piety in Medieval Ashkenaz: Men, Women, and Everyday Religious Observance.* Philadelphia: University of Pennsylvania Press, 2014.

Becker, Dan. *The Arabic Sources for Jonah Ibn Janaḥ's Grammar.* Tel Aviv: Tel Aviv University Press, 1998.

Beit-Arié, Malachi. "Commissioned and Owner-Produced Manuscripts in the Sephardi Zone and Italy in the Thirteenth–Fifteenth Centuries." In *The Late Medieval Hebrew Book in the Western Mediterranean*, ed. Javier del Barco, 15–27. Leiden: Brill, 2015.

———. "Stereotype and Individuality in the Handwriting of Medieval Scribes." In *The Makings of the Medieval Hebrew Book*, 77–92. Jerusalem: Magnes Press, 1993.

Bellver, José. "Al-Ghazālī of al-Andalus: Ibn Barrajān, Mahdism, and the Emergence of Learned Sufism in the Iberian Peninsula." *Journal of the American Oriental Society* 133, no. 4 (2013): 659–81.

Benjamin, Walter. *Illuminations.* New York: Schocken Books, 1969.

Bennison, Amira. *The Great Caliphs: The Golden Age of the Abbasid Empire.* New Haven, CT: Yale University Press, 2009.

Bennison, Amira, and María Ángeles Gallego. "Jewish Trading in Fes on the Eve of the Almohad Conquest." *Miscelánea de estudios árabes y hebreos* 56 (2007): 33–51.

Ben-Sasson, Menachem. "Varieties of Inter-Communal Relations in the Geonic Period." In *The Jews of Medieval Islam: Community, Society, and Identity*, ed. Daniel Frank, 17–31. Leiden: Brill, 1995.

Ben-Shalom, Ram. *Medieval Jews and the Christian Past: Jewish Historical Consciousness in Spain and Southern France.* Oxford: Littman Library, 2016.

Ben-Shammai, Haggai. "Is 'The Cairo Genizah' a Proper Name or a Generic Noun?" *From a Sacred Source: Genizah Studies in Honour of Professor Stefan C. Reif*, ed. Ben Outhwaite, 43–52. Leiden: Brill, 2010.

———. "Midrashic-Rabbinic Literature in the Commentaries of Sa'adya Ga'on: Continuity and Innovation." In *Heritage and Innovation in Medieval Judaeo-Arabic Culture*, ed. J. Blau and D. Doron, 33–68. Ramat Gan: Bar Ilan University Press, 2000.

———. "New and Old: Sa'adya's Two Introductions to His Translation of the Pentateuch." *Tarbiẓ* 69 (2000): 199–210.

———. "Observations of the Beginnings of Judaeo-Arabic Civilization." In *Beyond Religious Borders: Interaction and Intellectual Exchange in the Medieval Islamic World*, ed. David Freidenreich and Miriam Goldstein. Philadelphia: University of Pennsylvania Press, 2011.

———. "The Tension between Literal Interpretation and Exegetical Freedom: Comparative Observations on Saadia's Method." In *With Reverence for the Word*, ed. Jane Dammen McAuliffe, Joseph Goering, and Barry D. Walfish, 33–50. Oxford: Oxford University Press, 2003.

Ben-Shammai, Haggai, and Benjamin Hary, eds. *Esoteric and Exoteric Aspects in Judaeo-Arabic Culture*. Leiden: Brill, 2006.

Benvenisti, Meron. *Sacred Landscapes*. Berkeley: University of California Press, 2002.

Berlin, Adele. *Biblical Poetry through Medieval Jewish Eyes*. Bloomington: Indiana University Press, 1991.

Blau, Joshua. *The Emergence and Linguistic Background of Judaeo-Arabic*. Jerusalem: Magnes Press, 1981.

———. "On a Fragment of the Oldest Judaeo-Arabic Bible Translation Extant." In *Genizah Research after Ninety Years: The Case of Judaeo-Arabic*, ed. Joshua Blau and Stefan Reif, 31–39. Cambridge: Cambridge University Press, 2000.

———. "On the Status of Hebrew and Arabic amongst Arabophone Jews." *Leshonenu* 26 (1962): 281–84.

———. "Saadya Gaon's Pentateuch Translation and the Stabilization of Medieval Judaeo-Arabic Culture." In *The Interpretation of the Bible*, ed. J. Krašovec, 393–97. Sheffield: Academic Press, 1998.

Blau, Joshua, and Simon Hopkins. "On Early Judaeo-Arabic Orthography." *Zeitschrift für arabische Linguistik* 12 (1987): 9–27.

Bloch, Marc. *The Historian's Craft*. New York: Vintage, 1964.

Bonfil, Robert. "Reading the Jewish Communities of Western Europe in the Middle Ages." In *A History of Reading in the West*, ed. Guglielmo Cavallo and Roger Chartier, 149–78. Amherst: University of Massachusetts Press.

Borges, Jorge Luis. *Ficciones*. Reprint. Madrid: Alianza, 1999.

Bowman, Steven. "Review of Van Bekkum." *Journal of Jewish Studies* 48, no. 1 (1997): 166–68.

Boyarin, Daniel. *Intertextuality and the Reading of Midrash*. Bloomington: Indiana University Press, 1994.

———. *A Traveling Homeland: The Babylonian Talmud as Diaspora*. Philadelphia: University of Pennsylvania Press, 2015.

Boyarin, Shamma. "Diasporic Culture and the Makings of Alexander Romances." PhD diss., University of California, Berkeley, 2008.

———. "Hebrew Alexander Romance and Astrological Questions: Alexander, Aristotle, and the Medieval Jewish Audience." In *Alexander the Great in the Middle Ages: Transcultural Perspectives*, ed. Marcus Stock, 149–78. Toronto: University of Toronto Press, 2016.

Brann, Ross. "Andalusi Exceptionalism." In *A Sea of Languages: Rethinking the Arabic Role in Medieval Literary History*, 119–34. Toronto: University of Toronto Press, 2013.

———. "Andalusian Hebrew Poetry and the Hebrew Bible: Cultural Nationalism or Cultural Ambiguity?" In *Approaches to Judaism in Medieval Times*, vol. 3, ed. David Blumenthal, 101–31. Atlanta: Scholars Press.

———. "The Arabized Jews." In *The Cambridge History of Arabic Literature: The Literature of al-Andalus*, ed. María Rosa Menocal, Raymond Scheindlin, and Michael Sells, 435–54. Cambridge: Cambridge University Press, 2000.

———. *The Compunctious Poet: Cultural Ambiguity and Hebrew Poetry in Muslim Spain*. Baltimore: Johns Hopkins University Press, 1991.

———. "Constructions of Exile in Hispano-Hebrew and Hispano-Arabic Elegies." In *Israel Levin Jubilee Volume*, ed. Reuven Tsur and Tova Rosen, 45–61. Tel Aviv: Tel Aviv University Press, 1994.

———. "The Moors?" *Medieval Encounters* 15, no. 2 (2009): 307–18.

———. *Power in the Portrayal*. Princeton, NJ: Princeton University Press, 2002.

Brener, Ann. *Isaac ibn Khalfun: A Wandering Hebrew Poet of the Eleventh Century*. Leiden: Brill, 2003.

Brody, Robert. *The Geonim of Babylonia and the Shaping of Medieval Jewish Culture*. New Haven, CT: Yale University Press, 1998.

———. *Rav Sa'adya Gaon*. Jerusalem: Zalman Shazar Center, 2006.

———. "Saadya Gaon on the Limits of Liturgical Flexibility." In *Genizah Research after Ninety Years: The Case of Judaeo-Arabic*, ed. Joshua Blau and Stefan Reif, 40–46. Cambridge: Cambridge University Press, 2000.

Buresi, Pascal. *Governing the Empire: Provincial Administration in the Almohad Caliphate*. Leiden: Brill, 2013.

———. *Histoire du Maghreb medieval*. Paris: Armand Colin, 2013.

Camille, Michael. *Image on the Edge*. Reprint. London: Reaktion Books, 2012.

Cano Pérez, María José. "Los notables judíos de Cataluña y el sur de Francia según el Sefer Masa'ot de Benjamín de Tudela." *Miscelánea de Estudios Árabes y Hebreos* 53 (2004): 73–95.

Chartier, Roger. *The Order of Books*. Stanford, CA: Stanford University Press, 1992.

Chomsky, William. "The Growth of Hebrew during the Middle Ages." *Jewish Quarterly Review* 57 (1967): 121–36.

Cohen, Mark. "Medieval Jewry in the World of Islam." In *The Oxford Handbook of Jewish Studies*, ed. Martin Goodman and Jeremy Cohen, 193–217. Oxford: Oxford University Press, 2002.

———. "A Neo-Lachrymose Conception of Jewish-Arab History." *Tikkun* 6, no. 3 (1991): 55–60.

———. "On the Interplay of Arabic and Hebrew in the Cairo Geniza Letters." In *Studies in Arabic and Hebrew Letters in Honor of Raymond P. Scheindlin*, ed. Jonathan Decter and Michael Rand, 17–35. Piscataway, NJ: Gorgias Press, 2007.

——— *Under Crescent and Cross: The Jews in the Middle Ages*. Princeton, NJ: Princeton University Press, 1995.

———. "What Was the Pact of Umar?" *Jerusalem Studies in Arabic and Islam* 23 (1999): 100–157.

Cohen, Mordechai Z. "'The Best of Poetry . . .': Literary Approaches to the Bible in the Spanish Peshat Tradition." *Torah u-Madda Journal* 6 (1995): 15–57.

———. "Moses Ibn Ezra vs. Maimonides: Argument for a Poetic Definition of Metaphor (*isti'āra*)." *Edebiyat* 11 (2000): 1–28.

———. *Opening the Gates of Interpretation: Maimonides' Biblical Hermeneutics in Light of His Geonic-Andalusian Heritage and Muslim Milieu*. Leiden: Brill, 2011.

———. *Three Approaches to Biblical Metaphor: From Abraham ibn Ezra and Maimonides to David Kimhi*. Leiden: Brill, 2003.

Cole, Peter, and Adina Hoffman. *Sacred Trash*. New York: Schocken, 2011.

Corcos, David. "The Nature of the Almohad Rulers' Treatment of the Jews." Trans. Elisheva Machlis. *Journal of Medieval Iberian Studies* 2, no. 2 (2010): 259–85.

Cornell, Vincent. *The Realm of the Saint*. Austin: University of Texas Press, 1998.

Corriente, Francisco. "Again on the Metrical System of the Muwaššaḥ and Zajal." *Journal of Arabic Literature* 17 (1985): 34–49.

———. "La métrica hebrea cuantitativa." *Sefarad* 46 (1986): 123–32.

Dan, Joseph. "Ashkenazi Hasidism and the Maimonidean Controversy." *Maimonidean Studies* 3 (1995): 29–47.

———. *Studies in the Literature of the Ashkenazi Pietists*. Ramat Gan: Masadah Publishing, 1975.

David, Abraham. "Benjamin ben Jonah of Tudela." In the *Encyclopaedia of Jews in Islamic Lands*. Brill Online, 2016. http://ezproxy.library.nyu.edu:2447/entries/encyclopedi-of-jews-in-the-islamic-world/benjamin-ben-jonah-of-tudela-COM_0003980.

Davidson, Israel. *Thesaurus of Medieval Hebrew Poetry*. New York: Ktav Publishing, 1970.

Davies, Daniel. "Maimonidean Margins." In *Normative Judaism? Jews, Judaism and Jewish Identity*, ed. Daniel Langton and Philip Alexander, 15–27. Piscataway, NJ: Gorgias Press, 2008.

Decter, Jonathan. "Changing Landscapes of Hebrew Rhymed Prose Narrative." In *Studies in Medieval Jewish Poetry*, ed. Alessandro Guetta and Masha Itzhaki, 55–68. Leiden: Brill, 2009.

———. *Iberian Jewish Literature: Between al-Andalus and Christian Europe*. Bloomington: Indiana University Press, 2007.

———. "The Rendering of Quranic Quotations in Hebrew Translations of Islamic Texts." *Jewish Quarterly Review* 96 (2006): 336–58.

Del Valle Rodríguez, Carlos. "El testamento de Yehudah Ibn Tibbon: Notas para una historia de las bibliotecas en la España medieval." *Revista de archivos, bibliotecas, y museos* 82 (1979): 495–524.

Derrida, Jacques. *The Monolingualism of the Other: or, The Prosthesis of Origin*. Trans. Patrick Menash. Stanford, CA: Stanford University Press, 1998.

Doenitz, Saskia. "Alexander the Great in Medieval Hebrew Traditions." In *A Companion to Alexander Literature in the Middle Ages*, ed. Z. David Zuwiyya, 21–40. Leiden: Brill, 2011.

Drory, Rina. "Al-Ḥarīzī's Maqāmāt: A Tricultural Literary Product?" *Medieval Translator* 4 (1994): 66–85.

———. "The Hidden Context: On Literary Products of Tri-Cultural Contacts in the Middle Ages." *Pe'amim* 46 (1991): 9–28.

———. "Literary Contacts and Where to Find Them: On Arabic Literary Models in Medieval Jewish Literature." *Poetics Today* 14 (1993): 277–302.

———. *Models and Contacts: Arabic Literature and Its Impact on Medieval Jewish Culture*. Leiden: Brill, 2000.

———. "Words Beautifully Put: Hebrew versus Arabic in Tenth-Century Jewish Literature." In *Genizah Research after Ninety Years: The Case of Judaeo-Arabic*, ed. Joshua Blau and Stefan Reif, 53–66. Cambridge: Cambridge University Press, 2000.

Dunlop, M. D. "Ḥafṣ ibn Albar: The Last of the Goths." *Journal of the Royal Asiatic Society* 86, no. 3 (1954): 137–51.

———. "Sobre Ḥafṣ Ibn Albar." *Al-Andalus* 20 (1955): 211–13.

Edelman, Hirsch, and Judah Lieb Dukes. *Ginzei Oxford: An Anthology of Piyyutim and Other Poems by the Beloved Poets of Old Spain*. London, 1850.

Einbinder, Susan. *No Place of Rest: Jewish Literature, Expulsion, and the Memory of Medieval France*. Philadelphia: University of Pennsylvania Press, 2009.

———. "Pen and Scissors: A Medieval Debate." *Hebrew Union College Annual* 65 (1994): 261–76.

———. *Trial by Fire: Burning Jewish Books*. Kalamazoo, MI: Medieval Institute Publications, 2000.

Elinson, Alexander E. *Looking Back at al-Andalus: The Poetics of Loss and Nostalgia in Medieval Arabic and Hebrew Literature*. Leiden: Brill, 2009.

———. "Loss Written in Stone: Ibn Shuhayd's Rithā' for Cordoba and Its Place in the Arabic Elegiac Tradition." In *Transforming Loss into Beauty*, ed. Marle Hammond and Dana Sajdi. New York: American University of Cairo Press, 2008.

Engel, Edna. "Sephardi and Ashkenazi Attitudes toward Italian Script." *The Late Medieval Hebrew Book in the Western Mediterranean*, ed. Javier del Barco, 28–45. Leiden: Brill, 2015.

Eph'al, Israel. "Ishmael and the Arab(s): A Transformation of Ethnological Terms." *Journal of Near Eastern Studies* 35, no. 4 (1976): 225–35.

Even-Zohar, Itamar. "Polysystem Theory." *Poetics Today* 1, no. 1 (1979): 287–310.

———. "The Position of Translated Literature within the Literary Polysystem." *Poetics Today* 11, no. 1 (1990): 45–51.

Fauvelle-Aymar, François-Xavier. "Desperately Seeking the Jewish Kingdom of Ethiopia: Benjamin of Tudela and the Horn of Africa." *Speculum* 88, no. 2 (2013): 383–404.

Fierro, Maribel. "Alfonso X 'the Wise': The Last Almohad Caliph?" *Medieval Encounters* 15, no. 2 (2009): 175–98.

———. *The Almohad Revolution: Politics and Religion in the Islamic West in the Twelfth-Thirteenth Centuries*. Surrey: Ashgate, 2012.

———. "La religion." In *Historia de España*, ed. María Jesús Viguera Molins, 437–546. Madrid: Calape, 1997.

Fine, Lawrence. "The Arts of Calligraphy and Composition and the Love of Books." In *Judaism in Practice: From the Middle Ages through the Early Modern Period*, 318–24. Princeton, NJ: Princeton University Press, 2001.

Finklestein, Louis, ed. *Rab Saadya Gaon: Studies in His Honor*. New York: Jewish Theological Seminary of America, 1944.

Fleischer, Ezra. "On Dunash ben Labrat, His Wife and His Son." *Jerusalem Studies in Hebrew Literature* 5 (1984): 189–203.

———. "Towards a History of Secular Hebrew Poetry in Spain at Its Beginnings." In *Culture and Society in the History of Israel in the Middle Ages*, ed. M. Ben-Sasson, n.p. Jerusalem: Zalman Shazar Center, 1989.

Fletcher, Madeleine. "The Almohad Tawhīd: Theology Which Relies on Logic." *Numen* 38, no. 1 (1991): 110–27.

———. "Ibn Tūmart's Teachers: The Relationship with al-Ghazālī." *Al-Qantara* 18 (1997): 305–30.

———. *The Legacy of Muslim Spain*. Ed. Salma Khadra Jayyusi, 235–58. Leiden: Brill, 1992.

Forte, Doron. "Back to the Sources: Alternative Versions of Maimonides' Letter to Samuel ibn Tibbon and Their Neglected Significance." *Jewish Studies Quarterly* 23 (2016): 47–90.

Fraenkel, Carlos. "Beyond the Faithful Disciple: Samuel ibn Tibbon's Criticism of Maimonides." In *Maimonides after 800 Years*, ed. Jay Harris. Cambridge, MA: Harvard University Press, 2007.

———. "From Maimonides to Samuel ibn Tibbon: Interpreting Judaism and a Philosophical Religion." In *Traditions of Maimonideanism*, ed. Carlos Fraenkel, 171–212. Leiden: Brill, 2009.

———. *From Rambam to Samuel Ibn Tibbon: The Path from* Dalālat al-Ḥa'irīn *to* Moreh ha-Nevuḫīm. Jerusalem: Magnes Press, 2007.

———. "Legislating Truth: Maimonides, the Almohad and the 13th-Century Jewish Enlightenment." In *Studies in the History of Culture and Science Presented to Gad Freudenthal on His 65th Birthday*, ed. Resienne Fontaine et al., 209–25. Leiden: Brill, 2010.

Franklin, Arnold. "Cultivating Roots: The Promotion of Exilarchal Ties to David in the Middle Ages." *AJS Review* 29, no. 1 (2005): 91–110.

———. *This Noble House: Jewish Descendants of King David in the Medieval Islamic East*. Philadelphia: University of Pennsylvania Press, 2012.

Freidenreich, David. "The Use of Islamic Sources in Sa'adya's Tafsīr of the Torah." *Jewish Quarterly Review* 93, no. 3 (2003): 353–95.

Frenkel, Miriam. "Genizah Documents and Literary Products." *From a Sacred Source: Genizah Studies in Honour of Professor Stefan C. Reif*, ed. Ben Outhwaite, 139–56. Leiden: Brill, 2010.

Freudenthal, Gad. "Abraham Ibn Ezra and Judah Ibn Tibbon as Cultural Intermediaries." In *Exchange and Transmission across Cultural Boundaries: Philosophy, Mysticism, and Science in the Mediterranean World*, ed. Haggai Ben-Shammai, Shaul Shaked, and Sarah Stroumsa, 52–80. Jerusalem: Israel Academy of Arts and Sciences, 2013.

———. "Arabic into Hebrew: The Emergence of the Translation Movement in Twelfth-Century Provence and Jewish-Christian Polemic." In *Beyond Religious Borders*, ed. David Freidenreich and Miriam Goldstein, 124–43. Philadelphia: University of Pennsylvania Press, 2012.

———. "Les sciences dans le communautés juives médiévales de Provence." *Revue des Etudes Juives* 152, no. 1 (1993): 32–136.

Freudenthal, Gad, and Ruth Glasner. "Patterns of Translation Movements." In *De L'Antiquité tardive au moyen âge*, ed. Elisa Coda and Celia Martini, 245–52. Paris: Librairie Philosophique, 2014.

Friedlaender, Israel. "The Jews of Arabia and the Rechabites." *Jewish Quarterly Review* 1 (1910): 252–57.

Frojmovic, Eva. "Inscribing Piety in Late-Thirteenth-Century Perpignan." *The Late Medieval Hebrew Book in the Western Mediterranean*, ed. Javier del Barco, 107–47. Leiden: Brill, 2015.

Gallego, María Ángeles. "The Emergence and Development of Scholarship on Medieval Judaeo-Arabic in Spain." *Texts and Studies in Jewish History and Literature from Antiquity through the Middle Ages Presented to Norman Golb*, ed. Joel Kraemer and Michael G. Wechsler, 83–92. Chicago: Oriental Institute of the University of Chicago, 2012.

———. "The Languages of Medieval Iberia and Their Religious Dimension." *Medieval Encounters* 9, no. 1 (2003): 107–39.

García-Arenal, Mercedes. "Jewish Converts to Islam in the Muslim West." *Israel Oriental Studies* 17 (1997): 227–48.

———. *Messianism and Puritanical Reform: Mahdis of the Muslim West*. Leiden: Brill, 2006.

———. "The Religious Identity of the Arabic Language and the Affair of the Lead Books of Granada." *Arabica* 56 (2009): 495–528.

Garden, Kenneth. "Al-Ghazālī's Contested Revival: Iḥyā' 'ulūm al-dīn and Its Critics in Khrasan and the Maghrib." PhD diss., University of Chicago, 2005.

———. *The First Islamic Reviver: Abū Ḥāmid al-Ghazālī and His Revival of the Religious Sciences*. Oxford: Oxford University Press, 2014.

Geertz, Clifford. *Islam Observed*. Chicago: University of Chicago Press, 1971.

———. *Works and Lives: The Anthropologist as Author*. Stanford, CA: Stanford University Press, 1988.

Gibb, H.A.R. "The Social Significance of the Shu'ūbiyya." In *Studies in the Civilization of Islam*, 62–73. Princeton, NJ: Princeton University Press, 1982.

Gil, Moshe. *Jews in Islamic Countries in the Middle Ages*. Leiden: Brill, 2004.

Giladi, Avner. "A Short Note on the Possible Origin of the Title *Moreh ha-Nevukhim*." *Tarbiẓ* 48 (1979): 346–47.

Goitein, S. D. "Books, Migrant and Stationary: A Geniza Study." In *Occident and Orient: A Tribute to the Memory of A. Scheiber*, ed. Robert Dan, 179–98. Leiden: Brill, 1988.

———. "Dispositions in Contemplation of Death." *Proceedings of the American Academy for Jewish Research* 46, no. 1 (1986): 155–78.

———. *A Mediterranean Society*. Reprint. Berkeley: University of California Press, 2000.

———. Unpublished notecards, index numbers 100775, 101186, and 101188.

Goldberg, Jessica. "Goitein, Free Trade Zones, and the Writing of Economic History." Paper delivered at the Annual Meeting of the Medieval Academy of America, New Haven, CT, March 18, 2010.

———. "On Reading Goitein's *A Mediterranean Society*: A View from Economic History." *Mediterranean Historical Review* 26, no. 2 (2011): 171–86.

Goldfeld, Lea Naomi. *Moses Maimonides' Treatise on Resurrection: An Inquiry into Its Authenticity*. Jerusalem: Ktav Publishing, 1986.

Goldreich, Amos. "Possible Arabic Sources for the Distinction between Duties of the Heart and Duties of the Limbs." *Tecudah* 6 (1988): 179–208.

Goldstein, Miriam. "Arabic Book Culture in the Work of a Jerusalem Karaite: Abū l-Faraj Hārūn and His Glossary of Difficult Biblical Terms." *Zeitschrift der Deutschen Morgenländischen Gesellschaft* 164, no. 2 (2014): 345–73.

———. "Arabic Composition 101 and the Early Development of Judaeo-Arabic Bible Exegesis." *Journal of Semitic Studies* 55, no. 2 (2010): 451–78.

———. "Saadya's Tafsīr in Light of the Polemic against Ninth-Century Arabic Bible Translations." *Jerusalem Studies in Arabic and Islam* 36 (2009): 173–99.

Goldziher, Ignaz. "Alte und neue Poesie im Urtheile der arabische Kritiker." In *Abhandlungen zur arabischer Philologie*, vol. 1, 122–76. Leiden: Brill, 1896.

———. "Arab and Ajam" and "Shu'ūbiyya." In *Muslim Studies*, vol. 1, 98–168. Reprint. Chicago: University of Chicago Press, 1968.

———. "Die Shu'ūbijja unter den Muhammedanern in Spanien." *Zeitschrift der Deutschen Morgenländischen Gesellschaft* 53 (1899): 601–20.

Gonzalo Sánchez, José Luis. "Cisneros, el Colegio de San Idelfonso y la Biblia Políglota." In *V Centenario de la Biblia Políglota Complutense: La Universidad del Renacimiento, El Renacimiento de la Universidad*, ed. José Luis Gonzalo Sánchez, 91–131. Madrid: Servicio de Publicaciones, UCM, 2014.

Goodman, Lenn. "Saadiah Gaon's Interpretive Technique in Translating the Book of Job." In *Translation of Scripture*, ed. David Goldenberg, 47–75. Philadelphia: University of Pennsylvania Press, 1990.

Gould, Laura. "Inimitability versus Translatability: The Structure of Literary Meaning in Arabo-Persian Poetics." *Translator* 19, no. 1 (2013): 81–104.

Greenspahn, Frederick E. "How Jews Translate the Bible." In *Biblical Translation in Context*, ed. Frederick W. Knobloch, 43–61. Bethesda: University Press of Maryland, 2002.

Griffel, Frank. "Ibn Tūmart's Rational Proof for God's Existence and Unity, and His Connection to the Niẓamiyya Madrasa in Baghdad." *Los almohades: problemas y perspectivas*, ed. Patrice Cressier, Maribel Fierro, and Luis Molina, 753–813. Madrid: Consejo Superior de Investigaciones Científicas, 2005.

Griffith, Sidney. *The Bible in Arabic: The Scriptures of the People of the Book in the Language of Islam*. Princeton, NJ: Princeton University Press, 2012.

Gross, Henri. *Gallia Judaica*. 1897. Reprint. Leuven: Peeters, 1997.

Gutas, Dimitri. "Classical Arabic Wisdom Literature: Nature and Scope." *Journal of the American Oriental Society* 101, no. 1 (1981): 49–86.

———. *Greek Thought, Arabic Culture: The Graeco-Arabic Translation Movement in Baghdād and Early 'Abbāsid Society*. New York: Routledge, 1998.

———. "The Study of Arabic Philosophy in the Twentieth Century: An Essay on the Historiography of Arabic Philosophy." *British Journal of Middle Eastern Studies* 29 (2002): 5–25.

Gutwirth, Eleazer. "History and Intertextuality in Late Medieval Spain." In *Christians, Muslims, and Jews in Medieval and Early Modern Spain; Interaction and Cultural Change*, ed. Mark D. Meyerson and Edward D. English, 161–78. Notre Dame: University of Notre Dame Press, 2000.

Hacker, Joseph. "Jewish Book Owners and Their Libraries in the Iberian Peninsula, Fourteenth-Fifteenth Centuries." *The Late Medieval Hebrew Book in the Western Mediterranean*, ed. Javier del Barco, 70–104. Leiden: Brill, 2015.

———. "The Jewish Public Library in Spain." In *Rishonim ve-Aḥaronim: Studies in the History of Israel Dedicated to Abraham Grossman*, ed. Joseph Hacker, B. Z. Kedar, and Joseph Kaplan. Jerusalem: Zalman Shazar Center, 2010.

———. "Sephardi Book Culture: Jewish Book Owners in Late Medieval Aragon." Penn Seminar in the History of the Book, University of Pennsylvania, Philadelphia, April 28, 2014.

Halbertal, Moshe. *People of the Book: Canon, Meaning and Authority*. Cambridge, MA: Harvard University Press, 1997.

Hamilton, Michelle. "Hispanism and Sephardic Studies." *Journal of Medieval Iberian Studies* 1, no. 2 (2009): 179–94.

———. "Translating Desire." In *Representing Others in Medieval Iberian Literature*, 47–88. New York: Macmillan, 2007.

Hamori, Andras. *On the Art of Medieval Arabic Literature*. Princeton, NJ: Princeton University Press, 1974.

Harb, Lara. "Poetic Marvels: Wonder and Experience in Medieval Arabic Literary Theory." PhD diss., New York University, 2013.

Harkavy, A. *An Inedited Version of the Legend of Alexander the Great*. St. Petersburg, 1892.

Harvey, Steven. "Alghazali and Maimonides and Their Books of Knowledge." In *Be'erot Yitzhak*, ed. Jay M. Harris. Cambridge, MA: Harvard University Press, 2005.

———. "Did Maimonides' Letter to Samuel ibn Tibbon Determine Which Philosophers Would Be Studied by Later Jewish Thinkers?" *Jewish Quarterly Review* 83, no. 1 (1992): 51–70.

———. "The Introductions of Thirteenth-Century Arabic-to-Hebrew Translators of Philosophic and Scientific Texts." In *Vehicles of Transmission, Translation, and Transformation in Medieval Textual Culture*, ed. Carlos Fraenkel et al., 223–34. Turnhout: Brepols, 2011.

———. "A New Islamic Source of the Guide of the Perplexed." In *Maimonidean Studies*, vol. 2, ed. Arthur Hyman, 31–59. New York: Yeshiva University Press, 1992.

———. "Why Did Fourteenth-Century Jews Turn to Alghazali's Account of Natural Science?" *Jewish Quarterly Review*, 91, no. 3–4 (2001): 359–76.

Harvey, Warren Zev. *Physics and Metaphysics in Ḥasdai Crescas*. Amsterdam: Gieben, 1998.

Hary, Benjamin. "Judaeo-Arabic as a Mixed Language." In *Middle Arabic and Mixed Arabic: Diachrony and Synchrony*, ed. Arie Schippers, 125–44. Leiden: Brill, 2012.

———. *Multiglossia in Judaeo-Arabic*. Leiden: Brill, 1992.

———. *Translating Religion: Linguistic Analysis of Judaeo-Arabic Sacred Texts from Egypt*. Leiden: Brill, 2009.

Hary, Benjamin, and M. J. Wien. "Religiolinguistics: On Jewish-, Christian-, and Muslim-Defined Languages." *International Journal for the Sociology of Language* 220 (2013): 85–108.

Hawting, G. R. "Muḥammad ibn Abī Bakr." *Encyclopaedia of Islam*, 2nd ed. http://referenceworks.brillonline.com/entries/encyclopaedia-of-islam-2/muhammad-b-abi-bakr-SIM_5336. Accessed February 29, 2016.

Heinrichs, Wolfhart. "Istiʿāra and Badīʿ and Their Terminological Relationship in Early Arabic Literary Criticism." *Zeitschrift für Geschichte der Arabisch Islamischen Wissenschaften* 1 (1984): 80–111.

———. "Literary Theory: The Problem of Its Efficiency." In *Arabic Poetry: Theory and Development*, ed. G. E. von Grunebaum, 19–69. Wiesbaden, 1973.

———. "Prosimetrical Genres in Arabic Literature." In *Prosimetrum*, ed. Joseph Harris and Karl Reichl, 249–76. Cambridge: Brewer, 1997.

Heller-Roazen, Daniel. *Dark Tongues: The Art of Rogues and Riddlers*. New York: Zone Books, 2013.

Hershezon, Daniel. "The Arabic Portion of the Cairo Genizah at Cambridge." *Jewish Quarterly Review* 16, no. 1 (1903): 98–112.

———. "Traveling Libraries: The Arabic Manuscripts of Muley Zidan and the Escorial Library." *Journal of Early Modern History* 18 (2014): 535–58.

Hodder, Ian. *Entangled: An Archaeology of Relationships between Humans and Things*. Blackpool: Wiley, 2013.

Hoyland, Robert. "The Jewish Poets of Muḥammad's Hijāz." In *Le Judaïsme de l'Arabie antique*, ed. Christian Julien Robin. Turnhout: Brepols, 2015.

———. "The Jews of the Hijaz in the Qur'ān and in Their Inscriptions." In *New Perspectives on the Qur'ān*, ed. Gabriel Said Reynolds, 91–116. New York: Routledge, 2011.

———. "Mount Nebo, Jabal Ramm, and the Status of Christian Palestinian Aramaic and Old Arabic in Late Roman Palestine and Arabia." In *The Development of Arabic as a Written Language*, ed. M. MacDonald, 29–46. Oxford: Archaeopress, 2010.

Huici Miranda, Ambrosio. *La historia politica del imperio almohade*. Reprint. Tetuán: Editorial Marroquí, 1956.

Hughes, Aaron W. *The Invention of Jewish Identity: Bible, Philosophy, and the Art of Translation*. Bloomington: Indiana University Press, 2010.

Ivry, Alfred. "Moses of Narbonne's 'Treatise on the Perfection of the Soul.'" *Jewish Quarterly Review* 57, no. 4 (1967): 271–99.

Jabre, Farid. *Essai sur le lexique de Ghazali*. Beirut: Publications de L'Université Libanaise, 1970.

Johns, A. H. "A Humanistic Approach to I'jāz in the Qur'ān: The Transfiguration of Language." *Journal of Qur'ānic Studies* 13, no. 1 (2011): 79–99.

Kanarfogel, Ephraim. "Compensation for the Study of Torah in Medieval Rabbinic Thought." *Of Scholars, Savants and Their Texts*, ed. Ruth Link-Salinger, 135–48. New York: Peter Lang, 1989.

———. "The Impact of Halevi in Medieval Ashkenaz." Presentation at the Annual Conference of the Association for Jewish Studies, Baltimore, December 14–16, 2014.

———. *The Intellectual History and Rabbinic Culture of Medieval Ashkenaz*. Detroit: Wayne State University Press, 2012.

———. *Jewish Education and Society in the High Middle Ages*. Detroit: Wayne State University Press, 1992.

———. "Judah he-Ḥasid and the Rabbinic Scholars of Regensburg: Interactions, Influences, and Implications." *Jewish Quarterly Review* 96, no. 1 (2006): 17–37.

———. *Peering through the Lattices: Mystical, Magical, and Pietistic Dimensions in the Tosafist Period*. Detroit: Wayne State University Press, 2000.

Kassis, Riad. *The Book of Proverbs and Arabic Proverbial Works*. Leiden: Brill, 1999.

Kay, Sarah. *Parrots and Nightingales: Troubadour Quotations and the Development of European Poetry*. Philadelphia: University of Pennsylvania Press, 2013.

Kellner, Menachem. "Maimonides' Disputed Legacy." In *Traditions of Maimonideanism*, ed. Carlos Fraenkel, 245–76. Leiden: Brill, 2009.

Kennedy, Hugh. *Muslim Spain and Portugal: A Political History.* New York: Routledge, 2011.

Key, Alexander. "Arabic: Acceptance and Anxiety." American Comparative Literature Association State of the Discipline Report, 2014–15. http://stateofthediscipline.acla.org/entry/arabic-acceptance-and-anxiety. Accessed April 1, 2015.

Khan, Geoffrey. "Al-Qirqisānī's Opinions Concerning the Text of the Bible and Parallel Muslim Attitudes towards the Text of the Quran." *Jewish Quarterly Review* 81 (1990): 59–73.

Killito, Abedlfattah. *The Author and His Doubles: Essays on Classical Arabic Culture.* Syracuse: Syracuse University Press, 2001.

———. *Thou Shalt Not Speak My Language.* Syracuse: Syracuse University Press, 2008.

Kirschner, Robert. "Maimonides' Fiction of Resurrection." *Hebrew Union College Annual* 52 (1981): 163–93.

Knight, Christopher. "Medieval Hebrew Medical Poetry: Uses and Contexts." *Aleph* 11, no. 2 (2011): 213–88.

———. "Rechabites in the Bible and in Jewish Tradition to the Time of Rabbi David Kimhi." PhD dissertation, Durham University, 1988.

Kraemer, Joel. *Maimonides: The Life and World of One of Civilization's Greatest Mind.* New York: Doubleday, 2010.

Kraemer, Joel, and Josef Stern. "Shlomo Pines on the Translation of Maimonides' Guide of the Perplexed." *Journal of Jewish Thought and Philosophy* 8 (1999): 13–24.

Krinis, Ehud. *God's Chosen People: Judah Halevi's Kuzari and Shi'i Imami Doctrine.* Turnhout: Brepols, 2014.

Krstić, Tijana. "Self-Narratives of Conversion to Islam in the Age of Confessionalization." *Comparative Studies in Society and History* 51, no. 1 (2009): 53–63.

Kugel, James L. *The Idea of Biblical Poetry: Parallelism and Its History.* Baltimore: Johns Hopkins University Press, 1981.

Kuhne Brabant, Rosa. "Algunos aspectos de la literature didáctica entre los medicos árabes." In *Actas de las II Jornadas de Cultura Árabe e Islámica*, 273–80. Madrid: Instituto Hispáno-Arabe, 1985.

Langermann, Tzvi. "A Judaeo-Arabic Poem Attributed to Abu Hamid al-Ghazali." *Miscelánea de estudios árabes y hebraicos* 52 (2003): 183–200.

———. "A New Codex of Medieval Jewish Philosophy." *Qiryat Sefer* 64 (1993): 427–32.

———. "Samuel ben 'Eli's Epistle on Resurrection." *Kovetz al-Yad* 15 (2001): 39–94.

Larkin, Margaret. "The Inimitability of the Qur'ān: Two Perspectives." *Religion and Literature* 20, no. 1 (1988): 31–47.

Larsson, Goran. *Ibn García's Shu'ūbiyya Letter: Ethnic and Theological Tensions in Medieval al-Andalus.* Leiden: Brill, 2003.

Lassner, Jacob. *Islamic Revolution and Historical Memory: An Inquiry into the Art of 'Abbasid Apologetics.* Winona Lake, IN: Eisenbrauns, 1987.

———. *The Shaping of 'Abbasid Rule.* Princeton, NJ: Princeton University Press, 1980.

Lavee, Moshe. "Haggadic Midrash in the Cairo Genizah as Reflected in the Book Lists of Rav Yosef Rosh ha-Seder." In *Studies in Canonicity and Genizah*, ed. M. Ben-Sasson et al., 38–87. Jerusalem: Magnes Press, 2010.

Lavi, Abraham. "A Comparative Study of al-Ḥarīrī's Maqāmāt and the Hebrew Translations." PhD diss., University of Michigan, 1979.

Lazarus-Yafeh, Hava. "Was Maimonides Influenced by Al-Ghazālī?" In *Tehillah le-Moshe: Biblical and Judaic Studies in Honor of Moshe Greenberg*, ed. Mordechai Cogan, Barry Eichler, and Jeffrey Tigay, 163–93. Winona Lake, IN: Eisenbrauns, 1997.

Leder, Stefan. "Zubayr ibn Bakkār." *Encyclopedia of Islam*, 2nd ed. http://ezproxy.library.nyu.edu:2313/entries/encyclopaedia-of-islam-2/al-zubayr-b-bakkar-SIM_8190. Accessed February 2, 2016.

Lerner, Ralph. "Maimonides' Treatise on Resurrection." *History of Religions* 32 (1984): 140–55.

Levi, Israel. "Les traductions hébraiques de l'histoire légendaire d'Alexandre." *Revue des Etudes Juives* 7 (1883): 238–65.

———. "Sefer Toledot Alexander." In *Sammelband kleinter Beitraege aus Handschriften*, vol. 2. Berlin: Mekitzei Nedarim, 1886.

Lezra, Jacques. "On Contingency in Translation." In *Early Modern Cultures in Translation*, ed. Karen Newman and Jane Tylus, 153–74. Philadelphia: University of Pennsylvania Press, 2015.

———. "This Untranslatability Which Is Not One." *Paragraph* 38, no. 2 (2015): 174–88.

Lieberles, Robert. *Salo Wittmayer Baron: Architect of Jewish History*. New York: New York University Press, 1995.

Lobel, Diana. *A Sufi-Jewish Dialogue: Philosophy and Mysticism in Bahya Ibn Paquda's Duties of the Heart*. Philadelphia: University of Pennsylvania Press, 2007.

Loeb, Isidore. *Un procès dan la famile des Ibn Tibbon*. Paris: Alcan-Lévy, Imprimeur du Consistoire, 1886.

Lowin, Shari. *Arabic and Hebrew Love Poems in al-Andalus*. New York: Routledge, 2014.

———. "Khaybar." *Encyclopedia of Jews in the Islamic World*. http://referenceworks.brillonline.com/entries/encyclopedia-of-jews-in-the-islamic-world/khaybar-COM_0012910. Accessed February 2, 2016.

Magen, Ze'ev. *Virtues of the Flesh: Passion and Purity in Early Islamic Jurisprudence*. Leiden: Brill, 2004.

Mahallati, Mohammad Jafar. "Biography and the Image of a Medieval Historian." In *The Rhetoric of Biography*, ed. Louise Marlow, 21–40. Cambridge, MA: Harvard University Press, 2011.

Mahdi, Muhsin S. Preface to *The Thousand and One Nights* (Alf Layla wa-Layla). Leiden: Brill, 1995.

Malter, Henry. *Saadia Gaon: His Life and Works*. Philadelphia: Jewish Publication Society of America, 1942.

Maman, Aharon. *Comparative Semitic Philology in the Middle Ages*. Leiden: Brill, 2004.

———. "Medieval Grammatical Thought: Karaites Versus Rabbanites." *Meḥqarim be-lashon* 7 (1995): 79–96.

Marcus, Ivan. *Piety and Society: The Jewish Pietists of Medieval Germany*. Leiden: Brill, 1997.

Marino, John A. "The Exile and His Kingdom: The Reception of Braudel's Mediterranean." *Journal of Modern History* 76, no. 3 (2004): 622–52.

Martínez Delgado, José. "El uso de la métrica árabe en la obra Ben Tehillim de Samuel ibn Nagrela." *Sefarad* 72, no. 2 (2012): 269–94.

———. "Maimonides in the Context of Andalusian Hebrew Lexicography." *Aleph* 8 (2008): 15–40.

———. "Secularization through Arabicization: The Revival of the Hebrew Language in al-Andalus." *Simon Dubnow Institute Yearbook* 12 (2013): 299–318.

———. "Una carta literaria de la Guenizá de El Cairo en judeo-árabe." *Sefarad* 75, no. 2 (2015): 253–67.

May, George. *Les mille et une nuits d'Antoine Galland: ou le chef-d'oevre invisible*. Paris: Presses Universitaires, 1986.

McNeill, William. "Fernand Braudel, Historian." *Journal of Modern History* 73, no. 1 (2001): 133–46.

Melchert, Christopher. "The Destruction of Books by Traditionalists." *Al-Qanṭara* 35, no. 1 (2014): 213–31.

Menocal, María Rosa. "On Convivencia and Exile: The Enduring Power of Américo Castro's Vision." Unpublished typescript.

———. *The Role of Arabic in Medieval Literary History*. Philadelphia: University of Pennsylvania Press, 1987.

———. *Writing without Footnotes: The Role of the Medievalist in Contemporary Intellectual Life*. Binghamton: State University of New York Center for Medieval and Renaissance Studies, 2001.

Menocal, María Rosa, Raymond P. Scheindlin, and Michael Sells, eds. *The Cambridge History of Arabic Literature: The Literature of al-Andalus*. Cambridge: Cambridge University Press, 2000.

Metcalfe, Alex. *Muslims and Christians in Norman Sicily: Arabic Speakers and the End of Islam*. New York: Routledge, 2003.

Meyerhoff, Max. "Autobiographische Bruschstücke Galens auz arabischen Quellen." *Sudhoffs Archiv für Geschichte der Medizin* 22 (1929): 72–86.

Monferrer Sala, Juan Pedro. "Salmo 11 en ersión árabe versificada." *MEAH* 49 (2000): 303–19.

Montgomery, James. "Salvation at Sea? Seafaring in Early Arabic Poetry." In *Representations of the Divine in Arabic Poetry*, ed. Geert Borg, 25–47. Atlanta: Rodopi, 2001.

Monroe, James T. *The Art of Badīʿal-Zamān al-Ḥamaḏānī as Picaresque*. Beirut: American University in Beirut Press, 1984.

———. "Hispano-Arabic Poetry during the Caliphate of Cordoba: Theory and Practice." *Arabic Poetry: Theory and Development*, ed. G. E. von Grunebaum, 125–54. Wiesbaden: Harrassowitz, 1973.

———. *Islam and the Arabs in Spanish Scholarship*. Leiden: Brill, 1970.

———. "Maimonides on the Mozarabic Lyric: A Note on the Muwashshahat." *La Corónica* 17, no. 2 (1989): 18–32.

———. *Shuʿubiyya in al-Andalus: The Risāla of Ibn García and Five Refutations*. Berkeley: University of California Press, 1970.

Mourad, Suleiman. *Early Islam between Myth and History: Al-Ḥasan al-Baṣrī and the Formation of His Legacy in Islamic Legal Scholarship*. Leiden: Brill, 2005.

Mufwene, Salikoko. "Competition and Selection in Language Evolution." *Selection* 3 (2002): 45–61.

———. *The Ecology of Language Evolution*. Cambridge: Cambridge University Press, 2001.

Muranyi, Miklos. "*Genizah* or *ḥubus*: Some Observations on the Library of the Great Mosque of Qayrawān." *Jerusalem Studies in Arabic and Islam* 42 (2015): 183–99.

Na'eh, Shlomo. "On the Meaning of 'Igarta.'" *Meḥqarei Talmud* 3 (2005).

Neubauer, Adolf. *Catalogue of the Hebrew Manuscripts in the Bodleian Library*. Oxford: Clarendon Press, 1886.

———. *Catalogue of the Hebrew Manuscripts in Jews' College, London*. Oxford: Hart Publishers, 1886.

———. "Ḥafṣ al-Qouti." *Revue des Etudes Juives* 30 (1895): 65–69.

———. "Review of *An Inedited Version of the Legend of Alexander the Great*." *Jewish Quarterly Review* 4, no. 4 (1892): 685–89.

Nisse, Ruth. "Diaspora as Empire in the Hebrew Deeds of Alexander." *Alexander the Great in the Middle Ages: Transcultural Perspectives*, ed. Marcus Stock, 76–87. Toronto: University of Toronto Press, 2016.

Noorani, Yaseen. "The Lost Garden of al-Andalus: Islamic Spain and the Poetic Inversion of Colonialism." *International Journal of Middle East Studies* 31, no. 2 (1999): 237–54.

O'Callaghan, Joseph. *A History of Medieval Spain*. Ithaca, NY: Cornell University Press, 1983.

Olszowy-Schlanger, Judith. "Bilingual Hebrew-Latin Manuscripts." *Hebrew Scholarship and the Medieval World*, ed. Nicholas de Lange, 107–30. Cambridge: Cambridge University Press, 2001.

———. "Leaning to Read and Write in Medieval Egypt: Children's Exercise Books from the Cairo Genizah." *Journal of Semitic Studies* 48, no. 1 (2004): 47–69.

Ozick, Cynthia. *Metaphor and Memory*. New York: Vintage, 1980.

Pagis, Dan. *Innovation and Tradition in Hebrew Secular Poetry in Spain and Italy*. Jerusalem: Keter, 1976.

———. *The Secular Poetry and Poetics of Moses Ibn Ezra and His Contemporaries*. Jerusalem: Mossad Biyalik.

Pearce, S. J. "Matter, Meaning and Maimonides: The Material Text as an Early Modern Map of Thirteenth-Century Debates on Translation." In *Entangled Histories: Knowledge, Authority, and Jewish Culture in the Thirteenth Century*, ed. Elisheva Baumgarten, Ruth Mazo Karras, and Katelyn Mesler, 376–412. Philadelphia: University of Pennsylvania Press, 2016.

———. "Poetry on the Margins: Medieval Historiography's Marginal Verse." *Postmedival* 6, no. 2 (2015): 223–39.

———. "The Types of Wisdom Are Two in Number: Judah ibn Tibbon's Quotation from the Iḥyā' 'ulūm al-dīn." *Medieval Encounters* 19 (2013): 137–66.

Pearsall, Derek. "Towards a Poetics of Chaucerian Narrative." In *Drama, Narrative, and Poetry in the Canterbury Tales*, ed. Wendy Harding, 99–112. Toulouse: Presses Universitaires du Mirail, 2003.

Pellat, Charles. "Al-Djāhiẓ." *Encyclopaedia of Islam*. 2nd ed. http://ezproxy.library.nyu.edu:2447/entries/encyclopaedia-of-islam-2/al-djahiz-SIM_1935. Accessed February 2, 2016.

———. "Essai d'inventaire de l'oeuvre āḥiẓienne." *Arabica* 3, no. 2 (1956): 147–80.

———. *The Life and Works of Jāḥiẓ*. Berkeley: University of California Press, 1969.

———. "Note sur l'Espagne musulmane et al-Yahiz." *Al-Andalus* 21, no. 2 (1956): 277–84.

———. "Nouvel essai d'inventaire de l'oeuvre ˇgāḥiẓienne." *Arabica* 31, no. 2 (1984): 117–64.

Peretz, Ma'aravi. "Substitution of One Word for Another as an Exegetical Method." In *Studies in the Bible and Its Exegesis*, vol. 2, ed. Uriel Simon, 207–28. Ramat Gan: Bar Ilan University Press, 1986.

Perlmann, Moshe. "Eleventh-Century Andalusian Authors on the Jews of Granada." *Proceedings of the American Academy for Jewish Research* 18 (1949): 269–90.

Pines, Shlomo. "Shiite Terms and Conceptions in Judah Halevi's Kuzari." *Jerusalem Studies in Arabic and Islam* 2 (1980): 165–251.

Polliack, Meira. *Genres in Judaeo-Arabic Literature.* Tel Aviv: Tel Aviv University Press, 1998.

———. *The Karaite Tradition of Arabic Bible Translation.* Leiden: Brill, 1997.

———. "The Spanish Legacy in the Hebrew Bible and Commentaries of Abraham Ibn Ezra and Profiat Duran." In *Encuentros and Desencuentros: Spanish Jewish Cultural Interactions Throughout History*, ed. Aviva Doron, 83–101. Tel Aviv: Tel Aviv University Press, 2000.

———. "The Unseen Joints of the Text: On the Medieval Judaeo-Arabic Concept of Elision (iḫtiṣār) and Its Gap-Filling Functions in Biblical Interpretation." In *Words, Ideas, Worlds: Biblical Essays in Honour of Yairah Amit*, ed. Athalya Brener and Frank Polak, 179–205. Sheffield: Phoenix Press, 2012.

Poznansky, J. "Ein Altes Juedisch-Arabisches Buecherverzeichinis." *Jewish Quarterly Review* 15, no. 1 (1902): 76–78.

Pratt, Mary Louise. "Arts of the Contact Zone." *PMLA* 91 (1991): 33–40.

Qualey, M. Lynx. "Why Medieval Arab Scholars Thought It Was Classier Not to Cite Sources, and Other Stylistic Choices: An Interview with Devin Stewart." *Arabic Literature in English*. http://arablit.org/2015/04/14/why-medieval-arab-scholars-thought-it-was-classier-not-to-cite-sources-and-other-stylistic-choices/. Accessed April 31, 2015.

Rabassa, Gregory. *If This Be Treason: Translation and Its Discontents.* New York: New Directions, 2005.

Rapoport, S. L. "On the Independent Jews of Arabia." *Bikkurei ha-ʿittim* 4 (1824): 51–77.

Ravitzky, Aviezer. *History and Faith: Studies in Jewish Philosophy.* Amsterdam: Gieben, 1996.

———. "Samuel ibn Tibbon and the Esoteric Character of the Guide of the Perplexed." *AJS Review* 6 (1981): 87–123.

———. "Samuel Ibn Tibbon and the Secret of the Guide of the Perplexed." *Daʿat* 10 (1982): 19–46.

———. "The Thought of Zerahiah ben Isaac ben Shealtiel Hen and Maimonidean-Tibbonid Philosophy in the Thirteenth Century." PhD diss., Hebrew University of Jerusalem, 1978.

Reif, Stefan. *A Jewish Archive from Old Cairo.* London: Curzon, 2000.

Reiner, Elchanan. "The Attitude of Ashkenazi Society to the New Science in the Sixteenth Century." *Science in Context* 10, no. 4 (1997): 589–603.

Reynolds, Dwight, et al. *Interpreting the Self: Autobiography in the Arabic Literary Tradition.* Berkeley: University of California Press, 2001.

Ribera y Tarragó, Julian. *Libros y enseñanzas en al-Andalus.* Ed. María Jesús Viguera Molins. Reprint. Pamplona: Urgoiti Editores, 2008.

Rifaterre, Michael. *Textual Production.* New York: Columbia University Press, 1983.

Robinson, Cynthia. "Ubi Sunt: Memory and Nostalgia in Taifa Court Culture." *Muqarnas* 15 (1998): 20–31.

Robinson, James T. "The Ibn Tibbon Family: A Dynasty of Translators in Medieval Provence." In *Studies in Memory of Isadore Twersky*, ed. Jay Harris, 193–224. Cambridge, MA: Harvard University Press, 2005.

———. "Samuel ibn Tibbon's Perush ha-Millot ha-Zarot and al-Farabi's Eisagoge and Categories." *Aleph* 9, no. 1 (2009): 41–76.

———"Secondary Forms of Philosophy: On the Teaching and Transmission of Philosophy in Non-Philosophical Literary Genres." In *Vehicles of Transmission, Translation, and Transformation in Medieval Textual Culture*, ed. Carlos Fraenkel et al., 235–48. Turnhout: Brepols: 2011.

———. "Towards a Theoretical Study of Samuel Ibn Tibbon's Translation and Its Relationship to Arabic Sources." In *Alei Asor*, ed. Daniel Lasker and Haggai Ben-Shammai, 249–68. Beersheba: Ben Gurion University Press, 2008.

———. "We Drink Only from the Master's Water: Maimonides and Maimonideanism in Southern France, 1200–1306." *Studia Rosenthaliana* 40 (2007): 27–60.

Roldán Castro, Fatima. "De Nuevo sobre la mezquita aljama almohade de Sevilla: La versión del cronista cortesano Ibn Sāhib al-Salah." In *Magna Hispalensis: Recuperación de la Aljama almoade*, ed. A. Jiménez Martín, 13–22. Seville: Hernán Ruiz, 2002.

Ronell, Avital. *Loser Sons: Politics and Authority*. Urbana: University of Illinois Press, 2012.

Rosenthal, Franz. "Die arabisch Autobiographie." *Studia Arabica* 1 (1937): 1–40.

———. *Knowledge Triumphant*. Ed. Dimitri Gutas. Leiden: Brill, 2006.

———. "Of Making Many Books There Is No End: The Classical Muslim View." In *The Book in the Islamic World*, ed. G. N. Atiyeh, 33–55. Albany: State University of New York Press, 1995.

———. "Significant Uses of Arabic Writing." *Arts Orientalis* 4 (1961): 15–23.

Roth, Norman. "Jewish Reactions to the 'Arabiyya and the Renaissance of Hebrew in Spain." *Journal of Semitic Studies* 28, no. 1 (1983): 63–84.

———. *Jews, Visigoths, and Muslims in Medieval Spain: Cooperation and Conflict*. Leiden, Brill, 2004.

Ruggles, D. Fairchild. *Gardens, Landscape, and Vision in the Palaces of Islamic Spain*. University Park: Penn State University Press, 2003.

Ruiz Souza, Juan Carlos. "El Palacio de los leones de la Alhambra: ¿Madrasa, zāwiya, y tumba de Muḥammad V?" *Al-Qantara* 22 (2001): 77–120.

Rust, Martha. *Imaginary Worlds in Medieval Books: Exploring the Manuscript Matrix*. New York: Palgrave, 2007.

Rustow, Marina. "Formal and Informal Patronage among Jews in the Islamic East: Evidence from the Cairo Geniza." *Al-Qantara* 29, no. 2 (2008): 341–82.

———. "The Genizah and Jewish Communal History." In *From a Sacred Source: Genizah Studies in Honour of Professor Stefan C. Reif.*, ed. Ben Outhwaite, 289–318. Leiden: Brill, 2010.

———. *Heresy and the Politics of Community: The Jews of the Fatimid Caliphate*. Ithaca, NY: Cornell University Press, 2008.

———. "Karaites Real and Imagined: Three Cases of Jewish Heresy." *Past and Present* 197 (2007): 35–74.

Sadan, Joseph. "An Admirable and Ridiculous Hero: Some Notes on the Bedouin in Medieval Arabic Belles-Lettres." *Poetics Today* 10, no. 3 (1989): 471–92.

———. "Genizah and Genizah-Like Practices in Islamic and Jewish Traditions." *Bibliotheca Orientalis* 43, no. 1–2 (1986): 36–58.

———. "Identity and Inimitability: The Contexts of Inter-Religious Polemics and Solidarity in Medieval Spain, in Light of Two Passages by Moše Ibn 'Ezra and Ya'qov ben El'azar." *Israel Oriental Studies* 14 (1994): 325–47.

———. "Maidens' Hair and Starry Skies: Imagery System and Ma'ānī Guides as Demonstrated in Two Manuscripts." *Israel Oriental Studies* 11 (1991): 57–89.

———. "On Genizah Practices among Muslims and the Methods of Treating Worn-Out Holy Books." *Qiryat Sefer* 55 (1980): 398–410.

Sáenz-Badillos, Ángel. "Early Hebraists in Spain." In *Hebrew Bible/Old Testament: The History of Its Interpretation*, vol. 1, 96–109. Vandenhoek and Ruprecht: Göttingen, 2000.

———. "Hebrew Invective Poetry: The Debate between Todros Abulafia and Phineas Halevi." *Prooftexts* 16, no. 1 (1996): 49–73.

———. "La obra de Abraham Ibn Ezra sobre las críticas contra Se'adyah." *Abraham Ibn Ezra and His Age*, ed. Fernando Díaz Esteban, 287–94. Madrid: Asociación Española de Orientalistas, 1990.

———. "Late Medieval Jewish Writers on Maimonides." In *Traditions of Maimonideanism*, ed. Carlos Fraenkel, 223–43. Leiden: Brill, 2009.

Sáenz-Badillos, Ángel, and Judit Tarragona Borrás. *Los Judíos de Sefarad ante la Biblia*. Córdoba: Ediciones El Almendro, 1996.

Safrai, Shmuel, Zeev Safrai, Joshua Schwards, and Peter J. Tomson, eds. *The Literature of the Sages*. Assen: Fortress Press, 2006.

Safran, Janina. *Defining Boundaries in al-Andalus: Muslims, Christians, and Jews in Islamic Iberia*. Ithaca, NY: Cornell University Press, 2013.

———. *The Second Umayyad Caliphate*. Cambridge, MA: Harvard University Press, 2001.

Sairo, Anni, and Minna Palander Collin. "The Reconstruction of Prestige Patterns in Language History." In *The Handbook of Historical Sociolinguistics*, ed. Juan Manuel Hernández Campoy and Juan Camilo Conde Silvestre, 626–38. Chichester: Wiley Blackwell, 2012.

Salama, Mohammad. "Arabic and the Monopoly of Theory." *Arcade: Literature, the Humanities and the World*. http://arcade.stanford.edu/blogs/arabic-and-monopoly-theory. Accessed April 31, 2015.

Saleh, Walid. "The Psalms in the Qur'ān and in the Islamic Religious Imagination." *The Oxford Handbook of The Psalms*, ed. William P. Brown, 281–96. Oxford: Oxford University Press, 2014.

———. "Reflections on Muslim Hebraism: Codex Vindobonensis Palatinus and al-Biqa'I." In *A Sea of Languages: Rethinking the Arabic Role in Medieval Literary History*, ed. Suzanne Conklin Akbari and Karla Mallette, 71–80. Toronto: University of Toronto Press, 2013.

———. "Sublime in Style, Exquisite in Tenderness: The Hebrew Bible Quotations in al-Biqā'ī's Qur'ān Commentary." In *Adaptations and Innovations*, ed. Tzvi Langermann and Josef Stern, 331–47. Louvain: Peeters, 2007.

Saler, Michael. "Imagined Communities, Holistic Histories, and Secular Faith." *Soundings* 92, no. 1 (2009): 129–57.

Salvatierra, Aurora. "On Books and Poems: Poetic Exchanges in Hebrew Poetry in al-Andalus." In *Studies in Medieval Jewish Poetry*, ed. Alessandro Guetta and Masha Itzhaki, 71–84. Leiden: Brill, 2009.

Scales, Peter. *The Fall of the Caliphate of Córdoba: Berbers and Andalusis in Conflict*. Leiden: Brill, 1993.

Schacht, Joseph. "Waṣīya." *Encyclopaedia of Islam*. Leiden: Brill, 1913.

Scheiber, Alexander. "Autograph Manuscript of Maimonides from the Leningrad Genizah." *Acta Orientalia Academiae Scientarum Hungaricae* 33 (1979): 187–95.

Scheindlin, Raymond P. "Merchants and Intellectuals, Rabbis and Poets: Judeo-Arabic Culture in the Golden Age of Islam." In *Cultures of the Jews*, ed. David Biale, 313–88. New York: Schocken Books, 2002.

———. "Moses ibn Ezra." In *The Cambridge History of Arabic Literature: The Literature of al-Andalus*, ed. María Rosa Menocal, Raymond P. Scheindlin, and Michael Sells, 252–64. Cambridge: Cambridge University Press, 2000.

———. "Rabbi Moshe ibn 'Ezra on the Legitimacy of Poetry." *Medievalia et Humanistica* 7 (1975): 101–15.

Schippers, Arie. "Hafs al-Qutī's Psalms in Arabic Rajaz Meter." In *Law, Christianity, and Modernism in Islamic Society*, ed. Urbain Vermeulen and J.M.F. Van Reeth, 133–46. Leuven: Peeters, 2009.

———. *Spanish Hebrew Poetry and the Arabic Literary Tradition: Arabic Themes in Hebrew Andalusian Poetry*. Leiden: Brill, 1994.

Schirman, Hayyim. "The Function of the Hebrew Poet in Medieval Spain." *Jewish Social Studies* 6, no. 3 (1954): 235–59.

———. *The History of Hebrew Poetry in Christian Spain and the South of France*. Ed. Ezra Fleischer. Jerusalem: Magnes Press, 1997.

———. "Maimonides and Hebrew Poetry." *Moznayim* 3 (1935): 433–36.

———. *Studies in the History of Hebrew Poetry and Drama*. Jerusalem: Mossad Biyalik, 1979.

Schneidewind, William. *A Social History of Hebrew: Its Origins through the Rabbinic Period*. New Haven, CT: Yale University Press, 2013.

Schoeler, Gregor. *The Genesis of Literature in Islam: From the Aural to the Read*. Edinburgh: Edinburgh University Press, 2009.

Scholem, Gershom. "Reste neuplatonischer Spekulation in der Mystik der deutschen Chassidim und ihre Vermittlung durch Abraham bar Chija." *Monatsschrift für Geschichte und Wissenschaft des Judentums* 75, no. 5 (1931): 172–91.

Segal, David Simha. "Ben Tehilim of Shmuel Hanagid and the Book of Psalms: A Study in Esoteric Linkage." PhD diss., Brandeis University, 1975.

Septimus, Bernard. *Hispano-Jewish Culture in Transition*. Cambridge, MA: Harvard University Press, 1982.

Serrano Ruano, Delfina. "Why Did the Scholars of al-Andalus Distrust al-Ghazālī?" *Der Islam*, 83, no. 1 (2006): 137–56.

Shalev, Zur. "Benjamin of Tudela, Spanish Explorer." *Mediterranean Historical Review* 25, no. 1 (2010): 13–33.

Shear, Adam. *The Kuzari and the Shaping of Jewish Identity, 1167–1900*. Cambridge: Cambridge University Press, 2008.

Shiffman, Yair. "The Differences between the Translations of Maimonides' Guide of the Perplexed." *Journal of Semitic Studies* 44, no. 1 (1999): 47–61.

Shohat, Ella. "The Question of Judaeo-Arabic." *Arab Studies Journal* 23, no. 1 (2015): 14–78.

Silver, Jeremy David. *Maimonidean Criticism and the Maimonidean Controversies*. Leiden: Brill, 1965.

Simonet, Francisco Javier. *El Cardenal Ximénez de Cisneros y los manuscritos arábigo-granadinos*. Granada: Impresa la Lealtad, 1885.

Sirat, Colette. *Hebrew Manuscripts of the Middle Ages*. Cambridge: Cambridge University Press, 2002.

———. "Studia of Philosophy as Scribal Centers in Fifteenth-Century Iberia." In *The Late Medieval Hebrew Book in the Western Mediterranean*, ed. Javier del Barco, 46–69. Leiden: Brill, 2015.

Sklare, David. "Responses to Islamic Polemics by Jewish Mutakallimun in the Tenth Century." In *The Majlis: Interreligious Encounters in Medieval Islam*, ed. Hava Lazarus-Yafeh, 137–61. Weisbaden: Harassowitz, 1999.

———. *Samuel ben Ḥofni Gaon and His Cultural World*. Leiden: Brill, 1996.

———. "Yūsuf al-Baṣīr: Theological Aspects of His Halakhic Works." In *Jews of Medieval Islam*, ed. Daniel Frank, 249–70. Leiden: Brill, 1995.

Soifer, Maya. "Beyond Convivencia: Critical Reflections on the Historiography of Interfaith Relations in Christian Spain." *Journal of Medieval Iberian Studies* 1, no. 1 (2009): 19–35.

Spiegel, Gabrielle. *The Past as Text*. Baltimore: Johns Hopkins University Press, 1997.

Stahuljak, Zrinka. "Medieval Fixers: The Politics of Interpreting in Western Historiography." In *Rethinking Medieval Translation*, ed. Emma Campbell and Robert Mills, 147–62. Woodbridge: Boydell and Brewer, 2012.

Stearns, Justin. "Representing and Remembering al-Andalus: Some Historical Considerations Regarding the End of Time and the Making of Nostalgia." *Medieval Encounters* 15 (2009): 355–74.

Steiner, Richard C. *A Biblical Translation in the Making: The Evolution and Impact of Saadia Gaon's Tafsīr*. Cambridge, MA: Harvard University Press, 2010.

Steinschneider, Moritz. *Die Arabishe Literatur Der Juden*. Kaufmann: Frankfurt-am-Maim, 1902.

———. *Die hebraeischen Uebersetzungen des Mittelalters*. Berlin: Kommisionverlag des Bibliographischen bureaus, 1893.

———. *The Hebrew Translations of the Middle Ages and the Jews as Transmitters*. Ed. and trans. Charles Manekin et al. New York: Springer, 2014.

———. "Vorrede zu Maimonides' Teḥiyyat ha-Metim." *Israelitische Letterbode* 8 (1882): 99–101.

Stern, David. "The First Jewish Books and the Early History of Jewish Reading." *Jewish Quarterly Review* 98, no. 2 (2008): 163–202.

Stern, Josef. *The Matter and Form of Maimonides' Guide*. Cambridge, MA: Harvard University Press, 2013.

Stern, S. M. "A Collection of Treatises by 'Abd al-Laṭīf al-Baghdādī." *Islamic Studies* 1, no. 1 (1962): 53–70.

Stern, Samuel Miklos. "Maimonides' Correspondence with the Scholars of Provence." *Zion* 16 (1951): 18–39.

Stock, Brian. *Listening for the Text: On the Uses of the Past*. Baltimore: Johns Hopkins University Press, 1990.

Strauss, Leo. *Persecution and the Art of Writing*. Chicago: University of Chicago Press, 1952.

Stroumsa, Sarah. *Beginnings of the Maimonidean Controversy in the East*. Jerusalem: Ben-Zvi Institute, 1999.

———. "The Literary Corpus of Maimonides and Averroes." *Maimonidean Studies* 5 (2008): 193–210.

———. "On Jewish Intellectuals Who Converted to Islam in the Middle Ages." In *Medieval Islam: Community, Society, Identity*, ed. Daniel Frank, 179–97. Leiden: Brill, 1995.

———. *A Portrait of Maimonides as a Mediterranean Thinker*. Princeton, NJ: Princeton University Press, 2008.

———. "Prolegomena as Historical Evidence: On Saadia's Introductions to His Commentaries on the Bible." In *Vehicles of Transmission, Translation, and Transformation in Medieval Textual Culture*, ed. Carlos Fraenkel et al., 129–42. Turnhout: Brepols, 2011.

Suleiman, Yasir. *Arabic, Self, and Identity: A Study in Conflict and Displacement*. Oxford: Oxford University Press, 2011.

Szpiech, Ryan. "The Convivencia Wars: Decoding History's Polemic with Philology." In *A Sea of Languages: Rethinking the Arabic Role in Medieval Literary History*, ed. Suzanne Conklin Akbari and Karla Malette, 135–61. Toronto: University of Toronto Press, 2013.

———. "A Father's Bequest: Augustinian Typology and Personal Testimony in the Conversion Narrative of Solomon Halevi/Pablo de Santa María." In *The Hebrew Bible in Fifteenth-Century Spain*, ed. Jonathan Decter and Arturo Prats, 177–98. Leiden: Brill, 2012.

———. "The Original Is Unfaithful to the Translation: Conversion and Authenticity in Abner of Burgos and Anselm of Turmeda." *eHumanista* 14 (2010): 146–76.

Tanenbaum, Adena. *The Contemplative Soul: Hebrew Poetry and Philosophical Theory in Medieval Spain*. Leiden: Brill, 2002.

———. "On Translating Medieval Hebrew Poetry." *Hebrew Scholarship and the Medieval World*, ed. Nicholas de Lange, 171–86. Cambridge: Cambridge University Press, 2001.

Ta-Shma, Israel. *Rabbi Zerahya ha-Levi Ba'al ha-Me'or and His Circle: Towards a History of Rabbinic Literature in Provence*. Jerusalem: Magnes Press, 1992.

Taylor, Andrew. *Textual Situations: Three Medieval Manuscripts and Their Readers*. Philadelphia: University of Pennsylvania Press, 2002.

Teicher, J. L. "A Literary Forgery in the Thirteenth Century." *Melilah* 1 (1944): 81–92.

Tobi, Joseph. *Between Hebrew and Arabic Poetry: Studies in Spanish Medieval Hebrew Poetry*. Leiden: Brill, 2010.

———. *Proximity and Distance: Medieval Hebrew and Arabic Poetry*. Leiden: Brill, 2004.

Tolan, John V. *Saracens: Islam in the Medieval European Imagination*. New York: Columbia University Press, 2002.

Torres Balbás, Leopoldo. "La primitiva mezquita mayor de Sevilla." *Al-Andalus* 14 (1946): 425–39.

Tritton, A. S. "Ākhira." *Encyclopaedia of Islam*, 2nd ed. http://referenceworks.brillonline.com/entries/encyclopaedia-of-islam-2/akhira-SIM_0469. Accessed February 15, 2011.

———. "Dunyā." *Encyclopaedia of Islam*. 2nd ed. http://referenceworks.brillonline.com/entries/encyclopaedia-of-islam-2/dunya-SIM_2155. Accessed February 15, 2011.

Twersky, Isadore. "Aspects of the Social and Cultural History of Provençal Jewry." *Journal of World History* 11 (1968): 185–207.

———. *Studies in Jewish Law and Philosophy*. New York: Ktav Publishing, 1982.

Vajda, George. "An Analysis of the Ma'amar Yiqqavu ha-Mayim by Samuel ibn Tibbon." *Journal of Jewish Studies* 10 (1959): 137–49.

Van Bekkum, Wout Jac. "The Hebrew Grammatical Tradition in the Exegesis of Rashi." In *Rashi, 1040–1990*, ed. Gabriel Sed-Rajna, 427–35. Paris: Cerf, 1993.

———. "The Risāla of Yehuda ibn Quraysh." In *The History of Linguistics in the Near East*, ed. Kees Versteegh, Konrad Koerner, and Hans-Joseph Niederehe, 71–92. Amsterdam: John Benjamins, 1983.

Van Gelder, Geert. "Arabic Didactic Verse." In *Centers of Learning*, ed. Jan Willem Drijvers and Alisdair MacDonald, 103–17. Leiden: Brill, 1995.

———. *Beyond the Line: Classical Arabic Literary Critics on the Coherence and Unity of the Poem*. Leiden: Brill, 1982.

Versteegh, Kees. *The Arabic Language*. Edinburgh: Edinburgh University Press, 2001.

———. "Breaking the Rules without Wanting To: Hypercorrection in Middle Arabic Texts." In *Investigating Arabic*, ed. Alaa Elgibali, 3–18. Leiden: Brill, 2004.

———. "Dead or Alive: The Status of the Standard Language." In *Bilingualism in Ancient Society: Language Contact and the Written Word*, ed. J. N. Adams, Mark Janse, and Simon Swain, 52–76. Oxford: Oxford University Press, 2002.

Vidro, Nadia. "How Medieval Jews Studied Classical Arabic Grammar." *Jerusalem Studies in Arabic and Islam* 41 (2014): 173–244.

———. *A Medieval Karaite Pedagogical Grammar of Hebrew*. Leiden: Brill, 2011.

Viguera Molins, María Jesús. *Los reinos de taifa y las invasiones magrebíes*. Madrid: Editorial Mapfre, 1992.

Vollandt, Ronny. *Arabic Versions of the Pentateuch*. Leiden: Brill, 2015.

———. "Making Quires Speak: Multi-Block Bibles and the Quest for a Canon." *Intellectual History of the Islamicate World* 4 (2016): 173–209.

Von Grunebaum, Gustave. *Medieval Islam: A Study in Cultural Orientation*. Chicago: University of Chicago Press, 1946.

Wagner, Esther Miriam. *Linguistic Variety of Judaeo-Arabic in Letters from the Cairo Genizah*. Leiden: Brill, 2010.

———. "The Weakening of the Bourgeoisie: Social Changes Mirrored in the Language of the Genizah Letters." In *From a Sacred Source: Genizah Studies in Honour of Professor Stefan C. Reif*, ed. Ben Outhwaite, 343–56. Leiden: Brill, 2010.

Wasserstein, David J. "Jewish Élites in al-Andalus." In *The Jews of Medieval Islam: Community, Society and Identity*, ed. Daniel Frank, 101–10. Leiden: Brill, 1995.

———. *The Rise and Fall of the Party-Kings: Politics and Society in Islamic Spain*. Princeton, NJ: Princeton University Press, 1985.

Wasserstrom, Steven. *Between Muslim and Jew: The Problem of Symbiosis under Early Islam*. Princeton, NJ: Princeton University Press, 1995.

———. "Sharing Secrets: Inter-Confessional Philosophy as Dialogical Practice." In *New Directions in Jewish Philosophy*, ed. Aaron Hughes and Elliot Wolfson, 205–28. Bloomington: Indiana University Press, 2009.

———. "The Shiʿi's Are the Jews of Our Community: An Interreligious Comparison within Sunni Thought." *Israel Oriental Studies* 14 (1994): 297–324.

Webb, Peter. "Foreign Books in Arabic Literature: Discourses on Books, Knowledge, and Ethnicity in the Writings of al-Jaḥiẓ." In *Journal of Arabic and Islamic Studies* 12 (2012): 16–55.

Yakerson, Shimon. "An Unknown Book List from the Period of the Spanish Inquisition." *Jewish Studies* 40 (2000): 161–71.

Yellin, David. *Spanish Poetic Theory*. Jerusalem: Magnes Press, 1972.

Yeshaya, Joachim J.M.S. "In the Name of the God of Israel: Judaeo-Arabic Language and Literature." In *Scripts beyond Borders: A Survey of Allographic Traditions*, ed. J. van den Heijer, Andrea Schmidt, and Tamara Pataridze, 527–38. Leuven: Peeters, 2014.

———. "Some Observations on Jewish Poets and Patrons in the Islamic East, Twelfth–Thirteenth Centuries." In *Patronage, Production, and Transmission of Texts in Medieval and Early Modern Jewish Cultures*, ed. Esperanza Alfonso and Jonathan Decter, 79–97. Turnhout: Brepols, 2014.

Zackin, Jane Robin. "A Jew and His Milieu: Allegory, Polemic, and Jewish Thought in Sem Tob's Proverbios Moralems and Ma'aseh ha-Rav." PhD diss., University of Texas, 2008.

Zawanowska, Marzena. "Was Moses the Mudawwin of the Torah? The Question of Authorship of the Pentateuch according to Yefet ben 'Eli." In *Studies in Judaeo-Arabic Culture*, ed. Haggai Ben-Shammai et al., 7–36. Tel Aviv: Tel Aviv University Press, 2014.

INDEX

ʿAbd Al-Raḥmān III, 103
Abrahams, Israel, 49, 66, 150, 164, 204–205
After Proverbs (Samuel ibn Naghrīla), 57, 65–70, 75n67, 76n82, 76n86, 88, 111, 121
Alexander romance, 75–76n69, 179–83, 193n23, 193–94n28
Alfonso, Esperanza, 163–64, 194n29
Allony, Nehemiah, 49, 55, 71n9, 73n30, 92
Almohads, 13–14n4; connection with al-Ghazālī, 160–61; invasion, 1–2, 20, 23; religion and philosophy under, 30–31
Almoravids, 11, 161; invasion, 20
Arabic: Bedouin, 89–90, 92–93, 100n71; as devotional, 32, 80, 86–87; grammar, 84, 93; Hebrew Bible translations into, 57, 78–82; poetry and poetics, 101, 105, 115, 122, 123, 127n3, 131–32n49, 134n78; status within Islam of, 31–32. *See also* prestige language
ʿarabiyya, 105, 128n15
Ashkenazi. *See* Jews
assimilation, 28, 87–90
Assis, Yom Tov, 33
auctoritas, 45n79
autobiography, 15n14, 58, 134–35n78; as related to bibliographic writing, 46–48, 61, 67–68

Bahr, Arthur, 51, 69
Bakhtin, Mikhail, 9
Bar Hilai, Naṭronai, 86
Bedouins, 87–94, 98n48, 100n71
Bekkum, Wout van, 182
Ben David, Abraham, 23
Ben Elʿazar, Jacob, 149–50
Ben Jacob, Meshullam, 23
Benjamin of Tudela: *Itineraries*, 22–23, 91–92
Benjamin, Walter, 112, 131n48
Ben Labraṭ, Dunash, 56, 57, 81, 103–10, 127n7, 129nn22–23
Ben Makhir ibn Tibbon, Jacob, 27, 163
Ben Meshullam, Asher, letter from Judah ibn Tibbon to, 24, 113, 132n50, 200
Ben Mishlei. See *After Proverbs*
Ben ʿOvadiah, Jacob, 26
Ben Rekhav, Yehonadav. *See* Rechabites
Ben-Shammai, Haggai, 49, 56, 73n30, 76n83
Benvenisti, Sheshet, 3, 30
Bible, the Hebrew, 11; in the ethical will, 87–90, 94; reference works for, 24, 154; as source of poetics, 101–105, 114; translations into Arabic of, 57, 78–82
bibliographic writing, as related to autobiography, 46–48, 61, 67–68
bilingualism, 26, 184, 190. *See also* multilingualism
biography; of Alexander the Great (*see* Alexander romance); *tarjamah*, 198–99, 202n1. *See also* autobiography
Blau, Joshua, 28, 73–74n36, 202n1
book lending and borrowing, 59–61

book lists. *See* catalogues
Boyarin, Shamma, 182–83
Brann, Ross, 14n9, 21, 33, 90

Cairo Genizah, 4–7, 18n45, 28–29, 49, 55, 58, 67, 70, 71n9, 72–73n19, 74–75n55, 163
calligraphy. *See* handwriting
catalogues, 10–11, 47, 60, 69–70; ethical wills as, 50, 52–55; familial relationships in, 60–61; *mazkeret-sefarim* (memorandum of books), 53, 73n23; poetry in, 68–69, 76n82
Christian: communities, 1–2, 8, 10, 33, 43n66, 48, 49, 79, 82, 89, 129n24, 149, 163; exegesis, 130n37; translations, 79
chronograms, 124–25
close reading, 12, 190, 201
colophons, 124, 179–83; dates in, 14n8, 124–25
comparative Semitics, 81, 103–104, 127n7
conservation: cultural, 88; textual, 22, 36–37
contact zone, 199–200
conversion narrative, 61–65, 75n57, 75n61. *See also* Al-Maghribī, Samawa'l
copyists. *See* scribes
cost of books, 67–68
cultural history, 12, 201
cultural nationalism, 38n5, 80, 95–6n17, 126
cultural transmission, 10, 89, 165, 177

Dalālāt al-ḥā'irīn. See *Guide of the Perplexed*
Derrida, Jacques, 18n40
dhimmī, 1–2
dictionaries, 154, 166n15, 202n1; biblical (*see* Sa'adya Ga'on: *Sefer ha-Egron*); biographical, 46; *Kitāb al-Uṣūl* (Ibn Janāḥ), 84, 53, 54; by Menaḥem ibn Saruq, 103. *See also* lexicography
documentary versus literary, text as, 18n45, 49–51, 64, 66
Drory, Rina, 19n50, 94, 131–32n49, 134n78

egodocument, 17n33
ethical wills, 4–7, 15nn12–13, 134n73; audience of, 111; as autobiography, 23, 61; as curriculum, 4, 106; as library catalogues, 52–58. *See also* Ibn Tibbon, Judah; *musar av*; *waṣīya*; *ẓeva'ah*
Even-Zohar, Itamar, 12
exegesis, 29, 56–57, 68, 73n34, 78–83, 83–84, 95n14, 130n37; *derash* method, 82; lexicography in, 153–54, 166n15; *peshat* method, 82; *taqdīr* (supposition), 159
exile, from al-Andalus, 2, 8, 47, 86, 89, 94, 134n78; and exile from Jerusalem, 21; reading al-Ghazālī in, 163–64; Judah ibn Tibbon in, 10, 21, 30, 33, 53, 58, 121, 160, 165; Samuel ibn Tibbon in, 9, 26; Judaeo-Arabic in, 27–31; in poetry, 20; text as being in, 184, 190

faḍā'il (merits), 31; *al-Andalus* (merits of al-Andalus), 20
fantasy, 179, 191, 192n13
Al-Farābī, 24, 27, 39n15, 57, 85, 97n40
Al-Fāsī, Daūd ben Abraham: *Kitāb Jāmi' al-Alfāẓ* (The Book of Collected Meanings), 154
Al-Fāsī, Judah. *See* Ḥayyūj
fiction, 29, 158, 172, 174–79, 185–86, 191, 192n13, 196n50, 196–97n52, 201
Finkel, Joshua, 186, 189–90
Fleischer, Ezra, 103
Frenkel, Miriam, 18n45, 49, 55, 71n9, 73n30, 76n83
Freudenthal, Gad, 4

Galen, 35; *Ars Parva*, 27, 193n25; *My Books*, 47; *The Order of My Books*, 47
garden imagery, 106–11, 130nn32–33; Garden of Eden, 50, 106, 129–30n29; and libraries, 109, 111. *See also* land of al-Andalus
Genizah. *See* Cairo Genizah
Al-Ghazālī, Abū Ḥāmid, 6, 16n22, 27, 150, 166n10; Almohads' and Ibn Tūmart's connection with, 160–61; Andalusi exiles' use of, 163–65; *Iḥyā' 'ulūm al-dīn* (Revival of the Religious Sciences), 57, 150–59, 162, 164, 165, 168n32; *Tahāfut al-Falāsifa* (*Incoherence of the Philosophers*), 162–63, 167–68n32

Goitein, S. D., 6–7, 71n13, 91, 166n3
grammar controversies, Córdoba, 56, 81
Great Mosque of Seville, 1
Greek, 10, 44n74, 179; philosophy and logic, 26–27, 153, 165, 176, 178; translation to Arabic, 24, 27, 35, 117
Guide of the Perplexed (Maimonides), 2, 26, 27, 129n24, 132n49, 162, 168n32, 171, 174, 178, 191; Samuel ibn Tibbon's appendix to (*Explanation of Foreign Terms*), 97n40; Samuel ibn Tibbon's preface to, 39n17, 43–44n69; Maimonides on the translation of, 25, 35, 85; translation debates regarding, 34, 179–83

Hadassi, Judah, 91
ḥadīth, 150, 151, 174–75
Hai Ga'on, 56, 66
ḥakhamim. *See* sages
Halevi, Judah, 57, 68, 109, 111–12, 162, 167–68n32, 175; Judah ibn Tibbon's Hebrew translation of *The Kuzari*, 158; *The Kuzari*, 23, 104, 162, 168n32, 174; use by Ashkenazi pietists of *The Kuzari*, 176–77
Halkin, A. S., 28
handwriting, 2, 15n13, 26, 40n31, 48, 65, 75n66
Al-Ḥarīzī, Judah, 75n68, 177, 187, 195n44, 196n50; *Guide of the Perplexed* translated by, 180–82; *Sefer Taḥkemoni*, 90, 98n48, 105–106, 184, 187
Ḥasidut. *See* pietists
Ḥayyūj, 56, 66, 81, 157, 167n23
Hebrew: grammar, 15n14, 32, 81, 96n22, 157; Tibbonid, 9, 131n48, 173, 179. *See also* Bible, the Hebrew
heteroglossia, 9
Historia de Proeliis, 179, 181, 193n23
Ḥovot ha-levavot. *See* Ibn Paqūda, Baḥya: *Hidāya ilā farā'id al-qulūb*

Ibn Abī Ṭālib, 'Alī, *waṣīya* attributed to, 5–6
Ibn 'Alī, Yefet, 44n74, 79–80
Ibn Bakkār, Zubayr, 6–7
Ibn Chiquitilla, Moses, 81–82, 96n22
Ibn Danan, Sa'adya, 83, 96n28
Ibn 'Ezra', Abraham, 20–21, 23, 54, 82, 83, 93, 104, 155, 176, 201; *Safah Berurah* (Clear Language), 32–33
Ibn 'Ezra', Moses, 21, 33, 56, 66, 105, 119, 130n29, 132n49
Ibn al-Faraḍī, 'Abd Allāh: *Tarīkh 'ulamā al-Andalus* (History of the Learned Men of al-Andalus), 46
Ibn Gabirol, Solomon, 105, 163; Judah ibn Tibbon on, 113; *Kitāb iṣlāh al-akhlāq* (Improvement of Moral Qualities), 23, 36, 113; *Kitāb mukhtar al-jawāhir* (*Choice of Pearls*), 23, 57, 66, 88
Ibn Ḥazm, 20, 100n71, 168n32
Ibn Iṣḥāq, Ḥunayn, 35–36, 44n75, 47
Ibn Janāḥ, Jonah, 24, 53–54, 56, 66, 81, 83, 84, 85, 110, 158; *Kitāb jāmi' al-alfāẓ*, 56; *Kitāb al-Lum'a*, 24, 159; *Kitāb al-Usūl*, 24, 155
Ibn Kardinal, Joseph, 177
Ibn Naghrīla, Samuel, 14n9, 47, 56, 58, 65–70, 76n76, 105, 111, 123, 129, 130n29, 133n68; *After Proverbs*, 17n33, 57, 65–70, 75n67, 76n82, 76n86, 88, 111, 121
Ibn Paqūda, Baḥya, 36, 174; *Hidāya ilā farā'id al-qulūb* (*Duties of the Heart*), 3, 175. *See also* Ibn Tibbon, Judah: on *Duties of the Heart*
Ibn Saruq, Menaḥem, 81, 103, 105
Ibn Shapruṭ, Ḥasdai, 103, 167n23
Ibn Shu'ba al-Ḥarrānī, Ḥasan, 6–7
Ibn Shuhayd, Abū Amīr, 20, 130n29
Ibn Taqāna, Moses, 105
Ibn al-Ṭayyib al-Bāqillānī, Muḥammad: *I'jāz Qur'ān* (the Inimitability of the Qur'ān), 102
Ibn Tibbon, Judah: on *Duties of the Heart*, 3, 23, 36, 43n67, 167–69n32, 172; poetry of, 119–23, 126, 134n71, 135n78; *Sefer ha-Riqmah* (Book of Woven Patterns), 24, 28, 36, 82, 83; *Sefer ha-Shorashim* (Book of Roots), 24, 54, 82, 107, 108, 155, 156, 157. *See also* Hebrew: Tibbonid
Ibn Tibbon, Moses, 24, 27, 39n15
Ibn Tibbon, Samuel, 2, 40n33, 58–59, 64; Judah's critique of, 24–26, 30, 48; Mai-

monides's correspondence with, 18n42, 25–26, 35, 40n26, 40n31, 85, 132n49; as translator and writer, 26–27, 39n17, 43–44n69, 44n76, 75–76n69, 97n40, 174, 179–83, 184, 187–89

Ibn Tumart, 13n4, 160–61. *See also* Almohads

Iggeret, 52–55. *See also* catalogues

illiteracy. *See* literacy

inimitability doctrine (*i'jāz al-Qur'ān*), 29, 32, 78, 93, 102

Israel, 21, 155. *See also* cultural nationalism

Al-Jāḥiẓ, 116–17, 133n59, 167–69n32

Jerusalem, 21, 179

Jews: Arabized, 7, 8, 16n28, 28–30, 50, 86, 90, 105, 149; Ashkenazi, 174–79, 191 (*see also* pietists); Karaite, 44n74, 79–82, 91, 93, 97n39, 154; Khaybar, 91, 92; Rabbanite, 80–82, 91

jihād, 175

Jonathan of Lunel, 25

Judaeo-Arabic, as culture and language, 4, 27–31, 37, 41n35, 41n40, 81, 103, 167n32, 171, 187

Judah of Regensburg, 176

kalām, 87, 91, 160–61, 164

Killito, Abdelfattaḥ, 19n51, 116–17

Kister, Meir, 6–7

Kitāb iṣlāh al-akhlāq. *See under* Ibn Gabirol, Solomon

Kitāb mukhtar al-jawāhir. *See under* Ibn Gabirol, Solomon

Kitāb al-radd wa-l-dalīl fī l-dīn al-dhalīl (Book of Proofs and Refutations in Defense of the Despised Faith). See *Kuzari, The*

Kitāb al-Ṣila fī ta'rīḥ al-Andalus (A Continuation of Andalusi History) (Ḥalaf ibn Bashkuwāl), 46

Kitāb Takmila li-Kitāb al-Ṣila (Completion of the Book of Continuation) (Muḥammad ibn al-Abbār), 46

Kitāb uṣūl al-sh'ir al-'ibrānī. *See* Sa'adya Ga'on: *Sefer ha-Egron*

Kuzari, The (Judah Halevi), 23, 104, 162, 168n32, 174; Judah ibn Tibbon's Hebrew translation of, 158; use by Ashkenazi pietists of, 176–77

land of al-Andalus: lament over, 20–21; praise of, 20, 108. *See also* garden imagery

Latin, 45, 181; didactic poetry in, 134n73; manuscripts, 125; translation into, 27; translation of *Historia de Proeliis*, 179, 193n23

lexicography, 2–3, 54, 58, 80–82, 92, 93, 153–54; Arabic tradition of, 83–85, 90, 129n29; of Judah ibn Tibbon, 157, 158–59, 164–65; of Samuel ibn Tibbon, 97n40; Jewish, 154, 155–56; in poetry and poetics, 103–104. *See also* dictionaries

libraries, 37, 46, 67, 72n17; documents of, 48–50; and exile, 47, 54; of Judah ibn Tibbon, 47–48, 53, 56–58; as institutions, 74n48. *See also* catalogues

literacy, 9, 23, 55; relationship with orality, 52

literal translation. *See* translation: word-for-word

literary. *See* documentary versus literary, text as

Lunel, 2, 21, 22–23, 26, 85, 160

Maghreb, the, 3, 74–75n55, 80, 93, 105, 161, 198; grammatical tradition of, 85

Al-Maghribī, Samawa'l, 75n57; *Ifḥām al-yahūd* (The Silencing of the Jews), 61–65, 99n56

Maḥbarot ha-diqduq (The Grammatical Notebooks), 24, 36, 159

Maimonidean controversies, 175, 177, 178, 183–84, 189–90, 194n38

Maimonides, Moses, 13–14n4, 25, 30, 55–56, 73n34; *Mishneh Torah*, 162, 184. *See also Guide of the Perplexed* and *Treatise on the Doctrine of Resurrection*

Maman, Aharon, 83–84, 96n22, 127n7

Martínez Delgado, José, 66, 154
Menocal, María Rosa, 10
methodologies: translation, 80, 187 (*see also* translation); in this work, 11–12, 69, 199–200
Mivḥar ha-peninim. *See* Ibn Gabirol, Solomon: *Kitāb mukhtar al-jawāhir*
Moreh ha-nevukhim. See *Guide of the Perplexed*
"Mourners of Zion" (*avalei ẓion*), 79
Muḥammad, 6, 101, 150, 175
multilingualism, 28, 95n12, 200. *See also* bilingualism
musar av (a father's guidance), 4, 123
mutakallimūn (practitioners of *kalām*). See *kalām*
mu'tazilism. *See* rationalism

nationalism. *See* cultural nationalism
New Historicism, 11–12, 18n45
New Medievalism, 18n45
nostalgia, 20, 21, 30, 33, 93–94, 106

Orakh ḥayim, 86
oral transmission, 6, 7, 52, 72n18, 150–51, 198
orchards. *See* garden imagery

pietists, 91; Ashkenazi (*ḥasidei Ashkenaz*), 174–76; poets (*payetanim*), 104
Pines, Shlomo, 34, 44n70, 162
plays-on-words. *See* puns
poetry and poetics, 51, 135–36n92; Arabizing Hebrew, 20, 22, 29, 98n48, 105, 106, 111, 112, 119, 134n71; courtly, 20, 94; and the Hebrew Bible, 101–105, 114; liturgical, 57, 177; in relation to prose, 113, 118–26, 129n28; and Scripture, 80, 101–103; as untranslatable, 112–17; wine, 98n48. *See also* Arabic: poetry and poetics
polysystem theory, 12, 19n50, 199
Pratt, Mary Louise, 199
prestige language, 2, 4, 8–10, 31, 33, 37, 42–43n54, 48, 78–79, 83–84, 106, 126, 150, 172, 199
professional: use of Arabic as, 86–87; translation as, 14n6, 97n42
Provence, 30, 42n47, 82, 93, 116, 164, 177, 187; Judah ibn Tibbon in, 3, 23, 52. *See also* Lunel
puns, 98n47, 115–16, 132n55, 190

Qimḥi, David, 82, 93, 201
Qimḥi, Joseph, 82, 93, 201
Al-Qirqisānī, Ya'qūb, 79, 81, 91; *Kitāb al-anwār wa-l-murāqib*, 80
qualitative versus quantitative analysis, 72n17
quantitative poetic meter, 81, 104
Al-Qūmisī, Daniel, 79
Qur'ān, the, 11, 29, 31, 32–33, 63, 78–79, 101–102, 110, 151, 198; *ākhira* and *dunyā* in, 152, 166n12. *See also* inimitability doctrine
Al-Qurṭubī, 149–50

rationalism, 1, 6, 61, 80, 82, 83, 149, 153, 160, 174–78, 184; mu'tazilism, 79
reception: fictive, 183–91; of al-Ghazālī's work, 160–65; history, 132n51, 173–74; of poetry, 102–103, 119; of the Tibbonid project, 171, 201
Rechabites, 88–94, 97n43, 99n58. *See also* Bedouins
Ribera y Tarrago, Julian: *Libros y enseñanzas en al-Andalus*, 46
Robinson, James T., 4, 15–16n14, 23, 38–39n10, 97n40, 97n42, 120
Romance languages, 3, 30, 45n79, 181, 201
Ronell, Avital, 58–59
Rosenthal, Franz, 52, 72n19, 162
Rustow, Marina, 92–93

Sa'adya Ga'on, 43n67, 54, 81–82, 95n12, 103, 104, 175–76; in catalogues and library collections, 56–57, 61; *Kitāb al-amanāt wa-l-itiqadāt* (Book of Beliefs and Opinions), 23, 55, 67, 168n32; *Sefer ha-Egron* (The Thesaurus), 53, 80, 105, 153; *Tafsīr*, 80, 97n40, 131n47
Sabbath, reading on the, 87–88, 97n39

Sadan, Joseph, 149–50
sages: Arab, 149–52, 165n2; hierarchy of, 85, 149
scribes, 7–8, 69, 100n64, 130n37, 195n44; errors committed by, 111–12, 180–81; handwriting of, 15n13, 17n32, 48–49, 65; Yo'av, 124–26, 131n42, 135nn91–92
Seder Rav 'Amram Ga'on, 68, 86
Sefer emunot ve-de'ot. *See* Sa'adya Ga'on: *Kitāb al-amanāt wa-l-itiqadāt*
Sefer ha-riqmah. *See* Ibn Tibbon, Judah; Ibn Janāḥ, Jonah: *Kitāb al- Lum'a*
Shohat, Ella, 41n35
shu'ūbiyya, 128n15
Spiegel, Gabrielle, 12
Steinschneider, Moritz, 14n8, 35, 39n17, 40n27, 181, 185, 186, 189, 193–94n28, 195n47
Strauss, Leo, 129n24
syllabification, 119, 133nn67–68, 133–34n70

taifa kingdoms, 11
Targum Onkelos, 172–73
Tel Aviv poststructuralists, 12, 199
Tibbon, Profiat. *See* Ben Makhir ibn Tibbon, Jacob
Tiqqun middot ha-nefesh. *See* Ibn Gabirol, Solomon: *Kitāb iṣlāh al-akhlāq*
Tobi, Joseph, 104, 127n11
translation: cultural, 29, 37, 131n38, 199; inter-sectional, 79; of Islamic material, 166n10; loan, 156, 158, 159; omission in, 83–85, 110–11, 151–52, 167–69n32; sense-for-sense, 10, 34–35, 82, 112, 167n32, 172–73, 182–83, 188, 199; word-for-word, 3, 9–10, 22, 33–36, 84, 112, 152, 167n32, 171–83, 187, 199
Treatise on the Doctrine of Resurrection (Maimonides), 26, 195n41; preface to, 184–91, 192n13

Umayyads, 20, 29, 74–75n55, 93, 103
untranslatability, 112–17, 131n47. *See also* inimitability doctrine

waṣīya, 4, 52, 120, 199; attributed to 'Alī ibn Abī Tālib, 5–7. *See also* ethical wills; *ẓeva'ah*
wisdom literature, 25, 61, 76n82, 76n86, 114, 150
Wissenschaft des Judentums movement, 8, 17n35, 41n35

Yūsuf I, 1–2, 13n1

ẓeva'ah, 4, 120, 123. *See also* ethical wills; *waṣīya*

S. J. PEARCE earned her PhD in Near Eastern Studies at Cornell University in 2011 and is now assistant professor in the Department of Spanish and Portuguese at New York University, where her teaching and research focus on the intellectual history and literature of Jews, Christians, and Muslims in medieval Spain. She was awarded the John K. Walsh Prize from La Corónica/MLA Division of Medieval Hispanic Literature in 2016.

www.ingramcontent.com/pod-product-compliance
Lightning Source LLC
Chambersburg PA
CBHW060627310726
48982CB00003B/699

* 9 7 8 0 2 5 3 0 2 5 9 6 8 *